ASIAN EXPORTS

Edited by
Dilip K. Das

Published for the Asian Development Bank
By Oxford University Press

OXFORD
UNIVERSITY PRESS

OXFORD
UNIVERSITY PRESS

Oxford University Press is a department of the University of Oxford.
It furthers the University's objective of excellence in research, scholarship,
and education by publishing worldwide in

Oxford New York

Athens Auckland Bangkok Bogotá Buenos Aires Calcutta
Cape Town Chennai Dar es Salaam Delhi Florence Hong Kong Istanbul
Karachi Kuala Lumpur Madrid Melbourne Mexico City Mumbai
Nairobi Paris São Paulo Singapore Taipei Tokyo Toronto Warsaw

with associated companies in Berlin Ibadan

Oxford is a registered trade mark of Oxford University Press

Published in the United States by Oxford University Press Inc., New York

First published 2000
This impression (lowest digit)
1 3 5 7 9 10 8 6 4 2

Published for the Asian Development Bank by
Oxford University Press

British Library Cataloguing in Publication Data
available

Library of Congress Cataloging-in-Publication Data
available

ISBN 0 19 592100 3 (Paperback)
ISBN 0 19 592128 3 (Hardback)

Printed in Hong Kong
Published by Oxford University Press (China) Ltd
18th Floor, Warwick House East, Taikoo Place, 979 King's Road, Quarry Bay
Hong Kong

Foreword

Several Asian economies have recorded laudable export performances during the last three decades. Given the apparent importance of exports in the economic transformation of nations, the ability to achieve strong export-led economic growth has become a recurring theme in policy discussions in both successful and less successful developing member countries of the Asian Development Bank.

The most successful models of such growth are the four newly industrialized economies (NIEs) of Hong Kong, China; Korea; Singapore; and Taipei,China. They were the first to record extraordinary growth rates in their export performance. Several factors and policy measures that were crucial to the growth of the NIEs were subsequently found in the ASEAN-4 economies (Indonesia, Malaysia, Philippines, and Thailand), and later on in the People's Republic of China (PRC). Generally, exports in these successful Asian economies grew, both in real and nominal terms, much faster than the world average, thereby increasing their share in world exports. The World Trade Organization's 1998 league table of leading exporters has seven Asian economies among the 25 largest exporters in the world. However, a negative feature of the Asian success story is its highly concentrated nature: the 10 largest Asian exporters accounted for 96.3 percent of total Asian exports in 1997. Thus, export success in Asia is based on a small number of highly successful economies. It is far from a regionwide success story.

The rapid export expansion in Asia, particularly in the NIEs and the ASEAN-4 economies, benefited a great deal from the rapid improvement in the international trading environment, which in turn was the direct consequence of the seven rounds of multilateral trade negotiations (MTNs) under the aegis of the General Agreement on Tariffs and Trade. The MTNs succeeded in bringing down tariff barriers, particularly in the industrial economies which were substantial markets for Asia. The Uruguay Round, the eighth round of MTNs, was the most ambitious of such rounds and culminated in comprehensive achievements in terms of liberalization of tariffs and nontariff barriers. In addition, in 1997 three new trade agreements were signed as part of the "unfinished agenda" of the Uruguay Round. The Millennium Round, for which preparations are in full swing, is to be launched in November 1999 in Seattle.

Despite constant improvements in the international trading environment, the long-term trend of export growth in Asia came to an abrupt end in 1996, when export growth decelerated sharply. To exacerbate the situation, a financial and currency crisis struck several Asian economies in 1997, involving steep currency depreciations. It was initially expected that currency depreciations would lead to a spurt in Asian exports, which would work as a vehicle of recovery. However, largely due to various supply-side factors and some demand-side variables, this much-needed boost to exports did not occur.

The year 1998 saw the further unfolding of the Asian crisis. Growth in the NIEs and the Southeast Asian economies was the lowest in the post-World War II period in 1998. Private capital flows to emerging Asian economies, which had reached $110 billion in 1996, turned negative in 1998 as foreign investors scrambled to move out of supposedly risky markets. Until the first quarter of 1999, several Asian economies were in dire straits and were grappling to recover from a recession as well as an export slump, although at this point, several crisis-stricken economies were showing signs of stabilization and exports were beginning to rise in volume terms in these economies. During the second quarter of 1999, there were some indications that intra-Asia trade was beginning to pick up. However, a look at what is being traded shows that revival is only at the earliest stage.

It is one of the mandates of the Asian Development Bank to provide its developing member countries with policy guidance. This volume examines developing Asia's export performance at both regional and country levels. After providing a fresh analysis of trade regimes, it dwells on the causal factors behind the export deceleration of 1996 as well as the impact of the 1997 financial and currency crisis on export performance. In keeping with the Bank's mandate, it attempts to provide a policy prescription for the recovery of exports. It is also hoped that policymakers in the region will benefit from it in resolving the onerous issues they face and in arriving at the right decisions.

Jungsoo Lee
Chief Economist
Economics and Development Resource Center
Asian Development Bank

PREFACE

To help policymakers comprehend trade policy structure better, to improve their understanding of a dynamic scenario, and to enable them to appreciate the merits of alternative courses of action in the area of export strategy, in June 1997 the Asian Development Bank approved a regional technical assistance grant. This volume is an outcome of that effort. It is intended for policymakers and development practitioners, as well as for scholars in the area of international trade.

To keep the study manageable, while still reflecting the diversity among the Asian economies, five regional economies were selected for a detailed analysis of export regimes and the recent performance of the export sector. The selected economies included two newly industrialized economies of Asia (Korea and Taipei,China), two Southeast Asian economies (Malaysia and Thailand), and the People's Republic of China. Two workshops were organized for in-depth discussions of Asian export deceleration, its causes, and possible remedies. International and national consultants participated in these two workshops held in October 1997 and July 1998 to discuss various aspects of the study.

During the studies on the five economies, government agencies, chambers of commerce, and private citizens contributed information, ideas, and time. Central bank officials in various countries and those from multilateral institutions assisted in providing information and analyzing facts. In particular, Masamichi Kono of the World Trade Organization, Geneva, was of great assistance in providing trade-related data and other valuable information. A number of staff of the Asian Development Bank also offered meaningful suggestions. Several of them were involved in reviewing the various drafts of the chapters before they were finalized.

When various drafts of the chapters were being prepared, Dr. Jungsoo Lee took enormous interest in them and made large swaths of time available for discussions. Dr. M.G. Quibria and members of the Economic Analysis and Research Division provided extensive comments on various chapters of this volume.

In performing various project-related tasks I was ably assisted by Emma Banaria. She provided valuable research assistance and handled voluminous correspondence. Jonathan Aspin provided editing assistance and Lulu Antonio, Teresa Cabellon, and Rochi Harder-Ignacio supplied efficient secretarial services. Rose Arcano typeset the manuscript with the assistance of ADB's Printing Unit.

Dilip K. Das
Economics and Development Resource Center
Asian Development Bank

CONTENTS

9 Case Study: Thailand
by Peter G. Warr

10 Rejuvenating Asian Exports
by Dilip K. Das

List of Tables

List of Figures

Terms and Definitions

AFTA	ASEAN Free Trade Area
APEC	Asia-Pacific Economic Cooperation
ASEAN	Association of Southeast Asian Nations
BOI	Board of Investment (Pakistan/Thailand)
CEPD	Council for Economic Planning and Development (Taipei,China)
CET	common external tariff
CGE	computable general equilibrium
CIF	cost, insurance, freight
CIS	Commonwealth of Independent States
CMEA	Council for Mutual Economic Assistance
CNEER	competitors' nominal effective exchange rate
CREER	competitors' real effective exchange rate
CP	contracting party
CPI	consumer price index
CUSTA	Canada-United States Trade Agreement
DME	developed market economy
DRAM	dynamic random-access memory
DRC	domestic resource cost
EC	European Community
EEA	European Economic Area
EEC	European Economic Community
EER	effective exchange rate
EFTA	European Free Trade Association
EPZ	export processing zone
ERP	effective rate of protection
ESCAP	Economic and Social Commission for Asia and the Pacific
EU	European Union
FDI	foreign direct investment
FIE	foreign-invested enterprise
FKI	Federation of Korean Industries
FOB	free on board
FOGS	Functioning of the GATT System
FSU	Former Soviet Union
FTC	foreign trade corporation
GATS	General Agreement on Trade in Services
GATT	General Agreement on Tariffs and Trade

GDP	gross domestic product
GNP	gross national product
GSP	Generalized System of Preferences
HCI	heavy and chemical industries
HKTDC	Hong Kong Trade Development Council
HS	harmonized system
HSIP	Hsinchu Science-Based Industrial Park
IFCT	Industrial Finance Corporation of Thailand
IMF	International Monetary Fund
IS	import substitution
JETRO	Japan External Trade Organization
KDB	Korea Development Bank
KDI	Korea Development Institute
KIET	Korea Institute for Industrial Economics and Trade
KITA	Korea International Trade Association
KOTIS	Korea Trade Information Service
LAFTA	Latin American Free Trade Association
LAIA	Latin American Integration Association
LDC	less developed country
LNG	liquefied natural gas
MCBP	Multiple currency basket peg system
MFA	Multifiber Arrangement
MFN	most favored nation
MIDA	Malaysian Industrial Development Authority
MNC	multinational corporation
MOFTEC	Ministry of Foreign Trade and Economic Cooperation (PRC)
MTN	multilateral trade negotiation
NAFTA	North American Free Trade Agreement
NBKR	National Bank of the Kyrgyz Republic
NEER	nominal effective exchange rate
NEPR	net export performance ratio
NER	net export ratio
n.e.s.	not elsewhere specified
NESDB	National Economic and Social Development Board (Thailand)
NIC	newly industrializing country
NIE	newly industrialized economy
NRP	nominal rate of protection
NTB	nontariff barrier

OECD	Organisation for Economic Co-operation and Development
OLS	ordinary least square
PPP	purchasing power parity
PRC	People's Republic of China
PTA	preferential trading arrangement
R&D	research and development
RCA	revealed comparative advantage
REER	real effective exchange rate
RER	real exchange rate
RTA	regional trading arrangement
SAARC	South Asian Association for Regional Cooperation
SAPTA	South Asian Preferential Trading Area
SEZ	special economic zone
SITC	Standard International Trade Classification
SME	small and medium enterprise
SOE	state-owned enterprise
SSB	State Statistical Bureau (PRC)
TFP	total factor productivity
TPRM	Trade Policy Review Mechanism
TRIM	trade-related investment measure
TRIP	trade-related intellectual property
TVE	township-village enterpise
UK	United Kingdom
UN	United Nations
UNCTAD	United Nations Conference on Trade and Development
US	United States
VAT	value-added tax
VER	voluntary export restraint
WEFA	Wharton Economic Forecast Association
WPI	wholesale price index
WTO	World Trade Organization

Notes: References to Korea are to the Republic of Korea; and Taipei,China to the island of Taiwan. "$" as a currency notation refers to United States dollars unless otherwise specified. The symbol "—" in tables indicates that the amount is negligible. The symbol "..." in tables indicates that data are not available or not applicable.

CHAPTER ONE

Asian Exports: The Present Predicament

Dilip K. Das

> *Exports have more value to people than is commonly appreciated ... Exports enhance workers' remuneration, benefits, skills, productivity and future prospects. Exports enhance corporate innovation, economic stability and ability to endure external shocks. Exports benefit workers and owners in small businesses, as well as large. (Richardson and Rindal 1995)*

THE PAST

Over the past three-and-a-half decades, several developing Asian economies have performed the essential function of growth and export expansion better than most other economies. The successful subgroups of these economies, and their performance, can be divided in the following manner. The newly industrialized economies (NIEs)[1] were the first and the most successful in export-led or trade-induced growth, followed by four Southeast Asian economies in the Association of Southeast Asian Nations[2]—the ASEAN-4—and subsequently the People's Republic of China (PRC). The South Asian economies were the last to embark on this path. The process became known as the "flying-geese paradigm" of Asian growth.

Several policy measures and macroeconomic factors that were crucial to the growth of the NIEs were also to be seen, at a later stage,

[1] Hong Kong, China; Republic of Korea; Singapore; and Taipei,China.
[2] Indonesia, Malaysia, Philippines, and Thailand.

in the ASEAN-4 countries and the PRC. Consequently, if the gross domestic product (GDP) growth rates of these economies are plotted on a logarithmic scale, they show parallel trends. However, a caveat must be made here that these economies began their exports from a very low level, and therefore their trade statistics hide a low-base effect. The most recent and noteworthy example of this effect is the PRC. In the mid-1970s, its exports were barely $6.4 billion. At the time of its adoption of the "open-door policy" in 1979, the PRC's exports were still a paltry $12.6 billion. In fact, the economy opened up to the outside world at a disadvantageous time, for global recession in the early 1980s and the subsequent weak recovery greatly reduced import demand from developed market economies for its products. And since the PRC was a latecomer to the club of successful Asian exporters, it was not accorded the favorable treatment that the NIEs and ASEAN-4 countries enjoyed under the Generalized System of Preferences (GSP) when they launched their export-led growth programs. Nevertheless, the 1997 export figure for PRC was $182.9 billion, reflecting a radical change both in the structure of its economy and its macroeconomic management. The official target for 1998 is $200 billion. Such a dramatic increase in two decades is a remarkable achievement. However, several Asian economies—including those in South Asia—have not taken part in Asia's "miracle."

Table 1.1 shows clearly that, in 1965–1997, exports from developing Asian economies grew faster on average than world exports. In nominal terms, world export volume rose 32 times over this period. In comparison, the volume of developing Asian exports soared 86-fold. Among the various subgroups, the NIEs were far ahead of the rest, with a 193-fold increase in export volume. To see export growth in real terms, if the nominal series of Table 1.1 are deflated by the export unit value indexes, one again sees (Table 1.2) that developing Asia's exports grew much faster than world exports (between 1965 and 1997), and that the four NIEs achieved the fastest export growth rate in the region. While world exports, in real terms, grew about 7-fold during this period, developing Asia's exports grew about 20-fold. If we take a disaggregated view, the NIEs, in real terms, recorded a 64-fold rise during this period. The point that bears repeating here is that the low-base effect is easy to see. The ASEAN-4 economies, which followed the NIEs in this respect, were only able to quadruple their exports in real terms between 1965 and 1985, but their export growth rate picked up after this point. These two country

Table 1.1 Developing Asia, Nominal Exports, 1965–1997 ($ billion)

Year	World	Developing Asia[a]	NIEs	ASEAN-4	South Asia-3[b]	PRC
1965	172.4	12.1	2.7	3.3	2.2	2.6
1966	189.0	13.1	3.2	3.4	2.6	2.7
1967	198.4	12.8	3.6	3.4	2.3	2.4
1968	221.7	13.6	4.3	3.6	2.2	2.3
1969	253.3	15.5	5.4	4.1	2.2	2.4
1970	290.1	17.1	6.3	4.5	2.4	2.3
1971	327.1	19.4	7.7	4.8	2.5	2.8
1972	390.7	24.8	10.2	5.7	3.4	3.7
1973	541.8	38.4	16.3	9.7	4.2	5.9
1974	811.3	54.6	21.8	16.8	5.4	7.1
1975	835.2	54.4	21.6	15.4	5.7	7.7
1976	942.3	68.8	30.9	19.4	7.1	6.9
1977	1,066.3	81.7	37.3	23.5	8.0	7.5
1978	1,233.6	98.0	47.0	26.5	8.7	10.0
1979	1,584.3	128.8	60.5	36.5	10.5	13.6
1980	1,910.6	164.0	76.4	47.1	12.0	18.1
1981	1,878.5	176.4	86.6	46.7	12.0	21.6
1982	1,729.4	175.6	85.7	46.2	12.5	21.9
1983	1,695.9	183.6	93.3	46.5	12.9	22.2
1984	1,809.2	210.5	112.1	51.2	13.4	25.0
1985	1,820.1	208.6	114.0	45.8	12.9	27.6
1986	2,003.1	227.1	132.3	43.5	13.7	31.4
1987	2,355.3	295.3	177.9	52.4	16.5	39.5
1988	2,693.5	363.8	223.7	63.6	19.1	47.5
1989	2,906.6	405.5	246.3	75.0	21.9	51.9
1990	3,309.9	452.0	267.1	86.2	25.2	61.3
1991	3,477.6	515.7	305.6	101.1	25.9	70.5
1992	3,731.1	585.5	341.0	116.9	29.0	84.9
1993	3,730.6	646.4	376.2	131.8	30.5	91.0
1994	4,262.5	768.6	437.1	157.2	35.1	121.0
1995	5,094.5	933.6	528.7	193.4	41.9	148.8
1996	5,303.9	976.3	551.2	204.3	45.7	151.2
1997	5,483.3	1,041.6	571.0	214.8	46.7	182.9

[a] Afghanistan; Bangladesh; Bhutan; Brunei; Cambodia; PRC; Fiji Islands; Guam; Hong Kong, China; India; Indonesia; Kiribati; Korea, Republic of; Lao PDR; Macao; Malaysia; Maldives; Mongolia; Myanmar; Nepal; Pakistan; Papua New Guinea; Philippines; Samoa; Singapore; Solomon Islands; Sri Lanka; Taipei,China; Thailand; Tonga; Vanuatu; and Viet Nam.

[b] Bangladesh, India, and Pakistan.

Sources: Asian Development Bank (ADB) (various years); International Monetary Fund (IMF), *International Financial Statistics Yearbook* (various years); Council for Economic Planning and Developement (CEPD) (1997); and IMF (October 1997).

Table 1.2 Exports in Real Terms, 1965–1997
($ billion, 1990)

Year	World	Developing Asia[a]	NIEs	ASEAN-4	South Asia-3[b]	PRC
1965	805.6	51.1	8.7	10.0	-	-
1966	863.0	56.2	9.6	10.5	7.8	-
1967	905.9	55.7	27.3	10.5	7.0	-
1968	1,036.0	52.2	15.8	11.5	6.9	-
1969	1,151.4	57.0	19.1	12.7	6.7	-
1970	1,255.8	59.7	20.9	13.2	7.4	-
1971	1,329.7	67.0	24.3	14.6	7.5	-
1972	1,457.8	80.9	28.7	17.9	9.7	-
1973	1,641.8	92.6	38.1	20.5	9.7	-
1974	1,767.5	88.3	38.2	21.0	10.6	-
1975	1,677.1	91.7	40.2	20.8	10.0	66.2
1976	1,873.4	112.2	55.3	26.1	12.3	63.4
1977	1,938.7	118.2	61.3	28.5	12.6	62.1
1978	2,032.3	134.4	68.1	30.6	11.5	64.0
1979	2,188.3	145.9	76.7	31.3	13.1	62.5
1980	2,226.8	156.9	85.9	31.4	13.7	62.0
1981	2,233.7	170.6	91.7	31.9	14.3	62.1
1982	2,140.3	179.2	91.8	33.4	15.2	62.1
1983	2,205.3	196.2	100.7	36.2	15.7	62.1
1984	2,412.3	218.2	117.8	39.0	15.7	62.1
1985	2,476.3	232.6	124.4	40.8	15.0	62.1
1986	2,497.6	277.6	146.7	53.4	15.9	62.1
1987	2,646.4	338.7	191.1	58.6	18.7	62.1
1988	2,924.5	385.8	229.8	68.1	19.0	62.1
1989	3,128.7	414.2	251.9	79.2	21.7	62.1
1990	3,309.9	452.0	267.1	86.2	25.2	62.1
1991	3,523.4	517.3	301.1	97.6	24.5	62.2
1992	3,697.8	583.8	340.4	111.8	21.6	-
1993	3,894.0	645.7	370.8	129.1	30.5	-
1994	4,283.9	750.6	423.2	144.9	37.0	-
1995	4,656.5	848.7	480.7	150.0	44.1	-
1996	4,892.9	913.3	515.6	153.4	50.0	-
1997	5,328.8	1008.7	558.7	127.5	49.7	-

Note. The nominal value series have been deflated by the export unit value indexes (1990 = 100).

a, b As Table 1.1

Sources: ADB (various years); and IMF, *International Financial Statistics Yearbook* (various years).

groups recorded much faster export growth rates in real terms than the export growth rate of the world economy during the period under review. Unlike the NIEs and the ASEAN-4 economies, the export growth rate of the three South Asian economies only kept pace with that of world exports in real terms.

In terms of five-year average growth rates of exports between 1966 and 1995, developing Asia's averages were higher than world averages for all periods but 1966–1970, when some Asian economies had just launched their trade-induced growth process. During 1981–1985, when the world economy was in a downswing and world trade recorded a decline, developing Asia's exports grew by a healthy 5.1 percent. A comparison of five-year rates of the various subgroups reveals that the NIEs had the highest growth rates for almost all the periods, except for 1971–1975 and 1991–1995. During these two periods, the export growth rates of the ASEAN-4 countries were the highest. The latter period was an economically turbulent period for the NIEs. Krueger (1995) has made the point that in the NIEs, Malaysia, and Thailand the export growth rate exceeded that of GDP growth for much of 1965–1995.

Exports from Developing Asia on the Global Scene

The direct outcome of developing Asia expanding its exports faster than the rest of the world was an increasing share of its exports in the world total. In 1965, developing Asia accounted for 7 percent of world exports. Its share fell to 5.9 percent in 1970 because most developing Asia's economies were still following inward-oriented, import-substitution policy regimes. It was not, therefore, possible for them to keep pace with the rate of growth of world exports. This is evident from the slipping shares of the ASEAN-4 countries, South Asia, and the PRC in world exports (Table 1.3). But after 1970, driven by the strength of the NIEs' exports, the share of developing Asia's exports in world exports rose monotonically. It was 11.5 percent of world exports in 1985, 18.3 percent in 1995, and 19.0 percent in 1997. The NIEs recorded the highest proportional increase, with their exports accounting for 1.6 percent of total world exports in 1965, and 10.4 percent in 1997.

The share of the ASEAN-4 countries in total world exports began to rise gradually after 1970, and sharply during the 1990s (Table 1.3).

Table 1.3 Asian Exports as Share of World Exports, 1965–1997 (percent)

Year	Developing Asia[a]	NIEs	ASEAN-4	South Asia-3[b]	PRC
1965	7.0	1.6	1.9	1.3	1.5
1970	5.9	2.2	1.6	0.8	0.8
1975	6.5	2.6	1.8	0.7	0.9
1980	8.6	4.0	2.5	0.6	0.9
1985	11.5	6.3	2.5	0.7	1.5
1990	13.7	8.1	2.6	0.8	1.9
1995	18.3	10.4	3.8	0.8	2.9
1996	18.4	10.4	3.9	0.9	2.9
1997	19.0	10.4	3.9	0.9	3.3

[a, b] As Table 1.1.

Sources: As Table 1.1.

The South Asian economies continued on their lackluster inward-oriented policy path for much longer than the other Asian subgroups, with the result that their export expansion did not keep pace with export growth in the world economy. The share in world exports of Bangladesh, India, and Pakistan declined from 1.3 percent in 1965 to 0.6 percent in 1980. It has grown marginally since then because they gradually began to liberalize and reform their economies from 1991. The share of the PRC did not begin to improve substantially until 1980, but thereafter it recorded a dramatic rise. Between 1980 and 1990, its share of world trade more than doubled to 1.9 percent. Between 1990 and 1997, its share almost doubled again to 3.3 percent.

Because of the successful export performance of a few Asian economies, developing Asia's economies together have become a significant group in their own right in the international economy. The total share of the 10 largest developing Asia's exporters in world trade was 18.49 percent in 1997 (Table 1.4). This was 47 percent higher than that of the United States (US) (12.62 percent), 51 percent higher than that of Germany (9.38 percent), and more than double that of Japan (7.71 percent). According to the World Trade Organization (WTO 1997), in 1996 six Asian economies were among the 20 largest exporters in the world. Hong Kong, China, the largest exporter in the region, was ninth; PRC 11th; Republic of Korea (hereafter called Korea) 12th; Singapore 13th; Taipei,China 14th; and Malaysia 19th.

Table 1.4 Exports of the Ten Largest Developing Asia's Exporters, 1997

Country/Area	Value ($ million)	Share of World Exports (percent)
Hong Kong, China	188,063	3.45
PRC	182,877	3.35
Korea	136,164	2.50
Singapore	125,000	2.29
Taipei,China	121,744	2.23
Malaysia	83,027	1.52
Thailand	57,504	1.05
Indonesia	55,393	1.02
India	33,898	0.62
Philippines	25,088	0.46
Subtotal	**1,008,758**	**18.49**
US	688,697	12.62
Germany	511,642	9.38
Japan	420,957	7.71
Subtotal	**1,621,296**	**29.71**
World	**5,456,500**	**100.00**

Source: IMF, *International Financial Statistics Yearbook* (1998).

Table 1.4 also reveals a negative feature of the Asian trade, namely, the highly concentrated nature of Asian exporters: the 10 largest developing Asia's exporters accounted for 96.8 percent of total developing Asia's exports in 1997, while the 5 largest accounted for 72.4 percent of the total. As mentioned above, export success in Asia is clearly not regionwide, but the result of a small number of high-performing economies.

Export Growth and Structural Transformation

There is a body of literature in development economics that attributes brisk growth in Asia to successful export performance (see, among others, Balassa 1978, Krueger 1980, Feder 1982, Balassa and Williamson 1990, Edwards 1992). Several studies have highlighted various beneficial static and dynamic aspects of the export-international trade nexus. They include greater capacity utilization, resource allocation according to comparative advantage, exploitation of economies of scale, technological improvements, and efficient management, in response to competitive pressures from abroad.

These studies imply that since there are substantial differences in productivity between export-oriented and nonexport-oriented industries and sectors, economies that have adopted export-oriented strategies have benefited from closer to optimal resource allocation and higher growth rates than those which have not.[3]

For some time these precepts were considered the new orthodoxy in economics. However, in some recent studies, which were based on endogenous growth models, the hypothesis that exports played a special role in economic development was not convincingly proven. Some studies have either disagreed with this hypothesis or have found this relationship tenuous (Kormendi and Meguire 1985, Grossman and Helpman 1991, Young 1991, Levine and Renelt 1992). Empirical studies exploring cross-country evidence have shown that per capita growth rates had little correlation with the export/GDP ratios once the regression included other important variables, such as saving, investment in plant and equipment, and technology absorption.

However, the recent economic history of the NIEs, the ASEAN-4 countries, and lately the PRC would seem to provide ample evidence that these economies benefited from the successful promotion of exports. Export success—both to and beyond Asia—was responsible for faster growth in industrialization than in other developing economies during the same period. In many of these economies, particularly the NIEs, the phenomenal growth in export earnings was equivalent to about one third of the increase in output growth during the early phases of industrialization. Although the period of rapid economic growth differs for other developing Asia's economies, similar evidence is available for them. It is particularly conspicuous for Malaysia and Thailand during the latter half of the 1980s and the early 1990s, although it is less apparent for Indonesia and the Philippines.

The regression results of Fukuda and Toya (1995) show that the effect of exports on developing Asia's economic growth was significantly positive. Their rejection of the studies that came up with ambiguous conclusions regarding the link between export and economic growth is somewhat sweeping. They think that data problems and inappropriate dummy variables caused ambiguity in

[3] For a detailed survey of this literature, see Edwards (1993).

the results. However, what is convincing is their assertion that the standard endogenous growth model is not applicable to Asian economies of the 1980s and the early 1990s because the post-Plaza Accord[4] currency configuration led to a dramatic increase in the demand for exports of manufactured goods from developing Asia's economies. This big pull on the demand side had spillover effects in Asia's developing economies. It also contributed to a rapid growth rate in developing Asia without following the sequence of steps prescribed by the endogenous growth models. (Chapter 2 focuses on these and related issues.)

As stated above, export expansion in the successful exporting economies was accompanied by rising GDP, continued structural transformation, and maturing economic systems. We shall see later in the case studies of five economies in the region (Chapters 5–9) that as these economies moved up their growth curve, the product mix of exports continued to change. Initially, their product mix was confined to labor-intensive and low value-added products. The majority of these exports were concentrated in low-technology sectors such as textiles and clothing. But soon these economies began to step up the technological ladder. The capital/labor ratio continued to increase and currently some of them, particularly the NIEs and Malaysia, export highly sophisticated electronics, semiconductors, and other computer-related products.

According to the latest (1996) statistics, exports of manufactures from developing Asia's 10 largest exporters have reached $641 billion (Table 1.5). In 1970, these exports were only $6 billion. By 1996, manufactured products from Hong Kong, China; and Taipei,China accounted for almost 95 percent of total exports; even in the country with the lowest proportion, the Philippines, 44 percent of total exports were manufactures.

Direction of Developing Asia's Exports

As regards the direction of trade in the 1960s, the vast part of developing Asia's exports went to industrial economies. Singapore

[4] The (former) Group of Five leading industrial economies (G-5) arrived at this Accord in September 1985.

Table 1.5 Developing Asia, Exports of Manufactures, 1975–1996

	Exports of Manufactures ($ billion)[a]				Share of Total Exports (percent)			
	1975	1980	1990	1996	1975	1980	1990	1996
NIEs	15.2	55.0	189.2	356.7	69.7	78.2	88.6	89.6
Hong Kong, China	4.5	13.2	27.5	25.8	74.3	96.0	94.9	94.2
Korea	4.1	15.8	61.0	115.9	81.6	90.2	93.8	89.4
Singapore	2.3	8.6	38.0	105.9	41.8	44.7	72.3	84.7
Taipei,China	4.3	17.4	62.7	109.0	81.3	88.2	93.5	94.2
ASEAN-4	2.1	8.2	43.9	135.0	13.9	16.6	50.9	66.1
Indonesia	0.2	0.9	9.7	26.2	2.4	3.9	37.9	52.6
Malaysia	1.2	3.6	16.3	60.1	30.4	27.8	55.2	76.8
Philippines	0.4	1.4	3.4	9.0	16.3	23.5	40.9	43.6
Thailand	0.4	2.3	14.6	39.8	19.6	34.9	63.4	71.4
PRC	-	8.8	34.6	129.1	-	48.6	55.7	85.5
India	2.4	5.0	13.6	20.2[b]	50.7	58.8	73.4	76.6[b]

[a] Exports comprise chemicals, basic manufactures, machines, transport equipment, and miscellaneous manufactured goods.
[b] Data refer to 1994.

Source: ADB (various years).

and Thailand were the only exceptions, exporting more than half their total exports to other developing economies (within and outside Asia). During the early 1970s, the NIEs successfully penetrated the markets of industrial countries in an extensive range of products. The liberalizing international trade regime, under the various rounds of multilateral trade negotiations (MTNs) sponsored by the General Agreement on Tariffs and Trade (GATT), helped these economies enormously. This environment was more favorable for international trade than in the past. In addition, by this time the NIEs had acquired competitiveness in a whole range of skills-intensive, medium-technology products. The NIEs took advantage of these two factors and made profitable niches for their exports in industrial economies, particularly the US. They achieved this penetration of industrial country markets at the cost both of other developing countries outside the region, and of indigenous producers in the importing countries. Their success in exporting initially led to mild trade frictions between them and importing countries.

While Malaysia and Thailand gradually increased their share of exports to industrial countries, India, Pakistan, and Philippines were less successful. However, over the 1970s on balance, the relative importance of industrial countries for developing Asian exporters increased considerably, and that of other developing countries and centrally planned economies declined. The trends during the 1980s were markedly different from those in the 1970s, when mild protectionist tendencies became apparent in industrial countries. This threatened to turn into stringent protectionism and it became difficult for developing Asia's exporters to penetrate these markets. Gray area measures such as voluntary export restraints (VERs) and orderly marketing arrangements were applied. Consequently, exports from developing Asia began increasingly to go to other developing countries, and intraregional trade began to rise. Intraregional exports were 22.3 percent of total Asian exports in 1980, but rose to 31.6 percent by 1990. According to WTO (1997), intra-Asian exports reached 51.6 percent of total exports in 1996. This upward trend was favorably influenced by growing market size, political stability, physical proximity between the trading partners, cultural similarities, and membership in the Asia-Pacific Economic Cooperation (APEC) forum and, to a lesser degree, membership in ASEAN (Yu and Zietlow 1995). It should, however, be noted that different parameters affect intra-Asian exports in different ways in different periods (Cushman 1990).

With the passage of time, transformations in comparative advantage have taken place in the rapidly growing Asian economies. Although detailed product-wise analyses are available (Singer 1993, Das 1997), a broad pattern in this movement can be briefly depicted as follows. The NIEs had comparative advantage in labor-intensive goods and primary products in the 1960s. Singapore was an exception, with comparative advantage in capital-intensive goods. India and Pakistan had comparative advantage in low-technology manufactures, such as textiles and leather products. Other Asian economies had no comparative advantage in manufactures, and exported primary products. In the 1970s, the NIEs lost their comparative advantage in primary products (although they maintained it in some labor-intensive goods) but acquired it in other areas, namely, skills- and capital-intensive manufactures. India, Philippines, and Thailand gained comparative advantage in labor-intensive manufactures, but the first two could not exploit it because of a high degree of economic distortion and the continued inward-orientation of their trade regimes.[5]

In the 1980s, with the help of sustained high-technology imports, the NIEs enhanced their comparative advantage in skills- and capital-intensive manufactures, and Malaysia followed closely behind. The PRC acquired comparative advantage in chemicals and light engineering. India made some progress, but much less than the PRC and the NIEs. In the 1990s, the NIEs moved into higher-technology products and became large exporters of electronics, integrated circuits, semiconductors, and other computer-related products. In 1995, Korea and Malaysia were among the largest exporters of dynamic random-access memory (DRAM) chips. The growth of the high-technology sector in PRC and Malaysia was supported by heavy inflows of foreign direct investment (FDI). An important characteristic is that the specialization of most Asian economies remained confined to a relatively narrow range of products, which rendered their export revenues vulnerable.

The agreements made at the Uruguay Round (discussed below) will indisputably influence world trade, including Asian trade. The final year of implementation of the Uruguay Round is 2005. Although no one knows for sure what world trade will look like then, it will be decisively different from now. The global and Asian pattern of comparative advantage has been changing and is likely to continue. There is a strong possibility that the NIEs and ASEAN-4 will gain comparative advantage in the production of capital- and technology-intensive products. Hertel et al. (1996) believe that a projections approach to analysis of the Uruguay Round inspired policy reforms captures both the interaction between economic growth and changing comparative advantage.[6] They suggest that the implementation of the agreements inspired by the Uruguay Round will give rise to a 17 percent increase in the welfare gains in developing Asia, the largest of any region.

---

5 It should be mentioned that the Philippines made a short-lived attempt to liberalize its economy in the early 1980s, but it had to be abandoned because of macroeconomic instability.

6 They simulated a global trade analysis and projections (GTAP) model by shocking a relatively small number of fundamental determinants of output. The GTAP model is a relatively standard, multiregional, applied general equilibrium model, which assumes perfectly competitive markets and constant returns to scale technology. Unlike most such models, GTAP uses a sophisticated representation of consumer demands that allows for differences in the income responsiveness of demand in different regions, depending on both the level of development of the region and the particular consumption patterns observed in that region. Detailed documentation on the model and applications that demonstrate its properties is available in T. Hertel, ed. (1996).

Uniqueness of Asian Exports

Some commentators have seen something unique about Asian exports, but this would seem to be ill founded. Noland (1997) and Trefler (1995) have analyzed the commodity composition of exports from Asia. They investigated such hypotheses as Asian economies record very high (or low) exports in relative and absolute terms in certain products or sectors; Asian exports are concentrated in a few sectors; and a unique "Asian export pattern" exists.

To investigate whether there is a distinctively Asian export pattern, export similarity indexes were constructed. They were defined as

$$XS(a,b)=\sum_i min(X_{ia}, X_{ib})*100,$$

where X_{ia} (X_{ib}) is the industry *i* export share in country *a's (b's)* exports which have been calculated for nine Asian economies and a sample of 21 other non-Asian countries. The index varies from 0 to 100, with 0 indicating complete export dissimilarity, and 100 complete correspondence. Results show that Hong Kong, China; Korea; and Taipei,China share the highest export similarity values. The indexes for 1988 were higher than in 1968, implying that the export patterns of these three economies grew more similar over the two decades. There is some support for the hypothesis that Korea's and Taipei,China's exports followed Japanese export patterns. When Korea's export pattern for 1988 was compared with the sample countries' export patterns in 1968, the Japanese pattern had the highest similarity value (70), although it was lower than the contemporaneous value for Taipei,China. The results for Singapore were different from those of the other NIEs, perhaps reflecting its extensive investment relations with other Southeast Asian economies. In 1968, its highest export similarity pairings were with Indonesia (75), Malaysia (52), and Spain (50). In 1988 its highest values were with Malaysia (66), United Kingdom (61), and Taipei,China (58). When the noncontemporaneous pairings are calculated, Singapore's export similarity was the highest with Western European countries, e.g., Italy (60), Spain (54), Austria (51), and France (51), suggesting that Singapore is following a Western European pattern. It should, however, be noted that these results simply compare two points in time. If a different lag were examined (e.g., 10, instead of 20 years), a different similarity ranking might be obtained.

In the late 1960s, Malaysia consistently exhibited the highest degree of export similarity with its Southeast Asian neighbors, such as Indonesia, Philippines, Singapore, and Thailand. In contrast, over 1968–1988, the export similarities of Thailand shifted from non-Asian countries such as Brazil (70) and Mexico (59) to Asian countries such as Philippines (57), Taipei,China (57), and Korea (56). Interestingly, Thailand's export pattern in 1988 was more similar to that of Taipei,China in 1968 than any contemporaneous pairing, with the next highest noncontemporaneous pairing being Korea (53) and Hong Kong, China (51). In that sense, Thailand might be said to be following the export pattern of Hong Kong, China; Korea; and Taipei,China.

Somewhat similar results were obtained for the Philippines. In 1968 the highest export similarity pairings were with non-Asian countries such as Peru (53) and Brazil (42), but by 1988 the highest pairings were with Thailand (57) and Malaysia (53). The highest non-contemporaneous pairings were with Taipei,China (56) and Korea (54), suggesting that the Philippines, too, might be following in the NIEs' footsteps. The export similarity indexes for Indonesia exhibited the greatest change. In 1968 they were highest with Singapore (75), Malaysia (51), and Tunisia (49). In 1988, presumably due to its oil exports, its export similarity pairings were highest with Mexico (59), Norway (56), and Malaysia (52).

The export patterns of Japan, and to an extent Singapore, are more similar to those of some Western European economies, both contemporaneously and noncontemporaneously, than to other Asian countries, and there is little evidence that Asian countries, with the possible exception of Korea, are following the Japanese export pattern. However, there is some evidence that the two export patterns of Hong Kong, China; Korea; and Taipei,China on the one hand; and Malaysia, Philippines, and Thailand on the other, have grown similar over time.

The above results show, therefore, that none of the three hypotheses is supported by analysis, and that there is no such thing as a unique "Asian export pattern."

International Trading Environment

The rapid export expansion in developing Asia, particularly in the NIEs and the ASEAN-4 countries, benefited substantially from the rapid improvement in the international trading environment, which in turn was the direct consequence of seven rounds of MTNs held under the aegis of GATT in 1947–1979. Trade expansion in Asia fortuitously coincided with GATT-sponsored trade liberalization (see Chapter 4). These MTNs succeeded in bringing down tariff barriers, particularly in the industrial economies that were substantial markets for Asia.

The last round of MTNs, the Uruguay Round, started in September 1986 and ended after seven years of protracted negotiations in December 1993. This was the most ambitious of the rounds and culminated with significant achievements in terms of liberalization of tariffs and nontariff barriers. Implementation of the recommendations of this round will go a long way to improving the international trading environment. It was agreed that tariffs would be eliminated on pharmaceuticals, equipment for construction, agriculture and medicine, paper, furniture, toys, and beer. It was also agreed that tariffs would be reduced substantially on chemicals and certain electronics items such as semiconductors, electronics parts, and semiconductor manufacturing equipment. In addition, tariffs on many other items would be lowered by smaller amounts. All cuts would be staged over five to ten years, depending upon the product line. At the time of completion of implementation of the Uruguay Round recommendations, the average tariff rate for industrial countries should have declined from 5 percent to 3.6 percent.

The Uruguay Round negotiators also agreed that subsidies on agricultural exports would be reduced by 21 percent and the ban on rice imports to Japan and Korea would be lifted, to be replaced by an import quota of 4 percent of domestic consumption. Nontariff barriers, including the variable levies of the European Union (EU), various VERs, and import quotas would be replaced by tariffs that would be reduced gradually. The Multifibre Arrangement (MFA), which limited trade in textiles and clothing, would be phased out over a 10-year period. Many countries agreed to the comprehensive binding of reasonable (as defined by the importing countries) tariff rates. Export subsidies were prohibited. A framework agreement was also reached in the area of service transactions, which includes most favored nation (MFN) treatment, national treatment, and market access. At an organizational level, WTO was established in 1995, and the General Agreement on Trade in Services (GATS) was signed the same year. In addition, in 1997 three multilateral agreements were signed, on telecommunications, information technology, and financial services. However, despite such continued improvement in the international trading environment, the mid-1990s did not turn out to be a successful period for Asian exports.

THE PAST IS NO GUIDE TO THE FUTURE

The picture of Asian exports that has emerged from the foregoing exposition is positive and favorable. It sounds like an Asian success story. However, successful performance in the past need not vouch for the same in the future. The salutary long-term trend came to an end in 1996, when export growth rates began to decelerate. The deceleration was not only precipitous, but also struck all the high-performing economies of the region. For example, the average export growth rate of the 10 largest developing Asia's exporters in 1995 was 22.6 percent, a figure that fell to 4.3 percent growth in 1996. In 1997, their average growth rate rose to 7.2 percent, an improvement, but hardly a recovery. The performance of two Asian economies in 1996–1997 was noteworthy. First, the export growth rate of the Philippines did not decelerate. Second, exports from the PRC were the fastest to pick up after a decline during the first two quarters of 1996.

Judging by their quarterly growth rates in 1996, the magnitude of deceleration in the two traditionally successful country groups, namely, the NIEs and the ASEAN-4 countries, was of a similar magnitude (Figure 1.1). Economies that recorded the steepest deceleration in their export growth rates were the PRC; Hong Kong, China; and Thailand. The deceleration occurred because of a combination of three kinds of generic factors, namely, cyclical, structural, and country-specific. Among the NIEs, Hong Kong, China suffered from country-specific factors, and Korea; Singapore; and Taipei,China from cyclical and structural factors. Among the ASEAN-4 countries, deceleration in Indonesia was largely caused by country-specific factors, in Malaysia by cyclical and country-specific factors, and in Thailand by structural factors. In PRC, country-specific

Figure 1.1 Quarterly Growth of Asian Exports

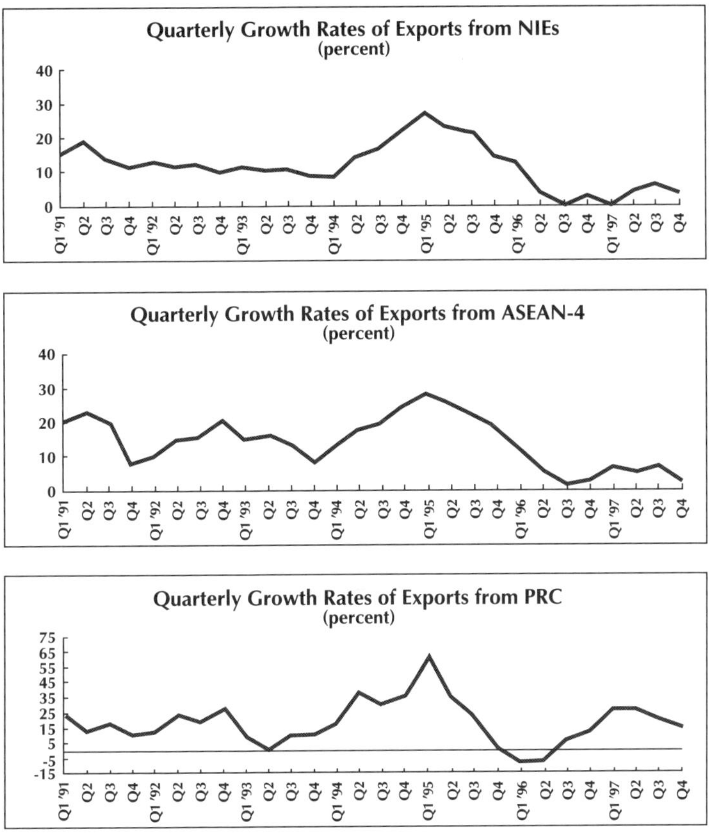

Sources: IMF, *International Financial Statistics,* (various years); Central Bank of China, *Financial Statistics, Taiwan District, The Republic of China*; Bank of Thailand Website; and Bank Negara Malaysia Website.

factors were the main causes of export deceleration. These issues are discussed further in Chapter 3 and Chapters 5-9.

Although the export performance of the ASEAN-4 countries improved in the first quarter of 1997, the NIEs recorded a negative growth rate, largely because of the poor performance of Korea and Singapore. Export growth in the PRC was relatively strong in the first three quarters of 1997, though it was affected by the economic and financial crisis in the region in the fourth quarter, then declined.

The financial and currency crisis, which struck Thailand in July 1997 and spread to other Asian economies, caused sharp currency depreciations. Between July 1997 and March 1998, the Korean won depreciated by 46.4 percent, the New Taiwan dollar by 12.7 percent, and the Singapore dollar by 11.4 percent, against the US dollar. (The Hong Kong dollar did not depreciate.) The Indonesian rupiah depreciated by 72.6 percent over the same period, the Malaysian ringgit by 31.4 percent, and the Philippine peso by 33.9 percent. The Chinese yuan resisted all pressures to depreciate through the crisis period, which was a respite to the other regional currencies. Finally, the currencies of India and Pakistan, countries that were not involved in the Asian crisis, recorded minor depreciations.

EXPORTS AFTER THE ASIAN CRISIS

When Asia's financial and currency crisis followed close behind the export deceleration of 1996, the general expectation was that large currency depreciations would lead to a spurt in exports, which in turn would act as a vehicle of recovery. The regional rescue programs of the International Monetary Fund (IMF) were partly based on this assumption. Currency depreciation implies that products exported from the stricken Asian economies should be less expensive in their export markets and so more price competitive; and indeed, though export volumes have grown in some Asian economies, by the third quarter of 1998, any expectations of a dramatic export revival have proved to be ill founded. It is increasingly felt that much of the post-depreciation export optimism was exaggerated. Conversely, imports recorded sharp declines in all Asia's crisis economies, falling by as much as half in Indonesia and Thailand.

To equate a depreciating currency directly with potential export gains is a little unrealistic because a currency's value is only one of the variables affecting export volume growth. The other variables include import content of exports, labor market conditions, liquidity in the domestic financial market, and export demand. Thus, both supply- and demand-side factors affect export performance. If we base our entire calculation of export demand on currency valuations, then we ignore the whole supply side. In addition, although a depreciating currency makes exports cheaper, the extent of this depends on the degree by which exporters' prices have fallen, on the price elasticity of demand in importing countries, and on how much of the price decline is passed on to importers by exporters.

Several supply-side factors are retarding exports in Asia. Many export products, such as electronics or shoes, have a significant import content.[7] Currency depreciation raises their input costs that offsets any advantage that low wages provide. In Indonesia, Malaysia, and Thailand exporters on average import over 30 percent of the raw materials and equipment used in their production processes. In the electronics and automobile assembly sectors, generally 60–90 percent of export value is derived from imported parts. By increasing input costs, currency depreciation contributes to a decline in export competitiveness.

Given such reliance on imports by exports, access to finance is vital to the prospects for an export-led economic recovery. This includes working capital, import finance, and trade (or export) finance. However, banks in the crisis Asian economies cannot lend because many of them are still struggling to meet the 8 percent capital-adequacy ratio required by IMF. If they fail to meet the requirement, they will be forced to shut down. Another problem is that banks in several Asian economies suffer from massive bad debts. There is consequently a severe credit shortage, and bank finance has virtually dried up in the affected economies. This is hampering the ability of Asian firms to take advantage of the steep currency depreciations. When export orders are received, there is no liquidity to purchase the necessary inputs. And since so many banks are in a poor state, their letters of credit are not acceptable to foreign banks. In addition, financial costs have soared with interest rates in some countries at around 30 percent, a level considered necessary by central banks and IMF to stabilize currencies. Finally, in Indonesia particularly, inflation has started to rise, threatening export competitiveness.

Large importers are aware of depreciating currencies, and are demanding price cuts in US dollars of 35–60 percent. However, exporters' costs have not fallen by that much (as mentioned above). They can barely afford 10 percent reductions, if anything. A small price decline will not raise export volumes substantially, unless the price elasticity of demand is extremely high. Unfortunately for Asian

[7] The import content of Nike shoes exported from various Asian locales is as high as 70 percent.

exporters, this is low for some of their major export items, such as electronics.

Intraregional and Japanese demands were weak in the latter half of 1997 and early 1998, and all the demand vigor had to come from the EU and the US. Monthly trade statistics show that export volumes increased for some of the affected economies during December 1997 and the early months of 1998. The US was a large market for these exports, even earning the sobriquet "market of last resort," as its trade deficit continued to swell. This also kept thriving US firms alert in much the same manner as the appreciating yen had forced the Japanese industry to keep growing more competitive in the early 1990s.

Large currency depreciations are having a distorting effect over comparative advantage in the crisis-stricken economies. Low-technology products that had lost their comparative advantage have begun to reappear; this occurrence is undesirable for the economic structures of these economies, as it amounts to economic and technological regression. In Korea, for example, the textiles, garments, and footwear industries have begun to revive after virtually disappearing a decade ago.

STRUCTURE OF THIS VOLUME

The foregoing commentary serves as an introduction to this volume. Chapters 2 to 4 comprise the first part, and deal with regional issues related to Asian exports. Chapters 5 to 9 are the second part, and consist of in-depth case studies on five economies in the region. Chapter 10 offers a summary analysis and makes certain policy recommendations.

In Chapter 2, Anne Krueger focuses on the determinants of Asian economic growth and the role played by the export sector. She looks at the policy instruments that directly affect exports, namely, the exchange rate, the overall cost of fiscal and monetary policies, and the trade regime. The last element includes both the degree of protection against imports and freedom of access of exporters to world markets for inputs. She also examines the factors that can sustain rapid growth of export earnings.

In Chapter 3, on the principal causes behind Asian export deceleration, Takatoshi Ito discusses the reasons for the "stalling of the export engine" in the region that led to a declining economic growth rate. Among several factors, he blames exchange rate appreciation for the export deceleration. In Chapter 4, David Greenaway assesses recent developments in regional and multilateral trading integration, prospects for further regional integration in Asia, and the impact of the new post-Uruguay Round trading environment on Asian exports.

The export sectors of five regional economies are examined: PRC; Korea; Malaysia; Taipei,China; and Thailand. Together, this group of economies represents a fair geographical distribution as well as differing degrees of success in export performance in the region.

The PRC adopted its open-door policy in 1979, which played an important role in economic development, particularly in export growth. Its contribution to the whole economy has been dramatic. During 1979–1997, the PRC was one of the fastest growing economies in the world, maintaining an average growth rate of over 10 percent. Chapter 5 addresses the country's export performance.

Korea and Taipei,China, until recently, were the two most successful Asian economies in terms of export performance. Their brisk GDP growth, stable prices, and equitable income distribution are partly attributed to their success on the export front. Both IMF and the World Bank have reclassified these two economies as advanced economies. Many developing countries, in their endeavor to improve their export performance, have tried to take policy lessons from these two high achievers. Chapters 6 and 7 provide a detailed account of their export sectors and their performance over the last three decades.

Although late starters, Malaysia and Thailand have also recorded high export growth since the early 1980s. Of the two, Malaysia has succeeded in transforming its export structure more and has become a significant exporter of electronics, and other computer-related and information technology (IT) products. Chapters 8 and 9 focus on their export performance.

Chapter 10 summarizes the present predicament and attempts to glance into the immediate future. An export forecasting exercise has been purposefully avoided because, first, the parameters it would be based on change frequently. Second, differing assumptions and minor changes in models would also change results dramatically, rendering the whole forecasting process of little value.

At the time of writing this volume, mid- to late 1998, the Asian economies that are still mired in macroeconomic and financial problems are seriously trying to reform their economic systems, particularly their financial sectors. And although the export growth rate improved marginally in 1997, any pattern of a long-term economic recovery cannot yet be discerned. However, if the reforms are carried out effectively and implemented in a timely manner, the country studies suggest the strong possibility of an export recovery in these economies over the medium term.

BIBLIOGRAPHY AND REFERENCES

Asian Development Bank (ADB). Various years. *Key Indicators of Developing Asian and Pacific Countries*. Oxford University Press for the ADB.

Balassa, B. 1978. "Exports and Economic Growth: Further Evidence." *Journal of Development Economics* 5:181-189.

Balassa, B., and J. Williamson. 1990. *Adjusting to Success: Balance of Payments Policies in the East Asian Economies*. Washington, DC: Institute for International Economics.

Council for Economic Planning and Development (CEPD). 1997. *Taiwan Statistical Data Book 1997*. Taipei,China.

Cushman, D. 1990. "US Bilateral Trade Equations: Forecasts and Structural Stability." *Applied Economics* 22(8):1093-1102.

Das, Dilip K. 1997. "Asian Exports: Past Trends and Future Prospects." February. Manila: ADB. Mimeo.

Edwards, S. 1992. "Trade Orientation, Distortions and Growth in Developing Countries." *Journal of Development Economics* 39: 31-57.

______. 1993. "Openness, Trade Liberalization, and Growth in Developing Countries." *Journal of Economic Literature* 31:1358-1393.

Feder, G. 1982. "On Exports and Economic Growth." *Journal of Development Economics* 12:59-74.

Fukuda, S., and H. Toya. 1995. "Conditional Convergence in East Asian Countries: The Role of Exports in Economic Growth." In T. Ito and A. O. Krueger, eds., *Growth Theories in Light of the East Asian Experience*: 247-262. Chicago: University of Chicago Press.

Grossman, G., and E. Helpman. 1991. *Innovation and Growth in the Global Economy*. Cambridge, Mass.: MIT Press.

Hertel, T. W., ed. 1996. *Global Trade Analysis: Modelling and Application*. Cambridge: Cambridge University Press.

Hertel, T. W., C. W. Bach, B. Dimaranan, and W. Martin. 1996. "Growth, Globalization, and Gains from Uruguay Round." Policy Research Paper No. 1614. May. Washington, DC: World Bank.

International Monetary Fund (IMF). Various issues. *International Financial Statistics Yearbook*. Washington, DC.

______. *World Economic Outlook.* October 1997. Washington, DC.

Kormendi, R. C., and P. G. Meguire. 1985. "Macroeconomic Determinants of Growth: Cross-Country Evidence." *Journal of Monetary Economics* 16:141-163.

Krueger, A. O. 1980. "Trade Policy as an Input to Development." *American Economic Review* 70:288-292.

______. 1995. "East Asian Experience and Endogenous Growth Theory." In T. Ito and A. O. Krueger, eds., *Growth Theories in the Light of the East Asian Experience.* Chicago: University of Chicago Press.

Levine, R., and D. Renelt. 1992. "A Sensitivity Analysis of Cross-Country Growth Regressions." *American Economic Review* 82: 942-963.

Noland, M. 1997. "Has Asian Export Performance Been Unique?" *Journal of International Economics* (43):79-101.

Richardson, J. David and Karin Rindal. 1995. *Why Exports Really Matter!* Washington, DC: Institute for International Economics and The Manufacturing Institute.

Singer, H. W. 1993. *Economic Progress and Prospects in the Third World.* Aldershot: Edward Elgar Publishing Co.

Trefler, D. 1995. "The Case of the Missing Trade and Other HOV Mysteries." *Journal of Political Economy* (101):1029-1046.

World Trade Organization (WTO). 1997. *Annual Report 1997.* Vol. I. Geneva.

Young, A. 1991. "Learning by Doing and the Dynamic Effects of International Trade." *Quarterly Journal of Economics* 106: 369-405.

Yu, C. M. J., and D. S. Zietlow. 1995. "The Determinants of Bilateral Trade Among Asia-Pacific Countries." *ASEAN Economic Bulletin* 11(3): 298-305.

CHAPTER TWO

Factors Affecting Export Growth and Performance and the Asian Case

Anne O. Krueger

INTRODUCTION

Ever since the world noticed that the newly industrialized economies (NIEs) of Asia—Hong Kong, China; Korea; Singapore; and Taipei,China—were growing rapidly while experiencing booming growth of export earnings, many policymakers and analysts have sought to understand the determinants of export growth, the reasons for rapid export growth, and its relationship to overall economic growth, with a view to achieving similar results in their own economies.

In this chapter, we focus on the determinants of export performance, in particular on the policy variables and changes in arrangements that can be conducive to more rapid export growth in support of sound overall economic growth. Policymakers want to achieve more rapid export growth because they believe it helps economic performance; and for this reason, it is important to understand why export growth can support better economic performance. Exports, even export earnings, are not an end in themselves: they are a means of efficiently utilizing resources to attain the goods and services desired by society.

The first section of this chapter, therefore, contains a discussion on the linkages between export growth and overall economic growth. Thereafter, the discussion turns to the determinants of economically efficient export performance and economic growth. In the following section, we look at those policy instruments that directly affect exports: the exchange rate, the overall expansiveness of fiscal and monetary policy, and the trade regime, including both the degree of protection against imports and freedom of access of exporters to world markets for needed inputs.

In the third section, we examine those domestic markets and policy variables that indirectly, but significantly, affect exports. These include such things as the flexibility or rigidity of the labor market, the structure and enforcement of taxes, the efficiency of infrastructure, and the workings of capital markets. In the fourth section, we look into those factors that can sustain rapid growth of export earnings and those that can lead to a deceleration in export growth. The fifth section applies these broad generalizations to the differential performance of various Asian economies. The final section then analyzes current prospects for the Asian economies.

EXPORT PERFORMANCE AND OVERALL ECONOMIC GROWTH

Definitions

In considering the relationship between export performance and economic growth, it is useful to start from cyclical factors and world demand conditions.[1] While it is true that export earnings increase when the terms of trade turn very favorable, and decrease when they turn unfavorable, these fluctuations in the terms of trade are transitory, and do not affect the long-term growth of export earnings. Even for countries with an abundance of a "good" primary commodity such as petroleum, long-term growth of export earnings is much more a function of policies with respect to exports from the rest of the economy than it is of the fortunes of the petroleum sector.[2] Many countries have seen stronger, but temporary, economic growth when their terms of trade have improved or when demand for one or more of their exports has risen with the cyclical expansion of the world economy, only to discover that export growth and overall economic

1 Chapter 3 discusses cyclical factors that affect export performance.

2 An interesting example is Mexico. Since Mexico undertook economic reforms and began encouraging export growth, export earnings from petroleum, which accounted for more than half of all export earnings as recently as 1985, have fallen to about 8 percent of all export earnings.

growth plummet when the world business cycle enters a new phase. In this chapter, therefore, export growth is defined as the long-term trend in a country's foreign exchange earnings from exports of goods and nonfactor services. Nonfactor services are included because they can be important for some countries, e.g., the financial services of Hong Kong, China; Panama; and Singapore.[3]

Even with this definition, it is useful to note an important distinction between export growth arising from a reasonably economically efficient set of incentives and export growth induced by other factors. "Reasonably economically efficient" incentives are relatively uniform and across the board. They provide equal incentives for producers to spend domestic resources to earn a dollar of foreign exchange in most lines of exporting activity, and do not provide differential rewards (depending on the nature of the export).

In some countries, discriminatory and ad hoc incentives have been provided to different economic activities under the guise of export promotion. Such export promotion accords various exports different rates of subsidy, and targets some activities for more incentives than others. It is not a sustainable strategy, and has not led to increases in overall growth rates—even when export growth has temporarily accelerated—any more than import-substitution strategies (which are selective and nonuniform by nature). The reasons are the same. When incentives are ad hoc and discriminatory, resource misallocation and other difficulties offset the gains that might otherwise accrue to improved export performance. In addition, export subsidies divert producers' attention from seeking ways to expand their export markets (and cut their costs) to lobbying for larger export incentives for their products. Indeed, it can be persuasively argued that more rapid

---

[3] Some countries, such as the Philippines, whose economic growth has been relatively slow, have experienced significant periods of increasing foreign exchange receipts from workers' remittances. These are factor service income. Workers leave for work overseas because of their inability to find sufficiently rewarding work at home, so rapid growth in workers' remittances is usually a consequence of sluggish export growth. While the remitted earnings permit a more liberal import regime (and hence somewhat more rapid growth) than would otherwise be possible, the rapid growth of workers' remittances has not normally been associated with accelerated overall economic growth. Countries where workers' remittances have grown rapidly over a decade or more include Turkey in the 1960s (workers went to Europe), Pakistan in the 1970s (the Middle East), and several countries in North Africa in the 1970s and 1980s. Peter Lloyd presents data on workers' remittances for selected Asian countries in 1980, 1985, 1990, and 1993. Among these countries, workers' remittances accounted for less than 0.3 percent of GDP in PRC, Indonesia, and Korea. At the other end of the range, workers' remittances were over 8 percent of GDP in Pakistan in 1980 and 1985, and over 5 percent of GDP in Sri Lanka in 1993. See Quibria (1996).

export growth leads to faster economic growth, largely because the across-the-board incentives that induce the speedup in export growth simultaneously reduce misallocation and attendant waste in the economy.

The second circumstance under which rapid growth of export earnings has not led to more rapid overall economic growth has already been mentioned, i.e., when export growth has been largely attributable to changes in the terms of trade, even when they are long lasting. One need think no further than the oil price increases of 1973 and 1979 and the failure of the members of the Organization of Petroleum Exporting Countries (OPEC) to achieve rapid economic growth to realize this.

In general, however, consensus seems to have been reached that openness is a prerequisite for satisfactory and sustained rates of economic growth, with exports as a leading sector.[4]

In this chapter, therefore, we are concerned with export growth achieved under policies that provide for reasonably uniform export incentives to most economic activities and do not differentiate significantly between activities in terms of rewards (except insofar as some activities are more profitable than others because of comparative advantage). This does not mean that there might not be some, probably relatively small, rewards to first-comers in new exports. The Korean Government, for example, provided certain incentives to producers in the first year that they exported either a new product or to a new country. These incentives were "one-offs," and were offered to any first-time exporter, regardless of the product. Such incentives, while not necessarily desirable, can be defended as encouraging would-be exporters to shoulder the risks of entering new markets (a variant of the infant-industry approach). In any event, such incentives relate only to the first year or so of exporting, and exporters must anticipate that they will, in future, receive the same rewards as other foreign exchange earners.

In this chapter, policies that provide reasonably uniform and across-the-board incentives for production of both exportable and import-competing goods will be referred to as "outer-oriented" or "export-oriented" trade strategies. While some have tried to distinguish between "outer-oriented" and "export-oriented," any

---

[4] See Sachs and Warner (1995), and Edwards (1993).

distinction makes little sense. In practice, there have been no instances of countries where the average incentive for production of exportables is above that for production of import-competing goods. Others have argued that "outer-oriented" implies further intervention (possibly even ad hoc and industry-specific) to encourage export production—perhaps offsetting incentives provided by tariffs and quantitative restrictions for import-competing production. In fact, successful policies that have resulted in rapid and sustainable growth of exports and real GDP have provided fairly uniform and across-the-board incentives for exporting. And, over time, the degree of discrimination against exports has been reduced, but generally not eliminated for a fairly long period. Incentives for exporting in the early stages of outer-oriented trade strategies have usually been fairly uniform and have, at most, partially offset incentives for import-competing production.[5]

Policies that provide for significantly higher incentives for production of import-competing goods than would prevail under free trade will be referred to as "import-substitution" strategies.[6] Such incentives include tariffs, quantitative restrictions on imports, domestic content requirements, and tax breaks and credit subsidies for import-competing producers.

To simplify terminology later, it is useful to define the "bias" of the trade and payments regime as the degree to which domestic prices of exportables relative to importables and import-competing goods diverge from the international price ratio that would prevail under free trade. For example, if all imports were subject to a 100 percent duty, while exports were shipped at the official exchange

---

5 See Frank et al. (1975), for a good account of the Korean regime during its switch to an outer-oriented trade strategy.

6 It is well known that free trade is only optimal when certain conditions are met. These conditions include the absence of monopoly power in trade (the small-country assumption), as well as a lack of imperfections in the domestic market. Since export growth comes about primarily through expansion of new lines of goods and services, countries typically do not have any monopoly power in the export markets they are entering; similarly, it is increasingly recognized that trade policy instruments are a very poor substitute for correction of domestic distortions at the source. For that reason, we shall couch the discussion of trade policy in terms of a small country, i.e., one unable to influence its terms of trade for the goods and services affected by the outer-oriented trade strategy. Likewise, we shall assume that domestic market imperfections are to be addressed (as they must anyway be for healthy growth) through policy instruments other than the trade regime. These assumptions have been broadly met for the Asian countries that have successfully employed outer-oriented trade strategies.

rate, the bias of the trade regime would be two—that is, the domestic incentives to produce import-competing goods would be twice the economically efficient incentives.[7] A more protectionist regime would, therefore, be one with a higher bias toward import-competing goods. An outer-oriented trade regime would be one with little or no bias toward either import-competing or exportable goods. The use of the concept of "bias" strongly underlines the important proposition that a trade regime cannot discriminate in favor of all tradables, and to the extent that there is protection for import-competing goods, there is discrimination, or bias, against exportables. To a very significant degree, it is relative prices that pull resources toward or away from particular activities.

The bias of the trade regime is neither identical to, nor even necessarily highly correlated with, its restrictiveness, though restrictions on foreign exchange normally entail some protectionist (and therefore antiexport) bias. The term restrictiveness usually refers to the degree to which quantitative restrictions on imports are binding or, alternatively, to the gap between the landed cost of imported goods and the domestic price of those goods. In practice, an outer-oriented trade regime cannot be very restrictive, because the price differential accorded to import-competing goods through quantitative restrictions is so high that exportables are discouraged and the bias is toward the import-competing activities. However, one could have a regime with very high tariffs (and thus a high bias toward import-competing goods) that was not restrictive, i.e., there would be no quantitative restrictions on imports.

The concept of bias is an average concept, expressing the difference between the average incentive to produce import-competing goods and the incentive to export. The variance in incentives across activities both within import-competing and exportable goods sectors is also important. With a genuine outer-oriented trade strategy, incentives for exporting have always been fairly uniform and, therefore, the variance in incentives across exportable activities has been quite small. This is because outer-oriented trade strategies require reasonably uniform incentives for

7 In this example, it is assumed that tariffs are the only intervention in trade. If quantitative restrictions provided additional protection against imports, the bias of the regime would be calculated including the additional protection provided by the quantitative restrictions (that is, the tariff equivalent of the restrictions).

exporting, not item-specific interventions. The latter give rise either to administrative delays (as officials decide which category an export belongs to) or to corruption (as exporters vie to be classified among the high-incentive categories).

It is also true that no export-oriented strategy has succeeded when protection against imports has remained very high for goods that are domestically produced. Consequently, the variance of protection (and protection-equivalents) across import-competing goods has tended to be smaller under outer-oriented, than import-substitution, trade regimes. Thus, while variance as well as mean bias of the trade regime is significant, a fairly strong correlation tends to be seen in practice between the height of the bias and the variance of incentives across activities, especially among import-competing goods.

There can also be measures that differentiate between the sale of the same good in different markets. Thus, export incentives increase the price of the good overseas relative to the domestic market (unless there is protection against imports of the good as well). In Korea in the 1960s, for example, there were some import-competing goods (in which the domestic market was protected from import competition by tariffs) where producers found it profitable to take advantage of the export incentives available. Frank et al. (1975) and other authors have found that they had to distinguish between exports of import-competing goods and exports of exportables. This distinction largely vanished by the 1980s, both because of the unification of the exchange rate regimes in Korea and because of reductions in tariff levels.

Determinants of Linkages between Export Growth and Economic Growth

The relationship between export growth and overall economic growth depends on a number of factors.[8] Countries differ in their factor endowments, their stages of development, size, location, and their

[8] That there is a positive and significant relationship between more rapid, sustained export growth and more rapid, continuing growth of real GDP is not questioned. See Dollar (1993) and Edwards (1992).

previous development strategies. These differences influence the optimal composition of trade (and exports), the optimal size of trade in relation to GDP, and the ways in which exports affect overall economic performance.

With regard to factor endowments, in countries with more land relative to labor, real wages of unskilled workers may be significantly higher than in countries where there is much less land per person. In this case, the benefits to growth based on rapid expansion of exports that use unskilled labor intensively are significantly smaller than for countries with much higher man-land ratios and lower real wages in the early stages of growth. Thus, for a given set of policies providing for incentives of a specified magnitude for exports, one would expect that Argentina, for example, with its abundant land and relatively high real rural unskilled wages would experience less export growth and less satisfactory overall growth than Pakistan, with its much higher man-land endowment. In fact, although Korean real wages are now much higher than those in, e.g., Argentina, unskilled real wages in Korea in the 1960s at the start of the outer-oriented trade strategy were much lower than in Argentina.

Stages of development matter to a degree, because policies that can induce satisfactory export and economic growth in the early stages of development may be inadequate to sustain performance when economies are more advanced. In an early stage, the population is largely rural, and there is little industry. Generally, comparative advantage lies in unskilled labor-intensive manufacturing, and there is a wide range of policies (including directed credit and tax incentives) that can be consistent with rapid export growth, at least for an initial period. As the economy becomes more complex, however, policymakers are unable to discern the relative merits of alternative seekers of subsidized credit (and other government-allocated privileges) and the costs of credit rationing and other selective controls and incentives increase rapidly. Maintaining export growth under an outer-oriented trade strategy requires constant attention to the reform of policies whose economic costs increase as the economy becomes more complex and as exports grow in relative and absolute importance.

This does not mean that selective policies are ever optimal, even in the early stages of an outer-oriented trade strategy. Rather, the "slack" in policy permissible while achieving satisfactory economic performance is probably much greater in countries in the earlier stages of development. To give a concrete example, policies that were quite conducive to rapid economic growth in Korea in the 1960s, such as directed credit to export industries, are no longer so in the 1990s. And even here, Korea's policy was so successful partly because there was no discrimination among exporters with regard to credit and other incentives.

Thus, successful export (and probably overall) growth from a very low base normally requires ongoing policy reforms. Those changes in incentives that are sufficient to induce an export response become inadequate to sustain it. Success itself breeds the need for more change. Sustained economic growth requires the breaking of rigidities and other factors that become new bottlenecks to growth, and it is the policymaker's challenge to identify the key bottlenecks at any given time.

In the early 1960s in Korea, for example, policymakers sustained the uniform and across-the-board set of export incentives in real terms by adjusting the "export subsidy," the "credit subsidy," and the "tax incentives" as domestic inflation rose, while maintaining a fixed nominal exchange rate. Thus, the real exchange rate (RER) for exporters was relatively constant, while imports were still constrained by quantitative restrictions. This system worked reasonably well initially, as exports were equivalent to only 3 percent of GDP, so that the cost of the subsidies was relatively small. Meanwhile, with domestic inflation, the RER for imports appreciated, so that incentives for exporting and import-competing activities were becoming more equal even though tariffs remained in place. However, by the late 1960s, Korean exports had grown to a much larger share of GDP, and the system of export incentives had to be replaced with a uniform exchange rate for all transactions.[9] Over the years, Korean policymakers have been repeatedly confronted with slowdowns in growth, and have had to identify the key bottlenecks and take appropriate measures.

A country's economic size and location also undoubtedly affect its potential for rapid export and overall growth. The economic costs of a given level and structure of protection are almost certainly higher in economies whose small internal markets make the effects of

[9] Very early in the Korean outer-oriented drive, quantitative restrictions were removed or relaxed and exporters were given very easy access to imported inputs. It was not until 1967, however, that a "positive list" of permitted imports was replaced with a negative list of prohibited imports—a much more liberal trade stance. Korean tariff reforms were made on several occasions after 1967, with the average tariff level falling over time. By the early 1990s, the average Korean tariff is estimated to have been around 4-5 percent. See Krueger (1996).

import-substitution policies even more uneconomic than in larger ones. Location may also affect the potential gains from exporting: countries distant from major markets (and perhaps especially when they are landlocked) may have different potential gains from opening up their economies than countries closer to major markets with significantly lower transport costs. However, little is known about how large the impact of size and location is. For example, it was widely expected that Chile would not experience significant export growth when policies were changed, because it was reasoned that the country was small and distant from most major markets. However, the Chileans' experience of rapid export growth is well known, and suggests that the disadvantages of distant location may be far less important than previously thought.[10]

Development strategy, before the adoption of an outer-oriented trade strategy, is clearly important in its impact both on potential export growth, and on the overall economic growth that can result. For policymakers in a country where incentives have been highly distorted and economic growth has been very slow, the potential for rapid export and overall growth, once policies are changed, is enormous. The real rate of return on investments in exportables is very high, as the opportunities that were earlier neglected can be employed.

However, policymakers in countries that have a history of failed or half-hearted reform efforts (with occasional backsliding) may have difficulty convincing the business community and others that they are serious about reform, and that a new incentive structure will be sustained. When there are doubts that such a structure in an outer-oriented regime will be sustained, response to changes in the incentives can be greatly delayed, often by several years. This has been seen in South Asia.

For countries where there has been far less bias toward import substitution (or the bias has persisted for a significantly shorter time), the potential gains from changing to an outer-oriented trade strategy, and the initial pickup in growth rates, may be slower. As rapid export growth continues, however, the opportunities for further large gains are necessarily somewhat reduced, and the rate of export growth inexorably slows. For our purposes, two of the important questions

[10] For a general analysis of the role of size and location, see Srinivasan (1986).

are (i) how long can rapid export growth be sustained, and (ii) what are the factors that influence the timing and magnitude of the slowdown in export growth that must inevitably take place? (These questions are addressed in the section *At What Rate Can Export Growth Be Sustained?* of this chapter.)

Why Do Outer-Oriented Trade Strategies Matter for Economic Growth?

Policymakers keen to raise living standards and to achieve rapid economic growth must choose between an import-substitution and an outer-oriented trade strategy. For reasons to be discussed below, it is possible to select parts of each: the very policies (tariffs and protection) that encourage import substitution serve as powerful disincentives for the flow of new resources into export industries. One strategy or the other is necessary because, in virtually all circumstances, the process of rapid economic growth entails increases in productivity in existing lines of economic activity, as well as expansion of new lines of activity, especially in manufacturing. Here, we focus on the components of such a strategy and how they affect growth. It should first be stressed, however, that the government's increasing of agricultural productivity (through investment as well as through agricultural extension, provision of infrastructure and education, and other activities) is essential for economic growth. When productivity does increase, it enables the release of some resources for nonagricultural production. In most countries, this translates into a more rapid rate of growth of output and employment in nonagricultural pursuits than in agricultural activities. Since much of industry is new, the trade strategy determines the relative profitability of alternative investments in new industries (including expansion of ones already established). When import-substitution investments are more profitable, a higher fraction of new investible resources goes into new activities, once the capacity of existing units has expanded to replace imports.

Either an import-substitution or outer-oriented industrialization strategy requires, in addition, complementary policies and investments. (These are discussed in the section *Indirect Policies* of this chapter.) The new lines of activity that are entered or expanded must sell either on the domestic market (import-substitution strategy) or abroad (outer-oriented trade strategy).

Import-substitution strategies are not necessarily inimical to growth initially, especially in the very early stages of development. Then, there are usually profitable investments in activities for which there is a fairly sizable domestic market that use relatively large amounts of one factor of production in which poor countries have a comparative advantage, i.e., unskilled labor. These activities usually have fairly low incremental capital/output ratios, and initial growth rates under import substitution can be reasonably satisfactory. Of course, in many instances, an optimal incentive structure would result in new industries producing for both the home and the foreign markets, even in the early stages of growth.

However, the ability of import-substitution policies to sustain growth over time weakens. After the initial phase of "light" industry development (of unskilled labor-intensive consumer goods industries), new investments are typically directed toward industries that are economically less advantageous to the country. Aside from the obvious consideration that much the same set of industries would likely be encouraged in the early stages of development under either strategy, many observers question the wisdom of embarking upon the import-substitution strategy even if it can deliver relatively rapid growth in the short run. This is because of the difficulties associated with shifting from an import-substitution strategy to an outer-oriented trade strategy. Those producers who entered and expanded their activities under import substitution generally strenuously oppose a shift in trade strategy, making it politically difficult to change strategies before the economic costs have mounted sharply and growth has slowed severely. Many observers have pointed out that Korea and Taipei,China switched strategies before the import-substitution policies had induced investments in products other than light consumer goods.

Growth weakens for several reasons. First, the "easy" industries are picked off initially and subsequent investments—which must be for goods and services to be sold in the home market because of the nature of the incentives offered—are usually for activities further away from the country's comparative advantage. Developing countries' comparative advantage usually consists of goods and services that are intensive in the use of unskilled labor, while their comparative disadvantage is strongest in goods and services that use human and physical capital intensively. Depending on the educational level of the population, there can be slight differences in relative endowments, but there are no examples of countries with abundant physical capital and little human capital, or vice versa. Human capital and physical capital seem to be somewhat complementary in the early stages of development, so that sound development programs entail increasing the educational level of the population at the same time that the capital stock per person is growing. For simplicity, we shall talk about physical capital in what follows. It should be understood, however, that both physical capital and human capital are in short supply in the early stages of development, and that countries adopting import-substitution policies find themselves developing industries with higher ratios of both physical and human capital to unskilled labor. This is among the many reasons why employment in industry tends to grow very slowly in countries adopting import substitution.

The second reason for the weakening of growth is that most developing countries, especially in the early stages of development, have fairly small domestic markets and, as import substitution continues, investments necessarily take place in activities where the domestic market is so small that investments are on too low a scale to be economic. In India, for example, the incremental capital/output ratio was estimated to be about 1.5:1 at the beginning of the Second Five-Year Plan, the start of the big industrialization-through-import substitution effort there. The ratio was estimated to have risen to about 8:1 when the country began policy reforms in the early 1990s.[11] Thus, while India (and most other countries adopting import-substitution policies) increased savings from the 1950s to the 1990s by even more than policymakers in the 1950s had hoped for, the growth rate did not accelerate. All the increase in the savings rate was offset, or more than offset, by increases in the incremental capital/output ratio. Obviously, factors other than the choice of trade strategy contributed to this, but the increasing capital intensity of new import-substitution industries was a major factor.

There are other reasons for weaker growth. Because of the small size of the domestic market, policymakers are in a difficult position when they provide protection. They can either permit entry and

[11] See Srinivasan (1994).

encourage many firms, each of too small a size, or they can limit entry and encourage the development of monopolies (or duopolies) in a variety of domestic industries. Efforts to find a middle path have usually resulted in a situation where one or two firms have a market power that is, in any event, predetermined by their shares of imports, and where incentives for quality improvement and cost reduction are consequently very weak. As a result, even when policies have been adopted to try to foster competition, domestic monopolies have frequently resulted, with attendant losses in productivity growth. The importance of competition as a spur to domestic producers for economic efficiency was greatly underestimated in the early days of development. In many countries, economic efficiency—with falling capital/output ratios, rising output, but no increase of investment—has risen markedly after a shift to an outer-oriented trade strategy.[12]

Further, as already mentioned, in the early stages of development it is not difficult for policymakers to identify the "deserving" import-competing producers, awarding them directed credit, import licenses, or other privileges. While there may be some inefficiencies, the economic costs of these decisions are not high. When virtually all manufactures are imported, it is fairly straightforward to support investments in clothing, footwear, vegetable oil refining, and other relatively labor-intensive manufacturing activities that have quite large consumer markets in the domestic economy, and that generally are not used as inputs into other manufacturing processes. As demand for these products is met largely by domestic production, however, these lines of activity can expand only with an increase in incomes or population. New lines of activity must be undertaken. As more and more new lines are added, the economy becomes increasingly complex, and it becomes far more difficult for officials to ascertain the relative economic merits of the alternatives, especially as most producers have strong incentives to represent, or misrepresent, their lines of activity as being especially "deserving." Mistakes become more costly as well, as a low-quality intermediate good can increase production costs and reduce the productivity of manufacturers using the output as an input in their process. In short, the economic inefficiencies associated with bureaucratic allocation of resources are not as great in the early stages of import substitution as they are in the

[12] See Krueger and Tuncer (1982) and Levinsohn (1993) for an analysis of the Turkish case.

later stages, when the economy is far more complex and when, therefore, it is far more difficult for officials to determine the economically efficient uses of resources. This assumes that officials want to make choices that lead to economically efficient results, which is surely true of many of them. Over time, however, lobbying for licenses and the high value attached to bureaucratic decisions influence outcomes, even when the economic choice is evident.

It should also be noted that the economic incentives for producers who know that there will be no other entrants permitted to an activity are quite different from the incentives facing them under free entry (with the same policies). It is likely that some, who might be low-cost and economically efficient producers under the competition induced by an open trade regime, remain economically less efficient under a protectionist trade regime.

Import-substitution strategies have also provided such a level of disincentives for export development, that most import-substitution countries have encountered increasingly severe "foreign exchange shortages." These strategies result in disincentives for exporters in a variety of ways. First and perhaps most important, the use of protection to encourage new industries provides new investors with a reasonably assured rate of return on investment, contrasted with the difficulties and uncertainties of entering the international market. As such, new investments are likely to be more attracted to import-competing than to export industries.

Second, because there are some products that potential exporters would need to purchase on the home market at relatively higher prices (because of protection to import-competing industries and the use of high-cost domestically produced import substitutes in home goods), would-be exporters face higher costs than their foreign competitors. Even when provisions are made for exporters to obtain needed imports without duties, bureaucratic delays in issuing licenses and supplying foreign exchange can lead to high costs. Alternatively, rebates of duties paid can be significantly delayed. Either way, these costs serve as a major deterrent to would-be exporters.[13]

---

[13] In the 1960s, Turkey opened the Eregli Steel Mill and it was expected that the mill would provide flat and rolled steel products for most Turkish industries. Until that time, Turkey had been exporting canned tomato paste and tomato sauce. But after producers had to use Eregli steel, those exports ceased. The cost to exporters of the tinplate used in the cans exceeded the price they received for the canned tomato paste or tomato sauce in Europe. While this example may be extreme, it vividly illustrates the impact of protecting some industries on the cost structure of other industries.

Third, when some high-cost import substitution industries are protected, there are inevitable temptations for smuggling and false invoicing to import lower-cost (and often higher-quality) products. The result is that the authorities seek to prevent this by tightening up customs entry procedures and changing licensing processes, among other methods. The resulting delays affect potential exporters as well as other importers, and constitute a significant barrier to potential exporters' abilities to meet deadlines, reduce inventory levels, and otherwise maintain a competitive cost structure for tackling the international market.

Fourth, pressures on the authorities to maintain a realistic exchange rate are greatly reduced under an import-substitution strategy, both because producers lobby to maintain an overvalued exchange rate (to keep the costs of imported inputs and capital equipment low) and because there is less feedback to the authorities regarding the exchange rate. To the extent that there are longer lags in adjusting the nominal exchange rate in import-substitution countries, exports are further discouraged.[14]

Foreign exchange shortages under import substitution have intensified inefficiencies, both because the authorities resorted to import licensing (with its attendant inefficiencies) to "conserve scarce foreign exchange" and because people began investing resources in obtaining scarce foreign exchange, with the attendant costs of rent-seeking that accompany quantitative restrictions. Since outer-oriented trade regimes of necessity are accompanied by realistic exchange rates and few (if any) quantitative restrictions, monopoly power is largely eliminated in tradable goods industries and, at the same time, the incentives to allocate resources for securing government favors are greatly reduced.

Over time, each of the negative consequences of import-substitution policies intensifies. So, after an initial phase when growth rates are satisfactory, they then start slowing. By the 1980s, most of the development community recognized this, and efforts have begun in many countries to change policies. The developing countries as a

[14] In many countries with import-substitution policies, the overvaluation of the exchange rate has become severe. In Ghana, for example, prior to the start of reforms with the 1984 Structural Adjustment Program, the black market premium on the official exchange rate was 980 percent.

whole have dramatically raised their savings rates since the late 1960s, but their growth rates have not appreciably risen.[15]

An outer-oriented trade strategy is recognized as having a number of advantages, many of which are on the opposite side of the coin of the disadvantages of import substitution. If there is a profitable activity, its expansion is not limited by the size of the domestic market because producers can expand sales abroad. Likewise, because producers can expand profitable activities abroad in unskilled labor-intensive activities in which there is comparative advantage, domestic employment in new industries rises more rapidly. Simultaneously, increased savings rates are not offset (or are offset to a much smaller degree) by the rapidly rising capital intensity of production. Since the market for some labor-intensive activities in developing countries is very small, the ability of producers to sell on the international market enables the development of a wide variety of economic activities, especially in manufacturing, that would not be viable under import substitution because of limited domestic demand at low levels of per capita income. Probably of equal importance is that an outer-oriented trade strategy confronts domestic producers with competition on the international market. Producers may learn from being forced to meet their competitors' quality standards and/or costs. Learning to compete is itself an important skill.

More generally, an outer-oriented trade strategy can succeed only when the framework of incentives for potential exporters and other producers provides for reasonable economic efficiency. (The policies that provide such a framework are discussed below.) There is little disagreement as to appropriate policies, although questions remain about the precise mechanisms through which they affect overall economic growth, the rate at which policy reform is desirable, and the necessary degree of reform in the various stages of development.

What is clear is that the misallocation of resources that can result from unrealistic exchange rates, severe quantitative restrictions, and bureaucratic selection of industries is greatly reduced. For the private sector, the profitability from obtaining government favors under an outer-oriented trade strategy is much less than from producing goods and services, and hence fewer resources are wasted in seeking

---

[15] See World Bank, *World Development Report*, various years, for data documenting these developments.

bureaucratic favors. Even the relative profitability of seeking ways to cut costs and improve quality, as contrasted with seeking favors and permits from officials, changes drastically.

The importance of each of these effects can vary considerably from country to country. In India, it would seem that many of the gains achieved to date as a result of policy reform have originated in the reduced profitability of seeking licenses and in increased competition. The size of the domestic market has meant that the previous inefficiencies of small-scale domestic production were probably much less (though not absent) than in smaller countries. By contrast, in the Chilean case, there seems little doubt that the reallocation of resources toward exportable industries (in agriculture as well as manufacturing) was a much more significant factor in accelerating growth.

While these questions of relative importance remain, and while the precise nature of the links between export growth and overall growth is still debated, there is no doubt that more satisfactory and sustainable overall economic growth is achieved under an outer-oriented trade strategy, with uniform and across-the-board incentives for producing tradable goods.

POLICIES AFFECTING EXPORT PERFORMANCE

Direct and Indirect Policies

Although a distinction between "direct" policies and "supporting" or "indirect" policies is somewhat arbitrary, it is nonetheless useful in attempting to assess the determinants of a successful outer-oriented trade strategy. As a general idea, "direct" policies impact on the allocation of resources between the production of exportables and the production of import-competing goods. They are necessary for an outer-oriented trade strategy. Without appropriate "signals" for resource allocation, satisfactory and sustainable export growth will not occur. The most important "direct" policy is the real exchange rate (RER), or the relationship between domestic and foreign costs for producers of exportables.

"Indirect" policies, on the other hand, are conducive to more satisfactory overall economic growth, and without them, the degree to which direct policies can affect export performance is limited. An example of an "indirect" policy is the provision of adequate educational opportunities for the population. Such a policy would contribute to economic growth under any strategy, but, if educational attainments do not increase, the returns from an outer-oriented trade strategy (as well as any other) will be highly limited. Provision of adequate infrastructure to provide economical transport and communications is another indirect policy, and represents an essential part of any satisfactory growth strategy. Failure to expand such infrastructure can impose a severe constraint on the attainable rate of export growth, even with appropriate direct policies in place.

Some countries, when shifting trade strategies, have had in place the types of supporting policies that permit the rapid acceleration of growth. Even then, as export growth has picked up, the authorities have had to pay careful attention to ensuring that infrastructure capacity has kept pace with the growing demands of increasing trade. In other countries, the lack of supporting policies has limited the extent to which gains might be realized by the switch to an outer-oriented trade strategy. In Chile, for example, it would appear that the educational attainment of the population by the early 1970s was adequate to support the shift to an outer trade orientation. Although further increases in educational attainments were desirable, there is no evidence that a lack of qualified labor force served as any kind of brake on economic growth. Of course, had Chilean policymakers not taken measures to ensure that the educational attainments and training of the labor force would increase with rapid growth, there would have come a time when the skills of the labor force were a bottleneck. But, initially, Chile could change trade strategies (and the macroeconomic framework) without immediately encountering significant bottlenecks in the skills of the labor force.

In present day India, by contrast, there are grave concerns over the sustainable rate of economic growth unless the rate of growth of infrastructure capacity is significantly accelerated. Already, power outages and other impediments from overstretched infrastructure are imposing sizable costs on many Indian producers.

In Korea's case, it is evident that rapid growth under an outer-oriented trade strategy could not have been sustained for long had the authorities not focused on the expansion of infrastructure and the provision of additional educational opportunities at a rapid rate.

When Korea switched strategies, the existing transport and communications infrastructure appears to have been adequate for existing demands, but not to support a rapid increase in the volume of traffic. Of course, with a double-digit rate of economic growth, capacity would eventually have had to increase rapidly, but Korea's growth required attention to infrastructure from the outset.

In Turkey, when policies were switched in the early 1980s, the lack of infrastructure was a major bottleneck. Large investments in improving telecommunications, port facilities, and domestic transport routes were essential if exporters were to have a chance of success on the international market. This created major policy difficulties, as the demands for fiscal balance were in conflict with the need for improved infrastructure capacity. The result has been ongoing difficulties with macroeconomic balance for Turkey.

Direct Policies

Direct policies determine the relative incentives for producing for export and for the domestic market. Such incentives are not quite the same thing as incentives for producing import-competing and exportable goods, but they are closely related. Incentives for producing for the domestic market include anything that increases the profitability of selling domestically: an export tax shifts incentives toward the domestic market, while an export subsidy shifts them in the opposite direction. A large fiscal deficit and expansionary demand pressures increase the profitability of selling on the domestic market for producers of both exportable and import-competing goods. The relative incentive for producing import-competing goods, however, is determined by the level of protection (the bias for that particular good) accorded to it through tariffs, quantitative restrictions, and other measures. In addition, for developing countries over the past half century, the incentives to sell abroad have been closely related to the orientation of the trade regime.

Without appropriate direct policies, export performance will not be conducive to overall economic growth at the rate that would otherwise be attainable. Historically, there has been a positive and high correlation between a lower bias toward import-competing goods and the delivery of appropriate indirect policies to support rapid growth. However, analysis of the reasons for this relationship goes far beyond the scope of this chapter.[16]

Exchange Rates

The exchange rate is the key policy variable that links the domestic economy with the rest of the world, and establishes the price of tradable goods relative to nontradable goods. For any given structure of tariffs,[17] the nominal exchange rate determines the landed cost of an import in domestic currency, and hence the domestic price[18] of import-competing goods. It also determines the domestic currency received per unit of foreign exchange earned for exportables. For nontradable goods, of course, domestic supply and demand conditions determine price.

A change in the nominal exchange rate results (usually with only very small lags) in equal proportional changes in the domestic prices of tradable goods. Since nontradable prices adjust only to changing domestic demand and supply conditions, they do not tend to change immediately on a change in the nominal exchange rate.[19] Consequently, in the short run, changes in the nominal exchange rate bring about virtually equal changes in the RER, defined as the relative price of tradable goods to home (or nontraded) goods.[20] Over the longer run, prices of nontradable goods tend to change as producers switch their production toward the now relatively more expensive goods (tradable goods, in the case of devaluation) and consumers switch toward the now relatively cheaper goods. Together, this brings about a gradual realignment of relative prices. But the evidence is strong that, over periods of one to two years, changes in the nominal exchange rate result in changes in the RER.[21]

---

16 See Krueger (1993) for a discussion.

17 For expository purposes, we shall assume that the only intervention with trade is tariffs. This greatly simplifies the discussion. The reader can think in terms of the tariff-equivalent of quotas in cases where protection was provided through quantitative restrictions on imports (including import prohibitions).

18 Between landed costs and the final consumer, there are of course distribution costs. But these tend to be determined in a competitive environment and tend not to change significantly with small changes in the exchange rate.

19 Of course, when the prices of tradable goods rise (because of a change in the nominal exchange rate) the demand for domestic goods rises because their relative price has fallen.

20 See Mussa (1986).

21 See Mussa (1986).

Moreover, when policymakers are willing to adopt quantitative restrictions to "defend" the exchange rate, a nominal exchange rate can be maintained for some time, regardless of the rate of domestic inflation. During this time, the quantitative restrictions on imports become increasingly binding, so that the domestic price of import-competing goods rises. Unless the authorities take action, the domestic price of exportables remains fixed in nominal terms because of the unchanged nominal exchange rate. The result is that when a nominal exchange rate is maintained over a considerable period of time in a country experiencing inflation significantly above world rates, the bias against exports and in favor of import-competing goods increases.

When, instead of restricting imports, countries rely on capital inflows to sustain a nominal exchange rate in the face of domestic inflationary pressures, the RER appreciates as the price of nontradable goods—especially real estate and services—rises relative to the price of tradable goods. A shift of real GDP toward construction and away from investment in manufacturing is a strong symptom of such appreciation of the RER.

The concept of effective exchange rates proves useful here. The effective exchange rate is defined as the number of units of domestic currency paid for different purchases and sales of a unit of foreign currency. In a fully open, outer-oriented trade regime, the effective exchange rate for exports is the nominal exchange rate, as is the effective exchange rate for import-competing goods. This is known as a *unified exchange-rate regime.*[22]

When, instead, tariffs and surcharges are imposed on imports, the effective exchange rate for imports is above the nominal exchange rate by the amount of these tariffs and surcharges. Nominal exchange rates can differ for different categories of import-competing goods, but the presence of differing effective exchange rates for different categories of goods can be dealt with analytically through measures of effective exchange rates. When, in addition, there are quantitative restrictions on imports, these restrictions are reflected in the value of the *premiums* on import licenses. The premium is, by definition, the difference between the effective exchange rate and the domestic price of the import-competing good in question. In other words, it is

---

[22] See Bhagwati (1968).

the profit accruing to the holder of the import license, or the amount the holder earns simply by virtue of having received the right to import the good.

For our purposes, there are two crucial points. The first is that for an outer-oriented trade strategy to be effective, there cannot be a significant bias of the trade and payments regime toward import-competing goods. That, in turn, means that the bias of the regime, as reflected in the ratio of the average effective exchange for exportables to that for import-competing goods, must be very close to one. Hence, if there are tariffs and other measures raising the domestic price of import-competing goods above the level determined by the nominal exchange rate, then offsetting export incentives would be required to mitigate the bias of the regime toward import-competing activities. This was evidently the rationale behind the use of "export credits," "export subsidies," and "tax incentives" for exporters in Korea in the early years of its outer-oriented trade strategy, when it could not immediately reduce tariffs. These incentives, which were uniform across all exports, offset the bias that would otherwise have remained toward import-competing production.

Under WTO rules, however, export subsidies are not permitted. Hence, to achieve a reduction in the bias of the trade regime toward import substitution, reduction of protection has become an essential part of any effort to achieve an outer-oriented trade strategy. Many developing countries have been lowering their tariffs and protective barriers over the past decade and a half, though in many countries the remaining high level of protection is sufficient to serve as a significant pull of resources toward the home market and import-substitution industries.

The second crucial point regarding the exchange rate is that, since quantitative restrictions on imports are in any event incompatible with a successful outer-oriented trade regime (for reasons that are discussed below), a unification of the exchange rate, and a regime in which nominal rates are effective rates, are prerequisites for satisfactory long-run growth in countries applying an outer-oriented trade strategy.

The reason for the necessity of bringing the nominal and effective exchange rates together lies in the increasing complexity of the regime that otherwise results once an outer-oriented trade strategy encounters initial success. As exports increasingly represent a larger share of GDP (as they virtually must in the early stages, if the outer-oriented trade strategy is to be successful), the complexity increases of administering a trade regime that has strongly differentiated effective exchange rates. With greater complexity, the incentives for evasion and resource misallocation increase, and as that happens, the incentives for export production are commensurately diminished. On the export side, export subsidies become subject to abuse as producers misrepresent their exports; on the import-competing side, a multiplicity of rates invites over/underinvoicing, and pulls resources toward production of goods with high effective exchange rates and away from production of exportables.

Thus, while in principle a trade regime could be outer-oriented with an "overvalued" nominal exchange rate offset by an import duty of x percent and export subsidies in similar proportion, in practice, such a regime does not function well for very long. With initial success, it becomes increasingly important to unify the exchange rate and to eliminate both the quantitative restrictions and the differentials between categories.

As already mentioned, Korea operated its outer-oriented trade regime with export subsidies and import duties in the 1960s. In the 1990s, some of these measures would be in violation of WTO rules; the Koreans started at a time when exports represented 3 percent of GDP, so that export subsidies did not constitute a major drain on budgetary resources. It should also be noted that the best estimates of the effectiveness of these "nonexchange-rate" incentives suggest that a 1 percent increase in the additional incentives for export was about half as effective as a similar increase in the exchange rate in bringing additional resources into production of exportables.[23]

In addition to maintaining a unified exchange rate, an outer-oriented trade strategy requires reasonable stability of the RER. Especially in countries where significant fluctuations in the RER for exporters have occurred in the past, it is likely that potential exporters will at first be skeptical that a new RER for exportables will be sustained. In many such countries, there has been very little initial response to an altered real rate until exporters felt sure that the new RER for exports would be maintained. In many Latin American countries, there has been virtually no long-run export response to even very large increases in nominal (and hence real) exchange rates

[23] See Frank et al. (1975).

because, with high domestic rates of inflation, producers believe that the newly realized value of the RER will be eroded over time and that, if they invest at the time when the RER has depreciated, they will be exporting later when their domestic costs have risen relative to the prices at which they can sell their products.

It may be noted, however, that almost always when the nominal exchange rate is changed, there is an increase in realized foreign exchange receipts by the central bank. In part, this is because exporters have anticipated the change in rate and earlier withheld exports and built up inventories prior to it. In addition, some producers may be operating below capacity and can sell goods on the international market for a price above their marginal cost. These producers may not expand capacity to increase exports, however, because they believe that they will be unable to continue to realize the existing price-cost margin.

For countries experiencing inflation at rates significantly different from those of their largest trading partners, the necessity of assuring stability of the real rate for exporters implies the need for a policy regime that allows changes in the nominal exchange rate to offset inflation differentials. While the appropriate RER might change over time due to a variety of causes, there is no reason to believe that the RER should appreciate at the rate of the differential between domestic and foreign inflation. One solution that has been tried in countries with high inflation is to adjust the nominal exchange rate at frequent intervals to maintain a relatively constant RER. This permits changes in the real rate (and thus requires frequent devaluations) when foreign exchange reserves begin accumulating more rapidly than desired for sustained periods. This mechanism, known as the "crawling peg" system, was reasonably successful in several countries for periods in the 1960s and 1970s. However, as capital has become more mobile internationally, the problems with this system have increased.[24]

Regardless of whether the nominal exchange rate is fixed, whether it is permitted to crawl within a band, or whether a controlled crawl is in operation, the possibility of speculative attack has become so great as to question the wisdom of exchange rate management through any

[24] It was always recognized that efforts to support an inappropriate real exchange rate over the longer term could have highly inflationary consequences. This could be avoided, however, if the authorities adjusted the target real exchange rate in line with changes in foreign exchange reserves and the current account balance.

of these techniques. The case for maintaining a realistic exchange rate through a floating exchange rate with appropriate fiscal and monetary policy is very strong, and is discussed further in the following section.

Many officials have difficulty in evaluating the adequacy and appropriateness of the RER, for there is no guarantee that the appropriate RER will—or should—remain constant over time. Indeed, it is evident that the RER should depreciate when the terms of trade deteriorate, and vice versa. There is also some evidence that the appropriate RER may appreciate somewhat (and relatively slowly) during the early years of an outer-oriented trade strategy as foreign importers increasingly recognize the quality and products of the new exporters. Less well recognized, but perhaps equally important, is the fact that the RER should depreciate as the trade regime is liberalized. The RER that is appropriate to support an open trade and payments regime with an average tariff level of, e.g., 50 percent, will clearly be overvalued when tariffs are greatly reduced or eliminated.

For purposes of analyzing outer-oriented trade policies and their prospects of success in achieving accelerated economic growth, the important point is that the authorities must find some way of achieving two aims: providing a realistic RER that enables exporters to achieve profits when they are successful, comparable to those they could achieve if undertaking import-substitution activities (that are inherently less risky); and permitting potential exporters to have confidence that, if they succeed in the difficult international market, their real returns from exporting will not diminish significantly. As already noted, there is ample evidence that fluctuations in the RER have been as important as overvaluations of exchange rates in countries where export growth has been relatively slow.[25]

In recent years, concerns have been expressed over the role that capital inflows may play, and over the ways in which sudden speculative attacks can destabilize a currency, as well as an economy. As capital flows have become increasingly important, it has become even more crucial for policymakers to ensure that their combination of monetary, fiscal, and exchange rate policies are mutually consistent. The risks associated with attempting to set an unrealistic

[25] See, for example, Edwards (1989).

exchange rate are considerably greater, and a crisis can occur considerably more rapidly, than was true in earlier years. In the economics community, a great deal of research is currently being undertaken about the nature of currency crises and their determinants. While the outcome of this research is not yet certain, the results appear to point toward the desirability of maintaining a flexible exchange rate, and of ensuring that domestic credit creation is not undertaken too rapidly. Most analysts conclude that "sound fundamentals" are inconsistent with a currency crisis, and that the latter can occur only when the "fundamentals" are weak.

Macroeconomic Policies

Linkages between exchange rate policy and overall macroeconomic policy are numerous. In the days when most countries fixed their nominal exchange rates, monetary and fiscal policies that resulted in domestic inflationary pressures, of course, also resulted in RER appreciation. Once countries with inflation rates above those of their major trading partners found ways of maintaining their RER through a crawling peg or other means, macroeconomic policy still affected export performance, but through other channels and with somewhat less and slower impact. Then, when developing countries began opening their capital accounts and liberalizing their trade regimes, the importance of monetary policy, and attendant interest rates, in affecting capital flows increased.

It has always been true that large inflationary pressures in a domestic economy are inimical to satisfactory export performance even under a crawling peg regime with a constant RER. This is largely because the excess demand that results in inflation also provides producers with an assured and profitable home market, in the same way as protection under import substitution does. Especially when producers are inexperienced in the international market, the lure of excess demand in the domestic market is simply too great to resist. In addition, when domestic prices are rising rapidly, producers and consumers are relatively more insensitive to the relative price changes (because there is considerable uncertainty as to whether a given price increase reflects the inflation adjustment or signals an underlying change in relative prices) and thus do not respond as much to changes in exchange rates and other incentives. Finally, the very fact of excess demand in the domestic market implies that there will be additional demand for exportables domestically, and that the quantity available for export will be reduced.

For these reasons, there is no instance since World War II of any country successfully mounting a sustained outer-oriented trade strategy during a period of high and accelerating inflationary pressure.[26] Most of the times that countries have successfully followed an outer-oriented trade strategy, monetary and fiscal policies have gradually been altered: first to reduce inflation and then to bring about price stability. In Chile, for example, the rate of inflation was immediately brought down from four digits to around 150 percent, and then to 20–30 percent by 1975. Since the 1980s, it has gradually been reduced further, and is now in the low single digits. Chilean fiscal discipline has increased greatly, and fiscal deficits are very small. In Korea as well, trade policy and exchange rate reforms started in 1960 when the rate of inflation was in double digits. Fiscal reforms were undertaken in 1964, and the rate of inflation was reduced to around 10 percent for the rest of the decade (and the RER for exports stayed relatively constant through adjustments in export credit subsidies and other export incentives). Inflation reemerged with the oil price increase of 1973, and remained at rates well above those of its trading partners until the mid-1980s, by which time domestic inflation rates had reached levels comparable to those of its Organisation for Economic Co-operation and Development (OECD) trading partners.

In these and other cases, measures were taken to ensure that excess demand did not divert production from the international market, which is of course crucial to the success of an outer-oriented trade strategy.[27] With increasing capital mobility in the 1990s, monetary policy has, as already noted, assumed greater importance. The sensitivity of mobile international capital to interest rate

---

[26] Turkey undertook a shift in trade strategy in 1980 at a time when inflation rose to over 100 percent. However, this shift was accompanied by a stabilization program with restrictive monetary and fiscal policies, so that inflation fell to a low of 35 percent. Moreover, the exchange rate was permitted to fluctuate so that the real exchange rate actually depreciated over the first five years of the outer-oriented trade strategy. Turkey was unsuccessful in maintaining the lower rate of inflation and still confronts major macroeconomic difficulties. See Krueger and Aktan (1992).

[27] See Thomas et al. (1990). See also the abbreviated version by the same authors, "Lesson in Trade Policy Reform," World Bank Policy and Research Series No. 10, Table 2, p. 8 for documentation that fiscal discipline increases more in countries undertaking more significant trade policy reforms.

differentials has increased, and the importance of realistic interest rate policies has risen sharply. Maintaining an appropriate domestic real interest rate is important for domestic resource allocation, but it is also necessary because its absence induces two negative side effects. First, foreigners can invest (or disinvest) at rates of return diverging from the real rates of return achieved with investible resources. This is at a cost to the domestic economy of an excess paid to foreigners above the real rate of return on capital (in the case of too high a real rate) or of an absence of capital inflows (in the case of too low a real rate). Second, when capital inflows are larger or smaller than warranted by the underlying fundamentals, there is pressure on the exchange rate—especially if it is floating—or on domestic prices, or both.

Trade Regime

Many policymakers, recognizing the benefits of export growth, have asserted that they would attempt to achieve a "half-and-half" strategy, i.e., protect some import-competing industries while encouraging some export industries. In practice, successful growth through an outer-oriented trade strategy is not achievable under such a "mixed" strategy.

Some of the reasons for doubting the prospects for success under a mixed strategy have already been mentioned. First, exporters need to have ready access to world markets for their capital goods and to inputs of intermediate goods and raw materials if they are to compete on a level playing field with exporters from other countries. Maintaining high protection for other domestic industries requires monitoring and other bureaucratic delays for importers that are not consistent with an outer-oriented trade strategy. In the early stages of development, means can be found to permit exporters to import needed goods expeditiously, but as exports grow, it becomes increasingly difficult if other parts of the trade regime are still strongly protectionist.

In Korea, for example, in the very early days of the outer-oriented drive, exporters were given a "wastage" allowance, as well as a fairly generous proportion of inputs permitted per unit of exports. If, for example, a producer had used \$0.35 of imported inputs per dollar of exports he would be given a "wastage" allowance in addition, so that he could import perhaps \$0.40 of inputs duty free. The process was virtually automatic, with the papers cleared as the exports were made, and it only required the goods to be exported within 12 months.[28] Every effort was made to ensure that the total allowance provided sufficient inputs for exporters' needs, with a little left over, enabling exporters to profit by selling that on the domestic market. The fact that a good might be domestically produced did not matter if exporters regarded the foreign product as better in terms of price or quality. When there was protection on domestic production for the domestic market, the wastage allowance could be used, if not needed, to produce or sell on the domestic market, thus reducing protection for import-competing producers and simultaneously encouraging exporters (by not putting them at a disadvantage relative to their foreign competitors).

While such a technique can work fairly well in the early days of an outer-oriented trade strategy, it becomes increasingly complex to administer as the volume and variety of exports grow. Over time, the desirability of unifying the system relying on exchange rates for incentives, and of removing tariff protection for imports, becomes increasingly evident. Lack of action to reduce tariffs and eliminate most nontariff barriers to trade becomes increasingly costly and, if continued, can result in a significant slowdown in export growth.

A second major consideration against a mixed strategy relates to the "safe haven" feeling that such a strategy apparently gives to potential producers of the import-competing good. Successful exporting is demanding, and requires the ability to learn and successfully market in foreign countries. It is also fraught with risks, such as the emergence of a new competing product in a foreign country. And, even when it carries big rewards, producers are naturally hesitant in the early stages of development, and regard the risks of exporting as great. When provided with a viable alternative (i.e., investing in domestic import-substitution industries), most producers understandably direct new resources into the safer, if not necessarily more profitable, haven. Generally, under import-substitution policies, policymakers have underestimated the extent to which the incentives provided for import substitution would deter exports. The same is normally true of efforts to insulate one or more economic activities in a "protected" sector while leaving the rest open:

---

[28] This technique was used in Turkey in the early 1980s and had a significant positive effect on incentives to exporters.

resources flock into the protected activity, diverting much more than anticipated from other activities.

A third consideration is one that has been mentioned repeatedly above. An outer-oriented trade strategy, by its nature, offers across-the-board and uniform incentives to exporters. It is not possible to operate even a partial import-substitution strategy without being selective. Once policymakers have agreed that a few industries will receive protection, the political pressures to extend its scope are almost irresistible. Resources, including particularly the attention of entrepreneurs themselves, that producers could productively use to become more successful on international markets, are instead diverted to efforts to become one of the privileged protected sectors.

Since a successful outer-oriented trade strategy is one that reflects the authorities' single-mindedness to achieve growth through reliance on the international market, the question arises as to how the rest of the trade regime should be structured. As was seen in the experience of Korea and Taipei,China, protectionist barriers need not be entirely dismantled initially, although there is reason to believe that Korea and Taipei,China might have grown even more rapidly without domestic protection. In the Korean case, whatever residual profits accrued to importing went to exporters, as only exporters were given import licenses, and there was thus no separate "profit center" associated with importing. Moreover, the rate of protection declined over time and producers expected (correctly) that they could not flourish solely by relying on the domestic market.[29]

Quantitative restrictions need to be removed at a fairly early stage of an outer-oriented trade strategy, as already noted. Removal or reduction of tariffs can proceed systematically, as long as private agents believe that tariff levels will indeed be reduced. In many countries, tariff reduction has proceeded by announcing a formula under which the highest permissible tariff is reduced (thus reducing both protection and variance in protection) and the other tariffs

[29] In the 1970s, after 10 years of very successful outer-oriented growth, Korean policymakers believed that they had arrived at the stage where they should adopt import substitution in heavy and chemical industries (HCIs). It is often argued that the long-term success of Korea proves that this set of policies encouraging HCIs was appropriate. In fact, the HCI drive was already in grave difficulty before the first oil price increase, and its costs were very high relative to the benefits. While some industries, such as shipbuilding, emerged as viable exporters at a later date, it would appear that the HCI drive retarded economic growth. See World Bank (1993), p. 309 for an estimate of the very high costs of the HCI drive relative to the benefits.

are reduced by a proportionate amount. Both the mean tariff and the variation among tariff rates are important. In Chile, policymakers have gone even further, for not only is the mean tariff 11 percent (as it has been for some years), but the tariff is uniform across all goods entering the country. Furthermore, it is scheduled for reduction to 8 percent. Even in Mexico, the average tariff level had fallen to 10 percent before entry into the North American Free Trade Agreement (NAFTA), and the highest tariff on any good was 35 percent. This may be one reason why Mexican exports grew so rapidly after the peso crisis of 1994, and were able to spearhead a sharp recovery in economic activity.

Finally, it should be evident that for an outer-oriented trade strategy to be effective, it is highly desirable that paperwork and procedures associated with exporting and importing be simplified and expedited as much as possible. Delays in shipping or receiving goods can have large (and not necessarily obvious) negative effects on export prospects, as can the diversion of managers' time from attending to customers, quality, and delivery dates.

INDIRECT POLICIES

Indirect policies are those domestic policies (other than the direct ones already discussed) that affect the efficiency of resource allocation and the costs of exporters (and other producers). Even in the short run, the flexibility of the labor market is a key factor in affecting the prospects for success of an outer-oriented trade strategy. And the costs and efficiency of transport and communications are key for assuring export success, as well as for productivity growth more generally.

For long-term economic growth, it is evident that policies conducive to encouraging savings and to efficient allocation of investible resources are crucial, as are measures designed to improve the quality of the labor force. Likewise, efficient functioning of the financial markets increases the productivity of resources, enabling savings to finance investment in the most profitable uses. Failure to achieve reforms in these markets can severely inhibit export performance and overall growth.

Labor Market Policies

Measures that thwart the efficient functioning of the labor market can have serious consequences for export potential, even when the direct policies are appropriate. For example, provisions that workers, once hired for a trial period, must be kept on the payroll for life serve as serious deterrents to employers, who tend to adopt more capital-intensive techniques of production to avoid the risks associated with having an excessive payroll if demand falls for their products. With such provisions, employers also tend to hire workers on a temporary basis, and do not provide the training that they would otherwise give.

There is considerable evidence that, in Chile's case, the removal of requirements to give workers lifetime tenure was the most important labor market reform, and contributed significantly to the economy's success.[30] Minimum wage laws, which set the minimum wage above the levels that it would find in the market, had also served as a significant deterrent to the rapid growth of exports. Indeed, anything that significantly raises the cost of labor to potential entrants in world markets can reduce the attractiveness of attempting entry.[31] In the early stages of an outer-oriented trade strategy, such deterrent measures can significantly slow the rate at which producers shift resources into exportables and attempt to enter the export market. When labor market regulations are extreme enough, of course, the potential for export growth can be choked off.

Infrastructure

In many countries that follow import-substitution strategies, bottlenecks in transport and communications have been major factors in lowering productivity in the whole economy. In addition, because all producers on the home market face the same bottlenecks, overstretched infrastructure has persisted alongside whatever economic growth has been realized. No particular industry is

---

30 See Corbo and de Melo (1987).

31 Even in well-functioning flexible labor markets, the wage paid to unskilled manufacturing workers is normally significantly above the average rural wage.

advantaged or disadvantaged, except to the degree that some are more dependent on transport and communications than others.

In highly competitive international markets, however, poor and overstretched infrastructure facilities can greatly limit the potential gains from an outer-oriented trade strategy. Buyers in the international market have a range of alternative suppliers, and they value dependability of on-time delivery, ease of communications with their suppliers, and other attributes that exporters can only achieve if infrastructure is adequate.[32]

It is evident that exporters must be able to communicate quickly and relatively cheaply with their buyers, and vice versa. Equally, the need for reliable transport facilities is evident to most policymakers.[33] But it has been less recognized that high-cost facilities can seriously impair an outer-oriented trade strategy. Recent experience in Chile, where port fees were lowered by over 70 percent, and the competitive advantage conferred to higher-cost producers in Argentina and Brazil, have dramatically illustrated the importance of attention to the efficiency of infrastructure. Efficient infrastructure is clearly significant in a successful outer-oriented trade strategy.

Financial Market Development

All of the successful outer-oriented economies have experienced dramatic increases in savings and investment rates in the course of their rapid growth. Sometimes, a shift in trade strategy can achieve initial success with little new investment because producers can rationalize and increase production from existing capacity. However, over the longer term it is evident that exports can only grow rapidly when capacity expands, not only in production of exportables itself, but in the other economic activities that support exportables (including infrastructure) and that meet the upward shifts in demand for nontradable consumer goods that accompany rapid economic growth.

Hence, policymakers need to attend to the markets and incentives that determine savings rates and the availability of resources for investment. In the early stages of growth, this requires the provision

[32] See Morawetz (1981).
[33] See World Bank, *World Development Report 1994*: "Infrastructure Development," for a thorough discussion of infrastructure provision.

of incentives for additional savings, in particular ensuring that real interest rates received by depositors are positive. As growth continues, measures to ensure the increasingly efficient functioning of financial markets are necessary. These include the removal of any credit rationing previously imposed by the authorities, and the development of nonbank financial intermediaries.[34]

As was pointed out above, in the early stages of development the resource misallocation that can arise through the direction of credit to individual firms is significantly less than in later stages. Over time, the economic costs of inefficient allocation of investible resources can rise sharply unless financial markets are developed to provide for an efficient allocation of investible funds to the activities where the risk-adjusted rate of return is highest.

AT WHAT RATE CAN EXPORT GROWTH BE SUSTAINED?

In the 1960s, Korea's exports and export earnings grew at an average annual rate of more than 40 percent. When this was accompanied by double-digit average annual real GDP growth, exports were growing at about three times the GDP growth rate. Obviously, the relative importance of exports in the economy was rising rapidly, as happens in any country in the initial phases of an outer-oriented trade strategy.

Continuing with the Korean example, when exports were only 5 percent of GDP (as they were in the early 1960s), a 40 percent export growth rate directly accounted for only 2 percentage points of GDP growth. If, when exports were already 30 percent of GDP, and they grew by 40 percent, other things being equal, that would in itself have accounted for 12 percentage points of GDP growth, with little or no scope for expansion of infrastructure or increases in production of nontradable consumer goods. Clearly, 40 percent export growth rates are not sustainable from the supply side, and they may not be from the demand side. And, as long as the real export growth rate exceeds the real GDP growth rate for sustained periods of time, there will be a tendency for the export growth rate to fall. In the Korean economy

[34] See McKinnon (1995).

today (where exports account for more than 30 percent of GDP), there would be strong inflationary pressures if producers attempted to increase the volume of exports by 40 percent.

For countries where exports are based on natural resources and constitute a sizable percentage of GDP prior to the authorities' adoption of an outer-oriented trade strategy, overall growth of exports is typically not as rapid as in resource-poor countries at a comparable stage. However, growth of nontraditional exports can be very high. This was the experience of Malaysia and Thailand as they opened up their economies.

There are thus two (separate) domestic reasons why export growth is initially higher in countries adopting outer-oriented trade strategies and why it may slow. First, with little or no bias in the trade regime toward import substitution, export growth will slow as the outer-oriented trade strategy succeeds and as exports (and imports) become a larger fraction of GDP. Such a retardation can take place at a sustained rate of overall economic growth as a lower export growth rate can contribute more to overall growth when exports are a larger share of GDP. However, after some time (which will presumably be longer the greater the degree of resource misallocation at the outset), the economy's capacity to grow at rates of 8 percent and higher inevitably slows. Clearly, Korea (and Taipei,China) could not have sustained their growth rates of the 1960s and 1970s for another several decades, although they still managed to grow very strongly, at rates well above those of other OECD countries, in the 1990s. Korea's export growth rate slowed from around 40 percent in the 1960s, to 23 percent in the 1970s, and to 12 percent in the 1980s (see Table 2.1). From 1990 to 1995, however, Korea had clearly not exhausted the potential for rapid export growth, even three-and-a-half decades after it had begun.

The second reason for an export slowdown arises from the authorities' failure, as the economy grows, to continue reforms of economic policies to achieve greater economic efficiency. Financial market rigidities in Korea, inadequate infrastructure and education in Thailand, and similar factors in other countries have led to pauses in export growth and overall economic growth. Whether these pauses have turned into permanent reductions in growth rates or whether, instead, the authorities have been able to identify the sources of difficulty and adopt appropriate remedies, is the important question.

Table 2.1 Growth of Exports of Selected Asian Economies 1970–1995 (average annual rates)

	1970–1980 (percent)	1980–1990 (percent)	1990–1995 (percent)
PRC	8.7	11.5	15.6
NIEs			
Hong Kong, China	9.7	14.4	13.5
Korea	23.5	12.0	13.5
Singapore	4.2	10.0	-
Taipei,China	15.6	11.0	10.9
NICs			
Indonesia	7.2	2.9	10.8
Malaysia	4.8	10.9	14.4
Thailand	10.3	14.0	14.2
Other Southeast and South Asian Countries			
Myanmar	1.5	-4.5[a]	-
Papua New Guinea	15.6	3.3	13.3
Philippines	6.0	3.5	9.4
Sri Lanka	2.0	6.8	11.0
South Asian Countries			
Bangladesh	3.8	7.7	14.2
India	4.3	5.9	12.5
Nepal	13.9	1.1	25.8
Pakistan	0.7	8.1	7.7

Notes: Growth rates are for the dollar value of exports of goods and services for 1980–1990 and 1990–1995. For 1970–1980, the growth rate is for merchandise exports only.

[a] 1980–1992.

Source: World Bank (various years).

For policymakers, the challenge is to identify the sources of any slowdown in export growth rates, so as to ascertain the extent to which these sources are the result of success and the reduced need for such rapid expansion to sustain overall growth, as contrasted with the impact of domestic bottlenecks or inadequate incentives. Analysis of the feasible rate of expansion of overall capacity, and the rate of economic growth that could accompany it without excess demand for infrastructure and nontradable goods, are the first steps in estimating the potential for growth.

To be sure, changes in international market conditions can also lead to a slowdown in export growth, especially if these changes are in areas where a country's exports are concentrated. Policymakers can, in general, easily ascertain whether cyclical factors of this sort are responsible for any slowdown in export growth by checking the share of their country's exports in the world market of the good in question. In situations where there are cyclical (or other) factors at play, the country's share will remain relatively stable. Transitory changes in export growth rates due to world conditions do not suggest the need for a change in policies. These changes can be sourced to external facts or the world economy, and in the medium term they are self-correcting.

DIFFERENTIAL EXPORT PERFORMANCES OF ASIAN COUNTRIES

The Asian countries represent the spectrum of experience with exports, trade strategy, and development among the world's developing economies. Although almost all of them followed import-substitution policies early on, the early abandonment of this strategy by the NIEs is well known. At the other extreme in Asia are the Central Asian republics, where growth has barely started. In between are resource-rich countries such as Malaysia and Thailand that have, nonetheless, had reasonable success with outer-oriented trade strategies; India, which has only in the past few years begun relaxing trade restrictions; and countries such as Bangladesh, Nepal, and Pakistan, where the vestiges of an inner-oriented trade strategy are still evident.

All attempts to categorize countries are somewhat arbitrary. This is inevitable as long as there are so many dimensions in which they differ. However, some existing classifications for Asia follow.

Sachs and Warner (1995) classify both Hong Kong, China; and Thailand as having always been open; Malaysia and Taipei,China as having been open from 1963; Singapore from 1964; Korea from 1968; Indonesia from 1970; Philippines from 1988; Nepal and Sri Lanka from 1991; and India from 1994. As with any other categorization, one can quibble: Korea in the 1960s was probably more open to imports than India after 1994; while the degree to which Korea and Taipei,China, as well as others, liberalized their import regimes increased over time.

Lloyd and Summers (1997) believe that there are three transitions: one from having a closed to an open trading regime; a second from experiencing net out-migration to net in-migration; and a third from being a net recipient of foreign investment to a net investor abroad. They classify Hong Kong, China; Japan; Singapore; and Taipei,China as having made all three transitions (albeit at different dates) with Korea, Malaysia, and Thailand as having made the migration transition only.

We will attempt a different categorization, using three criteria: first, the bias of the trade and payments regime; second, the length of time during which the bias has been sustained; and third, the relative importance of natural resources (especially agriculture) as a generator of foreign exchange.

As already seen, the determinants of a country's export growth rate are numerous, both because of differences in economic policies and because of differences in underlying structure and past performance. But, based on our three criteria, Asian countries can be divided into several groups. First of all there is Japan, the only country that has been "developed" throughout the postwar period. For purposes of learning about the ways in which export growth can be achieved and sustained by developing countries, therefore, the Japanese experience, while instructive, is essentially of economic growth at a different level. Japan, therefore, is ignored in the following discussion.

The PRC is another very large country in terms of economic influence in the region. Because its economic structure is so different from that of most other countries, with a much larger share of central direction and control, it is generally treated as separate from any other group.

The first major group of economies, classified by our three criteria, comprises those which began their outer orientation and successful development in the 1950s and 1960s, namely, Hong Kong, China; Korea; Singapore; and Taipei,China. These economies achieved very rapid growth, surpassing all expectations. By the 1990s, all four had achieved industrial countries' standards of living and in 1997 were grouped as high-income countries by the World Bank. To be sure, there are significant differences between the four. Perhaps the one most frequently noted is size: Hong Kong, China; and Singapore are essentially city-states, while Korea and Taipei,China, with large rural populations in the early stages of development, still have significant agricultural activity.

The second group is the group of Southeast Asian countries that began moving toward outer orientation in the 1970s or later, but that have achieved very high growth rates over the 1980s and 1990s: Indonesia, Malaysia, and Thailand, or, for our purposes, the newly industrializing countries (NICs). Again, there are significant differences within the group. Indonesia's oil sets it apart from the others in terms of its structure, and the Government has maintained much more protection for domestic manufacturing than the other two. But all three have successfully grown through reliance, primarily, on export markets, although none of them was as single-minded in its export growth policies as the NIEs. It may be significant that all three countries were considerably more resource rich than the NIEs when they shifted to an outer orientation.

This is the group[35] that encountered severe economic difficulties and a currency crisis in mid-1997 and later. (Chapter 3 addresses the issues involved in the export slowdown, which was one factor contributing to the overall crisis.) Here, it needs to be noted that fundamentals (in the form of a weak banking system, large borrowings from the international market with accompanying unsustainable current account deficits, and maintenance of an appreciating RER) were all contributory factors. Despite this, this group has experienced more than two decades of rapid growth, and it would be fair to say that they are all at the point where the challenge is to identify the policy issues that must be resolved prior to resumption of growth.

The next group covers other Southeast (and one South) Asian countries, namely, Cambodia, Lao People's Democratic Republic (Lao PDR), Myanmar, Papua New Guinea, Philippines, Sri Lanka, and Viet Nam. In these countries, there has been much less incentive for exports, and a less satisfactory growth experience. Cambodia, Lao PDR, and Viet Nam have all had extensive government control of economic activity, and have not yet fully moved to incentive-based economic policy formulation, much less to an outer-oriented trade strategy. Myanmar has to a large degree cut itself off from world markets. Papua New Guinea has not achieved export growth in other

[35] Korea was also caught in the Asian financial and currency crisis of 1997. But the evidence seems to suggest that the immediate problems were more the result of mismanagement of external debt than the symptoms of an unsustainable short-run policy set. In the Korean case, the next stage of growth will require both the removal of more "distortions" in the domestic economy, especially in loosening the links between the Government, bank lending, and behavior of the *chaebols*, and the liberalization of the labor market.

than primary commodities, and has experienced slow overall growth. The Philippines, until the 1990s, had incentives much more biased toward import substitution than did the NIEs, and overall growth performance was, partly as a consequence, considerably less satisfactory. Sri Lanka had a somewhat better experience than most of these countries and is raw-material abundant. But, like the Philippines, Sri Lanka has not moved far enough to warrant being classified with the NICs, although one could almost argue that it should be placed with them.

The final group comprises the South Asian countries (excluding Sri Lanka) that have been the most oriented toward import substitution. All of them have had considerably more bias in incentives toward import substitution, and are much less integrated with the world economy. Bangladesh, India, and Pakistan all, of course, have relatively large economies, while Nepal's is much smaller. They all have very low per capita incomes, though they are all in the process of altering their trade strategies and embarking on fundamental economic policy reforms.

Some key characteristics of these groups are shown in Tables 2.1 and 2.2. As can be seen, the export growth rates of the NIEs were very rapid, especially for Korea in the 1970s. After 1980, export growth slowed somewhat, but nonetheless remained faster than GDP growth.

The PRC's relative isolation prior to the 1980s is revealed in the relatively low share of exports in GDP at that time (Table 2.2). The move toward a greater emphasis on exports and an opening up of the economy began in 1978, and is evident in the increase from 6 percent of exports in GDP to 21 percent between 1980 and 1995. The NIEs started from a substantial export base in 1970 and their exports, as a proportion of GDP, went on rising constantly. The three NICs did not have the advantage of having a large export base in 1970, but their exports, using the same measure, went on rising at a steady pace. By 1995, the share of exports of NICs was much larger than in the past, but lower than that of the NIEs.[36] While it is dangerous to contrast export shares of GDP across countries where the fraction of

[36] It is important to remember that exports are a gross measure whereas GDP is a value-added measure. This is vividly illustrated by Singapore, where exports constitute more than 100 percent of GDP. In Singapore's case, a great deal of crude oil is imported and refined. Naturally, GDP statistics reflect only the value-added in refining, whereas exports reflect the value-added domestically plus the value of the crude oil.

Table 2.2 Share of Exports in GDP
Selected Asian Economies
(percent)

	1970	1980	1990	1995
PRC	-	6	18	21
NIEs				
Hong Kong, China	92	90	137	147
Korea	14	34	32	33
Singapore	102	207	-	-
Taipei,China	31	53	46	48
NICs				
Indonesia	13	33	26	25
Malaysia	42	58	79	96
Thailand	15	24	38	42
Other Southeast and South Asian Countries				
Myanmar	5	-	2	-
Papua New Guinea	18	43	37	61
Philippines	22	24	28	36
Sri Lanka	25	32	30	36
South Asian Countries				
Bangladesh	8	6	8	14
India	4	7	8	12
Nepal	5	12	12	24
Pakistan	8	12	16	16

Source: As Table 2.1.

domestic value-added in export value varies widely, this nonetheless illustrates the point that one could not expect as rapid growth of exports in the countries where natural resource-based exports already constituted a significant fraction of GDP as one could in countries where there were fewer natural resources.[37]

Among the other Southeast and South Asian countries, natural resource-based exports are still important, as reflected in the structure of exports and the overall growth rate of exports. South Asian countries did not begin to reverse trade strategies until the 1990s, and hence their exports grew slowly and remained a small fraction of GDP in earlier decades.

[37] It is often forgotten that Korea's exports consisted of 88 percent of primary commodities in 1960. However, overall exports were less than 5 percent of GDP.

It seems evident that all the developing Asian countries have many stages to go through in their drive to become mature industrialized economies. The NIEs are clearly furthest advanced, although their comparative advantage still lies in the "middle" range of industrial products. The NICs and other Southeast and South Asian countries are probably at the stage where their comparative advantage in unskilled labor-intensive products is diminishing and where policy adjustments to the next phase of development must be made. These adjustments would certainly include further reducing protectionist measures, strengthening education and training for the labor force, and attending to infrastructure needs. South Asia, by contrast, still has a long way to go in moving from import-substitution to outer-oriented trade strategies. And the Central Asian republics, not covered here, are clearly at the very early stages of the development process.

Although any analogy such as "flying geese" clearly oversimplifies reality, one wonders whether, 20 years from now, the countries that successfully adopt appropriate policies may not find themselves approximately where the group ahead of them is now. That is, the NIEs (while having grown successfully and having much higher incomes) may be facing structural problems similar to those of Japan today; the NICs may be in a somewhat similar position to that of the NIEs in the late 1990s; the South Asian economies may look quite a bit like the other Southeast and South Asian countries, and so on. However, there is nothing automatic about these progressions. As has been stated throughout this chapter, they depend crucially on the policies chosen by individual governments.

FUTURE PROSPECTS: UNCERTAINTIES AND ANXIETIES

As of mid-1998, the contagion of the Asian financial crisis has spread to many countries in the region and there are many uncertainties and anxieties about the prospects for future growth. The situation in each country has been exacerbated by the simultaneous difficulty of others, as the demand for exports from other Asian countries has declined, fueling existing downward pressures resulting from the crisis.

The prospects for the future depend both on external conditions and on the policy responses of the governments in the affected countries. On the external side, there are two key identifiable questions, and one less crucial. The first concerns Japan's economic prospects. Given Japan's economic size and importance as a trading partner with the other Asian countries, the key question for the region is the likely timing and speed of the Japanese recovery. Should Japanese economic activity start picking up quickly, the prospects for all Asian countries would improve markedly. On the other hand, should the Japanese recession prove prolonged and severe, the prospects for other Asian countries during the recession would be considerably dampened.

A second key external consideration pertains to the entire international economy. In 1997 and 1998, the impact of the crisis has at least been partially offset by the fact that the rest of the world has been experiencing cyclically rapid growth. Insofar as the growth rate of output and trade in the rest of the world maintains its pace, prospects for Asian recovery and growth of exports will be commensurately better. If, however, the rest of the world (either because the business cycle has run its course or because of "contagion" from the Asian difficulties) also enters a period of recession, prospects for the rapid growth of Asian exports (even when domestic policies are appropriately aligned) will obviously be less sanguine.

A subsidiary issue of some importance concerns the prospects for resumption of growth in demand for semiconductors. While the recession in the industry contributed to the slowdown of export growth in 1996 and may therefore have contributed to the timing of the crisis, it did not cause it. However, it certainly contributed to it, and resumption of growth in demand (and steadier prices) for semiconductors would help the recovery of exports and of the region's economies. As is well known, the semiconductor industry is characterized by very heavy capital requirements for new investments, ranging in billions of dollars. One result is that investors are reluctant to build new capacity unless prices appear fairly firm and demand is rising. In consequence, the semiconductor industry goes through periodic cycles, in which there is first a period of excess demand when capacity is inadequate to meet world demand (and firms even allocate their production among customers to retain their goodwill for the inevitable downturns), followed by a period of building new capacity. When that capacity comes on line, it does so in large, indivisible chunks, leading to overcapacity and plummeting prices. This happened in 1996. However, the semiconductor slowdown was accentuated by the apparent slowdown in the growth of demand for the end products that had characterized the industry, as the growth rate of new sales of personal computers fell from double to single digits.

Even if the rest of the world (and Japan) experiences satisfactory growth, governments in the Asian crisis countries will need to make appropriate policy adjustments before their economies can take full advantage of the global situation. A first critical question facing policymakers is whether the crisis has been contained, or whether other events (such as, perhaps, a devaluation by the PRC authorities) could trigger another round in the painful downward spiral. At the heart of the difficulty in each country lies the problem that, with a considerable degree of capital mobility and fixed exchange rates, domestic credit creation was equivalent to increased foreign exchange liabilities. When the exchange rates finally had to move, the domestic liabilities of many companies far exceeded their ability to pay. The result, as is well known, was not only a foreign exchange crisis and a sharp depreciation of currencies, but also a huge increase in the volume of nonperforming loans. The difficulties in the banking system are particularly important to resolve for, as long as banks have a large fraction of nonperforming loans on their books,[38] they will be unable to provide new credit to expanding firms at globally competitive interest rates, as they must cover the costs of (and roll over) their nonperforming loans. This means a credit squeeze of serious proportions.

For the crisis countries, resolution of the issues is paramount. In some countries (Korea and Thailand among them), firms are reported (as of mid-1998) to be unable to accept additional export orders for lack of credit. Domestic business is also hampered, but given the domestic recessions, the demand for credit may be small. If the banking system was healthy, the normal route to recovery would be for exporting firms to receive an increasing volume of orders (because of the attractiveness of the exchange rate) and for newly profitable

[38] In Malaysia, for example, it is reported that outstanding bank credit is equal to 170 percent of GDP, and that it is anticipated that perhaps a third of loans will be nonperforming by the beginning of 1999. *Financial Times*, 20 July 1998, p. 12.

import-competing firms (because of the higher domestic price of imports) to seek to expand their capacity to meet additional demand. As they did so, their output would replace that of the declining industries, and eventually spur the resumption of growth.

It is therefore crucial that this avenue for recovery be reopened, but that, in turn, requires resolution of the banks' problems. The speed of recovery will clearly depend on the alacrity with which that happens.[39] As long as the overhang of bad paper in the banking system impairs its functioning, credit will not be available for those activities that could otherwise be profitably expanded.

Again in the crisis countries, it is probably equally important that appropriate supervisory and prudential standards be set for banks. More evidence is becoming available that suggests that part of Asia's problem was that the expansion of bank credit was directed toward activities whose expected profitability was not as high as it should have been. Finding means to enable the banks to lend again will not be sufficient unless mechanisms are also in place to provide assurance that loans are directed toward those who can most productively employ them.

Until these issues are addressed, it is unlikely that exports can respond as they should to the stimulus of the new RERs. It is also improbable that foreign private capital flows will resume; they are, though, crucial for the crisis countries.

Each country has other structural problems that need addressing. In Korea, for example, a key issue appears to be the relationship among the *chaebols*, the banks, and the Government. It is important for the Government to achieve an arm's length relationship among these groups. In Malaysia, in addition to the problem of nonperforming bank loans (which is serious in all countries), issues arise in connection with the extent to which allocation of resources is driven by market forces in contrast to government direction. There are also questions about the efficiency of public sector investment. In Thailand, infrastructure bottlenecks may present a constraint on further growth, and concerns over the supply of educated labor are in evidence. In India, the momentum for economic reform appears to have stalled, and additional policy reforms are urgently needed.

---

[39] The Japanese have now waited for many years using the theory that recovery would reduce the magnitude of the nonperforming loan problem. In fact, nonperforming loans and the problems of the banks have been at the heart of the prolonged Japanese stagnation.

Among them, liberalizing imports of consumer goods, addressing the problems of state-owned enterprises, improving infrastructure, and freeing up the labor market appear to be paramount.

Even if one could be entirely confident about external prospects, there is no Asian crisis country that has yet addressed its policy problems sufficiently to provide assurance that longer-term growth will resume. While some countries appear to be further along the path than others, none has taken the decisive actions on the financial system that appear crucial for further growth. Countries' fortunes depend both on their own internal policies, and on the prospects for all the crisis-stricken countries and the world economy as a whole.

Over the longer term, as these problems are addressed, there is every reason to be optimistic about the prospects for resumed growth in Asia. In all likelihood, in a decade's time, the crisis that started in 1997 will be viewed as a watershed, when many countries exhausted the opportunities provided by their existing growth strategy (e.g., unskilled labor-intensive export growth, reliance on foreign investment for growth) and had to adapt to the challenges of the next level of growth to achieve rising living standards. In all cases, however, at some later stage, further policy reforms will be needed if this next level is to be reached.

BIBLIOGRAPHY AND REFERENCES

Balassa, Bela. 1989. "Outward Orientation." In Hollis Chenery and T. N. Srinivasan, eds., *Handbook of Development Economics* 2, Ch. 31. Amsterdam: North-Holland.

Bhagwati, Jagdish. 1968. *The Theory and Practice of Commercial Policy: Departures From Unified Exchange Rates*. Princeton: Princeton Studies in International Finance.

______. 1978. *Foreign Trade Regimes and Economic Development: Anatomy and Consequences of Exchange Control*. Lexington, Mass.: Ballinger Press for the National Bureau of Economic Research.

______. 1988. "Export-Promoting Trade Strategy: Issues and Evidence." *World Bank Research Observer* 3 (1).

Corbo, Vittorio, and Jaime de Melo. 1987. "Lessons from the Southern Cone Policy Reforms." *World Bank Research Observer* 2(2):111-142.

Corsetti, Giancarlo, Paolo Pesenti, and Nouriel Roubini. 1998. "What Caused the Asian Currency and Financial Crisis?" New York University. June. Mimeo.

Dollar, David. 1993. "Outward-Oriented Developing Countries Really Do Grow More Rapidly: Evidence from 95 LDCs 1976 – 1985." *Economic Development and Cultural Change* 40 (3):523-44.

Edwards, Sebastian. 1989. *Real Exchange Rates, Devaluation, and Adjustment*. Cambridge, Mass.: MIT Press.

______. 1992. "Trade Orientation, Distortions, and Growth in Developing Countries." *Journal of Development Economics* 1 (39):31-57.

______. 1993. "Openness, Trade Liberalization, and Growth in Developing Countries." *Journal of Economic Literature* 1(3):31-57.

Financial Times. 1998. 20 July. 12.

Frank, Charles R., Kwang Suk Kim, and Larry E. Westphal. 1975. *Foreign Trade Regimes and Economic Development: Korea*. New York: Columbia University Press for the National Bureau of Economic Research.

Ito, Takatoshi, and Anne O. Krueger. 1993. *Trade and Protectionism.* Vol. II. National Bureau of Economic Research East Asia Seminar on Economics. Chicago: University of Chicago Press.

Krueger, Anne O. 1978. *Foreign Trade Regimes and Economic Development: Liberalization Attempts and Consequences.* Lexington, Mass.: Ballinger Press for the National Bureau of Economic Research.

______. 1993. *Political Economy of Economic Policy Reform in Developing Countries.* Cambridge. Mass.: MIT Press.

______. 1996. "Fifty Years of Trade and Industrialization in Korea: 1945 – 1995." Paper prepared for the Korea Development Institute Conference Celebrating Fifty Years of Korean Independence, December.

Krueger, Anne O., and Okan Aktan. 1992. *Swimming Against the Tide: Turkish Trade Reform in the 1980s.* San Francisco: ICS Press.

Krueger, Anne O., and Baran Tuncer. 1982. "Growth of Factor Productivity in Turkish Manufacturing Industries." *Journal of Development Economics* 11(3):307-25.

Levinsohn, James. 1993. "Testing the Imports-as-Market-Discipline Hypothesis." *Journal of International Economics* 35:1-22.

Lloyd, Peter J., and P. M. Summers. 1997. "A Long Term View of Investment, Migration, and Growth in East Asia." University of Melbourne. Mimeo.

McKinnon, Ronald I. 1995. *Financial Liberalization in Developing Countries.* Oxford: Oxford University Press.

Michaely, Michael, Demetris Papageorgiou, and Armeane Choksi. 1991. *Liberalizing Foreign Trade.* New York: Basil Blackwell.

Morawetz, David. 1981. *Why the Emperor's New Clothes are Not Made in Colombia.* Oxford: Oxford University Press.

Mussa, Michael. 1986. "Nominal Exchange Rate Regimes and the Behavior of Real Exchange Rates: Evidence and Implications." In Karl Brunner and Allan H. Meltzer, eds., *Real Business Cycles, Real Exchange Rates, and Actual Policies.* Carnegie-Rochester Conference Series on Public Policy No. 25:117-213. Amsterdam: North-Holland.

Quibria, M. G. 1996. "Migration, Remittances and Trade, with Special Reference to Asian Developing Countries." In Peter J. Lloyd and Lynne S. Williams eds., *International Trade and Migration in the APEC Region*. New York and Melbourne: Oxford University Press.

Rodrik, Dani. 1995. "Trade and Industrial Policy Reform." In Jere Behrman and T. N. Srinivasan, eds., *Handbook of Development Economics*. Vol. 3A, Ch. 45. Amsterdam: North-Holland.

Sachs, Jeffrey, and Andrew Warner. 1995. "Economic Reform and the Process of Global Integration." *Brookings Papers on Economic Activity.*

Sharer, Robert. 1998. *Trade Liberalization in IMF-Supported Programs*. Washington, DC: International Monetary Fund. February.

Srinivasan, T. N. 1986. "The Costs and Benefits of Being a Small, Remote, Island, Landlocked, or Ministate Economy." *World Bank Research Observer* 2 (2):205-218.

______. 1994. "Indian Agriculture: Policies and Performance." In T. N. Srinivasan, ed., *Agriculture and Trade in China and India.* Ch. 3: 73-108. San Francisco: ICS Press.

Subcommittee on Asian Financial and Capital Markets, Committee on Foreign Exchange and Other Transactions, Takatoshi Ito, Chairman. 1998. "Lessons from the Asian Currency Crises: Risks Related to Short-Term Capital Movement and the '21st Century-Type' Currency Crisis." 19 May. Tokyo.

Thomas, Vinod, Kazi Matinh, and John Nash. 1990. *Strengthening Trade Policy Reform*. Baltimore: Johns Hopkins University Press.

Tornell, Aaron. 1998. "Common Fundamentals in the Tequila and Asian Crises." National Bureau of Economic Research and Stanford Center for Research on Economic Development and Policy Reform. July. Mimeo.

World Bank. 1993. *The East Asian Miracle: Economic Growth and Public Policy*. New York: Oxford University Press for the World Bank.

______. Various years. *World Development Report*. New York: Oxford University Press for the World Bank.

CHAPTER THREE

Principal Causes of Asian Export Deceleration

Takatoshi Ito

INTRODUCTION

At the conclusion of *The East Asian Miracle: Economic Growth and Public Policy* (World Bank 1993), exports were identified as a key element for the high performance of dynamic Asian economies. Export promotion, as opposed to import protection, contributed to innovation and growth. Indeed, the export performance of the Asian economies in the 1980s and the first half of the 1990s was astounding. Many economies achieved sustained export growth of 20 percent and more. Several countries, starting out as agricultural and textile goods producers, climbed a technological ladder and started to produce more sophisticated manufactured goods.

Within a few years of the World Bank study, export growth started to decline. From 1995 to 1996, export growth rates of many Asian countries fell from around 20 percent to single digits. The deceleration of export growth was most prominent in Thailand (25 percent growth to 1 percent contraction on a free on board [FOB] customs basis) and Korea (30 percent to 4 percent growth). Export deceleration is one of the factors that contributed to the Asian currency crisis in 1997. Exports have seemed to determine whether Asian countries would soar or sink.

Asian success in economic growth in the 1980s and the first half of the 1990s is reminiscent of Japan's success in the 1950s and 1960s. Japan's average economic growth rate in the 1960s was above 10 percent. The growth rates in Japan declined in the 1970s and 1980s, but remained higher than those of the US and Europe, and by the late 1980s Japanese per capita income, at market exchange rates, exceeded that of the US. The Japanese success, especially in the 1950s and 1960s, was the result of rapid export growth, since the domestic market was not enough to support scale economies of major manufacturing industries.

Hong Kong, China; Korea; Singapore; and Taipei,China became the next group of countries, the NIEs, that followed the Japanese path of export success. Their income level trailed Japan by 10–20 years, but they gradually gained. Then came the Southeast Asian economies of Indonesia, Malaysia, Philippines, and Thailand, or ASEAN-4, that started their rapid economic growth in the 1980s after abandoning import substitution and adopting export promotion. In the 1990s, the PRC started to register strong economic growth.

A general consensus exists that rapid economic growth in the region was made possible by rapid industrialization and strong exports. In fact, export growth has been an engine for economic growth in many Asian economies, and export promotion by governments, if not industrial policy, was viewed positively by policymakers. Most Asian economies have few resources, and many of their raw materials, especially oil, are imported. Therefore, exports are crucial to avoid balance of payments crises and indeed, exports from the NIEs and ASEAN-4 countries increased at double-digit rates from the early 1980s to the mid-1990s (Ito 1996).

From mid-1996 to 1997, however, export growth in the region suddenly decelerated, followed by economic growth deceleration. Japan though has had a stagnant economy since 1992, with an average growth rate of 1 percent a year. The growth rates of Korea and Taipei,China decelerated to their growth recession level. Export growth rates of the NIEs, which were typically above 10 percent, fell to less than 5 percent. Thailand recorded negative export growth, after 10 years of average export growth rates of nearly 20 percent; the export performance of the other ASEAN-4 countries was only slightly better.

The currency crisis erupted in Southeast Asia in mid-1997. Thailand moved its exchange rate regime from the basket system with a heavy weight to the US dollar, to the managed float on 2 July. The baht depreciated by more than 30 percent in the following two months. The Indonesian rupiah, Philippine peso, and Malaysian ringgit started to depreciate in mid-July, and all three currencies had depreciated by 30–40 percent by the end of September. Then, between October and January 1998, the currency crisis spread to Indonesia and Korea. By the end of January, the value of the Indonesian rupiah was less than one sixth of the precrisis level.

The Thai Government asked for IMF assistance in August 1997. An IMF package of $17.2 billion was organized in cooperation with Japan and other Asian countries. The Indonesian Government asked for IMF help in October 1997 and reached an agreement in November. The crisis reached Korea in November, as commercial banks in leading industrial countries started to refuse rollovers for Korean banks. Korea reached an agreement with IMF in December. The currencies of Indonesia and Korea continued to decline in December and January, in spite of IMF support packages.

One of the reasons for the baht crisis is Thailand's large current account deficits. Although they existed in 1995 and 1996, at about 8 percent of GDP, the crisis did not hit until 1997. The trigger seems to have been the deceleration of exports and resulting adverse effects on economic growth in the second half of 1996 and early 1997. Even with the same level of current account deficits, an economy with a low growth rate may be regarded as a riskier country. A sharp decline of exports and declining economic growth prompted pessimistic expectations on sustainability of the de facto nominal peg to the US dollar.

Therefore, an understanding of the sudden deceleration in exports is important in analyzing the evolving currency crisis in Asia. Beyond this is the question whether the Asian economic miracle has ended, or is the crisis a temporary setback? To answer this, we will try to ascertain whether exports will recover after large currency depreciations in the ASEAN countries and Korea.

EXPORT MOVEMENT AND HYPOTHESES

Comovement of Export Growth among the NIEs, ASEAN-4, and PRC

Export booms, or a lack of them, in the Asian economies show a fairly clear comovement. The three economies of Hong Kong, China; Korea; and Singapore had a remarkable comovement in their export growth rates between 1981 and early 1997 (measured by the quarterly growth rate of exports in US dollars over the same quarter of the preceding year). Their export boom (20 percent or more a year) of the mid-1990s rivaled their 1987–1988 export boom, although the increase in Hong Kong, China's exports was somewhat less in the mid-1990s. Taipei,China also moved with the other three economies, except for 1987–1989, when the growth rate was much lower. Exports decelerated in 1995–1996 in all four economies, especially Korea and Singapore. It is remarkable that in one year (from mid-1995 to mid-1996 for Korea and slightly earlier for Singapore) the growth rates plummeted from about 30 percent to zero in these two countries (IMF, various issues; Central Bank of China, various issues.)

The ASEAN-4 countries also had comovement in export growth between 1981 and 1996. Export performance in the first half of the 1980s was erratic, but has been remarkable since the second half of the 1980s. Export growth rates in 1987–1988 reached 30 percent a year. Except for Indonesia, which suffered from a decline in oil prices, export growth in 1994–1995 also reached 30 percent a year. However, the deceleration of 1995–1996 affected the countries slightly differently: export growth rates for Malaysia and Thailand fell from 30 percent a year to negative in a few quarters. Indonesia suffered least, although it did not experience the boom in 1994–1995 as mentioned earlier. (But in the last quarter of 1997 and early 1998, Indonesian exports collapsed.) The Philippines suffered a deceleration from 30 percent growth a year to 10 percent a year, but quickly rebounded in the latter half of 1996 (IMF, various issues).

The PRC and Taipei,China have performed quite well in exports since the mid-1980s, with growth rates of 10–25 percent most of the time. The PRC's export growth rate in 1995 reached 30 percent, became negative in mid-1996, and experienced a strong recovery in 1997. Hong Kong, China also had an export boom, with growth reaching 20 percent in 1995, followed by deceleration in 1996. The recovery in 1997 for Hong Kong, China was slow (IMF, various issues; CEPD, various years.)

Table 3.1 shows a correlation matrix using quarterly data from the first quarter of 1981 to the second quarter of 1997. It shows a strong correlation among the three economies of Hong Kong, China; Korea; and Thailand. It also shows a strong correlation among Indonesia, Malaysia, Philippines, and Singapore.

Table 3.1 Export Growth Correlation Matrix, Selected Economies Q1 1981–Q2 1997

	Korea	Hong Kong, China	Thailand	Singapore	Indonesia	Philippines
Hong Kong, China	**0.54**					
Thailand	**0.57**	**0.68**				
Singapore	**0.53**	**0.52**	**0.68**			
Indonesia	0.12	0.20	0.31	**0.63**		
Philippines	0.45	0.46	**0.57**	**0.68**	**0.50**	
Malaysia	0.31	0.40	0.44	**0.73**	**0.65**	**0.58**

Note: Bold type indicates 0.50 and higher.

Sources: IMF (various issues); Central Bank of China (various issues); CEPD (various issues).

Table 3.2 shows a correlation matrix of the Asian economies included in Table 3.1 and the PRC using quarterly data from the first quarter of 1989 to the second quarter of 1997. A strong correlation exists between some pairs among Korea; Hong Kong, China; Singapore; and Thailand. Malaysia also has strong correlation with Singapore and Thailand. The export growth rates of the PRC and Indonesia do not have a high correlation with those of other countries (except for the PRC with Singapore). Indonesia's export performance

Table 3.2 Export Growth Correlation Matrix, Selected Economies Q1 1989–Q2 1997

	Korea	Hong Kong, China	Thailand	Singapore	Indonesia	Philippines	Malaysia
Hong Kong, China	0.28						
Thailand	0.47	**0.67**					
Singapore	**0.51**	0.24	**0.54**				
Indonesia	0.02	0.26	0.07	0.41			
Philippines	**0.66**	-0.15	0.12	0.28	-0.10		
Malaysia	**0.53**	0.47	**0.66**	**0.77**	0.41	0.19	
PRC	0.37	0.25	0.37	**0.50**	0.15	0.31	0.48

Note: Bold type indicates 0.50 and higher.

Sources: As Table 3.1

may be dominated by oil prices, and oil prices have declined in the mid-1990s. The PRC's weak correlation coefficients suggest that its export base and markets are different from those of the other economies in the table.

In summary, the four NIEs, the ASEAN-4 countries (with the possible exception of Indonesia), and the PRC experienced an export boom from 1994 to mid-1995, followed by deceleration from mid-1995 to 1996. The deceleration experience is quite uniform to these economies, suggesting that shocks were regionwide.

Whether the deceleration of mid-1995 to 1996 is cyclical or permanent is difficult to determine at this point. The degree of deceleration is not unusual from these economies' export histories: their export growth rates fell simultaneously in 1985 and 1989. The way growth rates fell in 1995–1996 seems to be similar to the cyclical slowdown of earlier years. This is further analyzed below.

Comovement of Export Growth among other Asian Economies

Growth rate movements of four South Asian economies—Bangladesh, India, Pakistan, and Sri Lanka—are in general more volatile than those discussed above. Except for occasional strong export performance, the average growth rate was less than 20 percent a year in the late 1980s and 1990s, though it was somewhat stronger in 1994 to mid-1995. The deceleration of mid-1995 to 1996 was prominent only in Bangladesh and Pakistan; both countries had negative export growth in 1993. The slowdown of exports in mid-1995 to 1996 in this group seems much more cyclical than in the NIEs, the ASEAN-4 countries, and the PRC (IMF, various issues).

Tables 3.3 and 3.4 show that the export growth rates of five South Asian countries are not correlated, unlike the NIEs or the ASEAN-4 countries. None of the pairs has a correlation higher than 0.4. This does not change even when the sample is restricted to the more recent period (Table 3.4).

Table 3.3 Export Growth Correlation Matrix, South Asia Q1 1981–Q2 1997

	India	Pakistan	Sri Lanka	Bangladesh	Myanmar
Pakistan	-0.05				
Sri Lanka	0.38	-0.05			
Bangladesh	0.40	-0.01	0.32		
Myanmar	0.03	0.17	0.13	-0.02	
Nepal	-0.25	0.20	0.25	0.13	-0.07

Source: IMF, *International Financial Statistics* CD-ROM (various issues).

Table 3.4 Export Growth Correlation Matrix, South Asia Q1 1989–Q2 1997

	India	Pakistan	Sri Lanka	Bangladesh	Myanmar
Pakistan	0.04				
Sri Lanka	0.23	0.15			
Bangladesh	0.31	0.23	0.28		
Myanmar	0.01	0.20	0.12	0.08	
Nepal	-0.35	0.23	0.23	0.27	-0.03

Source: As Table 3.3.

Export Acceleration

Sustained export growth needs constant changes in industrial structures and export goods. If a country continues exporting the same goods, exports sooner or later slow, as its exports quickly saturate the world market. For example, over the years of rapid economic growth and subsequently, the major export items of Japan have evolved from toys and textiles to consumer durables (e.g., radios and televisions), to heavy and chemical products (e.g., steel and ships), to automobiles, and to high-tech electronics. Korea and Taipei,China also promoted heavy and chemical industries in the 1970s and 1980s.

The pattern of economic development where Japan upgraded its industrial structure, followed by the NIEs, and later the ASEAN-4 countries (and possibly the PRC) is often called the "flying geese" pattern. As Japan vacated the place of textile exporter, that position was first filled by Hong Kong, China; then the Philippines and Thailand, and then the PRC. As the region as a whole developed, whole countries developed in order. Comparative advantage was in operation, and the flying geese pattern was maintained. As NIEs quickly grew in the 1970s, the ASEAN-4 countries were in good position to fill the void created by the NIEs' surging even further ahead in the 1980s.

Foreign direct investment (FDI), in contrast to portfolio flows, is considered a long-term commitment of investors in a host country. The host country gains in several respects. FDI is more likely than portfolio investment to stay in the host country in times of economic and political difficulty. In addition, FDI usually brings technological transfer, considered to increase the productivity of the host country. Firms established by FDI also tend to train workers more efficiently than local firms, with well-trained managers from the parent firms passing on their management and other skills. Another aspect of FDI is its impact on competition. A country with firms established by FDI tends to see enhanced competition in its domestic market, leading to greater efficiency, especially when a characteristic of the sector was previously monopoly or oligopoly. As a result, FDI is often identified as another factor in export acceleration. In the 1980s, direct investment within the Asian region became much more pronounced. Not only Japan, but Korea and Taipei,China also started to invest in other countries in the region, most notably the PRC.

It is reasonable to consider a hypothesis that rapid economic growth among the NIEs, ASEAN-4 countries, and the PRC in the 1980s and 1990s was the result of FDI. According to IMF data, global capital flows (including FDI, portfolio investment, and other types of capital flows) increased from $46 billion in 1990 to $235 billion in 1996. The share of FDI increased from 41 percent in 1990 to 45 percent in 1996. Moreover, the FDI share in total capital flows has been higher in Asia (since 1992) than in any other region.

There are two ways in which FDI may be correlated with export growth of emerging markets in Asia. First, as the economy grows, foreign investors and manufacturers invest in the booming export sector. Growth prompts more optimistic expectations and contributes to more FDI inflows. Second, governments may invite foreign manufacturers into a sector that has not yet experienced a boom, in the hope that foreign investors will make the boom happen. Some countries, especially Malaysia, are known to make deliberate efforts to encourage technology transfer by targeting particular industries (sometimes with tax incentives). However, without detailed sector data, it is difficult to establish quantitatively by sector how FDI promotes export growth.

It has often been argued that portfolio capital flows have contributed to growth. If intermediated into fixed investment, portfolio flows help an economy grow faster. Indeed, portfolio flows as well as FDI have soared in the first half of the 1990s. Most portfolio capital flows before 1994 were directed to Latin America. However, after the Mexican peso crisis of 1994–1995, they fell substantially. Asia did not experience this sharp decline.

Khan and Reinhart (1995) warn of the difficulty in formulating macroeconomic policies when a large amount (e.g., more than 10 percent of GDP) of portfolio capital moves into a country. Its mismanagement can result in a real exchange rate appreciation and therefore loss in price competitiveness of exports. On the other hand, intervention in the foreign exchange market may take one of two forms. Unsterilized intervention (see below) can lead to overheating and inflationary pressure. Sterilized intervention may reduce inflationary pressure, but increase capital inflows due to higher interest rates. Greater indebtedness, in particular short-term debts, increases the vulnerability of the domestic financial markets to a large shock, such as a reversal of capital inflows. Hence, macroeconomic management of capital inflows has relevance to export movements. It would seem therefore, before the currency crisis of mid-1997, that Asian countries had managed capital inflows quite well.

A laissez-faire (nonintervention) policy in the face of large capital inflows will certainly appreciate the currency sharply, hurting export industries particularly, possibly destroying some of them. Once an industry is lost, even if the exchange rate depreciates to previous levels, the production and exports of that industry may not rematerialize. Such an asymmetric effect is called hysteresis. Because many manufacturing industries require fixed investment, volatility of the exchange rate has an adverse effect on investment (some from abroad), growth, and exports. Hence, unless the current account is in surplus, which is unlikely for most emerging market economies, a first macroeconomic response to large capital inflows is usually to intervene in the foreign exchange market to prevent a sharp nominal appreciation of the currency. If the exchange rate regime is a de facto fixed rate regime, then intervention is not a choice but a necessity. Intervention will lead to higher foreign reserves as well as a larger domestic monetary base. There are then two choices: the monetary base increase can be left alone (unsterilized intervention), or the increase can be offset by domestic open market operations (sterilized intervention),

With unsterilized intervention, unless an increase in money demand—sometimes observed in a rapidly growing economy—absorbs the expansion in the monetary base, this expansion results in lower interest rates, overheating, and inflation. This is undesirable. Sterilized intervention, on the other hand, can reduce the risk of inflation, but may increase the size of capital inflows. For example, suppose that the initial surge in capital inflows is in the form of FDI and portfolio investment. Then one-to-one sterilization will likely increase short-term interest rates, leading to an increase in short-term capital inflows, such as investment in interbank deposits, interbank lending, and short-term securities. In fact, sterilized intervention may adversely change the composition of capital inflows toward a greater proportion of short-term instruments, and from the viewpoint of the host country, such instruments are less preferable to FDI or portfolio investment.

It is difficult to examine how portfolio flows affect, positively or negatively, exports of host countries, since these countries intervene to absorb currency appreciation pressures; it is also difficult to ascertain how host countries' domestic capital and financial systems intermediate the foreign funds into investment for export industries. Even with large portfolio inflows, if they become foreign reserves as a result of intervention, they do not contribute to an increase in domestic investment in the host country, beyond an indirect effect of keeping the interest rates lower than otherwise. Even if portfolio inflows do not result in foreign reserve increases but are absorbed by the domestic capital market, it is not clear whether they encourage more consumption or more investment.

In addition to intervention, what other policy measures can the host country undertake to absorb portfolio inflows? If overheating (for example, as a result of unsterilized intervention) is a problem, fiscal tightening is a correct response, as it changes the savings-investment balance in favor of reducing inflows. Thailand succeeded in reducing fiscal deficits during the period of large capital inflows of 1989–1991. Tax incentives for increasing saving, or a more direct measure (e.g., introducing a compulsory pension plan), can help prevent a further deterioration in current account deficits for the same reason.

Hypotheses on Export Deceleration

We have seen that export deceleration is a regional phenomenon, and several hypotheses for it have been put forward. The first suspect is exchange rate appreciation. Since many Asian countries pegged their currencies to the US dollar, either explicitly or implicitly, the nominal exchange rate vis-à-vis the US dollar was quite stable (before the Asian currency crisis) for most NIEs and ASEAN countries. Therefore, a domestic inflation rate higher than that in the US results in a real appreciation of the currency. Second, many Asian countries have trading ties with Japan as strong as with the US. Hence, the stable exchange rate vis-à-vis the US dollar does not mean a stable real effective exchange rate (REER). The yen depreciated by about 50 percent from April 1995 to mid-1996. Hence, Asian products directly or indirectly became less competitive against Japanese products.

Third, sector shocks may have been large in 1995–1997. Commodity prices in general, and oil prices in particular, fell. Moreover, semiconductor prices came down in 1995–1996 due to overcapacity in the industry. Fourth, the Japanese economy has been sluggish for several years. As one of the absorbers of Asian exports, the business cycle of the Japanese economy has some impact on Asian exports. Fifth, the business cycles of neighboring economies are also important, since the economies in the region depend on each other. As one economy slows its imports will decline. Then neighboring countries that export their goods to this economy will in turn suffer lower demand for their goods.

In short, the factors influencing Asian exports are real exchange rate appreciations, sector shocks, Japanese stagnation, and multiplier effects among regional economies, in addition to low productivity—the Lau-Young-Krugman hypothesis. We will look at the last hypothesis and trade implications before examining other hypotheses.

The Lau-Young-Krugman Hypothesis on Productivity

Krugman (1994) popularized the idea of Young (1992, 1994, 1995) and Kim and Lau (1994) that Asian growth has been achieved by increasing factor inputs (capital and labor), and that the total factor productivity (TFP) increase has been minimal.

TFP growth is a key to output growth among the leading industrial economies. During the rapid economic growth of Japan, the TFP increase constituted about half of output growth. According to Denison and Chung (1976), the average growth rate of Japan from 1953 to 1971 was 8.8 percent, of which 4.9 percent was attributed to technological progress, while the average growth rate of the US from 1948 to 1969 was 4 percent, of which 1.9 percent was attributed to technological progress.

Young (1992) shows that Singapore invested much more in capital stock than Hong Kong, China in the 1970s and 1980s, although the output growth rates of the two economies were similar. Output growth of Singapore is explained entirely by factor accumulation, thus there was no TFP growth. Young (1994, 1995), extending his earlier study to the NIEs, concludes that most output growth can be explained by the dramatic rise in factor inputs, and little by TFP growth. Kim and Lau (1994) present a similar finding by estimating the production function of the five leading industrial economies (US, Japan, Germany, France, and United Kingdom), and the four NIEs, and tests a null hypothesis of no TFP growth. The null is rejected for the five industrial economies, but not for the NIEs.

Young (1992) suggests that Singapore has invested too much and moved into new industries too quickly, leaving little time to enjoy TFP benefits in a mature industry. Krugman (1994) argues that if growth of the NIEs (in particular, Singapore) is explained by increases in capital and labor, then the future of these economies is dim, since there is a limit to an increase in mobilization of productive factors, especially labor.

The deceleration of the Asian economies in 1996–1997 has revived interest in the Lau-Young-Krugman hypothesis. Is the deceleration an omen of future slow growth?

It is important to examine this argument carefully. First, it is well known that capital is difficult to measure. The change in capital is usually estimated by gross investment minus depreciation. Depreciation, in theory, should reflect technological obsolescence as well as physical wear and tear. But, in practice, it is usually adjusted by a rigid formula for depreciating the existing stock. Second, labor input should be adjusted for the quality of workers. Attempts to use education levels for quality provide only an approximate adjustment. Third, marginal productivity of capital and labor is hard to estimate. These coefficients may change over time, especially when economic structures are changing fast. For these reasons, estimates of TFP growth vary from onc author to another, as do estimates from one sample period to another. IMF (1997a) offers a range of TFP growth estimates by different authors covering different sample periods. Estimates for the later sample periods in the 1980s and 1990s tend to show higher TFP growth. Even for Singapore, the case in point for Young's result, TFP growth seems to have increased in the later years: whereas Young estimates the TFP average growth rate at 0.2 percent for 1966–1990, Sarel estimates it at 2.5 percent for 1979–1996.

Even if the estimates by Young are close to reality, the interpretations by Young and Krugman may not be appropriate. Growth, even if it comes from accumulation of factors, is definitely better than no growth. Many developing countries do invest, but invest in the wrong kinds of fixed capital and inventory, so that productivity does not increase. This was part of the problem in the old Soviet economy which Krugman compares with Singapore.

Technological progress may be realized at the end of, even if not during, the sequencing of industrialization. This is, in fact, suggested by the above estimates, namely, that TFP growth in Singapore in the 1980s and 1990s (estimates by Sarel) was higher than that of the 1960s and 1970s (estimates by Young). Suppose that the growth process follows a process of changing from simpler to more sophisticated manufacturing sectors, what Young describes as too much investment and too hasty a shift to the next industry may not imply a loss in national welfare. If the time discount factor is sufficiently low, it may be optimal to run up the ladder of industrialization quickly before reaping even larger benefits (TFP growth) later.

If productivity did not increase, as Krugman and Young suggest, then it might have an implication on trade competitiveness. The Balassa-Samuelson hypothesis applies best when tradable sector productivity growth exceeds that in nontradable sectors. The productivity differential results in higher consumer price index (CPI) inflation rates relative to those of trading partners, leading in turn to real exchange rate appreciation. Hence, one might think that given the Balassa-Samuelson hypothesis, the Krugman hypothesis implies a lack of real exchange rate appreciation for rapidly growing Asian economies. However, after examining all these arguments, it is too early to tell whether this deceleration is a turning point to the slower growth predicted by Krugman.

Ito et al. (1996) examine the Balassa-Samuelson hypothesis for fast-growing APEC countries for the period 1972–1993. According to them, the real exchange rate appreciated for the NIEs, while their economic growth rates were high. In contrast, the ASEAN-4 countries did not experience real exchange rate appreciation in the long run. It is unclear whether this observation—no real appreciation despite high growth rates—can be combined with Krugman's assertion of a lack of TFP growth.

EXPORT VOLUME AND PRICES

Export movements in the previous section illustrate how export earnings in US dollars have changed over time. Unfortunately, it is sometimes more revealing to decompose exports in dollars into export volume and prices. However, the appropriate series are not always available. The focus of this section is on the NIEs and the ASEAN-4 countries because of data availability. The export volume index for a country is usually obtained from the IMF's *International Financial Statistics* (code 72ZF).[1]

Table 3.5 shows the decomposition of export value growth for the NIEs into export volume and prices at the height of deceleration, from the second quarter of 1995 to the fourth quarter of 1996. Korean exports by value decreased by 8 percent from the third quarter of 1995 to the third quarter of 1996, while the volume *increased* by 10 percent. This implies that export prices declined by 18 percent. The situation is slightly different in both Hong Kong, China; and Singapore. Both values and volumes changed in parallel, while prices were largely flat or declined only slightly. In Taipei,China, the volume growth decreased to almost zero, while prices slightly increased, in sharp contrast to Korea. The Korean price decline was significant, and suggests a more structural, sector-based problem in Korean exports.

Table 3.6 gives information on export volume and prices for the ASEAN-4 countries, from the second quarter of 1995 to the fourth

[1] For Thailand, the export volume series ends in the first quarter of 1996. The export volume growth rates from the second quarter of 1996 to the second quarter of 1997 are calculated as the export value growth rate minus the wholesale price index (WPI) inflation rate. For Malaysia, the export volume series after the second quarter of 1992 is unavailable. The proxy is calculated as the export value growth rate minus the producer price index inflation rate. For the Philippines, the export volume series after the first quarter of 1992 is unavailable. The proxy is calculated as the export value growth rate minus the WPI inflation rate.

Table 3.5 Export Value Decomposition, NIEs, Q2 1995–Q4 1996

	Korea			Hong Kong, China			Singapore			Taipei,China		
	Value	Vol.	Price	Value	Vol.	Price	Value	Vol.	Price	Value	Vol.	Price
1995 Q2	0.34	0.25	0.09	0.20	0.09	0.10	0.17	0.13	0.04	0.17	0.06	0.11
1995 Q3	0.36	0.30	0.06	0.18	0.15	0.04	0.15	0.12	0.03	0.24	0.07	0.17
1995 Q4	0.21	0.19	0.02	0.17	0.15	0.02	0.09	0.07	0.02	0.17	-0.00	0.18
1996 Q1	0.20	0.23	-0.02	0.16	0.16	0.01	0.06	0.05	0.01	0.14	0.06	0.08
1996 Q2	0.04	0.19	-0.15	0.05	0.08	-0.03	0.03	0.04	-0.01	0.12	0.05	0.06
1996 Q3	-0.08	0.10	-0.17	0.00	0.01	-0.01	0.04	0.05	-0.01	0.04	0.05	-0.01
1996 Q4	0.02	0.28	-0.26	0.03	0.02	0.00	0.04	0.05	-0.01	0.04	0.07	-0.04

Sources: IMF (various issues); Central Bank of China (various issues); and author's calculations.

Table 3.6 Export Value Decomposition, ASEAN-4, Q2 1995–Q4 1996

	Thailand			Indonesia			Philippines			Malaysia		
	Value	Vol.	Price	Value	Vol.	Price	Value	Vol.	Price	Value	Vol.	Price
1995 Q2	0.29	0.13	0.16	0.12	-0.01	0.12	0.35	0.34	0.02	0.29	0.22	0.06
1995 Q3	0.24	0.13	0.10	0.10	0.16	-0.06	0.33	0.31	0.01	0.26	0.23	0.02
1995 Q4	0.19	0.10	0.08	0.13	-0.04	0.17	0.27	0.20	0.08	0.19	0.17	0.02
1996 Q1	0.07	0.04	0.03	0.10	0.01	0.10	0.22	0.11	0.11	0.17	0.16	0.01
1996 Q2	-0.02	-0.08	0.06	0.11	0.10	0.01	0.15	0.03	0.12	0.07	0.05	0.02
1996 Q3	-0.05	-0.08	0.03	0.09	-0.05	0.15	0.12	0.01	0.11	0.00	-0.02	0.02
1996 Q4	-0.04	-0.07	0.03	0.09	0.16	-0.07	0.19	0.16	0.04	0.01	-0.03	0.04

Sources: IMF (various issues.)

quarter of 1996. Export volume declines are common. Thailand experienced a parallel decline in volume and values, keeping prices relatively stable. Indonesia's data are hard to interpret because volumes and values are quite variable. The Philippines was least affected of the four in terms of export value deceleration; deceleration came mainly from volume. In contrast to the other countries, prices seem to have increased slightly in the Philippines. In Malaysia, values and volumes moved in parallel and prices were fairly stable.

Malaysia and Thailand seem to be in a similar situation. The decline in their volume of exports seems to reflect a general loss of competitiveness of their products.

With regard to South Asia, Pakistan's exports grew at a high pace in the second half of the 1980s. They slowed in the 1990s, but have maintained reasonably high growth rates, with occasional negative growth. The timings of increases and decreases in export volume tend to coincide with those of the ASEAN-4 countries for the 1990s. India could not be examined due to the unavailability of export volume data.

SECTOR PERFORMANCE

Korea

Long-Run Performance

Korea's industrial structure has changed rapidly over the last 20 years, and this change is reflected in its export structure. Figure 3.1 shows the time-series changes of shares of major export categories for Korea. Until the late 1980s, the leading export category with a share of more than 25 percent was bags and toys[2] (Bank of Korea 1998; author's calculations). From 1985, there was a sharp increase in electronics

---

[2] This category comprises handbags, travel goods, sports goods, apparel and accessories, footwear, watches and clocks, toys, and musical instruments and parts.

and machinery;[3] their exports surpassed bags and toys in late 1989, to reach 30 percent of the total in 1995. However, their share has been dropping in the last couple of years. The share of iron and steel increased sharply at the beginning of the 1980s, then gradually receded. In its place, automobile exports rose in the mid- to late 1980s.

Figure 3.1 Korea: Export Composition

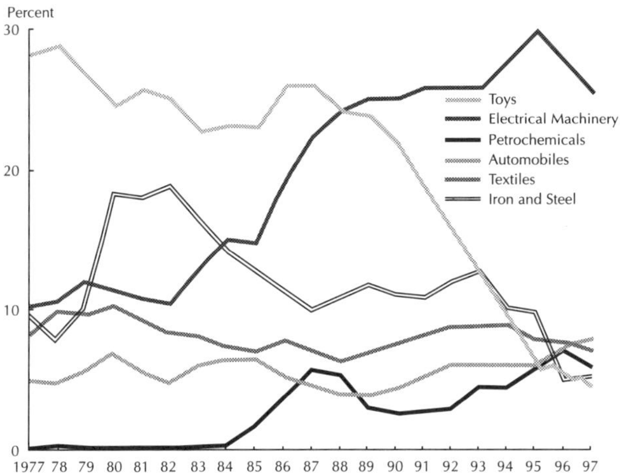

Source: Bank of Korea Website (1998).

Deceleration

The two sectors that suffered the largest declines in exports in 1995 and 1996 (in absolute terms) were iron and steel and semiconductors (Bank of Korea 1998). Combined, these sectors accounted for more than $6 billion of the export decline. The semiconductor slump was worldwide. The industry has a regular boom-bust cycle, and 1996 was a trough year. The industries—including semiconductors—that suffered most seem to be those competing with Japanese producers. The export surge of Korean industry from 1993 to 1995 appears to

[3] This category comprises power generating equipment, office machinery, televisions, radios, sound recorders and VTRs, telecommunications equipment, household electrical equipment, thermionic valves and semiconductors, and electrical power machinery.

have been helped by the yen's appreciation. The export deceleration from April 1995 to 1996 was a reaction to this surge, and can be attributed both to cyclical business patterns, particularly in the semiconductor industry, and to the fluctuation of the yen.

It was seen earlier (under Export Movement and Hypotheses, pages 77-78) that a prominent feature of Korea's export deceleration was the sharp decline in export prices (Bank of Korea 1998). Paper and wood products, iron and steel, and electronic tubes and electronics all had large price declines. The world price declines in these products must have been the reason for the export price declines, given that these products are highly competitive in world markets.

Combining these findings, it may be concluded that Korea's export deceleration in 1995 and 1996 was caused mainly by declines in semiconductors (world demand fell sharply) and iron and steel (world prices dropped significantly).

Malaysia

Long-Run Performance

Malaysia has made significant progress in industrialization in the last 20 years. (Figure 3.2 shows such a change.) In the 1970s, it exported mainly agricultural and mining goods (Bank Negara Malaysia, various issues).[4] During the 1980s, their share by value in total exports decreased from 70 percent to less than 40 percent. Exports of electronics and electronics products increased sharply during the 1980s. Textiles, manufacturing, chemicals, and other industries increased their shares also, but much more slowly than electronics. By the mid-1990s, the share of electronics exports exceeded 50 percent of the total, and indeed, high growth rates of total exports were largely the result of the boom in electronics industries. Hence it is not surprising that when the increase in the share of electronics exports fell to nearly zero over the 1995–1997 period, the growth rate of total exports decelerated.

---

[4] Comprise rubber, tin, sawlogs, sawn timber, palm oil, and petroleum, crude and partly refined.

Figure 3.2 Malaysia: Export Composition

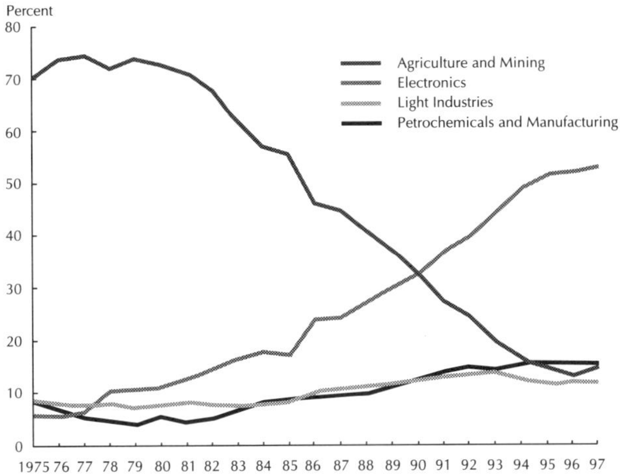

Source: Bank Negara Malaysia (various issues).

The Malaysian pattern of industrialization observed in export statistics is different from that of Hong Kong, China; Korea; and Taipei,China, in that no light manufacturing industries, such as bags, toys, and textiles, witnessed a surge in exports.[5] It seems to have jumped straight to the electronics stage.

Deceleration

The share of electronics in total exports was overwhelming in the mid-1990s, and consequently, any deceleration in exports must come from this industry. Exports of its subsector, semiconductors, increased by more than 30 percent in 1993, 1994, and 1995; in 1996, export growth decelerated to a mere 6 percent. In fact, for most months in 1996, negative export growth over the preceding 12 months was recorded for the electronics industry and semiconductors. This is consistent with what was seen for Korea. Besides semiconductors, consumer electronics products registered substantial declines in 1996. Therefore, both parts of the electronics industry suffered from an export decline.

---

5 Light industries cover food, beverages and tobacco, textiles, clothing and footwear, wood products, rubber products, paper and paper products, and toys and sporting goods.

Thailand

Thailand, as well as Korea and Malaysia, experienced a major decline in computer-related exports during 1996 and 1997. Export growth of machines, of which computers account for more than 90 percent, was increasing by more than 40 percent a year in 1995. However, in the second half of 1996, exports of machines increased by less than 10 percent. Electronic machinery was also a boom industry in 1995, only to become a stagnant, if not shrinking, industry in 1996. In this category, integrated circuits account for about 40 percent of the total, and their exports declined by about 5 percent in the second half of 1996. Textile exports, which had been booming at the beginning of 1995, suffered a severe decline in 1996, contracting by 20 percent. This is often attributed to a rise in the PRC's exports, which became competitive after the devaluation of the yuan in 1994.

Thailand's export composition has been changing from agriculture and light industries to more sophisticated industries. However, it has been squeezed from above and below in the technological product ladder. The deceleration of exports in 1996 was probably so evident in textiles because of the increased competitiveness of PRC products, while computer-related exports suffered from the worldwide demand recession in this area.

Our examination of export composition in these three countries reveals some sector shocks in 1996, namely in electronics-related markets, semiconductors, integrated circuits, and computers. In addition, Thailand suffered a decline in textiles, while Korea experienced a slump in iron and steel exports.

PRC

Exports from the PRC by value shot up in 1994 and 1995. However, the export growth rate fell sharply in 1996, and the major export items such as textiles and apparel suffered major declines. The textile industry was especially hard hit. Growth rates of apparel and shoes declined significantly. Later in 1996, steel started to suffer.

There is a hypothesis that one of the reasons for export declines in Thailand and other ASEAN-4 countries was the devaluation of the yuan in 1994 and the increased price competitiveness of competing

PRC export products. Textiles and apparel are obvious candidates. However, the fact that the PRC's exports also suffered a decline in the first half of 1996, including textiles and apparel, suggests that this hypothesis is untenable.

Exports of electronic and telecommunications equipment did not decrease in 1996, in contrast to Korea, Malaysia, and Thailand. It may be that the PRC produces and exports different types or grades of such equipment.

EXCHANGE RATE REGIME

De Facto US Dollar Peg

Many Asian countries adopted de facto US dollar peg regimes in the years preceding the currency crisis of 1997. Hong Kong, China has its currency board, with a nominal peg to the US dollar. Thailand adopted a currency basket system, but it was well known from the actual movement of the baht that the weight of the US dollar in the basket was more than 80 percent. Indonesia adopted a crawling peg against the US dollar. Malaysia adopted a managed float, but the ringgit remained stable against the US dollar. The movement of the Singapore dollar was more flexible compared with other currencies.

Frankel and Wei (1994) estimated the weights of the US dollar, Japanese yen, and other currencies in the currency baskets of nine Asian currencies (see Table 3.7). They regressed each Asian currency (vis-à-vis the Swiss franc) on the US dollar (vis-à-vis the Swiss franc) and the yen (vis-à-vis the Swiss franc), for various subperiods in 1979–1992, using weekly data. They showed that the US dollar had an overwhelming weight in all currencies in all periods.

The US dollar weight was typically about 95 percent for the won; that is, if the US dollar depreciated by 1 percent against the Swiss franc, the won depreciated by 0.95 percent that week. The Hong Kong dollar, New Taiwan dollar, rupiah, peso, and baht all had coefficients with the US dollar higher than 90 percent. For the Singapore dollar, the weight in the basket of the US dollar was about 75 percent, significantly lower than for the won. Similarly, the ringgit had a coefficient of 0.78 with the US dollar. The coefficient was 0.87 for the yuan.

Table 3.7 Asian Exchange Rate Baskets, 1979–1992

Currency	Constant	US Dollar	Yen	R^2/DW
Korean won	-0.0007[b]	0.96[a]	-0.1	0.82
	(0.0003)	(0.02)	(0.03)	1.94
Singapore dollar	0.0003[c]	0.75[a]	0.13[a]	0.86
	(0.0002)	(0.01)	(0.02)	2.28
Hong Kong dollar	-0.0007[b]	0.92[a]	-0.00	0.76
	(0.0003)	(0.02)	(0.03)	2.04
New Taiwan dollar	0.0005[b]	0.96[a]	0.05[b]	0.88
	(0.0002)	(0.02)	(0.02)	2.07
Malaysian ringgit	-0.0003	0.78[a]	0.07[a]	0.79
	(0.0003)	(0.02)	(0.02)	2.19
Indonesian rupiah	-0.0018[b]	0.95[a]	0.16[b]	0.44
	(0.0007)	(0.05)	(0.07)	2.04
Philippine peso	-0.0018[a]	1.07[a]	-0.01	0.54
	(0.0006)	(0.04)	(0.06)	2.06
Thai baht	-0.0004	0.91[a]	0.05[c]	0.75
	(0.0003)	(0.02)	(0.03)	2.24
Chinese yuan	-0.0018	0.87[a]	-0.04	0.54
	(0.0005)	0.04	(0.05)	2.05

Note: Standard errors in parentheses.

a Statistically significant at the 99 percent level.
b Statistically significant at the 95 percent level.
c Statistically significant at the 85 percent level.

Source: Frankel and Wei (1994).

Frankel and Wei examined whether adding other currencies—the deutsche mark, Australian dollar, and New Zealand dollar—would change the results. For the Singapore dollar, when these currencies were added, the coefficients of the US dollar and the yen were reduced to 0.71 and 0.12, respectively; the coefficient of the deutsche mark was 0.14, and that of the New Zealand dollar 0.02, both statistically significant. Similarly, for the ringgit, the value of the coefficient was reduced. (It is also possible that the Singapore dollar was the genuine basket currency, and the ringgit was pegged to the Singapore dollar.) For other currencies, one cannot reject the hypothesis that coefficients of the deutsche mark, Australian dollar, and New Zealand dollar were statistically significantly different from zero.

From Frankel and Wei we may conclude that only the Singapore dollar and the Malaysian ringgit had a genuine basket system. The former assigned to the US dollar a weight of 70 percent, with the yen and the deutsche mark splitting the rest. The weights were similar for the ringgit. Other than these currencies, the Asian currencies were de facto pegged to the US dollar, its weight in the basket at around 90 percent or higher.

Trade Linkages with Japan and the US

One of the reasons for the de facto US dollar peg in these countries is that a large part of their exports go to the US, and so the dollar denomination is convenient for avoiding fluctuations in export competitiveness. However, Japan is also a major trading partner of many Asian countries. In fact, for most Asian economies, Japan and the US are equally important as export destinations. Many Asian countries import parts and semifinished goods from Japan. Although the nominal or real exchange rate against the US dollar was stabilized by the exchange rate policy, the REER against the yen fluctuated widely, because the yen fluctuated against the US dollar.

If one examines exports and imports of 10 developing Asian economies[6] over the period 1990–1996, several features stand out (see Table 3.8). First, Japan is as important as the US as a trade partner of most of the economies. The trade linkage to Japan is especially strong for the ASEAN-4 countries. Second, Japan tends to be more important as an import origin than as an export destination. Except for India and Indonesia, the import share from Japan is higher than the export share. The export share of Japan is lower than the export share of the US, except for the PRC and Indonesia . The import share of Japan is higher than that of the US, except for India and Pakistan, and, in 1996 only, Korea.

Third, the 10 developing Asian economies collectively are also important mutual trading partners. For Hong Kong, China; Malaysia; and Singapore, about half their exports go to the other developing Asian economies. For the Philippines and Thailand, the share of these economies increased markedly in 1990–1996, reflecting the fact that trade linkages are now stronger among the ASEAN-4 countries. Fourth, the combined exports to US, Japan, and these economies account for

---

6 PRC; Hong Kong, China; India; Indonesia; Korea; Malaysia; Pakistan; Philippines; Singapore; and Thailand.

Table 3.8 Exports by Destination and Imports by Origin, 1996

	Exports to				Imports from			
	World	US	Japan	Asia	World	US	Japan	Asia
	(US$ million)	(percent)			(US$ million)	(percent)		
Korea	129,835	16.8	12.3	38.0	150,2122	2.2	20.9	16.7
Singapore	125,024	18.4	8.2	51.3	131,338	16.4	18.2	37.3
Thailand	55,789	18.0	16.8	36.8	73,484	12.6	27.8	28.2
Indonesia	49,814	16.0	27.8	25.4	42,292	10.3	23.6	27.7
Malaysia	78,246	18.2	13.4	46.8	78,422	15.5	24.5	34.6
Philippines	20,417	34.1	18.0	25.9	34,122	18.3	20.3	27.8
PRC	151,197	17.7	20.4	37.3	138,944	11.6	21.0	35.1
India	33,054	17.7	7.6	25.4	37,375	9.7	7.1	20.3
Pakistan	9,321	16.6	6.5	23.3	12,131	10.6	10.2	20.9

Source: IMF (1997b).

more than 70 percent of total exports for the NIEs, the ASEAN-4 countries, and the PRC. This figure is less than 50 percent for India and Pakistan; Japan accounts for less than 10 percent of their trade.

For all the NIEs and ASEAN-4 countries, mutual trade linkages have become so important that a recession in one country spills over to neighboring countries easily. Asian export deceleration reflects a "multiplier process" among the Asian countries. A recession in country A reduces demands for goods from neighboring countries B, C, D, etc., which results in a slowing down there, which in turn worsens the recession of country A.

Japan's Imports

In the 1990s, the Japanese economy turned in a weak performance that eventually became a recession in 1998. With high export shares of the 10 developing Asian economies to Japan, some assert that an unencouraging economic scenario in Japan has contributed to Asian export deceleration. Overall, Japanese imports as a percentage of GDP declined from 8 percent in 1990 to 5.7 percent in 1993, though they rebounded to 7.6 percent in 1996 (IMF 1997b). Despite stagnation at the time, the import ratio increased—though some would say that *because* of an increasing import ratio, the period of stagnation has been prolonged. The higher import ratio is partly due to a delayed response to the yen's appreciation (J-curve) from 1990 to 1995, and partly due to structural reasons (e.g., deregulation in various sectors promoting imports).

The increase in Japan's imports from 1993 to 1996 is most prominent among imports from Asia. The import share of many Asian countries increased in the period, while that of the US declined. The share of developing Asia's countries increased from 28.9 percent in 1990 to 34.7 percent in 1993, and to 37.7 percent in 1996. For example, Japan's imports from Thailand increased from $4.2 billion in 1990 to $10.3 billion in 1996, while its imports from Korea rose from some $12 billion in 1990–1993 to $16.0 billion in 1996 (IMF 1997b). Japan's rising import/GDP ratio and increasing share of imports from Asia contradict a popular notion that Japan's recession contributed to Asia's export deceleration.

Real Exchange Rates and Export Volume

One possible factor of the export deceleration in 1996 is the real appreciation of Asian currencies, mainly owing to the yen's depreciation. To observe the relationship between exchange rate movement and export performance, the real exchange rate of country AA vis-à-vis the Japanese yen (AA-RER-JA) is calculated with the CPI of country AA and Japan. The real exchange rate of country AA vis-à-vis the US dollar (AA-RER-US) is similarly calculated using the CPI of country AA and the US. Then it is plotted against the export volume (used in Tables 3.5 and 3.6). The following analysis is based on data from the early 1980s to early 1997 (i.e., before the currency crisis).

Hong Kong, China adopted the currency board, and fixed the Hong Kong dollar to the US dollar in the mid-1980s. This resulted in very smooth movement of the real exchange rate vis-à-vis the US dollar. As with Korea, Hong Kong, China's export volume also had a cyclical movement; major decelerations took place in 1986 and 1990. From 1995, the real appreciation of the Hong Kong dollar against the yen appears to have moderately affected export growth.

The *Indonesian* rupiah from 1987 to 1996 was fairly stable against the US dollar, since the crawling peg maintained its real value (as opposed to the nominal value in Thailand) against the US dollar. Despite exchange rate stability, export volume fluctuated widely because of the export structure. A major component of Indonesian

Figure 3.3 Korea: Real Exchange Rate and Export Volume

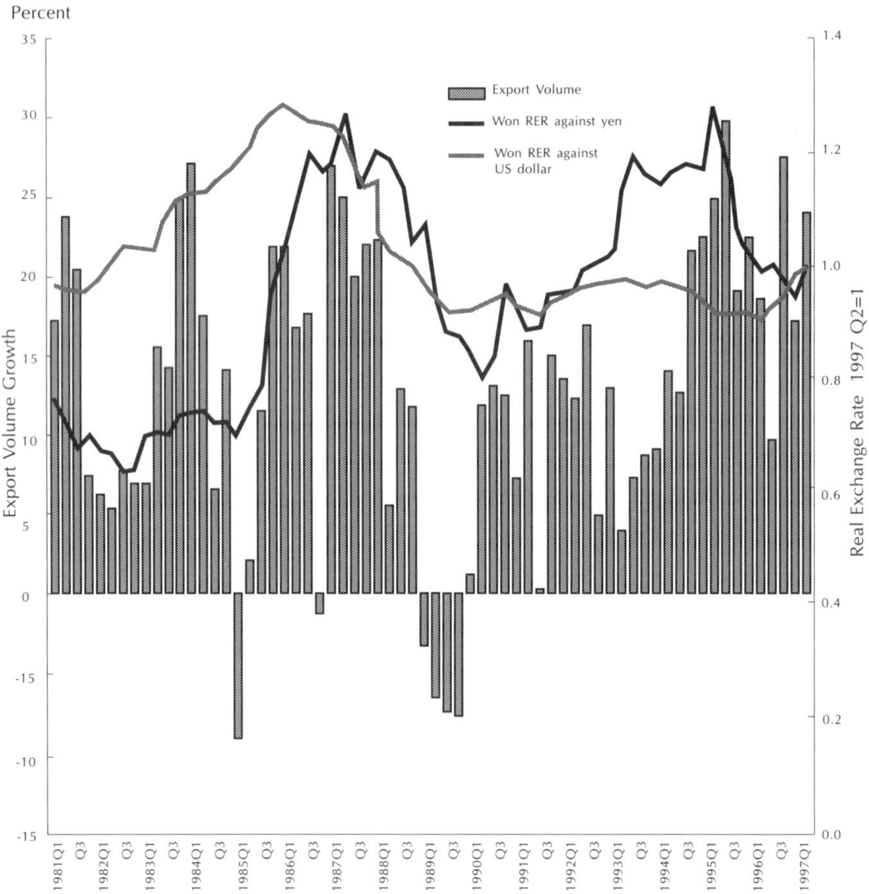

Source: Bank of Korea website (1998).

exports is oil and gas, which are subject to world market price fluctuations.

Korean export growth had a cyclical movement (as shown in Figure 3.3), and the average growth rate was very high. Major decelerations in exports took place in 1985 and 1989–1990. Export accelerations were recorded in 1987 and 1995. The peaks and troughs roughly corresponded to real exchange rate movements against the yen. Whenever the won depreciated against the yen, export volume increased, while appreciation against the yen resulted in deceleration.

However, in the second half of the 1980s, the won appreciated against both the yen and the US dollar. This was probably a reason for the major deceleration in 1989–1990. In the current phase of deceleration, 1995–1997, export volume did not decline; export prices did; and the won appreciated only against the yen.

Malaysia is another country that sustained very high export growth rates. There were fluctuations in the exchange rate and export volume, but the correlation between them was weaker than for the other cases mentioned above. This may be a result of the composition of exports, which changed from mainly agriculture in the 1980s to primarily electronics in the 1990s. It is expected that the correlation between the real exchange rate and the export volume will, from now on, become stronger, as Malaysia has become a major industrial (notably electronics) nation in the ASEAN-4 group.

Pakistan's export performance was erratic during 1987–1997. The exchange rate depreciated steadily, but export volume fluctuated every two or three years. Correlation between the exchange rate and export volume was low.

The *Philippines* also had fluctuations in the real exchange rate and export volume. In contrast to the NIEs and the other ASEAN-4 countries, export performance was much worse in the 1980s than the 1990s. This reflects political instability in the former period and political stability in the latter. Correlation between the exchange rate and export volume was fairly weak, except the major appreciations of 1988–1989, 1990–1992, and 1995–1996 that resulted in export deceleration. The depreciations of 1990 and 1993 seemed to restore export volume growth.

The cyclical movement of *Singapore's* export volume also had a common feature with Hong Kong, China; and Korea (see Ito et al., forthcoming, for relevant figures for economies other than Korea and Malaysia). Troughs were in 1985–1986, 1990, and 1995–1996, and the peaks were in 1989 and 1994–1995. There was also a deceleration in 1992. In the long run from 1985 to mid-1997, the Singapore dollar appreciated against both the yen and the US dollar. For Singapore, the deceleration in late 1996 was the most serious export decline since 1986, as the deceleration in 1990 was moderate.

Taipei,China's export volume movement was more volatile than that of the other NIEs, with cycles of only two or three years. Exchange rate movement appears to be more volatile than other NIE currencies. This may have contributed to export volume volatility.

Figure 3.4 Thailand: Real Exchange Rate and Export Volume

Source: IMF (various issues).

Thailand's remarkable sustained growth of export volume was accompanied by stable real exchange rate movement against the US dollar, after the baht's devaluation in 1984 (as shown in Figure 3.4). The major deceleration in 1995–1996 resulted in the first negative export growth since 1983. The export decline in 1983 had triggered the baht's devaluation in 1984, and this time again, the negative growth of 1996 resulted in devaluation in 1997, which triggered a whole Asian currency crisis. Although the average is high, export volume did fluctuate. The peaks and troughs are roughly correlated with the movement of the real exchange rate against the yen: the deceleration of 1995–1996 certainly coincided with the strong appreciation of the yen. A similar movement was seen in 1989–1990, though exports were growing at 10 percent a year at the trough.

Common Features

In general, there is a strong correlation between the real exchange rate of the yen and export volume growth rate in all the above economies, but most prominently Korea, Philippines, Singapore, and Thailand. In this sample period, the economies' real exchange rates vis-à-vis the yen saw two peaks: in 1987 and in 1995. In both periods, exports from the NIEs, the Philippines, and Thailand, increased before the peak, and decreased afterwards. If examined in detail, exports from the NIEs declined in 1985–1986, 1989–1990, and then 1995-1996. From these observations, the deceleration of exports in 1995-1996 may be considered cyclical, or at least, little different from past decelerations.

Data are too limited for Hong Kong, China for a general statement. For Malaysia, the correlation between exports and the real exchange rate became stronger in the 1980s, as its export structure became much more industrial. Indonesian exports do not seem correlated with its real exchange rate. This is because oil and other mineral resources account for a large share of the country's trade, and their export performance, which may not be directly related to the real exchange rate, has a large impact on export growth.

The movement of the real exchange rate of the US dollar is much smoother than that of the yen, reflecting the de facto US dollar peg. In many countries, the real exchange rate of the US dollar has shown an appreciating trend, with occasional jumps (depreciation), especially in Indonesia and Thailand, showing nominal devaluation.

As the real exchange rate of the US dollar is not volatile, its correlation with export volume is not apparent. The trend of real appreciation of these economies' currencies against the US dollar reflects mainly inflation differentials. The real exchange rate of the Hong Kong dollar has been constantly appreciating, as a result of fairly constant inflation differentials with the US. The real exchange rate of the US dollar against the baht was remarkably stable from 1984 to mid-1997, as a result of the de facto nominal US dollar peg and a very low inflation rate. Therefore, it is reasonable to conclude that baht exchange rate movements against the yen and their effects on

Thai exports are important, but this is a result of the policy of tying the exchange rate to the US dollar.

There is a weak correlation between the Pakistani rupee and the yen, while there is some connection between export volume growth and the real exchange rate against the US dollar. The weak rupee-yen correlation reflects Pakistan's trading relationships. More than a quarter of its exports go to the US, followed by Germany, UK, and Japan (the latter three each with 11–13 percent of the total).

When export volume growth and real exchange rates are plotted on a graph, the spike of RER in the second quarter of 1995 is very prominent. This reflects a sharp yen appreciation at the time, and the Asian currencies' de facto US dollar peg. In April 1995, the yen soared to 80 yen per US dollar, which was quickly reversed to the 100 level in the following six months. The yen showed an appreciating trend in the first half of the 1990s, reaching its peak in April 1995. This trend helped exports from most of the NIEs and the ASEAN-4 countries. In the two years after April 1995, the yen depreciated by 50 percent. This seems to have contributed to export volume declines in Hong Kong, China; Malaysia; Singapore; and Thailand. As mentioned before, Korea and the Philippines did not register export *volume* declines in 1996 and 1997.

The economies that adhered to the US dollar peg more strictly, such as Hong Kong, China; and Thailand, suffered most when the US dollar appreciated. For a given country, the more stable the real exchange rate of the US dollar is, the clearer the correlation between the real exchange rate of the yen and its export volume.

EXPORT REGRESSIONS

Calculation

To quantify the various factors in export movements of Asian countries, a regression analysis is carried out in this section. To explain the real exports of a country, a regression with the following specification is estimated with annual data from 1971 to 1996.[7] For the *j*th country, we estimate

[7] For a similar analysis with different datasets and frequencies, see Ito et al. (forthcoming).

$$(EXV_{j(t)}) = a + b(RER_{j(t-1)}) + c(RERy_{(t-1)}) + d_J(GrJ_{(t)}) + d_U(GrU_{(t)}) + d_A(GrA_{j(t)}) + Doil_{(t)} + e_{(t)}$$

where

$EXVj$	=	jth country export volume growth rate (calculated as the difference between export value growth minus CPI inflation rates)
$RERj$	=	jth country real exchange rate against the US dollar
$RERy$	=	real exchange rate of the yen against the US dollar
GrJ	=	real GDP growth rate of Japan
GrU	=	real GDP growth rate of the US
$GrAj$	=	weighted GDP growth rate of the ASEAN-4 countries
$Doil$	=	country-specific variable for Indonesia, namely, the real oil price

The dependent variable, EXV_j, is the export volume increase of the jth country, defined as the increase in the local currency value of free on board (FOB) exports less the CPI inflation rate of the jth country.

Right-hand side variables are as follows. The real exchange rate change, RER_j, is defined as the nominal exchange rate (jth country's currency against the US dollar) changes less the CPI inflation rate differential between jth country and the US. An increase in RER_j means real depreciation of the jth currency. A depreciation of the currency will increase export volume after a time lag (the J-curve effect). Therefore, the variable is lagged by one period. The coefficient measures how much the export volume increase will be accelerated in year t, if the real exchange rate change depreciates by 1 percent in year t-1. The expected sign of the coefficient is positive.

The real exchange rate of the yen, *RERy*, is defined as the yen/dollar nominal exchange rate changes less the inflation rate difference between Japan and the US. This variable is also lagged by one period for the same reason. The real yen/dollar exchange rate is considered to be important for Asian countries, partly because trade with Japan is a significant part of their total trade, and partly because their products compete with Japanese goods in the world market. When the yen depreciates against the US dollar, Asian goods lose their price competitiveness against Japanese goods. The expected sign of the coefficient is negative.

The growth rate of Japan, *GrJ*, is the real GDP growth rate of Japan. When Japan grows faster, it imports more from trading partners. For the *j*th Asian country, higher Japanese growth implies higher exports. The expected sign of the coefficient is positive.

Similarly, the growth rate of the US, *GrU*, is the real GDP growth rate of the US. A high proportion of Asian exports go to the US, and these exports are generally considered to be sensitive to US growth rates. The expected sign of the coefficient is positive. Neither *GrJ* nor *GrU* is lagged, because demand for Asian exports will rise as soon as the US economy expands.

Growth rates of neighboring economies also affect demand for exports. For the NIEs, exports to Southeast Asian countries may be important for their exports. The ASEAN-4 countries' average growth rate, GrA_j, is calculated as the nominal GDP-weighted average growth rates of the four countries. But, if the regression country is one of the four countries, then the weighted average is calculated excluding that country. This is done to make this variable an external factor in the export demand of that country. (Note that Singapore is not included in the definition of this variable, although it is an important member of ASEAN.) The expected sign for this variable is positive.

Since Indonesia is the only oil-exporting country, and its oil exports account for a significant share of total exports, the real oil price, *Doil*, defined by the oil price (Brent) increase less the Indonesian CPI inflation rate, is included in the Indonesian regression. The expected sign is positive, as Indonesian supply will expand when the world oil price, which is exogenous to Indonesia, rises.

Table 3.9 shows the regression results. In general, the expected signs are obtained for most of the time in each country, some statistically significant and some not significant, suggesting the general validity of a loose theoretical framework on which the examination of this chapter is based. No coefficient has the wrong sign and is statistically significant. Explanatory power varies from one country to another.

Interpretation of Regression Results

The dependent variable is the export volume increase, defined as the increase in the local currency value of FOB exports less the CPI inflation rate of that country.

Right-hand-side variables are as follows: RX_j is the real exchange rate of the local currency vis-à-vis the US dollar (increase means

Table 3.9 Export Determinants (annual data for sample period 1971-1996)

Economy	*Constant (t-stat) [signif lv]*	$RX_{j(t-1)}$	$RXyen_{(t-1)}$	*GrJapan*	*GrUS*	*ASEANX*	*Doil*	*AdjR^2 DW*
Korea	-27.90	2.035	-0.279	4.419	0.206	4.448	--	R^2 0.50
	(-2.35)	(3.54)	(-0.84)	(1.68)	(1.747)	(2.46)		DW 1.33
	[0.030][b]	[0.002][c]	[0.409]	[0.016][b]	[0.907]	[0.023][b]		
Taipei,	-6.655	0.692	0.029	2.782	2.227	0.486		R^2 0.46
China	(-0.725)	(1.95)	(0.10)	(2.06)	(1.45)	(0.35)		DW 1.83
	[0.477]	[0.065][a]	[0.918]	[0.053][a]	[0.163]	[0.722]		
Hong Kong,	1.248	0.907	-0.378	-0.699	1.611	1.277		R^2 0.35
China	(0.193)	(2.46)	(-1.84)	(-0.70)	(1.67)	(1.18)		DW 2.24
	[0.848]	[0.023][b]	[0.080][a]	[0.490]	[0.110]	[0.252]		
Singapore	-6.911	-0.102	-0.409	-0.870	0.748	2.783		R^2 0.30
	(-0.87)	(-0.282)	(-1.58)	(-0. 74)	(0.60)	(2.41)		DW 2.59
	[0.391]	[0.781]	[0.129]	[0.467]	[0.550]	[0.025][b]		
Singapore	-7.508	-0.098	-0.434			2.694		R^2 0.34
	(-1.04)	(-0.36)	(-1.91)			(2.51)		DW 2.67
	[0.306]	[0.720]	[0.069][a]			[0.020][b]		
Indonesia	5.492	0.166	-1.220	0.377	-0.977	1.071		R^2 0.04
	(0.34)	(0.40)	(-2.15)	(0.13)	(-0.36)	(0.47)		DW 1.96
	[0.733]	[0.687]	[0.444]	[0.894]	[0.719]	[0.642]		
Indonesia	0.417	0.399	-0.827			1.582	0.423	R^2 0.61
	(0.04)	(1.62)	(-2.31)			(1.12)	(5.21)	DW 2.34
	[0.964]	[0.119]	[0.031][b]			[0.274]	[0.000][c]	
Thailand	-2.261	0.825	-0.765	-0.022	0.263	2.056		R^2 0.46
	(-0.37)	(2.07)	(-3.61)	(-0.02)	(0.26)	(2.14)		DW 2.34
	[0.712]	[0.052][a]	[0.001][c]	[0.981]	[0.795]	[0.044][b]		
Thailand	-2.054	0.873	-0.786			2.116		R^2 0.51
	(-0.36)	(2.64)	(-4.17)			(2.45)		DW 2.35
	[0.715]	[0.015][b]	[0.000][c]			[0.023][b]		
Malaysia	-10.21	-0.418	-0.393	-0.526	1.400	2.975		R^2 0.23
	(-1.01)	(-0.78)	(-1.20)	(-0.34)	(0.98)	(1.94)		DW 2.47
	[0.321]	[0.444]	[0.241]	[0.731]	[0.337]	[0.066][a]		
Malaysia	-9.025	-0.355	-0.464			3.053		R^2 0.27
	(-0.95)	(-0.73)	(-1.52)			(2.11)		DW 2.45
	[0.348]	[0.471]	[0.142]			[0.046][b]		
Philippines	-26.83	-0.071	-0.297	-0.532	1.208	4.238		R^2 0.28
	(-2.51)	(-0.29)	(-1.04)	(-0.37)	(0.79)	(2.76)		DW 2.18
	[0.020][b]	[0.774]	[0.308]	[0.711]	[0.437]	[0.012][b]		
Philippines	-27.43	-0.007	-0.335			4.499		R^2 0.33
	(-2.70)	(-0.03)	(-1.24)			(3.25)		DW 2.08
	[0.013][b]	[0.974]	[0.227]			[0.003][c]		

[a] Statistically significant at 10 percent.
[b] Statistically significant at 5 percent.
[c] Statistically significant at 1 percent.

Source: Author's calculations.

depreciation of the local currency); *RXyen* is the real yen/dollar exchange rate (increase means depreciation of the yen); *GrJapan* is Japan's real GDP growth rate; *GrUS* is the US real GDP growth rate; *ASEANX* is the nominal GDP weighted average growth rates of Indonesia, Malaysia, Philippines, and Thailand, but without the regression country; and *Doil* is the real oil price, defined by the oil price (Brent) increase less the CPI inflation rate of Indonesia.

Korea's exports are very sensitive to the real exchange rate of the won: a 1 percentage point decrease in this accelerates export growth by more than 2 percentage points. They also heavily depend on Japanese and ASEAN-4 growth rates: a 1 percentage point increase in the growth rate of Japan or ASEAN-4 results in a more than 4 percentage point increase in Korean exports. These effects are consistent with theoretical predictions.

The dampening effect of the yen's appreciation on Korean exports is not statistically significant. According to the estimated results, the US growth rate has an insignificant effect on Korean exports.

For *Taipei,China,* the coefficients of its real exchange rate and the Japanese growth rate have the expected signs, and they are statistically significant. Their magnitude, however, is not as large as for Korea. The real exchange rate appreciation of the New Taiwan dollar by 1 percentage point reduces its exports by 2 percentage points. Qualitatively, the result is consistent with theory. A strong effect of Japanese growth on Taipei,China is consistent with the view that the Japanese economy is important for it. US growth also has a large effect on its exports, but with a statistical significance level of 0.16 (not very significant). ASEAN-4 growth has little impact on its exports.

For both Korea and Taipei,China, Japanese growth is important. The roles of the US and ASEAN-4 countries on exports differ between Korea and Taipei,China, with Korea more dependent on ASEAN-4 countries and Taipei,China on the US.

Although *Hong Kong, China* has maintained a fixed nominal exchange rate pegged to the US dollar since the early 1980s, the significant inflation differential has meant that the Hong Kong dollar has appreciated in real terms in the 1990s. The currency board arrangement severely limits the scope of domestic monetary policy. The result shows that Hong Kong, China's exports are sensitive to its own real exchange rate and yen/dollar movements. Even under the currency board arrangement, if inflation accelerates too much, it would put its exports in a difficult position. Exports also decline if the yen depreciates against the US dollar.

For Singapore and the ASEAN-4 countries, neither Japanese nor US growth is significant.

Exports from *Singapore* are sensitive to both the yen/dollar exchange rate and the ASEAN-4 growth rate. Although the effects of the yen on Singapore's exports are barely significant in a statistical sense, the effects of ASEAN-4 growth are strong. The coefficient on GrA shows that a 1 percentage point increase in ASEAN-4 growth rates accelerates Singapore's exports by 2.5 percentage points. This is consistent with theoretical predictions. However, its own exchange rate movement is not significant for exports.

The yen's appreciation would hurt exports from both Hong Kong, China; and Singapore. Considering the fact that these economies reexport many PRC and ASEAN-4 goods, respectively, it shows the general importance of the yen in Asian exports. However, the magnitude in either case is not large.

For *Indonesia* the most important factor seems to be oil. A 1 percentage point increase in the oil price from the preceding year increases Indonesian export volume by more than 0.4 percentage points, and this is statistically very significant. The yen/dollar rate is also statistically significant. Yen depreciation is not good for Indonesian exports: a 1 percentage point depreciation of the yen reduces Indonesian exports by 0.8 percentage points.

Thailand shows the clearest and most statistically robust result in this group of countries. Exports increase when the baht depreciates, the yen appreciates, or the ASEAN-4 growth rate increases, all consistent with theoretical predictions: a 1 percentage point depreciation of the baht increases the export growth rate by 0.8 percentage points, while a 1 percentage point appreciation of the yen increases exports by the same amount. A 1 percentage point increase in the other ASEAN-4 countries accelerates Thai export growth by 1 percentage point. This magnitude is similar to Singapore's, but less than that of Malaysia or the Philippines.

For *Malaysia* and the *Philippines,* neither their own exchange rates nor the yen has a statistically significant effect on exports. ASEAN-4 growth is important: a 1 percentage point increase in the average ASEAN-4 growth rate (excluding the country's own) accelerates export growth by 3 percentage points in Malaysia and 4.5 percentage points in the Philippines. The ASEAN-4 growth effect on their exports is consistent with theory.

It is interesting to note that the real exchange rate of the yen against the US dollar affects exports from Hong Kong, China; Indonesia; Singapore; and Thailand. These economies have significant ties with Japan through trade and investment. Their products need Japanese components, and their exports compete with Japanese products in the Japanese and world markets. It is somewhat puzzling that exports from Korea and Taipei,China which may, a priori, be considered as more directly competing with Japanese exports than those from other countries, are found to be insensitive to the yen's movement, but are sensitive to their own exchange rate movement. For Korea and Taipei,China, the growth rate of Japan has a bigger effect than the exchange rate.

It is also puzzling that for half the sample countries, their own exchange rates are not statistically significant for exports. The coefficients of RERj are significant for Hong Kong, China; Korea; Taipei,China; and Thailand, but are insignificant for Indonesia, Malaysia, Philippines, and Singapore.

There is also a strong effect of ASEAN-4 growth rates on exports from each other. For Malaysia, Philippines, Singapore, and Thailand, ASEAN-4 growth rates, as defined by GrAj, have a strong positive effect on exports.

In short, the above analysis shows that exports from Hong Kong, China; Korea; Taipei,China; and Thailand were sensitive to their real exchange rates against the US dollar over the period 1971–1996. Thai exports were most influenced by the yen/dollar rate (RXyen). For Indonesia and Singapore, the yen was also relevant to a degree. The Japanese growth rate was relevant only for Korea and Taipei,China. In general, ASEAN-4 growth rates were relevant for most countries. This shows the strong linkage within the ASEAN-4 countries (and Singapore) and strongly suggests that a recession, caused by a slump in exports, in one country is likely to reduce imports from neighboring countries, thus resulting in a slump in that economy.

CONCLUSIONS

On the basis of our examination of various factors, the following observations regarding the post-1996 export slowdown may be made. First of all, toward the end of the 1980s, fast-growing Asian economies became industrial states competing with other older industrial countries. Some of these countries started to specialize in particular industries (e.g., Malaysia in electronics) and continued to industrialize. Machinery and parts were imported from Japan and other advanced countries, and assembled into manufactured products for export to the US and Japan. This increased the sensitivity of the Asian economies' real exchange rates to movement against the dollar and the yen. This is established by the regression exercise attempted in this chapter.

In 1996, there were two principal shocks in the region. The yen depreciated by as much as 50 percent against the US dollar from the year before. This made non-Japanese Asian exports less competitive in the Japanese and US markets. Second, the worldwide computer-related recession hit the electronics and computer industries, especially semiconductor industries in Korea and Malaysia, and integrated circuit and computer industries in Thailand. These shocks were amplified, through the multiplier mechanism, because of the close trade relationships among the Asian countries.

Korea suffered export price declines, suggesting difficulties in exporting high value-added products. Iron and steel exports fell sharply, probably losing out to Japanese competitors. Thailand's textile exports also decreased, and likely gave ground to competitors in the PRC.

The deceleration that started in 1996 is likely to have been cyclical in nature, as the two principal shocks are expected to be reversed eventually, if not shortly. There was a sign of recovery in many sectors in some countries toward the middle of 1997. However, the Asian currency crisis that started with the baht's depreciation on 2 July 1997 changed the economic structure and competitiveness of the regional economy completely. In 1998, some economies are experiencing recessions. Despite countries' large currency depreciations, exports are not increasing because of problems in trade financing and a general disorder in their economies. And though some have fared better than others, all Asian countries are having difficulties. Meanwhile, the scenario of export recovery has become much more complicated with the variable rates of exchange among the NIEs and ASEAN-4 countries.

Although the problems in the coming months and years are beyond the scope of this chapter, it is hoped that the above analysis has at least given some insight into the reasons for the export deceleration that, to some extent, triggered the currency crisis in the region.

BIBLIOGRAPHY AND REFERENCES

Bank of Korea Website. 1998. *http://www.bok.or.kr.*

Bank Negara Malaysia. Various issues. *Monthly Statistical Bulletin.*

Bosworth, Barry and Susan M. Collins. 1996. "Economic Growth in East Asia: Accumulation versus Assimilation." *Brookings Papers on Economic Activity* 2:135-203.

Central Bank of China. Various issues. *Financial Statistics, Taiwan District, The Republic of China.* Taipei,China.

Council for Economic Planning and Development (CEPD). Various years. *Taiwan Statistical Data Book.* Taipei,China.

Denison and Chung. 1976. "Economic Growth and Its Sources." In H. Patrick and H. Rosovsky, eds., *Asia's New Giant.* Washington, DC: Brookings Institution.

Diehl, Markus and Rainer Schweickert. 1998. "Currency Crises: Is Asia Different?" *Kieler Diskussionsbeitrage.* No. 309, January.

Frankel, Jeffrey A., and Shang-Jin Wei. 1994. "Yen Bloc or Dollar Bloc? Exchange Rate Policies of the East Asian Economies." In T. Ito and A. O. Krueger, eds., *Macroeconomic Linkage: Savings, Exchange Rates, and Capital Flows.* Chicago: University of Chicago Press.

International Monetary Fund (IMF). 1995. *International Capital Markets 1995.* Washington, DC.

______. 1997a. *World Economic Outlook.* May. Washington, DC.

______.1997b. *Direction of Trade Statistics Yearbook 1997.* Washington, DC.

______.Various issues. *International Financial Statistics* CD-ROM. Washington, DC.

Ito, Takatoshi. 1996. "Japan and the Asian Economies: A 'Miracle' in Transition." *Brookings Papers on Economic Activity* 2: 205-260.

______. 1997. "What Can Developing Countries Learn from East Asia's Economic Growth?" Annual World Bank Conference on Development Economics 1997.

______. 1998. "Bail-out, Moral Hazard, and Credibility: IMF and World Bank Policies in Crises of the 21st Century-Type." Wharton Conference on Asian Twin Financial Crises, Tokyo, 10 March.

Ito, Takatoshi, Peter Isard, Steven Symansky, and Tamim Bayoumi. 1996. *Exchange Rate Movements and Their Impact on Trade and Investment in the APEC Region.* Occasional Paper No. 145. Washington, DC: International Monetary Fund.

Ito, Takatoshi, Eiji Ogawa, and Yuri N. Sasaki. Forthcoming. "How Did the Dollar Peg Fail in Asia?" *Journal of the Japanese and International Economies.* Vol. 12.

Khan, S. Mohsin and Carmen M. Reinhart. 1995. *Capital Flows in the APEC Region.* Occasional Paper No. 122. Washington, DC: International Monetary Fund.

Kim, Jong-Il and Lawrence J. Lau. 1994. "The Sources of Economic Growth of the East Asian Newly Industrialized Countries." *Journal of the Japanese and International Economies* 8: 235-271.

Krugman, Paul. 1994. "The Myth of Asia's Miracle." *Foreign Affairs:* 62-78 (November/December).

Ministry of Finance, Subcommittee on Asian Financial and Capital Markets, Committee on Foreign Exchange and Other Transactions, 1998. "Lessons from the Asian Currency Crises: Risks Related to Short-term Capital Movement and the '21st Century-Type' Currency Crisis." Japan.

Montes, Manuel, F. 1998. *The Currency Crisis in Southeast Asia.* Institute of Southeast Asian Studies.

Radelet, Steven and Jeffrey Sachs. 1998. "The East Asian Financial Crisis: Diagnosis, Remedies, Prospects." Brookings Panel. March.

Sarel, Michael. 1995. "Growth in East Asia: What We Can and What We Cannot Infer From It." Working Paper No. 98. Washington, DC: International Monetary Fund. September.

______. 1996. "Growth and Productivity in ASEAN Economies." Paper presented at the Conference on Macroeconomic Issues Facing ASEAN Countries. Jakarta, Indonesia, 6-8 November.

Young, Alwyn. 1992. "A Tale of Two Cities: Factor Accumulation and Technical Change in Hong Kong and Singapore." *NBER Macroeconomic Annual 1992*:13-54. Cambridge, Mass.: MIT Press.

———. 1994. "Lessons from the East Asian NICS: A Contrarian View," *European Economic Review* 38:964-973.

———. 1995. "The Tyranny of Numbers: Confronting the Statistical Realities of the East Asian Growth Experience." *Quarterly Journal of Economics:* August: 641-680.

World Bank. 1993. *The East Asian Miracle: Economic Growth and Public Policy.* Oxford: Oxford University Press for the World Bank.

Chapter Four

Multilateralism, Minilateralism, and Trade Expansion

David Greenaway

INTRODUCTION

Economic integration between states takes place when cross-border transactions in goods or services occur. These can be state-to-state but are overwhelmingly transactions between individuals and corporate bodies located in different states. The post-World War II period has seen a remarkable increase in integration that has affected all parts of the globe, including Asia. The exchanges that result in integration of economies are triggered by economic stimuli similar to those that trigger exchanges within economies, namely, declines in transactions costs. These are associated both with natural and man-made barriers. In the former, there has been a precipitous decline in the costs of transport and communications, which has been an enormous stimulus to international commerce. Declines in the latter have been no less dramatic, as governments have reduced or removed impediments to cross-border commerce. This has taken place unilaterally (i.e., unreciprocated actions by a single trading nation), multilaterally (i.e., reciprocated reductions in trade barriers that extend to all trading partners), and minilaterally (i.e., reciprocated reductions in trading barriers that extend to some subset of trading partners). All three forms of liberalization have been seen in the postwar period.

In this paper we concentrate on regional and multilateral integration in particular.[1] Both have considerably advanced over the

---

1 Surveys and assessments of recent unilateral liberalization can be found in Krueger (1997) and Greenaway et al. (forthcoming).

last decade. Developments in both have been extensively documented and analyzed. Our task in this chapter is fourfold. First, to assess recent developments in both multilateral and regional integration. Second, to evaluate the relationship between the two. In the terminology first used by Bhagwati (1991): Are regional integration arrangements a stepping stone or stumbling block to multilateral free trade? Third, to assess the economic impact of regional and multilateral trade liberalization with particular reference to growth. Finally, to consider the prospects for further regional integration in Asia.

MULTILATERALISM: THE URUGUAY ROUND AND WTO

Prior to focusing on minilateralism, we will set the context by reviewing briefly the process of multilateralism and its achievements. First, we focus on postwar multilateralism and trade liberalization. Second, we review the outcomes of the Uruguay Round, with particular reference to Asia's exports. Third, we comment on the prospects for multilateralism.

GATT and Multilateral Trade Negotiations

The General Agreement on Tariffs and Trade (GATT) has its origins in the Anglo-American vision for postwar reconstruction, which rested on three multilateral institutions: the International Monetary Fund (IMF), the World Bank Group, and what was meant to be the International Trade Organization (ITO) but which became the enabling treaty for that organization, i.e., GATT.

The overriding objective of GATT was to provide a framework for the orderly conduct of trade, as well as a process within which trade liberalization could take place. To this end, the key principles are nondiscrimination, reciprocity, and transparency. The first is important because it discourages the swapping of favors between trading partners and thereby encourages contracting parties to the negotiating table—countries negotiate in the knowledge that the agreements reached apply to all parties. The principle of reciprocity states that if one contracting party makes a trade concession to another (e.g., by cutting a tariff), the party that benefits is obliged to reciprocate with an equivalent concession. As we know from basic trade theory, in the absence of distortions, reciprocity is not necessary for a tariff-cutting country to benefit. However, it is important to the trade liberalization process. It encourages negotiators who are instinctively mercantilist to believe that "fairness" is being achieved by both parties making concessions; it also encourages them to claim that there are double benefits from any agreement—lower prices of imports for consumers and better market access for exporters. Transparency dictates that when intervention is necessary it should be via visible, rather than opaque, instruments.

The mechanism instituted by GATT to promote trade liberalization was the "rounds" system. Rather than negotiating continually, contracting parties came together as a group from time to time and agreed on a package of measures that was then implemented: eight rounds of multilateral trade negotiations (MTNs) have so far been completed. Several points should be noted. First, the number of countries involved has expanded dramatically, especially over the last two rounds. This is a reflection of the success of GATT and the multilateral liberalization process that has become more encompassing as time passed. Second, the value of trade involved has grown dramatically in real terms. This is clearly fashioned by more and more countries being involved. In addition, however, it is also fashioned by more and more trade impediments being addressed. This brings us to a third point: with the passing of time, it takes longer to secure agreements. Clearly this, too, must be fashioned by the increased number of contracting parties, but a more important factor is the growing complexity associated with multilayered negotiations relating to multiple instruments of intervention and growing sector coverage. Put simply, the early GATT rounds were essentially about tariff liberalization in manufactures and nothing else. Recent rounds, and in particular the Uruguay Round, have involved negotiations on tariffs, nontariff barriers (such as voluntary export restraints—VERs), contingent protection, new issues (such as intellectual property protection), and new sectors (such as agriculture and services). As a result, negotiations have become more protracted and complicated. As we shall see later, this is a possible contributory factor in explaining the upsurge of interest in the 1990s in regional trading arrangements (RTAs).

Uruguay Round Outcomes

The details of the negotiations, the evolution of bids and offers, and the convergence to an agreement in the Uruguay Round need not concern us here—reviews at various stages can be found in Greenaway (1993); Hoekman (1993); and Rayner et al. (1993). The final outcomes are of greater interest, details of which follow.

Market Access. There are essentially three ingredients to the tariff agreements: a zero-for-zero component that will result in tariff-free trade in some 11 sectors;[2] a liberalization component reflected in the fact that mean tariffs on industrial goods will decline by some 38 percent; and a harmonization component that results in higher tariffs being subject to deeper cuts. As a result, the trade-weighted average tariff in industrial countries will decline from 6.4 percent to 4 percent and some 40 percent of imports will enter duty free within seven years. Another crucial outcome is that the proportion of tariffs that are bound in industrial countries will increase from 78 percent to 97 percent; the proportion in developing countries will increase from 21 percent to 65 percent.

As tariffs have declined over the postwar period, so reliance on nontariff barriers has increased, most notably since the mid-1970s. Their discriminatory application and their opacity have been eroding GATT foundations. Although there was a separate nontariff barrier negotiating group, the issue crossed over with agriculture, safeguards, and antidumping negotiations. The outcome involved important commitments, including the prohibition of VERs, orderly marketing agreements, and other extralegal instruments.

Sectors. Agriculture was the single most contentious issue in the Uruguay Round. The market access agreement requires the tariffication of existing nontariff barriers, the binding of the resultant tariffs, and their reduction by 36 percent over 6 years in developed market economies (DMEs) and over 10 years in less developed countries (LDCs), with the least developed being exempted. Domestic support measures are to be reduced by 20 percent in DMEs and 13.3 percent in LDCs, with an exemption for interventions that are

---

2 These are pharmaceuticals, construction equipment, medical equipment, steel, beer, furniture, farm equipment, spirits, wood, paper, and toys.

decoupled from production, or that have a minimal impact on trade. Export subsidies are to be reduced by 36 percent in value terms and 21 percent in volume terms (on 1986–1990 bases) in DMEs. Lower reductions of 24 percent and 14 percent are required of LDCs, with no further concessions from the least developed countries. Although these reforms are to be phased in over a 6- to 10-year period, they represent a potentially very significant liberalization in a previously completely sheltered sector.

Trade in textiles and clothing has been subject to a legal derogation from nondiscrimination requirements for over 30 years. The web of quotas that makes up the Multifiber Arrangement (MFA) imposes significant costs on "Northern" consumers and "Southern" producers (see Silberston 1989; Trela and Whalley 1990). The Uruguay Round agreement commits contracting parties to a phased running-down of the MFA over 1995–2005 and the complete integration of textiles and clothing into the GATT system by 2005.

GATT System. This was the least glamorous area of the negotiations, yet the agreements reached are among the most important. On safeguards, several commitments were made to strengthen GATT Article XIX and encourage its use (in preference to extralegal interventions). First there is an outright prohibition of "gray area" measures, a vitally important outcome given the proclivity of DMEs toward instruments like VERs. Second, the criteria for recourse to Article XIX have been tightened, with tougher injury tests and a scheduled commitment to phasing out. Third, explicit arrangements for the termination of existing measures have been agreed. Fourth, discriminatory action is to be permitted under certain tightly defined circumstances. The last is a fundamental departure from the principle of nondiscrimination and one about which many LDCs are uneasy.

Subsidies and countervailing duties have been contentious for some time, in part because the Tokyo Round code on the former has not worked effectively and in part because the latter, like antidumping, has become a form of contingent protection. For the first time, the Uruguay Round agreement defines subsidies and identifies three categories: prohibited, actionable, and nonprohibited.[3] This "traffic

---

[3] The first are specific export subsidies tied to export promotion and import substitution; the second are those that could cause injury to another contracting party; the third are specific or nonspecific subsidies that are unlikely to have important trade effects or that involve assistance to research and development, disadvantaged regions, environmental protection, etc.

light" approach should prove more effective than the Tokyo Round code. Moreover, it will be complemented by strengthened disciplines on the use and termination of countervailing duties.

A whole series of GATT Articles were reviewed and in some cases amended. Potentially the most important development is the strengthening of antidumping provisions in Article VI. There is a growing body of evidence (e.g., Finger and Murray 1990; Messerlin 1989, 1990) to indicate that the US and European Union (EU) are using antidumping procedures as an instrument of protection, rather than a fair trade measure, and are using them in a discriminatory fashion against Japan and NIEs. The Uruguay Round agreement strengthens the procedures for calculating the dumping margin, as well as strengthening the injury test. Since many Asian NIEs and LDCs have been subject to antidumping action, more effective policing arrangements should be helpful.

The functioning of the GATT system group was also "unglamorous" yet delivered two major constitutional changes: the Trade Policy Review Mechanism (TPRM) and the World Trade Organization (WTO). The TPRM gives GATT an explicit audit function. All contracting parties will have their trade policies reviewed on a regular basis, from every two years for the large contracting parties (EU, Japan, and US), to every seven years for the smallest. This will help make more transparent the interventions of all contracting parties and will be an important source of pressure for reform.

WTO is the first serious systemic reform since GATT's inception. At its heart is a Ministerial Conference that will meet at least biannually. It will embrace GATT, the General Agreement on Trade in Services (GATS), the new bodies like the Safeguards Committee and the Textile Surveillance Body and all the Uruguay Round agreements. WTO will only be open to those GATT contracting parties that sign the Uruguay Round agreement. As with GATT, it will seek to adopt resolutions by consensus, but will be able to take a wide range of decisions on the basis of qualified majority. Unlike some other regimes (e.g., the EU or IMF) voting rights are not weighted; the system is one vote per contracting party. From a developing country standpoint this is important. Although WTO will have enhanced powers over GATT these do not include sanctions; enforcement will be effected by authorization of most favored nation (MFN) status withdrawal.

New Issues. For a time it looked as though the negotiations on trade-related investment measures (TRIMs) might resolve themselves with a traffic light approach. In fact, the key feature is essentially an affirmation of the applicability of existing disciplines, notably Articles III and XI. Those TRIMs that are inconsistent with these are prohibited. Preexisting measures have to be phased out within two years (DMEs), five years (LDCs), or seven years (least developed countries). There is also a commitment to evaluate the role of TRIMs in the wider context of competition policy. This is important given the symbiosis between TRIMs and other forms of anticompetitive interventions such as restrictive business practices (see Morrissey and Rai 1995).

The agreement on trade-related intellectual property (TRIP) is complicated. The general provisions and basic principles include national and MFN treatment. In addition, specific provisions relate to copyrights, trademarks, geographic indications, industrial designs, patents, layout designs of integrated circuits, and trade secrets. The obligations on the part of governments to ensure enforcement are set out in each case. The transition period for DMEs is short (one year), the assumption being that most have preexisting regimes. The transition is somewhat longer for LDCs (five years) and longest for least developed countries (11 years).

Services were controversial from the launch of the Uruguay Round. Given the diversity of philosophies and of regulatory regimes, it was also a complicated area. GATS is more limited in scope than seemed possible but takes an important first step in bringing disciplines to the area. It specifies a range of basic obligations that include national treatment and MFN commitments. A schedule is established for progressive liberalization and the specific institutional provisions required to accomplish this. For a number of sectors, such as financial services, telecommunications, and air transport services, detailed schedules were provided.

Uruguay Round and Asia's Growth

Asian countries played a major role in the Uruguay Round negotiations both unilaterally through one of the three main negotiating blocs (Japan) and through a number of coalition groupings on different issues (see Whalley 1991). The Asian region had an obvious interest in a successful conclusion. As a region of the world economy with relatively high trade ratios, it has the potential to gain from multilateral liberalization, as do other regions with high trade ratios. Arguably, however, the Asian region has the potential to be among the biggest winners in the Round, for several reasons. First, the market access agreements cover nontariff barriers as well as tariffs. There is an extensive literature which demonstrates that the pattern of nontariff barriers, as well as contingent protection measures, is nonrandom.[4] Specifically, developing Asia, together with Japan, tends to be subject to source-specific restraints to a greater degree than any other group of countries, and therefore has the potential for greatest gain from liberalization. Second, a formula for reform of the MFA was agreed. The MFA is a complicated and costly array of source-specific restraints that discriminates against growth of exports from Asia more than any other region globally. Third, some countries in Asia are well placed to benefit from agricultural liberalization. Finally, some are also well placed to benefit from services liberalization.

Clearly it is far too early to undertake an ex post analysis of the Uruguay Round agreements: that will not be possible for some time. It is, however, possible to undertake ex ante analyses using computable general equilibrium (CGE) technologies. This is an approach to economic modeling that is being increasingly used. It involves constructing a computational model of an economy and then working through the effects of policy shocks on it. In fact, quite a few CGE analyses of the Uruguay Round's outcomes have already been undertaken. Notwithstanding the well-known problems associated with the CGE methodology (mainly involving the need to assume fairly simple structures and to work at fairly high levels of data aggregation), it remains a useful tool for generating an idea of possible orders of magnitude and their sensitivity to alternative assumptions.

Table 4.1 reports results from eight CGE analyses of the Round's outcomes. These models vary in structure, dimensionality, and detail. They also vary in terms of their ingredients. Some focus only on "measurable" market access like changes in tariffs, while others factor in changes in nontariff barriers and services arrangements. All of them include an estimate of the net welfare gains to the world economy

[4] See, for example, Greenaway and Milner (1993).

Table 4.1 Impact of the Uruguay Round on Asia

Study		Welfare Effects (percent of GDP)	
		Asia	World
Brown et al. (1992)	Asian NIEs	2.0	0.7[a]
	Japan	0.8	0.6[b]
Goldin et al. (1993)	Lower-income Asia	0.2	0.1[a]
	Upper-income Asia	1.3	0.6[c]
	Japan	0.4	
Hertel et al. (1995)	PRC	1.5	0.4
	Indonesia	2.9	
	Malaysia	2.4	
	Philippines	6.6	
	Thailand	4.5	
	Japan	1.0	
Francois et al. (1994)	PRC	4.0	0.4
	East Asia	3.2	
	South Asia	3.1	
	Japan	0.4	
Harrison et al. (1994)	PRC	0.5	0.2
	East Asia	0.1	
	South Asia	1.1	
	Japan	0.2	
Brandao and Martin (1993)	Lower-income Asia	0.2	0.2[a]
	Upper-income Asia	1.1	0.6[c]
	PRC	0.1	
	India	0.4	
	Japan	0.6	
Nguyen et al. (1993)	Japan	2.0	1.1
OECD (1995)	Japan	1.8	0.9

[a] US only.
[b] Europe only.
[c] EU only.

and its subregions, expressed as a percentage of GDP. As we can see, the estimated global gain in welfare ranges from 0.2 percent to 1.1 percent of world GDP. What is interesting, however, is that practically all of these models estimate the Asian gains as being in excess of the global average. Comparisons are complicated by the fact that the regional/country breakdown differs from one study to another. Nonetheless, the PRC almost always turns out to gain more than the world average as does developing Asia, an outcome derived primarily by relatively high initial levels of protection. Even Japan,

Table 4.2 CGE Models of the Uruguay Round: Model Structures and Policy Experiments

Study	Policy Experiment	Model Structure
Brown et al. (1992)	*Industrial Tariffs* • Cut according to schedules *Agriculture* • Tariffs included NTB-equivalents cut according to the difference between estimated base rate and final offer rate. *Services* • NTB tariff-equivalents cut by 25 percent	• Agriculture: constant returns to scale, perfect competition products differentiated by country of origin • Manufactures and Services: Increasing returns to scale, monopolistic competition. Services are treated as tradables • The variety effect on utility and scale economies is dampened by 50 percent compared with the original Dixit-Stiglit specification. • Labor mobile between sectors, while capital specified as sector-specific • 29 Sectors (1 Agric., 1 Proc. food, 1 Primary, 20 Manuf., 6 Services), 9 Regions
Goldin et al. (1993)	*Industrial Tariffs* • Cut according to schedules *Agriculture* • Tariffs included NTB-equivalent cut according to schedules. • Input subsidies cut 36 percent for OECD and 24 percent for other countries.	• Two types of households: Urban manufacturing and rural farming • Constant returns to scale, perfect competition • Manufactured products differentiated by origin • Agricultural products treated as perfect substitutes • 20 Sectors (15 Agric., 1 Fertilizers, 1 Energy, 1 Equipment, 1 Services, 1 Other Manuf.) • 22 Regions • Recursive dynamic structure
Hertel et al. (1995)	*Industrial Tariffs* • Cut according to schedules *Agriculture* • According to the Agreement on Agriculture, *Textiles and Clothing* • MFA quotas lifted	• Constant returns to scale, perfect competition, products differentiated by origin • 10 Sectors (1 Agric., 1 Proc. Food, 1 Primary, 5 Manuf., 2 Services), 15 Regions • Exogenous projections of each region's growth of physical capital, human capital, state of technology, population, labor force, and arable land; world economy projected with and without the Uruguay Round policy changes from 1992 to 2005
Francois et al. (1994)	*Industrial Tariffs* • Cut according to schedules *Industrial QRs* • Safeguard QRs phased out	• Constant returns to scale, perfect competition, products differentiated by origin • Increasing returns to scale, monopolistic competition • 19 Sectors (3 Agric., 3 Primary, 12 Manufactures, 1 Services), 13 Regions

	Agriculture • Export subsidies cut 36 percent (24 percent) • Minimum market access commitments *Textiles and Clothing* • MFA quotas lifted	• Fixed savings rate (F) • Endogenous savings rate (E)
Harrison et al. (1994)	*Industrial Tariffs* • Cut according to schedules *Industrial QRs* • VERs (unclear which) eliminated *Agriculture* • Tariffs included NTB-equivalents cut according to schedules • Domestic support cut 20 percent (13 percent) • MFA quotas lifted	• Constant returns to scale, perfect competition, products differentiated by origin • Hybrid Armington-Monopolistic Competition (AMC) model • Regional increasing returns to scale • 22 Sectors (5 Agric., 3 Proc. food, 3 Primary, 9 Manuf., 2 Services), 24 Regions • Endogenous savings rate
OECD (1995)	*Industrial Tariffs and NTBs* • 36 percent across-the-board tariff cut *Agriculture* • Tariffs included NTB-equivalents cut 36 percent • Export subsidies cut 36 percent • Domestic support cut 20 percent	• Constant returns to scale, perfect competition • 4 Sectors (Manufacturing, Agricultural, Other traded goods, Nontraded goods) • 7 Regions (6 OECD regions/countries and rest of world)
Nguyen et al. (1993)	*Industrial Tariffs* • 30-50 percent cut depending on product category and region *Industrial NTBs* • Tariff equivalent of NTBs cut 40 percent • MFA phased out *Agriculture* • Broader measures cut 40 percent (20 percent) • Domestic support cut 20 percent *Services* • Tariff equivalent of NTBs cut 40 percent	• Constant returns to scale, perfect competition • 9 Sectors (1 Agric., 2 Prim., 5 Manuf., 1 Services) • 10 Regions
Brandao and Martin (1993)	*Agriculture* • Tariffs included NTB-equivalents cut 36 percent (24 percent) • Export subsidies cut 36 percent (24 percent) • Domestic support cut 20 percent (13.3 percent)	The RUNS model: (See above under Goldin et al. 1993.)

Note: Where two figures for tariff or nontariff barrier (NTB) reductions are quoted, that in parentheses applies to developing countries.

which is a potential loser from agricultural liberalization, tends to show welfare gains in excess of the world average.

These are summary statistics. What is important, however, is not the accuracy of a particular estimate but the relative orders of magnitude. The key point is the consistency across almost all of these (very different) studies to the effect that Asia gains from the Uruguay Round, and that it gains more than the world average. One can see from this why Asian countries were such strong advocates of a successful Uruguay Round and the interest they are likely to have in continued multilateral liberalization.

Prospects for Multilateralism

It is easy to criticize the Uruguay Round's process and focus on GATT's shortcomings. Rounds have become slow and cumbersome; sectors such as agriculture, textiles, and clothing have been sheltered from the liberalization process; nontariff barriers have proliferated as tariffs have declined; and contingent protection measures (in particular antidumping) have become more widespread. It is proper that deficiencies and shortcomings are highlighted. However, it is just as important to draw attention to the system's accomplishments. These number at least five.

First, average nominal tariffs have declined dramatically in industrial countries from an average of over 40 percent in the early post-World War II years to around 4 percent today. This is entirely an outcome of the MTNs. It is true that tariff peaks remain, especially in sensitive areas such as footwear, textiles, clothing, and agriculture. Moreover, it is also the case that nominal tariffs typically understate effective tariffs.[5] Nevertheless, the fact is that average nominal tariffs are in low single digits for the industrial countries. Second, average tariffs have fallen sharply in the NIEs and other developing countries. These declines are not as dramatic as in the industrial countries, neither are they solely attributable to the MTNs; there has been a

5 Nominal tariffs refer to the published/scheduled tariff rate. Effective tariffs calculate the protection accruing to value-added in a particular production process. Effective tariffs therefore take into account any nominal tariffs on imports of the final good concerned and any tariffs on imported inputs used in producing the import substitute. Tariffs on final goods are a subsidy to value-added whereas tariffs on inputs are a tax.

wave of unilateral liberalization since 1980 in developing countries. The MTNs have, however, helped. Third, the sector and instrument coverage of GATT has been extended quite dramatically in recent rounds. The early rounds focused only on tariff liberalization. Since the Kennedy Round, nontariff barriers, contingent protection, regulation, and other nonborder measures have figured prominently. It is easy to see how this complicates the process of negotiation but the fact is that important sectors that were sheltered are now encompassed, while important instruments that were not clearly within GATT's jurisdiction have been brought under it. Fourth, the institutional infrastructure underpinning the world trading system has been reinforced through improved auditing (TPRM), dispute settlement, and a range of strengthened disciplines. The TPRM is especially useful in bringing greater transparency to the trade policies of members. Finally, the number of members of WTO has continued to grow.[6] Newly independent states in Central and Eastern Europe and the former Soviet Union have fairly quickly acceded to GATT/WTO in the same way that newly independent developing countries did in the 1960s and 1970s.

The potential tensions between multilateralism and regionalism will be evaluated in detail later (see the section on *Minilateralism* and *Multilateralism* of this chapter). In the meantime we should note first that GATT has been the key institution for the promotion of international integration over the postwar period. We should also note that the prospects for WTO and its future promotion of multilateralism are far from bleak. Given the extension of WTO's jurisdiction and its broadened country coverage, it is well placed to continue the process. Moreover, there remains a substantial unfinished agenda from the Uruguay Round. These include environmental regulation, competition policy, investment measures, labor standards, and RTAs.

[6] Under GATT, participating countries were referred to as contracting parties; under WTO they are referred to as members.

MINILATERALISM: RTAs AND TRADE EXPANSION

Global Developments in Minilateralism

RTAs have been a feature of the global economy for centuries and should not be thought of only as a post-World War II phenomenon. There has, however, been a remarkable proliferation in RTAs since 1945: more than 100 agreements have been ratified. Despite the existence of GATT during this time, which has as one of its key pillars a commitment to nondiscrimination, in a strictly legal sense there is no inconsistency between GATT and RTAs. Article XXIV in effect offers a waiver to Article I and allows RTAs under certain conditions, and was included largely for political reasons, because, given preexisting RTAs, some major GATT signatories would not have signed up without it.

The key conditions of Article XXIV are that members eliminate restraints on "substantially all trade" between them and have a trade policy toward nonmembers which ensures that restraints are not "on the whole" more restrictive than those which prevailed prior to the RTA. In addition, Article V of GATS offers trade in services an equivalent waiver to Article XXIV of GATT.

The RTAs that have been signed since 1945 fall into two waves: the first in the 1970s and the second in the 1990s. The 1990s wave is often referred to as "the new regionalism." First, while the "old regionalism" of the 1950s and 1960s typically involved RTAs that were "North-North" or "South-South," the new regionalism has been typified by many "North-South" arrangements like the North American Free Trade Agreement (NAFTA) and the Asia-Pacific Economic Cooperation (APEC) forum. This offers obvious potential in terms of trade gains. However, it also creates the potential for adjustment problems and trade tensions. Second, whereas with the old regionalism, RTAs typically involved contiguous countries or near neighbors, many recent arrangements have been intercontinental. Third, many recent arrangements are not inclusive, and multiple membership is not problematic. Finally, whereas all arrangements under the old regionalism promoted shallow integration, e.g., liberalization of border measures, many recent agreements have aspired to deep integration with commitments to harmonization of regulatory measures, and freeing up of factor movements, etc. Since around one third of all postwar RTAs have been signed since 1990, the first issue to address is, what has triggered their dramatic growth?

Causal Factors behind the New Regionalism

There are many explanations for the resurgence in popularity of RTAs. A common view sees their proliferation as a reaction to frustrations with GATT in general and the Uruguay Round in particular. This sees RTAs as a reaction to concerns that the Uruguay Round would ultimately fail and some kind of insurance was required in the form of membership of an RTA. It is true that the timing of some recent RTAs is consistent with the prolongation of the Uruguay Round—but only for some. In fact, many postdate its successful conclusion.

A more sophisticated version of this explanation is associated with, among others, Krugman (1993) along the lines that RTAs are easier to negotiate and implement than multilateral agreements. He argues that this is partly a consequence of the number of negotiating parties involved. Multilateral agreements mean more parties, lower costs associated with noncooperation, and therefore more protracted negotiations. It is also a consequence of the fact that MTNs are no longer simply about tariffs but a much wider range of border and nonborder measures. The combination of a larger number of parties and a more complex array of issues is a recipe for protracted negotiation. By contrast, he argues that RTAs typically involve fewer negotiating parties endeavoring to reach agreement on a narrower range of issues.

Bhagwati (1993) advances a related argument in putting the new regionalism down to US interests in RTAs. He argues that US hegemony was vital not only to the sustenance of GATT but also to multilateralism more generally. As its dominance in the process waned and negotiations became more plurilateral, US policymakers were drawn to a more overt results-oriented approach to international trade policy. This manifested itself in two ways: first, "aggressive unilateralism," i.e., legislation that activated Super 301 and Special 301 instruments permitting the US Special Trade Representative to initiate unilateral action against, respectively, alleged unfair trading and alleged breaches of US intellectual property rights; and second, a greater regional focus on trade negotiations in which the putative benefits were superficially more transparent and more immediate, which resulted in the Canada-United States Trade Agreement (CUSTA) and NAFTA.

Baldwin (1997) contends that these explanations are not supported by facts. He points out that many RTAs go beyond simple tariff deals and confront liberalization and harmonization of nontariff measures which, by definition, are much more difficult to negotiate. He also argues that many of the key agreements in the new regionalism preceded, rather than followed, any apparent US conversion to the cause—the introduction of the Single European Market in 1992 and negotiations on CUSTA being good examples. As an alternative explanation, Baldwin puts forward his "domino theory" of regionalism. This builds on Viner's (1950) classic analysis and exploits the fact that any RTA results in some trade and investment diversion. This in turn generates pressures on excluded nations to be included. The greater the number of nations included, the greater the pressures on the nonparticipants. Thus, a single key agreement, if it is important enough, sets off a domino effect that stimulates expansion of that agreement and/or proliferation of others. In the context of the new regionalism, the Single European Market and NAFTA are key agreements.

A similar, though not identical, explanation is often cast in terms of defensive regionalism. This can be found, inter alia, in Whalley's (1991) analysis of regionalism in the western hemisphere and Greenaway's (1998) analysis of regionalism in Asia. Here it is not trade and investment diversion from growing blocs that is the threat, but the fear of market exclusion and the need to provide countervailing bargaining power. The "Fortress Europe" fears surrounding the Single Market discussions are a good example. Some of the threats perceived around this process were very real: for example, the first banking directive appeared to require "mirror-image reciprocity," which would have had a major exclusionary effect on US banks. This may well have stimulated further interest on the part of US policymakers in developing counterweights. The same can be said of APEC in the Asian and Pacific region.

There is therefore a range of complementary explanations for the rise of the new regionalism that include the following: frustrations with multilateral negotiations, the decline of US hegemony, reactions to trade and investment diversion, and a desire to avoid market exclusion. It is clear from the experience of the 1970s and 1990s that regionalism indeed generates its own dynamics. Thus one tends to observe just inflows to, and not outflows from, the stock of RTAs. Even ineffective RTAs find it easy to survive.

Minilateralism and Multilateralism

Is minilateralism in conflict with multilateralism? Put differently, are RTAs a stepping stone or stumbling bloc to free trade? This is a crucial question from an efficiency and political economy standpoint. If one believes, as theory suggests, that global free trade maximizes global welfare and RTAs are an impediment to global free trade, then there are clear welfare costs associated with the phenomenon. If this is indeed the case, then from a political economy standpoint one would wish to raise the costs of successfully forming RTAs relative to those for multilateral agreements.

One way of approaching the issue is to think of regional integration as a dynamic process. Following Bhagwati et al. (forthcoming) this can be approached through two analytical questions: If the time paths of MTNs and RTAs are completely independent, will a given RTA have expanding membership such that it will eventually equate to worldwide membership? If the MTN and RTA time paths, on the other hand, are embraced simultaneously, they will interact. This being so, will the policy undertakings in the RTA have a benign or malign impact on the progress along the MTN time path?

If one looks at Figure 4.1, an upward movement along an RTA path implies growing membership, while an upward movement along the MTN path means multilateral lowering of trade barriers. If the paths are independent, RTAs will neither accelerate nor decelerate progress to multilateral free trade and their goal should be thought of as aiming for U*. We can then think of the first question in terms of RTA paths I-IV. Thus, RTAs may improve welfare immediately. In either case, the time path could then be stagnant (as with time paths II and III), implying a fragmentation of the world economy through no further expansion of the initial preferential trading arrangement (PTA) or it can lead (as in time paths I and IV) to multilateral free trade for all at U* through continued expansion and coagulation of the RTAs. Under "process multilateralism," i.e., MTNs as a multilateral process of reducing trade barriers as distinct from multilateralism as the goal desired, the time path may fail to reach U* and instead fall

Figure 4.1 Alternative Time Paths under Multilateralism and RTAs

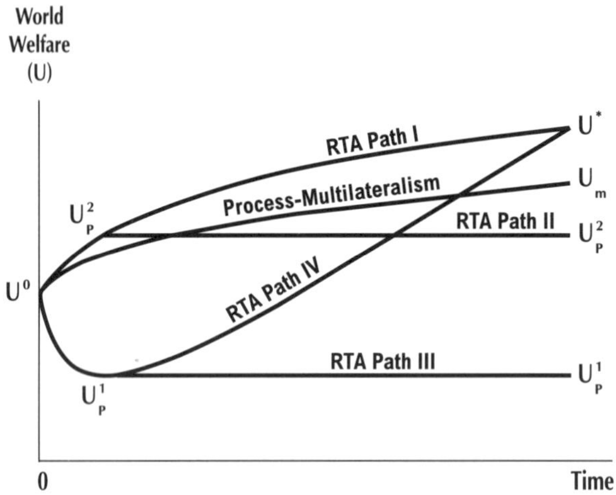

short at U_m because some countries "free ride." If the RTA and MTN time paths are interdependent, we can then address the second question: in that case the MTN time path becomes a function of whether the RTA path is traveled simultaneously. As we will see in the section *Regionalism in Asia* of this chapter, many hope that APEC's "open regionalism" will bring the RTA path into congruence with the MTN path.

Most analyses ignore the time path issue and treat expansion of membership as exogenous. However, some recent work has begun to address the question of incentives to add members. We have already mentioned Baldwin (1997). His model demonstrates that the incentive facing nonmembers will be positive. The RTA will create a domino effect, with outsiders wanting to become insiders. The argument is largely driven by the fact that the RTA implies a loss of cost-competitiveness by imperfectly competitive nonmember firms whose profits in the RTA markets decline because they face tariffs that inside firms do not have to pay. These firms then lobby for entry, tilting the political equilibrium toward entry demands in their countries. The countries closest to the present margin will then enter the bloc, assuming that the potential members have open entry, thus enlarging the market and thereby increasing the cost of nonmembership and pulling in countries at the next margin. This domino model therefore suggests that in principle the RTA time path can end at U*.

Some recent work also addresses the second question, i.e., whether the RTA possibility and/or time path helps or harms the MTN time path; examples are Krishna (1997) and Levy (1997), both of whom reach a conclusion of malign impact. Krishna models the political process via government acting in response to lobbying by firms as a "clearing house" and shows that the RTA reduces the incentive of member countries to liberalize tariffs reciprocally with nonmembers. With sufficient trade diversion, this incentive could be so reduced as to make impossible initially feasible multilateral trade liberalization. Levy, who models the political process instead as in a median-voter model, works with scale economies and product variety to demonstrate that bilateral RTAs can undermine political support for multilateral free trade. At the same time, a benign impact is impossible in this model: if a multilateral free trade proposal is not feasible under autarky, the same multilateral proposal cannot be rendered feasible under any bilateral RTA.

The literature is therefore limited. On balance it suggests that as a process RTAs are unlikely to be stepping stones to multilateral free trade; indeed there are some good reasons for believing that they could become stumbling blocks. The impact on growth and welfare is not independent of the dynamic time-path issue in relation to membership. This in turn is partly a function of the perceived benefits of membership; it is also a function, of course, of the perceived costs of nonmembership.

As an integration arrangement becomes deeper, the perceived benefits and costs of being in or out become greater. The Single European Market program is a good illustration of this. Its intention was to take integration beyond tariff liberalization, beyond even the elimination of nontariff barriers, and into the realms of harmonizing domestic policies. In the process, the notion of "Fortress Europe" became widespread. Its likelihood was certainly exaggerated. It had sufficient credibility, however, to generate a demand for entry and was instrumental in the accession of former European Free Trade Association (EFTA) countries under the most recent enlargement. The key point, however, is that RTAs do not treat nonmembers equally, and this, too, has consequences both for trade patterns and for the dynamics of trade relations and growth. Nonuniform treatment is most clearly evident where members are able to levy different tariffs against given nonmembers. This makes determination of origin important and gives rise to complicated and resource-consuming arrangements for rules of origin and content assessment.[7] However, even in customs unions the problem arises. Admittedly, it is less common to find differential access arrangements for given trading partners, though they are still present. It is though very common to find differential arrangements for different trading partners. Indeed, this is endemic and has given rise to what Bhagwati et al. (forthcoming) refer to as the "spaghetti bowl" phenomenon of numerous crisscrossing preferential arrangements and innumerable tariff rates. This is a systemic effect and can give rise to hidden protectionism. Ironically therefore, at the same time that something like the Single European Market program reduces transactions costs in trade among members, other forces raise transactions costs with nonmembers.

Clearly, the stepping stone or stumbling block issue is controversial. Equally clearly, much depends on the scope of membership and the degree and complexity of discrimination vis-à-vis nonmember countries. There is no doubt that RTAs can cut across multilateral liberalization efforts. Baldwin (1997) argues that, with one or two notable exceptions (like the EU's Common Agricultural Policy), there is not a large body of evidence to suggest that regional integration has in practice frustrated the process of multilateral liberalization. Foroutan (forthcoming) fails to find any relationship between RTAs and trade liberalization but notes that the latter typically precedes the former. This would fit in neatly with a recent explanation of RTAs by Ethier (1998) who argues that unilateral liberalization in developing countries is a necessary precondition for involvement in a "North-South" RTA. Thus it would seem that although MTNs have continued alongside the formation of RTAs, progress with the former might well have been further advanced without the proliferation of the latter.

TRADING BLOCS AND TRADE FLOWS

Clearly, the evaluation of integration is informed by theoretical analysis and, as we have seen, prevailing wisdom points to a number

[7] For a systematic review of rules of origin, see Falvey and Reed (1998).

of potential consequences of the formation of an RTA. This is helpful to both analysts and policymakers in thinking about possible integration arrangements. In addition, of course, it helps set a framework within which one might evaluate the impact of particular arrangements empirically, and, in fact, a substantial empirical literature has emerged. In general it addresses one of three questions: Has real integration occurred? Has integration affected trade flows? Has integration improved economic welfare? These questions have been addressed by reference to a number of RTAs. In this section we review the stock of evidence pertaining to these questions, almost all of which will be non-Asian. (The Asian evidence is reviewed in the following section, where we estimate a gravity model specifically targeted at searching for evidence of regional trade bias in Asia.)

Has Real Integration Occurred?

Answering this question is straightforward for an economist—look for evidence of price convergence. For, if real integration between two or more countries is taking place, this should manifest itself in a closer alignment of prices (and indeed wages).

One of the fundamental theorems of international trade theory is the Heckscher-Ohlin-Samuelson model. This provides an elegant proof of product price equalization and factor price equalization. The intuition is straightforward: countries specialize in and export those products that use their abundant (and therefore cheap) factor intensively and import those that use their scarce (and therefore expensive) factor intensively. As the export sector expands and the import sector contracts, the returns to the abundant factor increase while those to the scarce factor fall. This is an inevitable consequence of factor usage in the two sectors being different and is reflected in product price changes. Crudely, the domestic prices of imports fall with international competition, while those of exports rise. Since one country's exports are another country's imports, prices will eventually equalize across trading partners.

Thus, when looking for evidence of real integration, economists often begin by looking for a closer alignment of prices and wages. In practice, of course, this is a technically demanding task. Nevertheless, several studies have attempted to identify whether convergence of prices and/or wages has occurred, dating back to the work of Glejser

(1972) on the original EU six. Where price convergence is concerned, there is only limited evidence that integration has occurred, while the evidence on wage convergence is not much stronger. Several studies (e.g., Tovias 1982; van Mourik 1989) offer some evidence of limited convergence and it is not clear that it is greater than convergence with nonmembers.

Has Integration Affected Trade Flows?

Many studies have been directed at this question and a range of methodologies applied. Broadly speaking, they fall into three categories: *ex ante* elasticity models, *ex post* models, and CGE models. The first attempts to estimate trade changes using simple trade change models based on estimates of import elasticities. These have often been used to inform the debate about whether or not a country should join an RTA. They have the merit of simplicity, but a disadvantage is that the approach is partial equilibrium. CGE models are also *ex ante* but, as their name suggests, are general rather than partial equilibrium models. As a consequence, the information content of the output from such models is much greater and the capacity for modeling a range of scenarios is available. Although richer in structure than the simpler elasticity approach, the workings of these models are hidden. However, they have some utility and have been widely used in recent years.

As the name implies, *ex post* models attempt to disentangle the consequences of an integration agreement after the event. The oldest approach here is that of residual imputation whereby one estimates a model incorporating all known determinants of trade apart from integration, compares the model's estimated trade total with what the model predicts, and ascribes the difference to integration. The challenge, though, is in obtaining an accurate representation of what would have happened without integration. (An alternative to residual imputation is gravity modeling, discussed below.)

Surveys of the evidence on the trade enhancement effects of European integration can be found in Mayes (1978), Winters (1987), Greenaway et al. (1993), and Hine (1994). In reviewing the early work on the formation of the EU (European Economic Community, or EEC, at the time) Mayes (1978) concluded that it boosted trade by

15–30 percent. The CGE models that have been applied to recent enlargements and to the Single European Market also point unambiguously to trade expansion following integration, e.g., Cecchini et al. (1988) and Smith and Venables (1992).

The trade effects of both CUSTA and NAFTA have been simulated via CGE work. Cox and Harris (1984) were among the first on the former and predicted trade expansion. Subsequent work by Brown and Stern (1989) supported this conclusion. Analyses of NAFTA include Hummels and Stern (1994) and Brown et al. (1992). These and others point to trade expansion as a consequence of the formation of the RTA.

Finally, all the recent gravity models have produced evidence of an EU effect on trade (e.g., Panagariya et al. 1996). From the standpoint of pressing for further regional integration, this is encouraging. But two things must not be forgotten. First, the experiments in almost all these studies compare European integration with nonintegration, not with multilateral integration. Second, trade expansion can be associated with trade diversion as well as trade creation. What one should be interested in therefore is the balance between the two, and more broadly, the impact of integration on economic welfare.

Has Integration Improved Economic Welfare?

Early studies of the impact on welfare of the EU and its enlargement, such as Johnson (1958), Balassa (1975), and Waelbroeck (1976), attempted to assess welfare effects directly from trade effects. In other words, they worked out the balance between trade creation and trade diversion, and then calculated the effects on real income. This early work arrived at very small numbers, typically less than 1 percent of GDP as a one-off effect, which seems rather modest given the scale of the EU integration. The reason it is so modest is that in estimating welfare effects in this way, one is doing so very partially, thereby missing some very important effects, including the opportunities for scale economies that market expansion offers. For a great many manufactured products, the minimum efficient scale (MES) of production, i.e., the scale of operations necessary to fully exploit available economies, requires a level of output that exceeds the entire domestic markets of many EU member states.

Integration removes this constraint. It also has procompetition effects: domestic producers are exposed to greater competition that invariably results in costs and prices being driven down. Market deepening of the sort associated with the Single European Market also reduces transactions costs by eliminating or reducing nontrade policy impediments to commerce. Finally, as we saw earlier, integration can boost economic growth through various channels. All these effects were excluded from the early studies of welfare effects. They have been included in more recent work.

Owen (1983) concentrated on the scale economies effect. Based on detailed studies of the MES across the manufacturing industry, he put the total enhancement to GDP of the formation of EU at 3–6 percent of the combined GDP of the original six member states. Cecchini et al. (1988) estimated the gains from scale economies but also computed gains from procompetition effects and the abolition/harmonization of a range of nonborder measures. This study estimated a gain to GDP of the equivalent of 5 percent. In time this can be benchmarked against *ex post* estimates of the effects of the Single Market. It is certainly plausible given the reforms anticipated. Baldwin (1989) argues that it is, in fact, a significant underestimate of market completion on the grounds that the change in the GDP/capital ratio, which the Single Market will bring about, should result in a permanent increase in the EU's sustainable growth rate. In addition, he points to spillover effects across sectors that the Cecchini study ignores. Using a CGE framework, he estimates that the gains to EU will be 11–35 percent of GDP.

Again, there have also been analyses of the welfare effects of CUSTA and NAFTA, largely of a CGE nature. Where CUSTA is concerned, outcomes typically point to positive welfare gains, with Canada gaining more than the US. The orders of magnitude are generally quite small, well below 1 percent of GDP.[8] The major exception is Cox and Harris (1984) who suggest gains to Canada of some 9 percent of GDP, estimates which are driven partly by the exploitation of scale economies by Canadian firms and partly by procompetition effects. The general pattern of results for NAFTA is similar—gains for all parties—with the greatest gains accruing to Mexico but, with the exception of Mexico, the orders of magnitude are modest (see, e.g., Brown et al. 1992).

---

[8] See Markusen and Wigle (1990), Hamilton and Whalley (1985), and Brown and Stern (1989).

In recent years there has been a proliferation of growth modeling exercises partly stimulated by new growth theory, partly by a renewed interest in the effects of integration in Europe. De Melo et al. (1992) find no impact of regional integration on growth, though this is the exception rather than the rule. Henrekson et al. (1997) estimate that EU/EFTA has boosted the growth rates of member states by around 0.8 percent, a nonmarginal impact. Coe and Meghadam (1993) calculate that 0.3 percentage points of growth in France in the 1980s can be explained by EU membership. Many of these studies have also explored the impact on investment and/or research and development (R&D) spillovers. Coe and Helpman (1995) found that in the EU, foreign R&D tended to boost domestic investment while Baldwin and Seghezza (1996) found evidence to suggest that EU member states benefited from R&D expenditure to a greater extent than nonmembers. By contrast, Henrekson et al. (1997) could find no evidence of an investment effect.

REGIONALISM IN ASIA

Evolution

We earlier outlined global developments in regionalism. One of the striking features of RTAs approved under GATT Article XXIV is the overwhelming predominance of Europe. Only a small proportion involves Asian countries (the reasons for this are discussed below).

As is clear from Table 4.3, only *half a dozen* RTAs have been concluded since World War II. Of these, only three can be thought of as substantive agreements (at least on paper) involving predominantly Asian countries (APEC, ASEAN, and the South Asian Preferential Trading Area [SAPTA]). ASEAN has been in existence longest and involves a geographically contiguous group of countries. It incorporates a PTA, commitment to liberalization of some tariff measures, and an industrial cooperation agreement. However, in terms of promoting regional trade and investment, it has had very limited success. Balasubramanyam (1989) ascribes this to a combination of factors: first, the rather different development philosophies that prevailed until recently; second, the very selective and restrictive coverage of liberalization measures; and third, an

Table 4.3 RTAs in Asia

Agreement	Participating Countries/Areas	Foundation
Borneo Free Trade Area	North Borneo, Sarawak	1962
Association of Southeast Asian Nations (ASEAN)	Brunei Darussalam, Indonesia, Malaysia, Philippines, Singapore, Thailand	1967
Economic and Social Commission for Asia and the Pacific (ESCAP)	Bangladesh, India, Korea, Lao PDR, Philippines, Sri Lanka, Thailand	1976
South Pacific Regional Trade and Cooperation Agreement (SPARTECA)	Australia, Fiji Islands, Kiribati, New Zealand, Niue, Papua New Guinea, Samoa, Solomon Islands, Tonga, Tuvalu	1981
Asia-Pacific Economic Cooperation (APEC) Forum	Australia; Brunei Darussalam; Canada; Chile; PRC; Hong Kong, China; Indonesia; Japan; Korea; Malaysia; Mexico; New Zealand; Papua New Guinea; Philippines; Singapore; Taipei,China; Thailand; US	1989
South Asian Preferential Trading Area (SAPTA)	Bangladesh, Bhutan, India, Maldives, Nepal, Pakistan, Sri Lanka	1993

attempt at integration by regulation that was fundamentally flawed. This lack of progress has been recognized by the participating countries. In January 1991 they committed themselves to the formation of an ASEAN Free Trade Area (AFTA) by 2008. To advance this, a common external preferential tariff was agreed in 1994 and the deadline for the creation of AFTA brought forward to 2003. Clearly, the creation of a common external tariff is a step toward closer economic relations, but it does exclude broad product areas, for example, all agricultural products and natural resources, as well as trade in services. The past record of ASEAN, together with the present uncertainty, makes it hard to believe that a rapid transition to a free trade area is likely.

The South Asian Association for Regional Cooperation (SAARC) dates back to the early 1980s. For many years it was principally a discussion forum for the South Asian nations that are geographically contiguous, if rather diverse in terms of relative size and resource endowments. In 1993 the participating countries signed the SAPTA agreement though it still remains a framework for exchanging concessions at some unspecified time in the future. The grouping includes LDCs with a long-standing commitment to inward-oriented trade policies. Despite recent liberalization, they remain relatively protectionist, and the prospects for real minilateral liberalization seem remote.

Finally is APEC which, against this background, looks anomalous in terms of its scale and ambition. Although there had been earlier discussions around a similar initiative, for example, the 1968 proposal for a Pacific Free Trade Area, nothing on this scale had, before its formation, materialized in Asia. APEC began as a consultative forum in 1989. Since then, as, for example, through the Osaka Action Plan, it has set out principles for liberalization, as well as setting dates for complete liberalization of trade among members. Thus, 2010 is the target for free and open trade among developed country members and 2020 for all members, as set out at the Bogor Summit in 1994. Precise modalities for reaching these targets have not been agreed, beyond the fact that they will be reached by consensus. (APEC and its prospects are discussed further in the section *APEC: Prospects for the Future* of this chapter)

Generally, however, why have RTAs found such little favor in Asia? There are at least four factors that explain the relative unimportance of RTAs in Asia over the postwar period. First, in contrast to Western Europe where there has been the greatest proliferation, the immediate postwar pressures for regional cooperation were minimal. After the war, external pressures from the US reinforced internal forces that saw regional cooperation as desirable for fundamentally political reasons, i.e., it might help reduce the possibility of further military conflict. Second, the states of Western Europe coexist in a remarkably small geographic area, in contrast to the vast territorial domain of Asia. This close proximity, which through history has stimulated conflict, was conducive to regional cooperation when the political will existed. Third, despite the geographically disperse nature of the region, shares of intraregional trade in Asia have been consistently high over the postwar period, exceeded only by those in Western Europe (Norheim et al. 1993). The key point from Asia's view is that significant economic integration had occurred despite a lack of formal integration arrangements, and this was associated with very impressive growth rates. A fourth point, and related to the previous one, is that certainly where the NIEs were concerned, regional liberalization was not seen as a stepping stone to multilateral liberalization, nor as a substitute for it (as is the case in many developing countries). Substantial unilateral liberalization was undertaken by the NIEs as an ingredient in their outward-oriented trade strategies. The success of these policies meant, among other things, an absence of any phantom liberalization push toward regional integration arrangements.

APEC: Origins and Development

Given the history of regionalism in Asia, in particular a very small number of RTAs and agreements that have probably been ineffective, APEC's emergence is perhaps rather surprising. As we have seen, until now RTAs have touched relatively few Asian economies. Now we have an agreement involving some 12 Asian countries. Moreover, it is not confined to Asia but stretches across the Pacific to embrace countries in North, South, and Central America, and Australasia. In all there are 18 members. It is an agreement that is both "North-South" and "East-West," spans three of the five continents, includes the most populous country in the world and some of the least populous, brings together city states and continental economies, and embraces economic superpowers and economic minnows. Almost the only common characteristic seems to be a coastline on the Pacific Ocean.

APEC is gathering momentum. Its origins lie in the establishment of the Pacific Economic Cooperation Council in 1980, which lobbied hard for the creation of some kind of forum, ultimately APEC, in 1989. Initially this, too, was seen as a consultative forum but it has hardened somewhat with commitments to trade and investment liberalization being made. Advocates of APEC, like Bergsten (1994), emphasize the "differentness" of the agreement. In contrast to the EU and NAFTA, which are seen as exclusive, discriminatory arrangements in the classic customs union/free trade area mold, APEC is founded on the concept of "open regionalism." This means different things to different analysts. Garnaut and Drysdale (1994) define it as follows: "Open regionalism encompasses integrative processes that contain no element of exclusion or discrimination against outsiders." Drysdale et al. (1998) adopt a more precise definition in that they equate it with "concerted, unilateral, most favored nation liberalization of trade by a number of states." MFN liberalization eliminates the scope for trade diversion and avoids the complications of compliance with the "substantially all" trade condition of Article XXIV. Having concerted action across the group is seen as assisting in overcoming domestic obstacles to reform and maximizing improvements in market access. Finally, because liberalization is unilateral, individual members can proceed as quickly or slowly, and on as many fronts, as they wish. Bergsten (1994) clearly sees this as a concept whose time has come and sees APEC "at the center of a new era." He argues that it provides the potential for WTO-consistent liberalization, driven by a community of nations that is more powerful, economically and politically, than any other grouping. He also argues that the achievements thus far are very real. Is this so?

The objectives of APEC were first set out at the third Ministerial Summit held in Seoul, Korea, in 1991 as follows.

- Sustain the growth and development of the region for the common good of its people and in this way contribute to the growth and development of the world economy.
- Enhance the positive gains, both for the region and the world economy, resulting from increasing economic interdependence, by encouraging the flow of goods, services, capital, and technology.
- Develop and strengthen the open multilateral trading system in the interest of Asia-Pacific and all other economies.
- Reduce barriers to trade in goods and services among participants in a manner consistent with GATT principles where applicable and without detriment to other economies.

At its fourth meeting in Bangkok in 1992, it formed a Secretariat and established the "Eminent Persons Group" "...to develop a vision of trade in the Asia-Pacific region." It subsequently set out its vision in a report to the Seattle Summit in 1995, identifying three pillars of cooperation: trade liberalization, trade facilitation, and technical cooperation. The first essentially pointed to further GATT/WTO liberalization. The second called for commitments on an Asia-Pacific Investment Code, dispute settlement, mutual recognition on product standards, common testing and monitoring procedures, and mutual consultation on macroeconomic policies. On technical cooperation, the report urged action on human resources, transport, telecommunications, and energy. It did not set out an implementation program, but did stress the need for deeper institutionalization.

Follow-up reports from the Eminent Persons Group at the 1994 and 1995 Summits addressed "Achieving the Vision" and "Implementing the Vision," respectively. These reports, together with the momentum gathering behind APEC, resulted in explicit political commitments. Thus at the Bogor Summit in 1994, APEC leaders committed themselves to the goal of free trade and investment in the region by 2010 for industrial countries and by 2020 for developing countries. This was followed at the Osaka Summit in 1995 with the Osaka Action Agenda. This set out the key principles for liberalization and facilitation: WTO consistency, comprehensiveness, comparability, nondiscrimination, transparency, standstill, continuous process, flexibility, and cooperation. The delivery mechanism envisaged was "concerted unilateral liberalization." In other words, individual members each set their own targets and programs and aim for them, with the guiding objective of complete free trade by 2010 or 2020. Consultation and review can occur through annual summits, with peer pressure helping members keep their promises.

APEC: Prospects for the Future

Is APEC likely to endure? If so, is it likely to deliver real economic and political benefits to the region? The 1998 summit is APEC's tenth, to many commentators a surprise. APEC has endured for a decade and has undoubtedly progressed. Although it remains fundamentally a consultative forum, it has acquired some of the trappings of a "mature" RTA: a secretariat, an institutional identity, and commitments to regionally based actions. The last of these have been very visible and are very ambitious. If nothing else, these, together with the inherent flexibility of APEC, should ensure endurance (avoiding the problem noted earlier, i.e., that the bureaucracies set up as enabling devices sometimes become the ultimate driving force). The more interesting question, however, is whether APEC will deliver real benefits.

It can, if it can accelerate the process of multilateral liberalization. Arguably, though, there is a fundamental problem with the process selected for accomplishing this, i.e., unilateral, unreciprocated liberalization in an overall context of open regionalism. From an economic standpoint this is exactly what any liberal-minded economist would wish governments to commit to—it results in free trade at relatively low transactions costs, compared with, for instance, the MTN route. But the reason multilateral liberalization occurs through an MTN proccss is to minimize free-riding problems. If open regionalism really does mean "...regional cooperation whose outcome is not only the reduction of internal (intraregional) barriers but also the actual reduction of external barriers to economies not part of the regional enterprise" (Garnaut and Drysdale 1994, p. 3) then free riding is not only an intraregional issue. Put bluntly, is it plausible that the US will eliminate barriers to imports from, say, Japan (an APEC member) and, say, the EU (which is not an APEC member) on an unreciprocated basis? Clearly not. So the process must therefore either become truly multilateral, through WTO, or truly regional, on a discriminatory basis. Given the diversity of APEC membership and the members' very different protective structures, the latter is highly unlikely.

Of course, even if APEC fails to realize its goal of open regionalism through unilateral liberalization, it could nevertheless accelerate the process of multilateral liberalization by acting in concert through WTO. As a caucus it could be very effective. This is where its diversity allied to its economic power could be a real strength. The other area where it can deliver benefits to its members is in the political domain. This is where the EU, for example, has performed very well. If the arrangement and the process of summitry helps the cause of political stability in the region, then that must clearly be seen as a major benefit. If these were achieved without the hierarchy of preferences and complicated rules of origin that characterize many RTAs, then the benefit-cost ratio could be high.

CGE Modeling of APEC

In "Trading Blocs and Trade Flows" above, we referred to several CGE analyses of RTAs, most of which pertained to arrangements in Europe and North America. Although APEC is a much more recent phenomenon, several studies have attempted to evaluate its effects.

Inada (1996) takes the APEC tariff liberalization targets and assumes that they will be implemented in a linear fashion by 2003. In addition, he effects simulations that incorporate investment liberalization (in the form of increased investment inflows). Tariff reduction stimulates real exports and imports, with growth of the former exceeding the latter. Overall, the region's GDP growth accelerates, though the benefits of faster growth are not evenly spread, with Japan and Korea gaining relatively more. As one would anticipate, these benefits are reinforced when investment liberalization measures are incorporated. Anderson et al. (1997) also concentrate on tariff liberalization. Their policy experiment essentially involves an assumption that APEC economies liberalize trade to the full extent of their Uruguay Round commitments, plus a further 50 percent, and that these are fully implemented by 2005. They, too, find that substantial real output gains follow, with the level and distribution of these gains being particularly sensitive to whether or not agriculture is included.

Dee et al. (1996) take the analysis beyond tariff liberalization and use their model to analyze tariff and nontariff barrier liberalization in agriculture, manufactures, and services, as well as broader trade facilitation measures. Given the emphasis placed on trade facilitation in the APEC commitments, this is especially useful. As with Inada (1996) and Anderson et al. (1997) they identify substantial trade and real income gains from tariff liberalization in manufactures and agriculture. They also find very sizable gains from services trade liberalization. The novel ingredient of this study is the inclusion of trade facilitation measures which they benchmark by reference to the Cecchini et al. (1988) work on the Single Market and put at 5–10 percent of import values. The gains from these turn out to be as large as those from liberalization of merchandise trade.

Young and Huff (1997) and Lee et al. (1997) have a slightly different focus to their analysis. They concentrate on tariff and nontariff barrier liberalization, but their key policy experiments are comparisons of the gains from open regionalism with those from preferential trade within the region. Not surprisingly, the gains from the former exceed those from the latter. After all, concerted, unilateral MFN liberalization is closer to multilateral liberalization than preferential tariff reductions. As in other studies, the gains are unevenly distributed with those countries and areas with the highest prereform protection (ASEAN and the PRC) being the major gainers. This approach is also adopted by Yang et al. (1998) who introduce a further element, namely a comparison of MFN-based and FTA-based liberalization for both APEC and the EU. The open-regionalism, MFN-based approach agreed by APEC leads to gains to the region as a whole and gains to all individual participants. Moreover, it does so without imposing costs on the rest of the world. By contrast, a PTA, which also benefits APEC members, imposes such costs. Unsurprisingly, these results are mirrored in their outcomes for EU: this is an

RTA-based arrangement that has benefited its members but imposes costs on nonmembers; had it been an MFN-based arrangement, the benefits to members would have been greater and the costs to nonmembers less.

Thus, quite a substantial CGE-based literature has quickly grown as part of the debate on whether APEC will deliver real benefits to its members, and the potential size of those benefits. The outputs of these models suggest the following. First, there are likely to be substantial gains if the targets set for tariff and nontariff liberalization measures are implemented. Second, those gains will be enhanced if the proposed trade facilitation measures are implemented. Third, open regionalism has the potential to deliver greater gains than preferential liberalization. Fourth, the benefits of APEC will not be evenly distributed as some members will do better than others, depending upon initial protection levels and the composition of real output in member countries. Fifth, open regionalism can deliver benefits to the region without imposing costs on the rest of the world.

These results are encouraging, especially for those who see open regionalism as a concept whose time has come. They give a degree of reassurance that the process is worth pursuing. However, three caveats must be borne in mind. First, these are CGE models. Thus, the results are outcomes of computations fashioned by model structures, not forecasts based on past trends. Second, the models do not incorporate adjustment costs. Third, the models all assume that the APEC commitments will be realized in full, and that there will be no backsliding, and no shift from open regionalism principles to preferential trading. As we indicated earlier, this is the key point.

Is There a Regional Bias to Trade in Asia?

In the section *Trading Blocs and Trade Flows* of this chapter, we reviewed the existing literature on the trade effects of RTAs. We mentioned that several analysts have deployed the gravity approach. In this section we formally test for regional bias in Asian trade vis-à-vis other regions by estimating a series of gravity models.

The rationale behind the gravity model is simple and evolved by analogy to modeling gravitational force in the physical sciences. Gravitational force is inversely proportional to the distance between two objects and directly proportional to their mass. Extending the analogy to trade between nations is straightforward: greater distance between two countries should (other things being equal) result in less bilateral trade between them. Distance is effectively a proxy for natural barriers to trade. Other things being equal, the further away a trading partner is, the higher are communication and transport costs. By contrast, greater mass should result in more trade. Generally mass is proxied by either absolute size or effective purchasing power. The former is sometimes proxied by population but more usually by GDP. Effective purchasing power is generally proxied by GDP per capita.

There is a relatively long tradition of estimating gravity models as a basis for explaining trade flows. Until a few years ago they existed in something of a theoretical vacuum. Contributions by Deardorff (1994) and Frankel et al. (1995) have, however, given the model a more secure theoretical footing. Other gravity modeling exercises include Frankel (1993), Bayoumi and Eichengreen (1995), and Dhar and Panagariya (1996). They find mixed evidence of a regional bias. All find some evidence of a bias in Western Europe which they attribute to regionalism. Frankel (1993) identifies a strong regional bias in East Asia and rather interestingly uses this as an argument in favor of further RTAs, on the grounds that it is manifestly a "natural" trading bloc. By contrast, Dhar and Panagariya (1996) can find no such effect. Indeed they argue that, if anything, the bias is toward extraregional trade.

We use a large dataset on bilateral trade flows extending over a 40-year period to undertake a more comprehensive evaluation than hitherto of the potential trade impact of RTAs. Our basic specification is one that is typical of most gravity models including distance and GDP. Most studies go further in including other variables that are likely to shape trade flows, and we do likewise. Hence the estimating equation used also includes the per capita GDP of the two countries, whether they have a common border, and whether they have a common language. We conjecture that a common border and a common language will act as additional stimuli to trade and hence positive coefficients should be associated with these variables. In addition, since it would be expected that the greater the wealth of the country, the greater the demand for differentiated products and the greater the degree of specialization in production, it is anticipated that trading activity is positively related to the per capita GDPs of the countries concerned. Hence our estimating equation takes the form

$$\ln T_{ij} = \beta_0 + \beta_1 \ln(\text{Distance}_{ij}) + \beta_2 \ln(GDP_i) + \beta_3 \ln(GDP_j) + \beta_4 \ln(PCGDP_i) + \beta_5 \ln(PCGDP_j)\ \beta_6 (\text{BORDER}_{ij}) + \beta_7 (\text{LANGUAGE}) + \varepsilon_{ij}$$

where

i	= reporter country
j	= partner country
T_{ij}	= value of trade between country i and country j
Distance_{ij}	= distance between i and j
GDP_i	= gross domestic product of country i
PCGDP_i	= per capita GDP of country i
GDP_j	= gross domestic product of country j
PCGDP_j	= per capita GDP of country j
BORDERz	= countries share a land border or small body of water border
LANGUAGE	= countries share a common language

This equation is estimated separately for imports, exports, and total trade.

The dataset we use consists of a panel of 95 countries from 1965 to 1993. Bilateral trade data are taken from the IMF *Direction of Trade Statistics*, and GDP data from the World Bank's *World Debt Tables* (various issues).

Typically in previous studies of trading relationships the gravity equation specified is estimated as a pooled regression. While this vastly increases the degrees of freedom available to the researcher, it imposes a common gravity relationship on all reporting countries. As Polak (1996) has argued, this is likely to bias the results. Thus we allow individual countries to systematically deviate from the average gravity relationship. That is, we control for country-specific effects by adopting fixed and random effects panel data techniques. Robust standard errors are also used to control for the possibility of heteroscedasticity. The estimation results for the gravity model are reported in Table 4.4 (imports), Table 4.5 (exports), and Table 4.6 (total trade). The first column provides an estimation of the "base specification," with subsequent columns containing a number of augmentations.

Turning to column 1, the basic equation behaves much as we would expect, whether we consider imports, exports, or total trade.

Table 4.4 Gravity Model for Imports

	1		2		3		4		5	
Constant	-9.45728	-93.92	-9.27999	-84.211	-9.06429	-79.335	-8.33122	-81.335	-8.12455	-78.467
Ln(dist)	-0.70059	-168.35	-0.70055	-168.348	-0.70054	-168.487	-0.66678	-157.101	-0.6623	-155.388
Border	0.356344	20.086	0.356467	20.094	0.356248	20.099	0.26339	14.941	0.275599	15.579
Language	0.629241	70.137	0.629253	70.141	0.628633	70.126	0.621115	69.981	0.616869	69.124
GDP_i	0.851456	44.896	0.834438	42.912	0.862929	43.407	0.764376	40.629	0.800436	42.285
GDP_j	0.619548	331.327	0.619568	331.351	0.619132	331.291	0.595315	314.626	0.593649	313.985
$PCGDP_i$	0.243444	9.056	0.239581	8.906	0.173026	6.268	0.200361	7.53	0.121028	4.524
$PCGDP_j$	0.115619	45.998	0.115659	46.015	0.115755	46.094	0.108173	43.452	0.10979	43.928
In Bloc?			0.053866	3.959						
EEC					0.248018	8.783				
EFTA					-0.15875	-4.019				
LAFTA					0.051562	1.231				
ASEAN					0.12945	5.159				
LAIA					-0.02468	-0.719				
AUNZ					0.432778	2.87				
SAPTA					-0.08376	-3.263				
APEC					0.025472	0.93				
Same							0.882343	44.067		
Other							0.514585	48.755		
EC-EC									0.958441	29.436
EC-Other									0.645475	34.716
EFTA-EFTA									0.548896	12.163
EFTA-Other									0.591533	25.476
LAFTA-LAFTA									0.479089	6.535
LAFTA-Other									0.311066	7.616
ASEAN-ASEAN									1.828504	27.53
ASEAN-Other									0.550358	20.506
LAIA-LAIA									0.767177	19.037
LAIA-Other									0.222671	8.447
AUNZ-AUNZ									2.141321	9.861
AUNZ-Other									0.546426	10.766
SAPTA-SAPTA									0.144877	1.977
SAPTA-Other									0.125169	4.133
APEC-APEC									1.724371	19.811
APEC-Other									1.041531	26.284

Source: Author's calculations.

Table 4.5 Gravity Model for Exports

	1		2		3		4		5	
Constant	-9.61775	-98.372	-9.31499	-87.067	-8.81331	-79.59	-8.60887	-86.482	-8.48488	-84.358
Ln(dist)	-0.76789	-190.047	-0.76782	-190.056	-0.76739	-190.432	-0.73435	-178.035	-0.72722	-175.641
Border	0.283666	16.468	0.283877	16.482	0.285783	16.636	0.195564	11.415	0.222012	12.919
Language	0.559751	64.259	0.559771	64.27	0.559474	64.395	0.551941	63.99	0.561032	64.717
GDP_i	0.723653	39.3	0.69459	36.793	0.701618	36.415	0.643222	35.18	0.669883	36.429
GDP_j	0.536644	295.581	0.536679	295.641	0.536104	295.981	0.514205	279.637	0.511829	278.676
$PCGDP_i$	0.637109	24.408	0.630512	24.143	0.552318	20.644	0.598883	23.158	0.541133	20.823
$PCGDP_j$	0.088442	36.239	0.088509	36.271	0.088819	36.492	0.081619	33.736	0.082554	34.002
In Bloc?			0.09199	6.964						
EEC					0.41009	14.985				
EFTA					0.025789	0.674				
LAFTA					-0.4728	-11.643				
ASEAN					0.21616	8.888				
LAIA					-0.0786	-2.363				
AUNZ					0.667786	4.569				
SAPTA					-0.24265	-9.752				
APEC					0.256025	9.643				
Same							0.853506	43.862		
Other							0.462539	45.094		
EC-EC									1.110625	35.113
EC-Other									0.493327	27.314
EFTA-EFTA									0.575594	13.13
EFTA-Other									0.637729	28.274
LAFTA-LAFTA									0.151497	2.127
LAFTA-Other									0.272699	6.873
ASEAN-ASEAN									1.718382	26.633
ASEAN-Other									0.474229	18.189
LAIA-LAIA									0.562195	14.361
LAIA-Other									0.476601	18.613
AUNZ-AUNZ									1.556291	7.378
AUNZ-Other									0.479478	9.725
SAPTA-SAPTA									0.191803	2.694
SAPTA-Other									-0.10916	-3.711
APEC-APEC									1.59998	18.923
APEC-Other									0.893874	23.221

Source: Author's calculations.

Table 4.6 Gravity Model for Total Trade

	1		2		3		4		5	
Constant	-11.1548	-112.821	-11.0429	-102.054	-10.637	-94.902	-10.2464	-101.449	-10.1095	-98.95
Ln(dist)	-0.79588	-194.777	-0.79586	-194.774	-0.79557	-195.045	-0.77218	-184.509	-0.77048	-183.2
Border	0.373457	21.439	0.373534	21.443	0.374533	21.539	0.303744	17.474	0.312734	17.916
Language	0.681956	77.414	0.681963	77.417	0.681461	77.491	0.675979	77.241	0.67398	76.539
GDPi	1.049746	56.373	1.039006	54.416	1.05844	54.272	0.982137	52.942	0.996682	53.36
GDPj	0.653861	356.126	0.653874	356.137	0.653283	356.33	0.635108	340.409	0.633899	339.782
PCGDPi	0.345208	13.078	0.34277	12.977	0.261218	9.646	0.310045	11.816	0.269556	10.212
PCGDPj	0.110754	44.875	0.110779	44.885	0.111016	45.062	0.104914	42.739	0.107863	43.737
In Bloc?			0.033996	2.545						
EEC					0.336963	12.164				
EFTA					-0.10653	-2.749				
LAFTA					-0.32595	-7.93				
ASEAN					0.14059	5.711				
LAIA					-0.12555	-3.729				
AUNZ					0.752603	5.088				
SAPTA					-0.22979	-9.124				
APEC					0.110504	4.112				
Same							0.642903	32.563		
Other							0.413467	39.729		
EC-EC									0.585721	18.231
EC-Other									0.448672	24.456
EFTA-EFTA									0.290141	6.516
EFTA-Other									0.496048	21.651
LAFTA-LAFTA									0.22356	3.091
LAFTA-Other									0.253006	6.278
ASEAN-ASEAN									1.621979	24.749
ASEAN-Other									0.467272	17.644
LAIA-LAIA									0.678975	17.075
LAIA-Other									0.364551	14.016
AUNZ-AUNZ									1.666083	7.775
AUNZ-Other									0.638724	12.754
SAPTA-SAPTA									0.241435	3.339
SAPTA-Other									-0.04211	-1.409
APEC-APEC									1.37276	15.984
APEC-Other									0.741431	18.962

Source: Author's calculations.

Bilateral trade between country pairs is proportional to their respective GDPs and inversely related to the distance between them. Countries with contiguous borders or common languages are also more likely to trade with each other. Richer countries also trade more than poor ones.

The key question for our purposes is: How do regional integration agreements affect the volume and pattern of trade? To investigate this, subsequent columns of Tables 4.4 to 4.6 augment the basic equation in several ways. First, to investigate how regional integration agreements affect the total volume of trade, column 2 includes a dummy variable if the reporting country belongs to one of the following integration agreements: European Community (EC), EFTA, Latin American Free Trade Association (LAFTA), Latin American Integration Association (LAIA), Australia-New Zealand Free Trade Agreement (AUNZ), SAPTA, APEC, and ASEAN. As can be seen, the coefficient on this dummy variable is positive and significant for imports, exports, and total trade. Thus on average countries that belong to a regional integration agreement included in our sample appear to trade significantly more than countries that are outside such agreements. These are, however average effects. Moreover, they do not disentangle trade creation and trade diversion.

Column 3 includes dummies for each of the trading blocs individually to investigate the relative trading propensity of countries belonging to different blocs, with the results summarized in Table 4.7. Countries in those blocs highlighted in bold appear to have a higher than average propensity to trade.

On the basis of all measures of trade, the countries that are members of the EC, APEC, ASEAN, and AUNZ appear to trade to a greater extent than average, compared with LAIA, SAPTA, and LAFTA. This is not surprising where the EU and AUNZ are concerned, for reasons associated with their respective RTAs. Given the length of time that APEC has been in existence and given what we know about ASEAN, it may appear surprising in these cases, especially the latter. But it must be remembered that the dummy variable is not only capturing integration effects. In fact, coefficients on the dummy variables in the above regression are picking up all the ways in which countries in a particular trading bloc differ from those outside the bloc that are not controlled for either by the individual country-specific effects or the gravity model variables. Thus, for instance, if the existence of a trading bloc was coincident with a relatively rapid

Table 4.7 Relative Trading Propensities of Regional Integration Agreements

Trade	Imports	Exports
AUNZ	**AUNZ**	**AUNZ**
EC	**EC**	**EC**
ASEAN	**ASEAN**	**ASEAN**
APEC	**LAFTA**	**APEC**
EFTA	**APEC**	**EFTA**
LAIA	LAIA	LAIA
SAPTA	SAPTA	SAPTA
LAFTA	EFTA	LAFTA

Note: Blocs with a positive propensity to trade are shown in bold.

Source: Author's calculations.

expansion of regional trade stimulated by multilateral or unilateral liberalization, then the dummy associated with the trading bloc may partly reflect this. This is particularly the case with trading blocs that were/have been in existence for a relatively short time because in these cases, the possibility of coincidence is greater. We investigated this further in a number of ways.

First, we included dummies for the Southeast Asian "tigers" as a control group for ASEAN to see if they experience expansion at the same time as ASEAN. Second, a two-way random effects model allowing for time effects to vary effects was estimated. One can also use this framework to see whether members of regional integration agreements are more likely to trade with those within their blocs. Column 4 investigates this by including a dummy if trade is with a country in the same trading bloc as the reporting country. Dummies are also included if the partner country is in a "rival" bloc.[9] In all the tables the coefficient on the same trading bloc is positive and highly significant. Thus countries in regional integration agreements trade significantly more with each other than would be expected simply due to "gravity" considerations. Interestingly, if a country belongs to another trading bloc then trade is also greater than would otherwise be predicted. Column 5 examines this more closely by looking at the

[9] The reference group comprises countries that do not belong to a trading bloc.

relationship between pairs of trading blocs. Thus dummies are included to indicate the bloc of the reporting and partner country. The results of this exercise are summarized in Tables 4.8 and 4.9, which show for each arrangement the bloc with which they have the closest trading relationships in descending order. Thus the EC has the closest ties with ASEAN and APEC and weakest ties with LAFTA and SAPTA. These tables also shed further light on whether trading blocs alter the volume of trade by promoting trade internally or externally. Thus, for example, EC countries have a higher propensity to export to ASEAN and APEC countries than to each other, but are less likely to export to the other five trading areas. In these tables EFTA and SAPTA are perhaps conspicuous by the limited extent to which they promote trade internally, compared with the other trading groups.

This exercise suggests that there may well be a regional bias to trade patterns in AUNZ, EC, ASEAN, and APEC. In general, members of these arrangements trade to a greater extent than the average trading propensities across the 95 countries in the sample. However, three important caveats should be made. First, we must be wary of drawing welfare conclusions from this since we do not distinguish between trade creation and trade diversion. Second, in some of these cases, there is a higher propensity to trade with members of other blocs than with members of one's own bloc. Third, there may be other common factors at work that drive the regional bias and that are not included in our model.

Table 4.8 Propensity to Trade between Blocs: Exports

EC	APEC	ASEAN	EFTA	LAFTA	AUNZ	LAIA	SAPTA
ASEAN	ASEAN	APEC	APEC	EC	ASEAN	EC	AUNZ
APEC	APEC[a]	ASEAN[a]	ASEAN	LAFTA[a]	AUNZ[a]	APEC	EC
EC[a]	EC	EC	EC	EFTA	EC	LAIA[a]	APEC
AUNZ	SAPTA	AUNZ	AUNZ	ASEAN	LAIA	ASEAN	SAPTA[a]
EFTA	EFTA	SAPTA	EFTA[a]	AUNZ	EFTA	SAPTA	ASEAN
LAIA	LAIA	LAFTA	LAIA		LAFTA	EFTA	EFTA
LAFTA		EFTA	LAFTA			AUNZ	LAIA
SAPTA		LAIA	SAPTA				

[a] Indicates trade within group.

Source: Author's calculations.

Table 4.9 Propensity to Trade between Blocs: Imports

EC	APEC	ASEAN	EFTA	LAFTA	AUNZ	LAIA	SAPTA
ASEAN	ASEAN	APEC	APEC	EC	AUNZ[a]	EC	ASEAN
APEC	APEC[a]	AUNZ	ASEAN	LAFTA[a]	ASEAN	LAIA[a]	AUNZ
EC[a]	EC	ASEAN[a]	EC	EFTA	EC	APEC	APEC
LAFTA	EFTA	EC	EFTA[a]	ASEAN	EFTA	EFTA	EC
LAIA	LAIA	EFTA	LAFTA	AUNZ	LAIA	ASEAN	SAPTA[a]
AUNZ	SAPTA	LAFTA	LAIA		LAFTA	SAPTA	EFTA
SAPTA		LAIA	SAPTA			AUNZ	LAIA
EFTA		SAPTA	AUNZ				

[a] Indicates trade within group.

Source: Author's calculations.

CONCLUSIONS

Our purpose in this chapter has been fourfold: to assess recent developments in multilateral and regional integration; to evaluate the relationship between the two; to evaluate the economic impact of regionalism; and to assess the prospects for further regional integration in Asia.

We have seen that moves toward multilateral and regional integration have proceeded in parallel. In the late 1980s and early 1990s we saw the negotiation and conclusion of the most ambitious of all the GATT's rounds of multilateral trade negotiations. Around the same time we saw an upsurge in RTAs, which has been labeled "the new regionalism." This surge has been driven by a number of factors, including frustration with the process of multilateral liberalization, a desire to avoid being a victim of trade and investment diversion, and a desire to provide a counterweight to RTAs elsewhere. As a consequence of these forces, RTAs have been agreed in every continent of the globe and some are intercontinental. Although there is no long history of regionalism in Asia, the continent has not gone unaffected. Proposals to develop SAARC and ASEAN into SAPTA and AFTA respectively have recently been implemented, and APEC has been created and has gathered political and economic momentum. Moreover, it is probable that in the short to medium term at least, this momentum will increase rather than decrease.

Should we be concerned about these developments? As we have seen, this depends upon whether one sees RTAs as a stepping stone to multilateral free trade, or a stumbling block. Our analysis has demonstrated that, in principle, they could be either. In practice, it depends upon the reactions of members of a given RTA and the RTA's third-country effects. Membership of an RTA can serve as a distraction from the multilateral process, or even a substitute for it. For example, some commentators have argued that one of the reasons why the Uruguay Round was so protracted was that the EU was more concerned with its Single Market program. It has also been argued that the creation of RTAs among some groups of developing countries has been a convenient excuse for avoiding serious engagement in the MTN process. Third-country effects can be important, both via trade diversion and the proliferation of preferential arrangements. Evidence on the former is limited, but on the latter rather more readily available. Not only does this (together with the parallel development of complicated rules of origin) raise the transactions costs of trading, it also promotes significant trade deflection.

If there are potential dangers and potential costs associated with RTAs, how can we improve the "fit" with multilateralism? Since RTAs are unlikely to cease being a feature of the international trading environment, the key clearly lies in the approval and supervision arrangements, which brings us back to Article XXIV of GATT, and WTO. One of the leading commentators on GATT has described Article XXIV and the 1979 Enabling Clause as "... woefully inadequate for the tasks required of a multilateral trading system to provide some sort of adequate supervision and discipline on certain of the more dangerous tendencies of trading blocs..." (Jackson 1993). It is clear from experience that the review process for endorsement of new agreements requires strengthening beyond those agreed in the Uruguay Round, a necessity acknowledged by WTO (1995). It is equally clear, however, that third parties need some kind of WTO recourse to challenge "nullification and impairment" commitments that RTA members sign up to when they commit to an agreement. At present there are no embedded arrangements for taking action against third party damage, and WTO dispute-settlement procedures are the obvious mechanism. Finally, Jackson (1993) makes the interesting suggestion that RTAs could be subject to periodic reviews along the lines of the TPRM. As we argued earlier, this has turned out to be a useful mechanism for periodically auditing the trade policies of contracting parties and could, in principle, be extended to the RTA arena.

BIBLIOGRAPHY AND REFERENCES

Anderson, K., B. Dinaranan, T. Hertel, and W. Martin. 1997. "Economic Growth and Policy Reform in the Asia-Pacific: Trade and Welfare Implications by 2005." *Asia-Pacific Economic Review* 3(1):1-18.

Balassa, B., ed. 1975. *European Economic Integration.* Amsterdam: North-Holland.

Balasubramanyam, V. N. 1989. "ASEAN and Regional Trade Cooperation in South East Asia." In D. Greenaway, T. Hyclak, and R. Thornton, eds., *Economic Aspects of Regional Trading Arrangements.* London: Wheatsheaf Press.

Baldwin, R. E. 1989. "The Growth Effects of 1992." *Economic Policy* 2:247-281.

______. 1992. "Measurable Dynamic Gains from Trade." *Journal of Political Economy* 100(1):162-174.

______. 1997. "The Causes of Regionalism." *The World Economy* 20:865-888.

Baldwin, R. E., and E. Seghezza. 1996. "Growth and European Integration: Towards an Empirical Assessment." Geneva: Graduate Institute of International Economics. Mimeo.

Bayoumi, T., and B. Eichengreen. 1995. "Is Regionalism Simply a Diversion? Evidence from the Evolution of the EC and EFTA." Discussion Paper 1294. London: Centre for Economic Policy Research.

Bergsten, C. F. 1994. "APEC and World Trade: A Force for Worldwide Liberalization." *Foreign Affairs* 73(3):20-26.

Bhagwati, J. 1991. *The World Trading System at Risk.* Cambridge, Mass.: Massachusetts Institute of Technology Press.

______. 1993. "Regionalism and Multilateralism: An Overview." In J. de Melo and A. Panagariya, eds., *New Dimensions in Regional Integration,* Cambridge: Cambridge University Press.

Bhagwati, J., D. Greenaway, and A. Panagariya. Forthcoming. "Trading Preferentially: Theory and Policy." *Economic Journal* 107.

Brandao, A. S., and W. Martin. 1993. "Implications of Agricultural Trade Liberalization for the Developing Countries." Working Paper. Washington, DC: World Bank. March.

Brown, D. K., and R. M. Stern. 1989. "Computable General Equilibrium Estimates of the Gains from US-Canadian Trade Liberalisation." In D. Greenaway, T. Hyclak, and R. J. Thornton, eds., *Economic Aspects of Regional Trading Arrangements.* New York: New York University Press; distributed by Columbia University Press.

Brown, D. K., A. V. Deardorff, and R. M. Stern. 1992. "A North American Free Trade Area: Analytical Issues and a Computational Assessment." *The World Economy* 15 (1):11-29.

Cecchini, P., et al. 1988. *The European Challenge: 1992.* Aldershot: Gower Press.

Coe, D. T., and R. Meghadam. 1993. "Capital and Trade as Engines of Growth in France." *IMF Staff Papers* 40:542-566.

Coe, D. T., and E. Helpman. 1995. "International R and D Spillovers." *European Economic Review* 39:859-887.

Cooper, C. A., and B. G. Massell. 1965. "A New Look at Customs Union Theory." *Economic Journal* 75:742-747.

Cox, D., and R. Harris. 1984. "Trade Liberalization and Industrial Organization: Some Estimates for Canada." *Journal of Political Economy* 93:115-145.

Deardorff, A. V. 1994. "Determinants of Bilateral Trade: Does Gravity Work in a Neoclassical World?" University of Michigan. Mimeo.

Dee, P., C. Geisler, and G. Watts. 1996. *The Impact of APEC's Free Trade Commitment.* Canberra: The Australian Industry Commission.

Dhar, S., and A. Panagariya. 1996. "Is East Asia Less Open than North America and the EEC? No." Paper presented at IEA Roundtable Conference, Sydney.

Drysdale, P., and D. Vines, eds. 1998. *Europe, East Asia and APEC.* Cambridge: Cambridge University Press.

Drysdale, P., D. Vines, and B. House. 1998. "Europe and Asia: A Shared Global Agenda?" In P. Drysdale and D. Vines, eds., *Europe, East Asia and APEC.* Cambridge: Cambridge University Press.

Ethier, W. 1998. "Regionalism in a Multilateral World." In J. Piggott and A. Woodland, eds., *Trade Policy and the Pacific Rim.* London: Macmillan, for the International Economic Association.

Falvey, R. E., and G. V. Reed. 1998. "Economic Effects of Rules of Origin." *Weltwirtschaftliches Archiv* 134:209-229.

Finger, J. M., and T. Murray. 1990. "Policing Unfair Imports: The United States Experience." *Journal of World Trade* 24:39-53.

Foroutan, F. Forthcoming. "Does Membership in a Regional Preferential Trading Arrangement Make a Country More or Less Protectionist?" *The World Economy.*

Francois, J. F., B. McDonald, and H. Nordstrom. 1994. "The Uruguay Round: A Global General Equilibrium Assessment." Discussion Paper. London: Centre for Economic Policy Research.

Frankel, J. 1993. "Is Japan Creating a Yen Bloc in East Asian Pacific?" In J. Frankel and N. Kahler, eds., *Regionalism and Rivalry: Japan and the US in Pacific Asia.* Chicago: University of Chicago Press.

Frankel, J., E. Stein, and S. J. Wei. 1995. "Trading Blocs and the Americas: The Natural, the Unnatural and the Super-natural." *Journal of Development Economics* 47 (1):61-95.

Garnaut, R., and P. Drysdale. 1994. *Asia-Pacific Regionalism.* Sydney: Harper International.

Glejser, H. 1972. "Empirical Evidence on Comparative Cost Theory from the European Common Market Experience." *European Economic Review* 163:247-259.

Goldin, I., O., Knudsen, and D. van der Mansbrugghe, 1993. *Trade Liberalisation: Global Economic Implications.* Paris: OECD and World Bank.

Greenaway, D. 1993. "Liberalising Foreign Trade Through Rose-Tinted Glasses." *Economic Journal* 103:208-222.

———. 1998. "Current Issues in Trade Policy and the Pacific Rim." In J. Piggott and A. Woodland, eds., *International Trade Policy and the Pacific Rim.* London: Macmillan.

Greenaway, D., and C. R. Milner. 1993. *Trade and Industrial Policy in Developing Countries.* London: Macmillan.

Greenaway, D., S. J. Leybourne, G. V. Reed, and J. Whalley. 1993. *Applied General Equilibrium Modelling.* London: HMSO.

Greenaway, D., C. W. Morgan, and P. W. Wright. Forthcoming. "Trade Reform, Adjustment and Growth: What Does the Evidence Tell Us?" *Economic Journal* Vol. 108.

Hamilton, R. and J. Whalley. 1985. "Geographically Discriminatory Trade Arrangements." *Review of Economics and Statistics* 57:446-455.

Harrison, G., T. Rutherford, and D. Tarr. 1994. "Product Standards, Imperfect Competition and Completion of the Market of the European Union." Policy Research Working Paper 1293. Washington, DC: World Bank.

Henrekson, M., J. Torstensson, and R. Torstensson. 1997. "Growth Effects of European Integration." *European Economic Review* 41:1537-1557.

Hertel, T., W. Martin, I. Yanagishima, and B. Dimaranan. 1995. "Economic Growth and Policy Reform in the APEC Region: Trade and Welfare Implications by 2005." Discussion Paper. London: Centre for Economic Policy Research.

Hine, R. C. 1994. "International Economic Integration." In D. Greenaway and L. A. Winters, eds., *Surveys in International Trade.* Oxford: Blackwell.

Hoekman, B. 1993. "New Issues in the Uruguay Round." *Economic Journal* 103:1528-1539.

Hummels, D. L., and R. M. Stern. 1994. "Evolving Patterns of North American Merchandise Trade and Foreign Direct Investment." *The World Economy* 17:5-30.

Inada, Y. 1996. *The Economic Impact of Regional Integration with Special Reference to APEC.* Geneva: United Nations Conference on Trade and Development.

International Monetary Fund (IMF). Various Issues. *Direction of Trade Statistics Yearbook.* Washington, DC.

Jackson, J. 1993. "Regional Trade Blocs and the GATT." *The World Economy*: 121-132.

Johnson, H. G. 1958. "The Gains from Freer Trade in Europe: An Estimate." *Manchester School* 26:247-55.

Krishna, P. 1997. "Regionalism and Multilateralism: A Political Economy Approach." Economics Department, Columbia University. Mimeo.

Krueger, A. O. 1997. "Trade Policy and Economic Development: How We Learn." *American Economic Review* 87:1-22.

Krugman, P. R. 1993. "Growing World Trade: Causes and Consequences." *Brookings Papers* (1):327-377.

Lee, H., D. Roland-Holst, and D. van der Mensbrugghe. 1997. *APEC Trade Liberalization and Structural Adjustment: Policy Assessments.* Tokyo: Institute of Developing Economies.

Levy, P. 1997. "A Political Economic Analysis of Free Trade Agreements." Discussion Paper No. 718. Economic Growth Center, Yale University.

Markusen, J., and R. Wigle. 1990. "Explaining the Volume of North-South Trade." *Economic Journal* 90:1206-1215.

Mayes, D. 1978. "The Effects of Economic Integration on Trade." *Journal of Common Market Studies* 17:1-25.

Melo, J. de, C. Montenegro, and A. Panagariya. 1992. *"Regional Integration Old and New: Issues and Evidence."* Washington, DC: World Bank. Mimeo.

Melo, J. de, and A. Panagariya, eds. 1993. *New Dimensions in Regional Integration.* Cambridge: Cambridge University Press.

Messerlin, P. A. 1989. "The EC Anti-Dumping Regulations: A First Economic Appraisal." *Weltwirtschaftliches Archiv* 125:563-587.

———. 1990. "Anti-Dumping Regulations or Pro-Cartel Law?" *The World Economy* 13:465-492.

Morrissey, W. O. and Y. Rai. 1995. "The GATT Agreement and Trade Related Investment Measures: Implications for Developing Countries and Their Relationship with Transnational Corporations." *Journal of Development Studies* 31(5): 702-724.

Nguyen, T. T., C. Perroni, and R. M. Wigle. 1993. "An Evaluation of the Draft Final Act of the Uruguay Round." *Economic Journal* 103(421):1549-1558.

Norheim, H., M. Finger, and K. Anderson. 1993. "Trends in the Regionalization of World Trade, 1928 to 1990." In K. Anderson and R. Blackhurst, eds., *Regional Integration and the Global Trading System.* New York: St. Martins Press.

Organisation for Economic Co-operation and Development (OECD). 1995. *Regional Integration and the Multilateral Trading System.* Paris.

Owen, N. 1983. *Economies of Scale, Competitiveness and Trade Patterns within the European Community.* Oxford: Clarendon Press.

Panagariya, Arvind, M.G. Quibria, and Narhari Rao, eds., 1996. "The Emerging Global Trading Environment and Developing Asia." Occasional Papers No. 55, July. Manila: Asian Development Bank.

Polak, J. J. 1996. "Is APEC a Natural Regional Trading Bloc?" *The World Economy* 19:533-543.

Rayner, A. J., K. A. Ingersent, and R. C. Hine. 1993. "Agriculture in the Uruguay Round: An Assessment." *Economic Journal* 103:1513-1527.

Silberston, Z. A. 1989. *The Future of the Multifibre Arrangement: Implications for the UK Economy.* London: HMSO.

Smith, A., and A. J. Venables. 1992. "Completing the Internal Market in the EC: Some Industry Simulations." *European Economic Review* 32:1501-1525.

Tovias, A. 1982. "Testing Factor Price Equalisation in the EEC." *Journal of Common Market Studies* 20:165-181.

Trela, I., and J. Whalley. 1990. "Global Effects of Developed Country Trade Restrictions in Textiles and Apparel." *Economic Journal* 100:1190-1205.

van Mourik, A. 1989. "Countries: A Neo-Classical Model of International Wage Differentials." In W. Molle and A. van Mourik, eds., *Wage Differentials in the European Community, Convergence or Divergence?* Aldershot: Gower Press.

Viner, J. 1950. *The Customs Union Issue.* New York: Carnegie Endowment for International Peace.

Waelbroeck, J. 1976. "Measuring the Degree of Progress of Economic Integration." In G. Machlup, ed., *Economic Integration: Worldwide, Regional, Sectoral,* London: Macmillan.

Whalley, J. 1991. "Recent Trade Liberalisation in Developing Countries: What is Behind it and Where is it Headed." In D. Greenaway, ed., *Global Protection.* London: Macmillan.

Winters, L. A. 1987. "Britain in Europe: A Survey of Quantitative Trade Studies." *Journal of Common Market Studies* 25:315-335.

______. 1997. "What Can European Experience Teach Developing Countries About Integration?" *The World Economy* 20:889-914.

World Bank. Various Issues. *World Debt Tables.* Washington, D.C.

World Trade Organization (WTO). 1995. *Regionalism and the World Trading System.* Geneva.

Yang, Y., R. Duncan, and T. Lawson. 1998. "Trade Liberalisation in the European Union and APEC: What if the Approaches were Exchanged?" In P. Drysdale and D. Vines, eds., *Europe, East Asia and APEC.* Cambridge: Cambridge University Press.

Young, L., and K. Huff. 1997. "Free Trade in the Pacific Rim: On What Basis?" In T. Hertel, ed., *Global Trade Analysis: Modelling and Applications.* Cambridge: Cambridge University Press.

CHAPTER FIVE

Case Study: People's Republic of China

Larry D. Qiu

INTRODUCTION

The People's Republic of China (PRC) began its economic reforms, including its "open-door policy," in 1979. Since then, almost every sector of the economy has undergone changes to varying degrees. This chapter reviews both the pre- and post-reform foreign trade regime, analyzing the Government's foreign trade reform and current policies, with an emphasis on export performance.

Pre-Reform Foreign Trade

In the period of economic rebuilding and the establishment of the new foreign trade system, 1949–1957, the Government began to control foreign trade. In 1950, the Government established a number of national, specialized, state-owned foreign trade corporations (FTCs). In 1953, there were 14 FTCs and two specialized transport corporations. Together with their branches in many provinces, they accounted for 68.4 percent of the country's total international trade in 1950, 92.8 percent in 1952, and virtually all in 1955. During this period, the PRC's trade with the Soviet Union and other Eastern Bloc countries increased while that with Japan, Western Europe, and the US declined.

The rates of trade fluctuated during 1958–1965, as a result of the "Great Leap Forward" of 1958–1959, and the three-year natural disaster of 1960–1962. The PRC then changed its trading partners, switching from the Soviet Union and other Eastern Bloc countries to the West, especially Japan and Western Europe. However, during the Cultural Revolution of 1966–1976, every sector of the economy was severely damaged. From 1967 to 1969, the country's foreign trade declined substantially. Overall, during 1953–1978, the PRC's share of world trade fell from 1.2 percent to 0.8 percent. The overthrow of the "Gang of Four" in 1976 brought the Cultural Revolution to an end and helped revive the PRC's economy and trade. The open-door policy adopted in 1979 has played an extremely important role in the country's economic development, while the contribution of foreign trade to the economy has been extraordinary. Since 1979, the PRC's average growth rate for exports has been about 17 percent a year, and that for imports over 15 percent a year. In recent years, the PRC has become the world's tenth largest exporter and twelfth largest importer.

Open-Door Policy

Economic reform is predicated on "reform and open," meaning changing the domestic economy and opening it up to the outside world, with particular emphasis on liberalizing foreign trade and investment—the open-door policy. Such foreign trade liberalization involves three main elements. First, there was a significant reduction of state control and planning, giving producers and consumers a higher degree of autonomy. Second, the Government has adopted various incentive schemes to stimulate exports and to improve foreign trade efficiency. Third, the country's trade policies have been changed so as to be more compatible with international practices, such as the requirements of WTO.

Economic and Trade Performance

Since their inception, the reforms have wrought dramatic changes on the PRC economy. During the past two decades, the PRC has been the fastest growing economy in the world, maintaining an annual average of about 10 percent GDP growth. During this period, the PRC has maintained current account and capital account surpluses most of the time. Its strong export performance and its ability to attract foreign direct investment (FDI) have helped. As a result, the country has become the second largest holder of foreign exchange reserves in the world, reaching $140.9 billion by end-May 1998.

Table 5.1 indicates some important aspects of the PRC's export growth in the 1980s and 1990s. For most years since 1980, the PRC has had double-digit export growth rates, significantly outpacing the world average. As a result, its share of world exports has increased, from only 0.9 percent in 1980 to 3.3 percent in 1997. In 1997, the PRC was the tenth largest exporter in the world (WTO 1998). The PRC economy has also become more open to the world economy. Its export/GDP ratio rose from below 10 percent in the early 1980s to about 20 percent in 1997.

Table 5.1 Export Performance, 1980–1997

Year	Total Exports ($ million)	Annual Growth	Share of Goods Exports	Share of Services Exports	Share of World Exports (percent)	Exports/ GDP
1980	18,119	-	-	-	0.9	7.4
1981	22,007	21.46	-	-	1.1	7.9
1982	22,320	1.42	94.65	5.35	1.2	8.0
1983	22,226	-0.42	93.17	6.83	1.2	7.5
1984	26,139	17.61	91.45	8.55	1.4	8.3
1985	27,350	4.63	91.80	8.20	1.4	9.5
1986	30,942	13.13	83.24	16.76	1.5	11.2
1987	39,437	27.45	88.07	11.93	1.6	13.0
1988	47,516	20.49	86.40	13.60	1.7	12.6
1989	52,538	10.57	82.26	17.74	1.7	12.2
1990	62,093	18.19	82.97	17.03	1.8	16.6
1991	71,842	15.71	82.01	17.99	2.0	18.6
1992	84,940	18.23	81.90	18.10	2.3	18.5
1993	91,763	8.03	82.45	17.55	2.5	16.7
1994	121,038	31.90	84.73	15.27	2.9	23.6
1995	148,770	22.91	86.11	13.89	3.0	21.1
1996	151,066	1.54	-	-	2.9	18.4
1997	182,700	20.94	87.25	12.75	3.3	19.9

Sources: IMF(1996); Editorial Board (various years); IMF (1998); State Statistical Bureau (various years); and author's calculations.

In 1980, the contributions of primary goods and manufactured products to total exports were almost the same (50.3 percent and 49.7 percent, respectively). However, the share of primary goods has fallen steadily to only 14.5 percent in 1996. Apart from beverages and tobacco, all subcategories have fallen in their share of total exports.

The share of manufactured products has risen steadily since 1980, reaching 85.5 percent in 1996. The labor-intensive product group, sundry products, has more than doubled its share of total exports, from 15.7 percent in 1980 to 37.4 percent in 1996. The capital- and technology-intensive product group, machinery and transport equipment, has grown even faster, from 4.7 percent to 23.4 percent over the same period.

POLICIES ON EXPORTS, IMPORTS, AND CAPITAL FLOWS

Overview of the Foreign Trade Regime

Pre-Reform Foreign Trade System

Before 1979, the PRC had a planned economy. Foreign trade was therefore also subject to economic planning. The main characteristics were as follows: foreign trade rights were controlled by the State and a few national specialized FTCs; the Government administered exports following the overall economic plan; export taxes played a small role; the domestic currency was overvalued for a long time; the country kept itself outside the international economic and trade systems; and import-substitution policies were adopted.

In general, the Government planned both exports and imports. Specifically, the State Planning Commission and the Ministry of Foreign Trade jointly made the general import and export plans as part of the country's overall economic plan. Many layers of government units and FTCs then implemented these export plans. FTCs were the only bodies legally entitled to conduct foreign trade.

Before the reforms, all trade was conducted by a relatively small number of FTCs that strictly followed the state import/export plans. FTCs and some state-owned enterprises (SOEs) exported their products, not according to profitability, but according to government fiat. Because the economy was still very closed and domestic price reform had not been completed, domestic prices were not in line with international prices. Under the trade plans, FTCs were required to purchase some domestically produced goods, such as certain machinery and electronics products, at high domestic prices and export them at lower international prices. For some import products, however, such as grain and chemical fertilizer, FTCs had to purchase them at high international prices and sell at low domestic prices. As a result, FTC profits or losses mainly reflected the distortions of the price system rather than their efficiency.

Reforming the Foreign Trade System

The Ministry of Foreign Economic Relations and Trade (MOFERT) was established in March 1982 as an amalgamation of four former institutions. It was later renamed the Ministry of Foreign Trade and Economic Cooperation (MOFTEC). The reforms of the export system were intended to encourage exports through decentralization of export decisions, reform of the foreign trade system, combination of mandatory and advisory export plans, and introduction of a series of export incentives. (A more detailed discussion of the PRC's foreign trade decentralization is given in the section *Decentralization of Foreign Trade Management* of this chapter.)

There have been two major reforms in the foreign trade system with regard to FTCs. First, during 1988–1990, was the introduction and wide application of the *contract responsibility system* to all FTCs and the *profit-loss self-responsibility system* to all FTCs in light industry, arts and crafts products, and garments. For example, a typical contract between an SOE and the Government specifies that the SOE should supply the State a certain amount of output at certain prices. If the SOE produces more than the targeted amount (quota), it can sell the above-quota output to the Government at a higher price or sell it to the market. The Government began to apply this system to FTCs in 1988. These contracts specified three targets: the amount of foreign exchange earnings, the amount of foreign exchange to be remitted to the central government, and the amount of subsidies (in the form of domestic currency) on loss-making exports. The profit-loss self-responsibility system would seem to be self-explanatory.

Second, from 1991, was the application of the profit-loss self-responsibility system to all FTCs. The main elements of the reforms of this period were to abolish government export subsidies, unify the foreign exchange retention rates, adjust the official exchange rates, and encourage industry-trade linkages (or vertical mergers between FTCs and manufacturing enterprises). The scope of government trade planning was reduced: the share of exports subject to national planning was reduced from 45 percent in 1988 to 15 percent in 1992. In addition, foreign exchange retention for regional governments was increased, while export subsidies were removed in 1992.

Foreign Trade Financial Management

In terms of profit distribution, there has been a gradual evolution from the rigid centrally planned system before the reforms, through experimentation with the contract responsibility system in 1984–1986, to the widespread adoption of the profit-loss self-responsibility system in 1991.

Taxes on domestically produced products include product tax, value-added tax (VAT), and special consumption tax. The same taxes are levied on imported products, in addition to tariffs, though there are many exemptions (see below). When goods are exported, a rebate on any of these three taxes is paid to FTCs or enterprises that export their products directly. The policy was first introduced in 1983, and covered almost all products by the end of the 1980s. The VAT rebate policy has been modified twice since 1995. Exporters now receive a rebate of 6 percent on agricultural goods and 9 percent on industrial goods.

In terms of *pricing of imports and exports,* in the pre-reform period, FTCs imported goods at world prices, though after 1963 a premium was added to the conversion (Lardy 1992). In contrast, exporters received only domestic (i.e., much lower) prices.

Foreign Exchange Regime

Foreign Exchange Controls

Prior to 1979, all foreign exchange from exports had to be sold to the State, which allocated it centrally for imports. The yuan exchange rate was set by the State. All foreign exchange receipts and payments associated with foreign trade had to be made through the People's Bank of China (the central bank) in cooperation with the Ministry of Foreign Trade.

The reform of the foreign exchange regime has been wide ranging. In March 1979, the State Council established the State Foreign Exchange Management Bureau to manage foreign exchange within the country. In 1982, this function was transferred to the People's Bank of China. To provide incentives to exporters, local governments, FTCs, and export enterprises are now allowed to keep some foreign exchange from exports, after submitting a proportion to the Government.

The relaxation of foreign exchange controls and moves toward a market system were seen in three ways. First, the foreign exchange retention policy led to a situation where some enterprises with foreign currency did not spend it all, and others without foreign exchange needed some. To redress this imbalance, the State started, in 1980, to allow enterprises to trade through foreign exchange management departments in various provinces and major cities using "adjustment rates," which were higher than the official rates.

Second, from 1986, to encourage FDI, foreign-invested enterprises (FIEs), which include both joint ventures and wholly foreign-owned enterprises, were allowed to trade foreign currency among themselves. Furthermore, the establishment of foreign exchange markets in Shenzhen and Shanghai in the late 1980s moved foreign currency trading closer to a market system. In these markets, FIEs and local importers and exporters are allowed to participate in buying and selling foreign exchange. Third, in addition to the Bank of China and the People's Bank of China, domestic specialized banks, some financial institutions, and foreign banks have been allowed to conduct business in foreign exchange trading.

Evolution of Exchange Rate Policies

Between 1949 and 1952, foreign exchange instability prevailed. This was the period of rebuilding the domestic economy, and the private sector was still the driving force, including for foreign trade. The Government adopted a fixed exchange rate policy, based largely on the US dollar. Although it tried to maintain a fixed exchange rate system, the yuan/US dollar exchange rate was adjusted frequently and substantially.

However, from 1953 to 1970, the yuan/US dollar rate remained unchanged at 2.46 yuan per dollar. There were two reasons for this. First, the domestic economy was dominated by SOEs while the state-owned FTCs conducted all foreign trade. The economy was centrally planned. As one of the elements in this planned economy, the exchange rate was also fixed. Second, the Bretton Woods system adopted in 1947 by many Western countries used a fixed exchange rate system, with a peg to the dollar. The system ended in 1971 with the US's withdrawal from it.

From 1971 to 1980, as the major foreign currencies fluctuated, the yuan exchange rates were frequently adjusted under a fixed exchange rate system based on an adjustable basket of foreign currencies. However, the yuan was always overvalued. Between 1981 and 1984, to encourage exports and increase foreign exchange earnings, the Government adopted the "two-tier" system, and lowered its exchange rate for imports and exports. This rate, the "foreign trade exchange rate," was kept at 2.80 yuan to the dollar. However, the "basket currency" fixed exchange rate still remained, but only for non-foreign trade transactions, such as yuan purchases by foreign tourists or investors and foreign currency sales by PRC citizens going abroad. This was 1.45 yuan per dollar in July 1980 and 2.30 yuan per dollar in July 1984.

The "dual-track" system was applied from 1985 to 1993, and the Government used the foreign trade exchange rate as the sole exchange rate. However, after a while the fixed level (2.80 yuan per dollar) no longer reflected true supply and demand pressures, because of rising average export costs and increases in domestic prices. The yuan was then devalued by 24.5 percent to 3.70 yuan per dollar on 15 August 1986, and at various times thereafter to more reasonable levels. An important aspect of the exchange rate policy was the coexistence of the official exchange rate and the (sanctioned) swap market rate. In 1986, the Government established many foreign exchange markets and adjustment centers, where supply and demand largely determined exchange rates. Initially, the official rate differed substantially from the swap market rate but then closed up, reflecting market pressures to a greater extent.

On 1 December 1996, the PRC announced that it had removed all restrictions on payments or transfers for current account transactions and had formally eliminated discriminatory currency arrangements and multiple currency practices. This means that the PRC has achieved yuan convertibility on the current account, but not the capital account. Full convertibility may take several years (see Sylvester 1997).

Several administrative restrictions remain. For example, an FIE can open only one settlement account for trade-related receipts and payments. There is also a ceiling on the amount of foreign exchange an FIE may hold, according to its registered capital and trade volume. Excess foreign exchange must be sold to designated banks. In addition, to open a foreign exchange bank account, an FIE must obtain a certificate from the Government, and to continue using the account, it must undergo an annual inspection that focuses on whether the firm has paid its capital contribution on schedule, registered all its bank accounts, and fulfilled its contracted export commitments. (The last target, however, is not taken seriously any more.)

Nominal and Real Effective Exchange Rates

The yuan/US dollar exchange rate used above is only one exchange rate among many. Since the dollar has also appreciated and depreciated in the 1980s and 1990s, the changes in this rate alone do not give the full information needed. Thus this section discusses the yuan's effective exchange rate, based on the currencies of the PRC's major trading partners, i.e., Germany, Japan, Singapore, United Kingdom, and US. Accordingly, the PRC's exports to these countries are used as weights to calculate the average export exchange rate, i.e., the nominal effective exchange rate (NEER) of exports and the real effective exchange rate (REER) of exports; the PRC's imports from these countries are used to compute the average import exchange rate, i.e., the NEER of imports and the REER of imports.

Although Hong Kong, China is also one of the PRC's largest trading partners, it is excluded for three reasons. First, much trade between the PRC and Hong Kong, China comprises reexports, i.e., Hong Kong, China provides the import and export services for the PRC and the rest of the world. The share of reexports in Hong Kong, China's total export trade has been rising since the late 1970s. The share of reexports has been higher than 80 percent of Hong Kong, China's total trade since 1994. Imports and exports between the PRC and third countries via Hong Kong, China are affected by many factors, including the yuan exchange rate against that country's currency and against the Hong Kong dollar. But the effect of the yuan/Hong Kong dollar exchange rate on these reexports should be much less than that of the yuan exchange rate against the third country's currency.

Second, even though the yuan/Hong Kong dollar exchange rate has only a small effect on reexports, its effect on the PRC's exports to Hong Kong, China that are actually consumed there and on the PRC's imports of Hong Kong, China's domestically made products should be considerable. That is to say, the yuan/Hong Kong dollar exchange rate should not be omitted from the construction of the effective exchange rates. However, available data do not permit their disaggregation. There are many commodities that Hong Kong, China imports from the PRC, consumes, and reexports. But statistics show only how much it imports and reexports, but not how much it consumes. It might be thought that total imports minus reexports would be equal to local consumption of imports. This would be true if the data were reported on volume, but not if the data were reported on value, which is the case. The value-added is the difference.

Last, the Hong Kong dollar has been pegged to the US dollar since 1983. Therefore, the changes of the yuan against the Hong Kong dollar and the US dollar have been in line since that date.

When calculating the PRC's trade with another country, both the direct trade between the two countries and their indirect trade—through Hong Kong, China—are included. The formula used for the PRC's effective exchange rate is

$$NEER = \Pi E_i^{wi}$$

where

Π = product of all the variables to its right

E_i = yuan exchange rate to country *i* (i.e., the units of country i's currency per 100 yuan)

w_i = share of the PRC's exports to (or imports from) country *i* in the PRC's total exports to (or imports from) all the countries used in the calculation.

To compute for the real effective exchange rate, we use

$$REER = NEER\ (P/P^A)$$

where

P = PRC's GDP deflator

P^A = average of all other countries' GDP deflators.

The results of the NEER and REER estimation for both exports and imports, using the above formula, are shown in Tables 5.2 and 5.3.

In terms of the *effective exchange rates of exports,* the following may be noted.

(i) Both the NEER and REER are greater than 100 units of foreign currency per 100 yuan for some periods. This is because of the small value of the Japanese yen. For example, the nominal exchange rates of each 100 yuan in 1995 are \$11.97, S\$16.97, £7.60, DM17.14, and ¥1,120.76.

(ii) Because the PRC had higher inflation than the average inflation of the other five countries in this period, the REER decreased more slowly than the NEER (comparing the NEER index and the REER index).

(iii) Both the NEER and REER decreased continually except in 1987 and 1995. This suggests that the yuan has depreciated not only against the dollar, as mentioned above, but also against the basket of foreign currencies.

(iv) By comparing the NEER index with the nominal dollar exchange rate index, we find that the yuan/US dollar exchange rate decreased more slowly than the NEER of exports. That is, the yuan depreciated

Table 5.2 Effective Exchange Rates of Exports, 1986–1995

Year	NEER		REER		Nominal $ Exchange Rate	
	Per 100 yuan	Index	Per 100 yuan	Index	Per 100 yuan	Index
1986	200.99	100.00	200.99	100.00	28.96	100.00
1987	212.02	105.49	217.64	108.29	26.87	92.75
1988	194.12	96.58	216.20	107.57	26.87	92.72
1989	156.49	77.86	181.95	90.53	26.55	91.65
1990	103.49	51.49	121.74	60.57	20.91	72.18
1991	86.04	42.81	103.79	51.64	18.79	64.86
1992	73.85	36.72	93.14	46.34	18.13	62.58
1993	64.60	32.14	90.56	45.06	17.36	59.92
1994	46.99	23.38	76.93	38.28	11.60	40.14
1995	53.36	26.55	96.94	48.23	11.97	41.32

Sources: General Administration of Customs of the PRC (GAC) (various years); State Statistical Bureau (various years); Editorial Board (various years); Census and Statistics Department of Hong Kong (CSD), *Hong Kong Review of Overseas Trade;* CSD, Annual *Review of Hong Kong External Trade;* and IMF (1998).

Table 5.3 Effective Exchange Rates of Imports, 1986–1995

Year	NEER		REER		Nominal $ Exchange Rate	
	Per 100 yuan	Index	Per 100 yuan	Index	Per 100 yuan	Index
1986	612.37	100.00	612.37	100.00	28.96	100.00
1987	403.25	65.85	413.95	67.60	26.87	92.75
1988	331.56	54.14	269.27	60.30	26.87	92.72
1989	276.20	45.10	321.14	52.44	26.55	91.65
1990	190.03	31.03	223.56	36.51	20.91	72.18
1991	205.43	33.55	247.81	40.47	18.79	64.86
1992	233.41	38.12	294.39	48.07	18.13	62.58
1993	247.76	40.46	347.32	56.71	17.36	59.92
1994	149.91	24.48	245.42	40.08	11.60	40.14
1995	129.25	21.11	234.83	38.35	11.97	41.32

Sources: As Table 5.2.

more against the basket of foreign currencies than against the US dollar. There are two factors in this. First, the US dollar has also depreciated against other major currencies during this period. Second, the relative importance of the PRC's exports to the US among the PRC's exports to the five countries has increased. In this case, devaluation has not played a critical role in affecting the PRC's export structure. If it had, then we should have observed that the PRC's exports would have shifted more toward other countries from the US, since the yuan has depreciated more against these countries' currencies than the US dollar.

In terms of the effective exchange rates of imports, all the observations on the effective exchange rate of exports and the explanations given apply. Thus, what remains to be discussed is a comparison of them.

(i) The NEER of imports was greater than the NEER of exports, and the REER of imports was greater than the REER of exports. First, this is because of the small weighting of the yen in the currency basket. Second, the PRC imported more from Japan, and exported less to Japan, than the other four countries.
(ii) The NEER of imports decreased faster than the NEER of exports, especially before 1992. The same result holds for the REER of imports and of exports. That is, the yuan's depreciation against its major trading partners was greater for imports than for exports. As pointed out above, the yuan depreciated against the US dollar less than against the other currencies. On the other hand, the PRC exported more to and imported less from the US, in comparison with the other countries. Again, the export and import structure and the relative movement of the US dollar against the other currencies help explain this result.

Export Policies

Since 1979, the Government has recognized the importance of exports to its economic growth. New policies have been introduced and then modified to promote exports. The four most important aspects of the export promotion program in the PRC are discussed in the following sections.

Decentralization of Foreign Trade Management

The most significant feature of the pre-1979 foreign trade management system in the PRC was that only FTCs were allowed to trade directly with foreigners. That is, final users of imported goods received the goods from the domestic allocation system, and the producers of exported products sold their products to the FTCs for exports. However, even the FTCs did not have the freedom to make their trade decisions. Foreign trade was conducted in accordance with the state economic plan so as to keep the PRC economy in balance. Moreover, FTCs had to surrender all foreign exchange earnings from exports to the central bank, and they were not responsible for profits and losses.

Consequently, there was hardly any incentive to engage in foreign trade, and so export growth was retarded. This led to the following problems. First, domestic producers were cut off from foreign consumers of their products. This made it difficult to improve product quality and design and to compete in the international market. Second, since neither the FTCs nor the producers were responsible for profits and losses, the FTCs lacked the incentive to improve their trading services, while the producers were neither motivated to improve the quality of their products nor reduce their production costs. Third, such a structure enlarged the organization required to manage the PRC's foreign trade, creating many bureaucratic layers and, therefore, problems.

The above drawbacks of the centralized foreign trade system were clearly recognized by the Government at the beginning of the reform period. If the centralized structure was too rigid and inefficient before 1979 when trade was only a means to balance the country's planned domestic production and consumption, and when trade volumes were still relatively small, the problem was bound to become more serious after 1979 when other parts of the economy were reformed and international trade grew. Hence decentralization became the most crucial element of foreign trade reform. The Government devolved foreign trade decision making to lower administrative and enterprise levels. First, in addition to MOFTEC, other ministries were encouraged to set up their own FTCs to export the products from their respective industries directly. The advantage of this shift was that the trading corporations generally had more knowledge about their export products and about the international markets for such products than the more generalist FTCs.

Second, an increasing number of provinces, autonomous regions, and municipalities were granted the authority to organize trading companies to export their own areas' products. Unlike the branches of the national specialized FTCs, these trading companies had more autonomy in their export decision making since they did not have headquarters in Beijing. By 1985, all of the 29 provinces, autonomous regions, and provincial-level municipalities had the right to export their areas' products.

Third, although the national specialized FTCs still maintained their local branches, they became less and less dependent on their headquarters. Fourth, and perhaps more important for the future, highly productive enterprises selected by the Government were granted the right to export their products directly, and no longer through FTCs or other foreign trade enterprises. Among the first of these enterprises were the iron and steel manufacturers in Wuhan, Anshan, and Beijing. By 1991, 600 large enterprises had received such permission, the number increasing to 1,360 by 1993. More recently, some large township and village enterprises (TVEs) have also been granted direct trading rights. (FIEs have always had this right to trade their own products directly.)

As a result of decentralization, by 1994 the number of active, direct exporters stood at 58,500 and the number of importers 107,500 (Zhao 1996). Exports by the national and regional FTCs still accounted for over 50 percent of the PRC's exports and those by SOEs for almost 20 percent. In contrast, collective enterprises' exports accounted for less than 1 percent of total exports; there was almost no export activity by domestic private enterprises. FIEs accounted for 28.6 percent of exports, higher than SOEs. (The impact of FDI is analyzed below.)

In the mid-1990s, there was one notable difference between the FTCs' exports and imports (Zhao 1996). The national FTCs conducted more imports than the regional FTCs, but the regional FTCs made more export transactions than the national FTCs. This was because of the fact that the export—but not import—regime had been significantly liberalized.

In September 1984, the Government launched a comprehensive reform of the trade structure. MOFTEC lost its direct managerial authority over the national specialized FTCs, keeping control only over general trade policy making and world market research. The

FTCs performed the actual business of foreign trade and were responsible for their own profit and loss. In addition, the State no longer imposed any mandatory plan for the procurement of exported goods except for a small number of strategic products. In some products, the mandatory plans were replaced by guidance plans. Three years later, the Government instigated the agency system. Under this system, producers and end users take an active role and it is they who initiate trading. When people want to import products, they ask an FTC to find the products on the world market and import them, and pay for the imports at the actual price. In return, the FTC receives a commission, normally 1–2 percent of the import value, from them. Similarly, in the case of exports, producers set the price range for their export products and ask an FTC to sell the products for them. The FTC receives commission (3 percent) from the producers for this. However, because import and export contracts with foreigners can be signed only by FTCs, and thus in case of default by any party, the FTCs have to bear the cost, the benefits (commission) and the risks (default) are misaligned. Originally, commission trades were fairly important as many importers and exporters had little information and experience in the international market. But as they have gained more market information and experience, they have come to rely less on FTCs, and commission trades are declining: the share of commission trades in total exports in 1990 was 7.2 percent and in 1994 1.4 percent.

As a result of decentralization of foreign trade management, there are now many provincial and municipal trading corporations providing import and export services for their areas. There are also many ministerial trading firms authorized to export the products made by their industries. The immediate benefit of decentralization has been that it has reduced the monopoly power of FTCs.

Special Economic Zones and Open Coastal Cities

In the late 1970s, the Government created four special economic zones (SEZs): Shenzhen, Zhuhai, Shantou, and Xiamen, along the coastal area of southern China. Later in 1988, Hainan Island became a province and an SEZ. The main purpose for their establishment was to use them as windows and experimental locations through which foreign businesses and investors could learn about the PRC, while the PRC could learn how to develop a market system and open up its economy. The success of the SEZs later led to the formation of 14 open coastal cities along the PRC's eastern and southern coasts.

The SEZs are subject to more favorable policies than the rest of the country. Tax incentives are their major attraction. For example, while the corporate income tax rate for the country is more than 30 percent, enterprises in SEZs are required to pay only 15 percent. In addition, for certain enterprises, tax is not payable for the first two profitable years and, in the following three years, only half of the 15 percent is paid. (This is known as the "two-plus-three" policy.) Regarding imports and exports, the incentive comes in the form of duty-free imported materials used for producing export goods and a duty reduction for goods imported and sold within SEZs.

While the SEZs are successful in many aspects, the focus here is on their trade performance and impact. From 1987 to 1995, the average annual growth rate of exports by SEZs was 44.7 percent, compared with 18.2 percent for the whole country (SSB 1995). Their shares of total exports rose from under 7 percent in 1987 to over 20 percent in 1993. This is spectacular as the population of all these SEZs together is less than 1 percent of the country's total population.

However, their relative export performance has been declining in recent years: export growth was 28.9 percent in 1994 and 12.0 percent in 1995, compared with 31.9 percent and 22.9 percent, respectively, for the entire country. The share of SEZs' exports in the country's total exports declined to 21.8 percent in 1994 and to 19.9 percent in 1995 from its high of 22.3 percent in 1993. This trend is explained by the facts that the policy differences between the SEZs and the rest of the economy have been reduced in recent years, and that the 14 open coastal cities have achieved high growth in their exports.

Shenzhen is the leading SEZ in terms of exports. Its export share of 4 percent in the late 1980s rose to over 15 percent in 1993 (though down to under 14 percent in 1995), nearly six times that of Xiamen, the second largest SEZ for exports.

New Forms of Trade

As a result of foreign trade decentralization and overall reform of foreign trade, several new patterns of trade emerged, and made a significant contribution to total trade. First was the export of processed goods based on imported materials: domestic producers imported materials, processed them, and exported the semifinished or finished products. Processing equipment was frequently imported because it was high-technology equipment that contributed to improved productivity and high value-added. By the early 1980s, this pattern of producing exportable products had become fairly common and accounted for approximately 30 percent of total export earnings. Among its benefits were that it provided both machinery and equipment, and raw materials, for producing world-class exportable products. In addition, it made it easier to compete in the international market. Under this method, exporters were exempt from import duties on raw materials and equipment, from VAT, and from export duties.

The second new mode involved exports based on supplied inputs. This mode was similar to the first except that materials were not imported by domestic producers but supplied by foreign contractors or buyers. They supplied raw materials for processing, blueprints and samples for production, and parts and components (and sometimes equipment). The exporter only had to provide the local skilled and unskilled labor and produce goods to the specifications of the contractor or buyer. In return, the exporting firm was paid the wages of the labor and commissions on the volume or value of the exported goods. This mode of exports had several advantages. First, the domestic producers did not have to invest their own capital. Second, they learned to produce technologically advanced products and move up the technology ladder. Third, it enabled domestic producers to use their international partners' marketing networks.

Current Export Policies

The main features of current export policies in the PRC are as follows (see Liu et al. 1993). From 1983, the Government has implemented a system of export tax rebates, including those for product tax, sales tax, and VAT. Retained foreign exchanges by enterprises can be used freely and are allowed to be sold in the foreign exchange markets or to designated banks. To a limited extent since 1984, but more so since 1988, all regions (provinces, autonomous regions, and municipalities) and national specialized FTCs have been able to meet targets for foreign exchange earnings from exports, submit these targeted earnings to the State, and keep most of any excess earnings. Also from 1984, the administration of most branches of the specialized FTCs was shifted to local governments. By the end of 1995, the number of controlled products under the export plans, quotas, and licenses had been reduced significantly, so that the number of goods subject to export licensing was 114 (Li 1997).

Export planning was, in principle, eliminated in 1991. Instead, export licenses and quotas have become the main tools for export management. According to the Government, two categories of export products are subject to export quota restrictions. The first consists of products that are subject to bilaterally negotiated quantitative restrictions. The main items are products under the Multifiber Arrangement (MFA). Other examples include products subject to bilateral quantitative restrictions and therefore to quotas and licenses. For example, in February 1994, the European Union (EU) unilaterally decided to impose quantitative restrictions on seven categories of products, including bicycles, medical equipment, toys, and footwear.

The product items in the second category are those of which the PRC is a major supplier and can exploit market power. Agricultural exports such as beef, pork, and vegetables to Hong Kong, China belong to this category. This category also includes products for which domestic prices are set artificially below international prices to ensure an "orderly" domestic market. To avoid too great an outflow of these products, prompted by higher international prices, they are subject to quotas and licenses. Some large-scale traditional commodities such as edible oil, food, industrial raw materials, petroleum, and petroleum products fall into this category. The number of product items in this category has been gradually reduced—from 258 to 138 in January 1993—as part of the PRC's effort to join WTO. Further reductions are anticipated in the future.

Foreign Capital Inflows

FDI has played a significant role in the PRC's economic growth and export expansion. According to official statistics, the accumulated value of realized FDI up to the end of 1995 reached $133.16 billion and exceeded $200 billion by the end of 1997. In 1995, foreign investment accounted for 15.8 percent of the PRC's total fixed investment. This percentage, though remarkable, is an understatement of the importance of FDI, which not only brings much needed capital but also superior technology to the country. Moreover, FDI brings in management skills, business organization systems, and marketing channels that are completely new to domestic enterprises. Although FDI in the PRC has been increasing since 1979, the growth path is by no means smooth. Because of shifts in government policies, there have been fluctuations. The last two decades can be divided into four periods.

1978–1985. Before 1979, the PRC allowed virtually no FDI. The opening up of the economy in 1978 started to attract large amounts of foreign capital. The Government promulgated a joint venture law to provide guidelines for foreign investment in the PRC. Thus, starting from nothing, average annual growth of FDI was very high. In 1983–1985, the average annual rates were 88.4 percent for contracted FDI and 64.9 percent for realized FDI. Cumulative contracted FDI reached $14.9 billion in 1985 and cumulative realized FDI $4.7 billion. However, many restrictions on foreign investment remained, while many foreign investors remained lacking in confidence about the investment environment.

1986–1988. Because of the lack of experience in business cooperation between PRC firms and foreign investors, the latter encountered many restrictions on investment and other difficulties. Contracted FDI dropped in 1986 and realized FDI grew by only 13.1 percent. This, together with complaints from foreign investors, alarmed the Government. Consequently, it issued 22 new regulations in 1986 to provide more incentives for FDI and encourage foreign investment. As a result, FDI quickly picked up and the average annual growth rates in 1986–1988 were 36.8 percent for contracted FDI and 30.7 percent for realized FDI.

1989–1991. The June 1989 incident in Tiananmen Square caused great concern among many foreign investors, who became more cautious as the country's political and economic future seemed uncertain. The growth rates in 1989 slowed to only 5.7 percent for contracted FDI and to 6.2 percent for realized FDI.

1992–present. The PRC Government reiterated, in the early 1990s, its intention to continue economic reform and to welcome foreign investment. In 1992, FDI started to climb at unprecedented rates: 385.3 percent for contracted FDI and 152.1 percent for realized FDI. The average annual growth rate of realized FDI in 1992–1996 was 87 percent.

Direct and Indirect Export Effects of FDI

In terms of the direct effects, there are two major reasons behind foreign investment in the PRC. Some investors seek to enter and produce for the national market by moving production there. They normally have advantages over local competitors in their superior technologies and better managerial skills. Others, aiming at the world market, are attracted by the low-cost production factors available in the PRC, such as cheap land, labor, and natural resources. They therefore move their production base to the PRC and export most of their products. This latter type of FDI, clearly, contributes to the PRC's exports directly. Even the former type, which targets the local market, contributes directly to exports, as producers are required by law to export certain proportions of their products.

With little FDI in the mid-1980s, the share of exports from FIEs in total exports was also small, at only 0.3 percent in 1984. With higher inward flows of FDI, FIEs not only increased their exports dramatically (from $70 million in 1984 to $46.9 billion in 1995), but their share in total exports also increased rapidly to 31.5 percent in 1995. These shares are especially high in electronics, machinery, footwear, toys, travel goods, textiles, and clothing (ERC and SSB, various years; Zhou 1997).

The indirect effects of FDI on exports are much harder to calculate, partly because of the difficulty of obtaining data, and partly because, with 87 percent of FDI received since 1992, many of the long-term effects have yet to become apparent (ERC and SSB, various years). However, it would seem that FDI has not only linked production between the PRC and the rest of the world, but also facilitated trade linkages between the PRC and the world market through the transfer of capital, technology, and human resource skills, including modern business methods.

The entry of foreign firms into the PRC, either through joint ventures, affiliates, or wholly foreign-owned enterprises, has increased competition among PRC industries that were previously either dominated by a few large SOEs or many inefficient SOEs. As a result, many domestic firms have responded to the new entrants' greater efficiency and better technology through improving their own efficiency. This is particularly true in export-oriented industries, including textiles and clothing, electrical appliances, food processing, footwear, and travel goods. As their efficiency improves, they become more competitive in the world market with consequent advantages for exports.

FDI affects the economy in many other ways. To encourage FDI, the Government has stressed the improvement of the general investment infrastructure, and as a result, domestic firms have also benefited from a better business regulatory framework. In this sense, FDI has helped accelerate institutional reform and bring the economy closer to a market-oriented environment. A side-benefit of this is that the Government can let the market determine the economy's comparative advantages, reducing distortions to trade.[1]

Other Policies

Macroeconomic Policies

High inflation is typically associated with economies in transition and economies during a rapid development stage. During the last 20 years of economic reform and rapid growth, the PRC has experienced inflation, but managed to keep it under control. High domestic inflation is usually a strong disincentive to exports, as it pushes up factor prices. However, data on the PRC do not seem to bear this out: during two of the high inflation years of 1988, 1989, and 1994, exports grew rapidly (in 1988 and 1994), but not in 1989. Similarly, during the low inflation years of 1990–1992 and 1997, exports grew rapidly. In 1996, both the inflation rate and the export growth rate were low.

Labor-Intensive Exports

With a comparative advantage in labor-intensive products, such products constitute a large share of the PRC's exports. SITC 8 (miscellaneous manufactured articles) contains mainly labor-intensive products. This category has accounted for about 40 percent of total exports in recent years, rising from about 15 percent in the early 1980s. This increase reflects both the country's comparative

[1] See Zhan (1993) for more discussion on the impact of FDI on the PRC.

advantage in this sector, and the success of liberalization of foreign trade.

In many countries, long-term growth of exports of labor-intensive products has pushed up labor costs and reduced these countries' competitive advantages. As a result, labor-intensive production has frequently moved on to other low-cost countries. Consequently, as the PRC is still a low-cost producer, its labor policies will have a great impact on exports, through their effects on wage rates, labor mobility, and labor training.

Before the economic reforms, labor mobility was virtually absent. Control over the movement of workers has been gradually eased with the reforms, and private sector workers are now free to move. Without such a policy change, high export growth from Guangdong—the country's leading province in terms of exports—would not have been sustained as demand for labor—and consequently, all other things being equal, wages—would have gone up, thereby impinging on the province's export competitiveness. Labor-intensive production might have relocated to the inland and western provinces. In reality, because of the reforms, labor has been able to move from these provinces to Guangdong, not production relocating in the other direction. According to Li (1993), in 1982 only 1.5–2.0 percent of the total labor force in the Pearl River Delta had come from other areas. In 1990, the number of outside laborers working there had reached 35–40 percent of the local labor force. Because of the large inflow of labor from other areas, wage rates have been kept low. Basic wages for unskilled workers are 500–600 yuan ($60–72) per month, exclusive of other benefits. For semiskilled and skilled factory labor, wage rates are 1,000–1,600 yuan ($120–193) per month. These figures are not much higher than those in many other cities. The inference, therefore, is that labor mobility has kept the wages at par with other cities in the country. This, in the ultimate analysis, has prevented the cost of production from rising, keeping exports competitive.

Agricultural Reform and Exports from TVEs

In addition to the above policies, agricultural reform has had a significant effect on economic growth and exports. Among the first sectors to be reformed, agricultural reform was also one of the most successful. Prior to this, productivity was extremely low, with no incentives to farmers. Between 1981 and 1996, agriculture grew by 6.9 percent a year (SSB 1997). However, the most important aspect of reform has been agriculture's contribution to industrial growth, through the release of a huge labor force. Most of these laborers remained in the countryside to build TVEs, defined as any enterprise in a rural area funded by the collectively owned rural economic organization or by rural residents. Their output in 1994 was 42 percent of the nation's gross value of industrial output (SSB 1995). Their contribution to exports is equally impressive: their exports stood at $27 billion in 1993, or more than 40 percent of the total.

DETERMINANTS OF EXPORTS

Comparative Advantage

Here we use revealed comparative advantage (RCA) to examine some of the determinants of the PRC's exports. Yeats (1991) studies the PRC's comparative advantage, but with export information only up to 1987. Lui and Qiu (1997) have studied all APEC economies, using data up to 1994. Together, these studies suggest that the PRC has its greatest comparative advantage in SITC 8 (miscellaneous manufactured articles), which has mainly labor-intensive products such as clothing, footwear, travel goods, watches and clocks, toys, and office supplies. These studies also suggest a moderate comparative advantage in SITC 6 (manufactured goods classified chiefly by material), which includes material-intensive products such as processed food, wood manufactures, textiles, tin, zinc, and pottery.

Table 5.4 shows the PRC's RCA, based on the SITC 1-digit sections. The PRC has comparative advantages in SITC 0, SITC 2, SITC 3, SITC 6, and SITC 8. All of these are either resource-intensive or labor-intensive products. The comparative advantages in SITC 2 and SITC 3 have been declining over time and have disappeared in recent years. This can be at least partly explained by the price reforms in the PRC. In their early stage, the Government suppressed the prices of producer goods while liberalizing those of consumer goods. Consequently, exporting producer goods is more profitable than selling them in the domestic market. Because the prices of these goods have risen during the recent period of further reform and because of their strong

Table 5.4 RCAs, SITC 1-Digit Level, 1983–1994

Year	SITC 0	SITC 1	SITC 2	SITC 3	SITC4	SITC 5	SITC 6	SITC 7	SITC 8	SITC 9
1983	1.52	0.15	1.49	2.01	0.89	0.63	1.15	0.16	1.69	3.66
1984	1.59	0.14	1.65	2.41	0.78	0.61	1.20	0.17	1.82	2.55
1985	1.90	0.15	1.83	2.71	0.76	0.55	1.01	0.08	1.21	4.75
1986	1.91	0.17	1.85	2.06	1.54	0.59	1.14	0.09	1.37	6.50
1987	1.70	0.20	1.79	2.27	0.53	0.59	1.41	0.24	1.32	6.01
1988	1.72	0.21	1.69	2.07	0.47	0.63	1.30	0.34	1.99	1.41
1989	1.70	0.25	1.59	1.97	0.56	0.66	0.94	0.45	2.21	0.29
1990	1.60	0.24	1.31	1.75	0.00	0.66	1.24	0.43	2.18	0.66
1991	1.22	0.27	0.95	1.02	0.64	0.55	1.16	0.44	1.98	0.31
1992	1.30	0.35	0.88	1.15	0.56	0.59	1.22	0.39	2.77	0.18
1993	1.27	0.41	0.78	0.95	0.73	0.58	1.20	0.40	2.90	0.14
1994	1.18	0.35	0.88	0.85	1.11	0.57	1.31	0.43	2.87	0.10

Source: Lui and Qiu (1997).

domestic demand, growth of such exports has naturally slowed, and volumes even decreased.

A rapid increase in the RCA index of SITC 8 can be seen, including textiles and clothing—the PRC's major exports. However, exports of these products are constrained by the MFA and so it is reasonable to expect that without it, the country's comparative advantage in SITC 8 would have been even higher. According to the commitments made during the Uruguay Round, the MFA is gradually going to be dismantled. Therefore, the international environment for textiles exports is gradually going to improve.

Table 5.5 breaks the commodity group down further to the SITC 3-digit level. It reports the RCAs in 1994 for some selected commodities that have traditionally enjoyed an important place in the country's exports. As the figures indicate, the PRC has sustained a comparative advantage in numerous textile-related manufactures, some crude materials such as silk and coal briquettes, miscellaneous labor-intensive products, and several food products, as well as its usual natural resources, including tin and other nonferrous metals. One chemical product category, pyrotechnics, is also included in the top 20 RCAs.

Table 5.5. Exports and RCAs in Selected Commodities, SITC 3-Digit Level, 1994

SITC Heading	Description	Value of PRC's Exports ($ m)	Value of World Exports ($ m)	RCA
261	Silk	405	625	20.23
848	Nontextile Clothing Accessories	2,453	11,613	6.60
658	Made-up Textile Articles	2,186	108,722	6.28
842	Men's Outergarments, Textile	5,465	27,164	6.28
844	Undergarments, Textile	2,357	12,360	5.96
666	Pottery	982	5,164	5.94
831	Travel Goods, Handbags, etc.	2,365	12,437	5.94
843	Women's Outergarments, Textile	6,613	37,763	5.47
687	Tin	207	1,230	5.26
323	Briquettes, Coke	283	1,774	4.98
851	Footwear	5,707	36,801	4.84
894	Baby Carriages and Toys	5,093	32,900	4.83
056	Vegetables, Preserved, Prepared	849	5,675	4.67
899	Other Miscellaneous Manufactures	2,422	16,216	4.66
652	Cotton Fabrics, Woven	2,711	18,424	4.60
572	Explosives and Pyrotechnics	155	1,080	4.48
074	Tea and Maté	294	2,263	4.06
845	Outergarments, Knitted	3,908	31,470	3.88
689	Nonferrous Base Metals	271	2,313	3.65
671	Pig Iron, etc.	758	6,627	3.57
044	Barley, Unmilled	944	8,334	3.54
846	Undergarments, Knitted	2,332	20,728	3.51
847	Textile Clothing Accessories	665	5,973	3.48
522	Inorganic Chemicals	1,349	12,240	3.44
075	Spices	154	1,630	2.95
612	Manufactures of Leather	445	4,741	2.93
885	Watches and Clocks	1,742	19,110	2.85
613	Fur Skins, Tanned, Dressed	101	1,114	2.82
042	Rice	515	5,780	2.78
655	Fabrics, Knitted	745	8,411	2.77
659	Floor Coverings	762	9,009	2.64
653	Synthetic Fabrics, Woven	2,148	28,529	2.35
651	Textile Yarn	1,778	27,699	2.00
771	Electric Power Machinery	1,087	17,041	1.99
264	Jute	4	73	1.85
661	Cement and Fabr. Const. Materials	533	9,139	1.82
222	Oil Seeds, etc.	666	11,636	1.79
246	Pulpwood	83	1,504	1.73
775	Household-type Equipment	1,566	28,260	1.73
014	Meat, Prepared, Preserved, etc.	268	4,975	1.68
656	Tulle, Lace, etc.	181	3,369	1.68
111	Nonalcoholic Beverages	202	3,922	1.61
001	Live Animals Chiefly for Food	445	8,736	1.59
322	Coal	771	15,494	1.55
895	Office Supplies	243	5,630	1.35
034	Fish, Fresh, Chilled, Frozen	661	15,912	1.30
061	Sugar and Honey	403	10,143	1.24
335	Residual Petroleum Products	175	5,051	1.08

Source: Author's calculations based on United Nations (UN) (1994).

Township-Village Enterprises

TVEs produce goods in which the PRC enjoys a comparative advantage. Their exports, as mentioned above, account for more than 30 percent of the country's total exports. Consequently, their export behavior can shed some light on the understanding of the country's exports generally. Wu and Cheng (1998), in a study on what determines export incentives, use cross-regional data on TVEs. They regress TVEs' export intensity, i.e., the ratio of exports to total output of each TVE, over a number of factors. They find that the TVEs' export intensity is negatively related to unit labor cost, indicating that their products are mainly labor intensive. Moreover, FDI is an important factor, contributing positively to the TVEs' export performance. Finally, the Government's financial support to TVEs, though limited, appears to have enhanced their export performance.

Exchange Rate Variations

In the PRC, the effectiveness of devaluation on export expansion was very limited in the early reform period, but became more effective later. This was because, in the 1980s, a large percentage of trade in the PRC still followed government plans, and due to the lack of an incentive system, devaluation did not provide a strong enough motive for export activity. In fact, Wu and Cheng (1998) find that the impact of level and changes of the exchange rate on the export intensity (for TVEs) across regions in the PRC is, if anything, moderate. This is supported by other studies that use total export data, rather than TVE export data only. Both Qiu (1998) and Zhang (forthcoming) show that the changes in exchange rates in the PRC did not lead to corresponding changes of imports and exports.

Since 1992, when the profit-loss self-responsibility system was adopted by FTCs, they have been increasingly motivated by profit. In addition, the profit motive has generated a higher percentage of exports from large manufacturing enterprises and FIEs. It is expected that once the economy has opened further to the world market and the domestic market has been reformed more completely, the impact of any currency depreciation on trade will be greater than in the past.

RECENT EXPORT DECELERATION

The export growth rate for the whole of 1996 compared with 1995 was only 1.5 percent (Table 5.1). Export growth was negative in every month from January to June of 1996 compared with the same periods of 1995. The growth rates were -8.7 percent for the first quarter of 1996 and -7.9 percent for the second. Exports began to register positive growth in July and remained positive to the end of the year. The growth rates for the third and fourth quarters of 1996 compared with the same periods of 1995 were 7.4 percent and 12.9 percent.[2] The questions at issue are: What caused the PRC's negative export growth in the first six months in 1996? How was the PRC able to reverse the declining trend in the second half of the year?

Three policy changes would seem to have been mainly responsible for the export growth slide in the first half of 1996. The first is the rebate of VAT for exporters, which was lowered considerably twice, in July 1995 and January 1996. As discussed earlier, the rebate policy was first introduced in 1983 for a number of products and by the end of the 1980s it covered all export products. It has been used by the Government to encourage exports because it acts exactly like an export subsidy. Generally, the tax rates are 13 percent for agricultural products and 17 percent for industrial products. Before July 1995, exporters received a full refund. Thus, it was equivalent to export subsidies of 13 percent and 17 percent, respectively. While it was an effective policy in stimulating exports, it created some other problems, which had led the Government to modify it twice since 1995. The main problem was that many people provided false export invoices and VAT invoices to obtain money when they in fact did not export any products or did not pay any VAT. The system of taxation collection was partly responsible for this type of misconduct, because the local governments collected the VAT and later submitted it to the central government, the latter providing the money to finance the VAT rebates. Thus, the system did not provide adequate incentives for local governments, which were acting on behalf of the central government, to check carefully before rebating. It has been reported that this had resulted in a huge financial loss to the central

---

[2] Calculated from data in *International Financial Statistics Yearbook* (various years), IMF.

government, although the exact figure was never released and is difficult to estimate. A natural response by the central government was to change the policy. From July 1995 to the end of the year, the rebate rates were reduced to 10 percent for agricultural goods and 14 percent for industrial goods. In January 1996, the rebate rates were further lowered to 6 percent and 9 percent, respectively. In addition, the rebate procedure was considerably slowed. This administrative impediment, together with the cutback in tax rebate (or export subsidy), militated against the country's exports.

The second policy change concerned the duty exemption for imports of machinery and equipment by FIEs and processing enterprises. Before 1996, both these types of enterprise were exempted from tariffs on imports of machinery and equipment for their own production purposes. The new policy adopted in early 1996 eliminated this privilege. This measure is one of the government policy changes under the Ninth Five-Year Plan (1996–2000) and is an important component of the "national treatment" policy aimed at gradually unifying the tax policies on FIEs and domestic enterprises and creating a level playing field for them. The changes of the VAT rebate policy had a direct and negative effect on exports. The indirect negative effect was potentially large as in 1995 FIEs accounted for almost one third of the country's exports, while the processing trade amounted to 47 percent of the nation's total foreign trade volume. Of the companies responding to a survey conducted by the Hong Kong Trade Development Council (HKTDC) in 1997, 38.1 percent considered the negative impact on their investment in the PRC to be "serious" and 33 percent "moderate." Once their investments have been affected, exports by their enterprises established in the PRC will, of course, also be affected. The negative effect of this policy change on exports from processing trade is dramatic and quick.

The third policy that adversely affected export growth was the introduction of the "duty security account" at the end of 1995 for the processing trade. Processed exports, based on imported raw materials, account for almost half the PRC's exports. Initially, the imported or supplied raw materials for this type of export were free from tariffs. However, some industries and exporters abused this privilege. They avoided paying duties on the pretext that the final products from their imported raw materials would be exported. Sometimes they succeeded in proving this with false documents. Consequently, the Government introduced duty security accounts at designated banks, and all importers of raw materials had to pay duty into these accounts. However, once the output of the imported raw materials was exported, the duty was reimbursed to the exporter by the bank. This was found to be cumbersome by the exporters because reimbursements were made after bureaucratic foot-dragging. It increased their transactions costs, adversely affecting exports. The same survey by the HKTDC indicates that the duty security system has had quite a strong and negative impact on investment in the PRC and related exports: 35.5 percent of the companies in the survey considered the impact to be "serious" and 40.6 percent "moderate."

However, this negative scenario did not last long. The export slide in the first half of 1996 was reversed and the PRC sustained firm growth in the latter half of the year. There were several factors contributing to this. First, local governments, fearful of losing FDI and exports, tweaked the new regulations that were detrimental to exports. For instance, in Guangdong Province, FIEs were released from paying duty on their imports of machinery and equipment. All they were required to do was "register and go," i.e., instead of paying tariff duties, simply register the imports with customs. If the central government insists on implementing the new policy, the FIEs will be asked to pay the duties accordingly. Also, to minimize the costs incurred from the duty security account system, importers of raw materials for processing exports were only required to deposit a symbolic amount in the account, rather than the full amount.

Second—and more important—the Government made a policy adjustment to combat the export slide. According to Zhou (1998), four new measures adopted in 1996 helped stop the export drop. The first was the speeding up of the export tax rebate process. As a result, VAT rebates for exports rose 50.5 percent in 1996 compared with 1995, reaching $9.9 billion (*China Economic Review*, June 1997). The other measures are related: enlarging the export credit scale, increasing trade-related finance, and fostering the export of machinery and electronic products through more export credits. The macroeconomic austerity policy introduced in late 1993 and early 1994 to combat inflation and economic overheating at that time severely limited credits for almost all investments and foreign trade business. While the country continued to adopt a tight fiscal and monetary policy in 1996, the Government relaxed credit control and lending to enterprises producing exports. This had a positive impact on exports. Moreover, the Government phased in an insurance system for export credit risk and strengthened the links between economic cooperation and foreign trade by granting foreign trading rights to more companies engaged in foreign economic cooperation. It is extremely likely that these policies, to different degrees, helped boost export growth in the second half of 1996.

As the above policy changes are unique to the PRC, they explain not only the reversal of the export slide in early 1996, but also perhaps the strong and steady export growth in the second half of 1996 and later in 1997, compared with the weak export performance of many other countries in the region. In addition, the PRC began to adopt a market diversification strategy in 1996. It held three large-scale export fairs in key new markets such as Africa and Latin America. As a result, the share of the country's trade in 1996 with its four largest traditional trade partners, i.e., Japan; US; Hong Kong, China; and EU, dropped from 1995's 67.2 percent to 63.2 percent, a reduction of 4 percentage points. In contrast, trade with the Russian Federation increased by 24.5 percent in 1996 compared with 1995.

As seen in Table 5.1, exports picked up in 1997, growing by 20.9 percent. Thus, unlike some other Asian economies, there is no trend of an export slowdown in the PRC. According to IMF (1998), the PRC's exports during the first three quarters of 1997 were \$129.1 billion, having grown by 24.1 percent compared with the same period of 1996 (\$104.0 billion). The growth rates of the first three quarters were 26 percent, 26.7 percent, and 20.5 percent, respectively. During the last quarter of 1997, the Asian financial crisis started to affect the PRC's exports, and export growth slowed to 13.6 percent compared with the same period in 1996.

Thus viewed, the government policy changes in 1995 were mainly responsible for the export slowdown during the first half of 1996, and the policy reversals in 1996 not only stopped the export slide but also stimulated export growth. Were the policies so effective? It has been noted above that trade policy reforms and export incentives contributed a great deal to export expansion in the PRC. Therefore, it is not difficult to comprehend that policy reversals can and did affect export performance significantly in a negative manner. The policies that had caused export deceleration were identified and corrected without delay. Consequently, the 1996 export deceleration in the PRC was a temporary phenomenon.

The Impact of tbe Asian Financial Crisis

Although the crisis broke out in July 1997, it did not have an immediate effect over the PRC export performance. The PRC reported export growth of 21 percent for 1997; of this, exports to Asian economies grew by 22.7 percent. Thus, the immediate impact of the crisis over export performance was nil. This is not to imply that there will be no lagged effect either; if anything, it is expected to be strong. MOFTEC warned that in 1998 exports will grow by less than half (8 percent) the 1997 rate. This forecast is not pessimistic as the PRC will find it hard to maintain a robust export growth rate in a regional environment of financial turbulence. During 1998, PRC export growth was 12.6 percent and 2.5 percent in the first and second quarters, respectively. Although intra-Asian exports had risen by 16.6 percent during the first quarter of 1998, qualitative evidence of a contraction existed after that. The contraction was caused by the competition effect and the demand effect. Since the renminbi yuan was not devalued while currencies in Indonesia, Malaysia, Philippines, and Thailand were, exports from the PRC will become less competitive in the world market. In addition, the regional economies went into a steep recession—some in contraction—in 1998, which drastically cut down on their purchasing power. Consequently, the PRC export will suffer from weak demand. In addition, the Japanese economy was also in recession. The five crisis-stricken Asian economies and Japan together accounted for 27.4 percent of the PRC exports. Therefore, weak demand effect may be large (WTO 1998).

To minimize the negative effect of the Asian crisis, MOFTEC has adopted some practical policy measures. Three measures were announced in April 1998. First, it removed export quotas and licensing administration on 27 commodities. Second, the quota allocations have been rearranged in favor of enterprises of high competence. Third, it has accelerated the grant of import and export operational right to qualified manufacturers. Some other amendments have been made. For instance, tax breaks on imports of capital goods by FIEs have been resumed and the value-added tax rebates for exporters were increased since June 1998. The tax rebates will be particularly beneficial to exporters of steel, cement, and ships. Guangdong Province, which accounts for more than 40 percent of the PRC's total exports, has taken even bolder policy initiatives. Among the eight key measures taken by the provincial government, the strongest one is the full corporate profit tax rebate, which is 33 percent.

FUTURE PROSPECTS

Many areas of the economy have benefited from the reforms carried out since 1979. Markets have replaced government plans and have started playing an increasingly important role in directing resources to their most productive uses. This has been the most important driving force of the PRC's export growth since 1979. Moreover, the open-door policy and the policy reforms in foreign trade have directly contributed to the rapid growth of trade. In addition, foreign exchange policy has also played an important role, through the devaluation of the yuan to more reasonable levels and its greater convertibility. On the management side, exporters are now allowed to keep their foreign exchange earnings, rather than surrender them all to the Government. All these reforms have raised incentives for exporting. However, the reforms discussed above have not been completed yet. For example, FTCs still dominate foreign trade business in the PRC; most small and medium enterprises do not have the appropriate import and export rights; the currency is not fully convertible; and major reforms in the SOEs and in finance and banking have only just started. As reforms in these areas are consolidated, the country's exports can still maintain their momentum of rapid growth.

As seen in the section on *Comparative Advantage* of this chapter, the PRC used to have comparative advantages in SITC 2 (crude materials) and SITC 3 (mineral fuels), but these comparative advantages have been lost in recent years. On the other hand, the RCA indexes of SITC 7 (machinery and transport equipment) and SITC 8 (miscellaneous manufactured articles) have shown an increasing trend during 1983–1994, especially the latter because of economic reform allowing the PRC to benefit not only from its cheap labor but also from advanced technologies.

However, the RCA indexes alone may not give adequate information on which sectors have become relatively more important to the PRC's export growth. If a product has a constant share in the country's exports, but the average world export share of that product has decreased over time, then that product's RCA increases. On the highly aggregate level, the primary sectors (SITC 0–SITC 4) are the "sunset" export industries and the manufacturing sectors (SITC 5–SITC 9) are the "sunrise" export industries. Although the export values of the primary sectors have also grown over time, their average growth rate is much lower than that of total exports. As a result, their relative contribution to exports has fallen from 50.3 percent in 1980 to only 14.5 percent in 1996, while that of the manufacturing sector has increased rapidly from 49.7 percent in 1980 to 85.5 percent in 1996.

The contributions of the leading export items from 1986 to 1995 are given in Table 5.6, ranked by 1995 figures greater than $1 billion. With the exception of crude oil, all commodities have double-digit export growth rates. If the other two materials-based products—cotton cloth and coal—are omitted, the remaining items have export growth rates higher than 20 percent a year.[3] These are the industries that not only contribute most to exports, but also show very strong growth. They are the most important "sunrise" export industries.[4] This is reinforced by two factors. First, the Government has reiterated the importance of science and technology. More and more resources have been directed to innovation and advanced technology development, while industrial and FDI policies are also in favor of high technology. Second, the PRC will surely maintain its advantage in labor-intensive manufacturing products because, in contrast to the newly industrialized economies, wage rates are unlikely to rise rapidly in the near future. This is because, though wages for skilled workers in rapidly growing coastal regions have increased, the supply of unskilled labor is almost unlimited, as it has become highly mobile, especially from "poor west" to "rich east."

Against this rosy scenario must be seen the impact of the Asian financial crisis that began in 1997. There are at least two effects the crisis may have on the PRC's exports: the competition effect and the demand effect. First, the competition effect. The devaluation of the currencies in Indonesia, Korea, Malaysia, Philippines, and Thailand will make the PRC's exports in the world market less competitive, if the yuan is not devalued or if the devaluation is too small. As a result, the country's export growth will slow. This is the most direct effect.

[3] Semifinished products of iron or steel, with data for only two years, are not statistically representative.
[4] There are of course many other sunrise export industries. However, they have been left out because they contribute less to exports than those in Table 5.6.

Table 5.6 Major Export Items, 1986–1995
($ million)

Category	1986	1987	1988	1989	1990	1991	1992	1993	1994	1995	Avg. Growth Rate (percent)
Textile Garments	2,422	3,086	3,999	5,064	5,705	7,540	14,384	15,706	20,081	19,953	28.40
Toys	152	280	393	508	574	711	2,371	2,629	3,064	3,431	51.53
Cotton Cloth	1,270	1,525	1,487	1,600	1,602	1,739	2,057	2,230	2,678	3,411	12.00
Leather Shoes		125	173	158	428	691	1,782	2,352	2,608	2,737	58.52
Crude Oil	2,392	3,141	2,557	2,750	3,402	2,957	2,774	2,409	2,000	2,236	0.71
Sound-Recording Apparatus		113	224	383	593	634	1,314	1,430	2,003	2,193	49.57
Rolled Steel		119	296	347	700	729	665	447	606	2,190	65.94
Peripheral Units of Data Processing Machines						128	268	510	866	2,019	100.52
Plastic Footwear					263	462	829	1,276	1,596	1,926	50.91
Vegetables	274	339	476	524	592	664	834	932	1,257	1,571	21.87
Parts of Data Processing Machines		171	519	699	1,019	1,448	81.66				
Garments of Leather				109	168	246	579	796	1,157	1,360	56.12
Plastic Bags and Boxes							587	679	953	1,224	28.20
Containers						202	323	267	616	1,180	66.13
Furniture	105	174	228	264	310	446	487	603	844	1,106	30.82
Semifinished Products of Iron or Steel									143	1,038	624.35
Wrist Watches				100	166	156	667	778	951	1,033	72.40
Coal	400	476	515	554	654	748	743	702	771	1,011	11.31

Sources: SSB, *China Foreign Economic Statistical Yearbook* (various years); and author's calculations.

Second, the demand effect. As the economies of most other Asian countries have already slowed, demand for the PRC's exports from them will be reduced as their purchasing power decreases. This further dampens the PRC's exports, though if Japan is excluded, the effect may be limited as the five most-affected countries (as above) together import only 8.3 percent of the PRC's exports (WTO 1998). However, including Japan, which alone absorbed 19.1 percent of the country's exports in 1995, the effect could be large, depending on how the Japanese economy moves.

As mentioned above, the Asian financial crisis is affecting the PRC's exports through reduced demand in Asia, and through increased competition in EU and the US. The figures for the first four months of 1998 (*South China Morning Post,* 12 May 1998) show that the demand effect has been large, but the competition effect has been in favor of the PRC's exports. Compared with the same period of 1997, in the first four months of 1998 the PRC's exports to Korea fell by 24.5 percent and to Japan by 3.1 percent. However, exports to the US rose by 20.6 percent and to EU by 29.7 percent. Thus, we have not seen the PRC's loss of competitiveness to other Asian countries in export markets. This is not surprising. Devaluation in those countries has pushed up the prices of imports that their exports rely on. Especially in Southeast Asia, a large percentage of exports are assembled products that depend heavily on imports of components and parts. Moreover, what has happened in those Asian economies is not only devaluation. They are experiencing currency, financial, and economic crises. Even though domestic labor and land have become cheaper in dollar terms, this does not necessarily help domestic exporters as most of them find difficulty in obtaining credit from the banking system to finance imports and production.

Evidence of an export slowdown can already be seen, and some areas of the country will be hit more than others. For example, Beijing's trade has been affected significantly because its export pattern is similar to that of exporters in the Association of Southeast Asian Nations (ASEAN), especially for electrical machinery (more than half its exports), metals, and light industrial goods. In the first 10 months of 1997 exports of electrical machinery to ASEAN countries fell by 16.5 percent to $68.75 million, while imports from them rose by 88.1 percent to $73.89 million.

According to the most recent figures from PRC Customs, in the first quarter of 1998, the PRC's total trade was $69.66 billion—$40.1

billion of exports and $29.56 billion of imports. Compared with the same period of 1997, exports grew by 2.8 percent and imports by 2.6 percent. It is expected that due to a time lag, the negative effect of other countries' currency devaluations on export growth will become more pronounced during the rest of 1998. It would seem reasonable to forecast a slowdown in export growth in 1998 to 7–10 percent.

It is still too early to distinguish the long-term effects of the crisis—and the effects of the crisis will be changed considerably if the Government devalues its currency. This is unlikely at this stage but cannot be ruled out. However, the Government has made a strong commitment to maintain high growth in exports and GDP. For example, in a bid to boost exports, it is likely to adopt practical policy measures such as optimizing export structures and further improving the export tax refund (*South China Morning Post,* 10 February 1998). Given this and the effectiveness of the PRC's export policies, and the unlikely erosion of the PRC's competitiveness in world markets, it is not unrealistic to predict moderate export growth for the PRC for the next few years.

BIBLIOGRAPHY AND REFERENCES

Balassa, Bela. 1965. "Trade Liberalization and 'Revealed' Comparative Advantage." *The Manchester School of Economic and Social Studies* (2): 99-124.

Census and Statistics Department of Hong Kong (CSD). Various issues. *Hong Kong Review of Overseas Trade.*

______. Various years. *Annual Review of Hong Kong External Trade.*

China Economic Review. 1997. "Rebates Boost Surplus." June.

Economic Research Centre (ERC) and State Statistical Bureau (SSB). Various years. *Almanac of China's Economy.* Beijing: Modern Cultural Company Ltd.

Editorial Board. Various years. *Almanac of China's Foreign Economic Relations and Trade.* Beijing: China Economics Publishing House and Hong Kong, China: Economic Information and Agency.

General Administration of Customs of the People's Republic of China (GAC). Various years. *China Customs Statistical Yearbook.*

Hong Kong Trade Development Council (HKTDC). 1997. "Building on the Present, Creating the Future: A Survey Report on Hong Kong Companies' Views on China's Changing Economic and Trade Environment under the Ninth Five-Year Plan." Hong Kong, China: HKTDC Research.

International Monetary Fund (IMF). 1996. *Balance of Payments Statistics Yearbook.* Washington, DC.

______. (IMF). 1998. *International Financial Statistics Yearbook 1998.* Washington, DC.

Lardy, Nicholas R. 1992. *Foreign Trade and Economic Reform in China 1978-1990.* New York: Cambridge University Press.

Li, Dongsheng. 1997. "Positive Results Achieved in the Reform of the Import and Export Administrative System." *Almanac of China's Foreign Economic Relations and Trade 1996/97*: 45-47. Beijing: China Economics Publishing House and Hong Kong, China: Economic Information and Agency.

Li, Ruo Jian. 1993. "The Development of Labour Power Markets in the Pearl River Delta in the Context of the Situation of Labour Power Markets in South China." *Pearl River Delta Economy* 7:8-11.

Lin, Justin Yifu, Fang Cai, and Zhou Li. 1995. *China Miracle.* Hong Kong, China: The Chinese University of Hong Kong Press.

Liu, Xiandong, et al., eds. 1993. *A Guide to China's Foreign Economic and Trade Policies.* Beijing: Economic Management Publishing Ltd. In Chinese.

Lui, Francis, and Larry D. Qiu. 1997. "Cost and Productivity Trends and Patterns of Specialization in APEC." Hong Kong Special Administrative Region Government.

Qiu, Larry D., and Changqi Wu. 1997. "Investment Strategies." Report D in *Research Reports on Doing Business in China: Current Issues,* Shui On Center for China Business and Management, School of Business and Management, Hong Kong University of Science and Technology.

Qiu, Larry D. 1998. "Comments on 'Exchange Value of the Renminbi and China's Balance of Trade: An Empirical Study.' " In T. Ito and A. O. Krueger, eds., *Changes in Exchange Rates in Rapidly Developing Countries.* National Bureau of Economic Research-East Asia Seminar on Economics, Vol. 7. Chicago: University of Chicago Press.

South China Morning Post. 1998. "Wu Slashes Trade Forecast." 10 February.

______.1998. "Regional Turmoil Retards Exports." 12 May.

State Statistical Bureau (SSB). Various years. *China Statistical Yearbook.* Beijing: China Statistical Publishing House.

______.Various years. *China Foreign Economic Statistical Yearbook.* Beijing: China Statistical Publishing House.

Sylvester, Kirsten. 1997. "On the Road to RMB Convertibility." *The China Business Review (* January-February).

United Nations (UN). *International Trade Statistics Yearbook 1994.* New York.

Wang, Hong. 1993. *China's Exports Since 1979.* New York: St. Martin's Press.

World Bank. 1994. *China: Foreign Trade Reform.* Washington, DC.

______.1997. *China 2020: China Engaged – Integration with the Global Economy.* Washington, DC.

World Trade Organization (WTO). 1998. "World Trade Growth Accelerated in 1997, Despite Turmoil in Some Asian Financial Markets." 19 March .

Wu, Changqi and Leonard Cheng. 1998. "Determinants of International Competitiveness of China's Township-Village Enterprises." Hong Kong University of Science and Technology. Mimeo.

Yeats, Alexander, J. 1991. "China's Foreign Trade and Comparative Advantage: Prospects, Problems, and Policy Implications." Discussion Paper No. 141. Washington, DC: World Bank.

Zhan, Xiaoning James. 1993. "The Role of Foreign Direct Investment in Market-Oriented Reforms and Economic Development: The Case of China." *Transnational Corporations* 2(3).

Zhang, Zhaoyong. Forthcoming. "Exchange Value of the Renminbi and China's Balance of Trade: An Empirical Study." In T. Ito and A. O. Krueger, eds., *Changes in Exchange Rates in Rapidly Developing Countries.* National Bureau of Economic Research-East Asia Seminar on Economics, Vol. 7. Chicago: University of Chicago Press.

Zhao, Haiying. 1996. "China in the New World Trading Environment after the Uruguay Round." Manila: Asian Development Bank. October. Mimeo.

Zhou, Jie. 1997. "Growth Amid Opportunities and Challenges." *Almanac of China's Foreign Economic Relations and Trade 1996/97*: 43-44.

______.1998. "Advancement and Development of China's Foreign Trade Amid Difficulties and Transformation." *Almanac of China's Foreign Economic Relations and Trade 1997/98*: 47-49.

Zhu, Guoxin, et al., eds. 1995. *Handbook of China's Foreign Trade and Foreign Economic System Reform.* Beijing: The University of International Business and Economics Press. In Chinese.

CHAPTER SIX

Case Study: Republic of Korea

Sang Kyom Kim and Inkyo Cheong

INTRODUCTION

Among the many factors contributing to the outstanding economic performance of the Republic of Korea (henceforth Korea) in recent decades, export-oriented industrialization has been one of the most influential and has received the greatest attention from economists. This export-oriented growth strategy, adopted in 1961, minimized the role of the free market and instead emphasized active government direction and support of research into, and exploitation of, new export markets. Such support has largely involved the Government's funneling of foreign capital obtained through exports to manufacturers engaged in promising new industries.

Economic growth in Korea has been driven by industrial development, which in turn has relied largely on export expansion. Although trade in goods has accounted for the majority of current account earnings since the 1970s, trade in services has also constituted an important component. As seen in Table 6.1, exports were merely $835 million in 1970. Expanding at a steep rate, they crossed the $21 billion mark in 1981 and $30 billion mark in 1985. Their 1990 level was more than double ($65 billion) the 1985 level. In 1997, Korean exports were $136 billion. Such dramatic export expansion led to deeper integration with the world economy. Between 1961 and 1997, the share of Korean exports in total world exports increased from 0.1 percent to 2.5 percent. In the late 1980s, swelling domestic demand and external calls to reduce import restrictions helped fuel a rapid structural shift of exports to capital- and technology-intensive products.

Table 6.1 Exports and Imports, 1970–1997

Year	Exports		Imports		Share of World Exports (percent)
	Amount ($ million)	Change (percent)	Amount ($ million)	Change (percent)	
1970	835	34.2	1,984	8.8	0.3
1971	1,068	27.8	2,394	20.7	0.3
1972	1,624	52.1	2,522	5.3	0.4
1973	3,225	98.6	4,240	68.1	0.6
1974	4,460	38.3	6,852	61.6	0.6
1975	5,081	13.9	7,274	6.2	0.7
1976	7,715	51.8	8,774	20.6	0.9
1977	10,047	30.2	10,811	23.2	1.0
1978	12,711	26.5	14,972	38.5	1.1
1979	15,056	18.4	20,339	35.8	1.0
1980	17,505	16.3	22,292	9.6	1.0
1981	21,254	21.4	26,131	17.2	1.1
1982	21,853	2.8	24,251	-7.2	1.2
1983	24,445	11.9	16,192	8.0	1.4
1984	29,245	19.6	30,631	16.9	1.6
1985	30,283	3.6	31,136	1.6	1.6
1986	34,715	14.6	31,584	1.4	1.7
1987	47,281	36.2	41,020	29.9	2.0
1988	60,696	28.4	51,811	26.3	2.2
1989	62,377	2.8	61,465	18.6	2.1
1990	65,016	4.2	69,844	13.6	1.9
1991	71,870	10.5	81,525	16.7	2.1
1992	76,632	6.6	81,775	0.3	2.0
1993	82,236	7.3	83,800	2.5	2.2
1994	96,013	16.8	102,348	22.1	2.3
1995	125,058	30.3	135,119	32.0	2.5
1996	129,715	3.7	150,339	11.3	2.4
1997	136,164	5.0	144,616	-3.8	2.5

Source: Korea Trade Information Service (KOTIS) database.

As a result, the importance of such sectors as textiles and iron and steel to the overall economy declined, while reliance on electrical appliances, electronics products, and transport equipment grew.

While the Korean experience was regarded by some economists as a showcase of a successful export-oriented development strategy,[1]

1 Cho and Kim (1995), for example, point out that when Korea embarked on its industrialization process in the early 1960s, it had a weak industrial base and little accumulated capital or technology. It was aid-dependent and its per capita income lagged behind many sub-Saharan countries, including Kenya and Ghana, and most Latin American countries.

the country's economic growth and industrial development demonstrate not only the possibilities, but also the limitations, of rapid export expansion policies. Despite its rapid economic growth being closely associated with export expansion, between 1961 and 1996 the country posted a chronic trade deficit, interrupted briefly by trade surpluses from 1986 to 1989. In this regard, Korea's experience, both good and bad, will provide a useful example of export-led growth to economists and policymakers in developing countries currently mapping out economic strategies.

POLICY REGIME AND EXPORTS

Overview of Trade Regime

The Korean external development strategy can be understood better if the period under review is split into five subperiods, based on the contemporary characteristics of the major government policies.

1950s: Import Substitution

When the Government of Korea was established in August 1948, the southern part of the Korean peninsula possessed all the familiar characteristics of an extremely underdeveloped economy, such as high unemployment, and budget and balance-of-payments deficits. Furthermore, the Korean War of 1950–1953 destroyed most industrial facilities and led to negative economic growth and high inflation. During postwar reconstruction, financed mainly by aid from the US and the United Nations,[2] no serious efforts were made to increase either domestic saving or export earnings. The Government's main aim was to maximize foreign aid to rebuild industry and to finance imports.

By the middle of 1957, with most of the postwar recovery tasks nearly achieved, the Government began to tackle inflation and to focus on alleviating economic imbalances that had resulted from both

[2] From 1953 to 1960, this aid totaled $1.8 billion.

inflation and trade deficits. In fact, throughout the 1950s, the Government used an import-substitution policy, characterized by trade restrictions, a repressive financial system, and an inward-looking industrial policy. Meanwhile, to control the balance of payments, the Government protected domestic industries with high tariffs and quantitative restrictions, including quotas and a strict import licensing system.

The import-substitution policy was, on the whole, unsuccessful. According to Hong (1987), import substitution induced a trade deficit followed by a deep recession. Nationwide excess capacity in the primary sector, largely caused by manufacturers churning out products in which both the domestic and export markets had little interest, caused sharp inventory accumulation. Excessive imports and unsold stocks led to increased unemployment and low capacity utilization. The Government periodically altered exchange rates under a multiple exchange rate system, but any benefits were quickly negated by inflation.[3] In 1959, per capita income and exports remained at $80 and $0.9 (in nominal terms), respectively. In the same year, the volume of trade (exports and imports) registered less than $330 million and the trade deficit stood at $290 million in nominal terms (Korea National Statistical Office, various years).

1960s: Export-Oriented Industrialization

The military Government, which assumed power in May 1961, began redirecting economic policy to outward-looking development objectives, with a drastic devaluation of the official exchange rate from 65 to 130 won to the US dollar. With the launching of the first Five-Year Economic Development Plan (1962–1966), the Government introduced a series of reform packages aimed at stimulating the development of key industries, modernizing industrial infrastructure, and building an adequate supply of infrastructure.[4] It also implemented measures to increase exports and restrict imports. However, this first phase of economic reform failed to meet its objectives, largely because

[3] Exchange rates became overvalued in real terms as a consequence of inflation throughout the 1950s. Therefore, exchange rate control was not conducive to export promotion.

[4] These early reforms included budget and tax reforms along with exchange rate controls.

it was not supported by restrictive monetary and fiscal policies. Instead, the expansionary measures geared to promote growth resulted in a sharp acceleration of inflation and an increase in import demand. These macroeconomic problems obliged policymakers to intensify their use of quotas and quantitative controls with regard to purchases of foreign exchange (Krueger 1979).

The second stage of reform started with the further devaluation of the won. In May 1964, the Government devalued it from 190 to 256 against the dollar and announced the adoption of a unitary floating exchange rate system. Other important policies were the introduction of comprehensive export promotion schemes, gradual attempts to liberalize import controls, and the encouragement of the inflow of foreign loans to fill the domestic resource gap (Nam 1990).[5] Export expansion measures included a preferential tax system, automatic credit access, and a number of subsidy programs for export-oriented industries, with administrative support by the Government. On the import side, only minor progress in the area of nontariff barriers, such as a partial replacement of quantity restrictions by tariffs and a gradual increase of importable items, was made.

As seen in Table 6.2, the export promotion strategy and other reform programs of 1964 to 1969 produced substantial results. The expansive growth of exports fueled and sustained high output growth rates during the latter part of the 1960s. Export volume grew by 15 times from $41 million in 1961 to $623 million in 1969, with an average annual GNP growth rate of 8.8 percent. At the same time, the average wholesale price index (WPI) moderated to around 8 percent. From the late 1960s, Korea sustained high export growth rates and emerged as a major competitor in an increasingly wide range of international markets.

1970s: Greater Government Control and Diversification of Industry

Following rapid growth and industrialization during the first two Five-Year Economic Development Plans (1962–1971), real wages and capital intensity increased sharply in the manufacturing sector, which

---

[5] For details on the various incentives used at the early stage of export promotion see Hong (1987), Yun-Hwan Kim (1994), and Nam (1990).

Table 6.2 Key Macroeconomic Indicators (percent)

	1954–1959	1960–1964	1965–1969	1970–1974	1975–1979	1980–1984	1985–1989	1990–1996
GNP Growth Rate	4.18	5.52	10.04	8.52	9.26	6.26	10.40	7.54
Exports/GNP	1.78	0.87	11.22	21.18	29.45	36.31	38.61	30.45
Saving/GNP	4.70	4.87	12.90	17.91	25.40	24.24	34.90	35.53
Current Account Balance/GNP	-1.61	-1.69	-4.23	6.50	-3.74	-4.61	4.27	-1.90
WPI	25.52	17.73	8.01	16.17	15.61	12.95	0.82	3.02

Note: Average of annual rates in each period.
Source: Bank of Korea, *National Income Accounts,* various years.

accounted for the majority of exports. This was a sign that the country's comparative advantage had shifted to skilled labor- and technology-intensive products, such as machinery and sophisticated electronics.

To maintain rapid economic growth, the Government enacted a series of special laws promoting the Heavy and Chemical Industries (HCI) drive. In addition to the oil shock in 1973, rising protectionism abroad against light industry imports limited export expansion. Furthermore, the emergence of other developing countries pursuing export-oriented growth strategies pushed the Government to a major industrial restructuring.

The HCI drive was vast in scope and called for massive investment over a prolonged period. The Government targeted six major industries—steel, nonferrous metals, machinery, shipbuilding, electronics, and chemicals—as future core industries. To finance them, it had to provide increasingly distorted incentive schedules facilitated through a system of preferential loans, many of which were funded by massive foreign loans. However, the HCI drive made the trade and investment regime increasingly rigid in the late 1970s, to the point where it began displaying many of the features commonly associated with import-substitution regimes.

Compared with previous economic development strategies, the HCI drive was broader in scope and yet more detailed. It included precise construction and investment schedules over a seven-year time frame. However, these industrial and trade initiatives ran into serious difficulties. The country's economic capacity in the 1970s was simply unable to absorb such massive, capital-intensive investment. Excess capacity in relatively unproductive industries was generated because of the misallocation of human and physical capital resources. The severe world recession caused by the second oil shock of 1979, combined with a tight monetary policy at home, exacerbated the problem, setting the stage for another overhaul of economic policy. The Government abandoned the HCI policy in 1979 and announced a new approach, the Comprehensive Measures for Economic Stabilization. However, despite the many economic difficulties of the HCI drive, the excess capacity in terms of human and physical capital resources it created laid the foundations for the export boom of the heavy and chemical industries that began in 1983.

1980s: Structural Adjustment and Opening of Markets

HCI-led growth produced a number of structural imbalances by the late 1970s, including relatively underdeveloped small and medium enterprise (SME) sectors and an excessively high level of protection on the domestic market. Coupled with the second oil shock, this led, by 1980, to an annual WPI increase rate of 40 percent. Furthermore, a large rise in domestic demand combined with a decline in demand in many export markets resulted in a large deficit on the current account: in 1980, this represented 8.7 percent of GNP, or 6.6 percentage points higher than in 1978.

The severity of the economic hardship and the obvious inefficiencies of such extensive government economic direction convinced economic planners that unfavorable external developments or domestic political instability were not solely to blame. The Government reacted by allowing the role of the market in the economy to expand, including a gradual reduction of government intervention in banking and in investment decision making. Concurrently, government policy made a priority of stabilizing the economy, including combating inflation, reducing the excess investment of the HCI era, and eliminating price distortions. The Government also initiated trade liberalization to increase competition in domestic markets and reduce the cost of protection.

In fact, import liberalization was the main means to increase the role of the market, as the Government hoped that increased foreign competition would improve the quality and competitiveness of local products. The Government also partially deregulated foreign investment and strengthened domestic antimonopoly regulations to eliminate market distortions caused by the increasing dominance of the conglomerates, or *chaebols.*

Industrial policy also underwent a significant overhaul. Most subsidized loans were eliminated and the Government no longer targeted areas of the economy for preferential treatment. In 1985, it passed the Industrial Development Act, which assigned to the Industrial Development Council the responsibility for restructuring and streamlining industrial policy. This council, comprising experts from all segments of the economy, advised the Government on how to streamline its role in the industry sector, foster private sector initiatives, and enhance the role of the market.

This new direction in industrial policy was reflected in the Fifth Five-Year Economic Development Plan (1982–1986). First, the industry-specific support system was replaced by functional support related to development of technology and human resources, and to energy conservation. Second, a fairer and more competitive market environment was encouraged through the removal of import restrictions and other barriers to entry. Third, the Government provided temporary support only to those industries that were essential to the national economy, but that lacked sufficient infrastructure to realize sustained growth. By the end of the plan in 1986, and with a current account surplus, the Government came under increasing pressure to open up its financial markets and further liberalize its trade regime. However, no significant efforts were made.

1990s: Globalization and Financial Crisis

In the 1990s, policymakers have favored general economic liberalization and a further opening of domestic markets through trade reform. However, the economy is again confronted by economic difficulties stemming from structural weaknesses. Labor disputes led to increased wages in the late 1980s. Moreover, inflation soared, quickly undermining the competitiveness of Korean industries.

In the late 1990s, the pace of international economic integration is accelerating. Thus, if the Government is to maintain both a strong export sector and a strong economic growth, it must further liberalize the economy. This includes complying with World Trade Organization (WTO) industrial and trade policies. For example, it has abolished the direct subsidy system for export activities (as well as some traditionally government-managed trade systems). In its place, the Government has introduced the indirect functional system for export activities. In addition, it has begun efforts to transform producer-oriented trading practices into consumer-oriented ones.

In the face of an ongoing financial and currency crisis that hit the country in November 1997, a shift toward a new blueprint for the economy seems inevitable. In a broad sense, the crisis originates from the cumulative burdens on the Korean economy—excessive borrowing by the corporate sector, inflexible labor markets preventing or slowing restructuring attempts by companies, overinvestment in some sectors, and an inefficient, heavily regulated, and protected financial sector.

A key condition of the agreement between the Government and the International Monetary Fund (IMF) of December 1997 is that restructuring of key sectors be undertaken.[6] As part of the restructuring program, a timetable will be set for the elimination of trade-related subsidies, restrictive import licensing, and a further liberalization of current import restrictions (including the lifting of restrictions on a number of Japanese products). Furthermore, import certification procedures will be streamlined and transparency enhanced. Government economic targets and intervention are being phased out. Instead, government industrial policy will focus on providing the infrastructure to promote technological innovation through private initiatives. In this sense, the current financial crisis provides Korea not only with great challenges but also excellent opportunities.

Exchange Rate Policies and Trade

Maintaining a realistic and competitive exchange rate is integral to achieving sustainable export growth. In the 1960s, the Korean

[6] The IMF program proposes a tight macroeconomic and structural adjustment policy, categorized under macroeconomic policies, financial sector liberalization, corporate sector reform, capital account liberalization, labor market reform, trade liberalization, and information provision.

Government initiated an exchange rate policy that periodically devalued the won to encourage exports. At the same time, the authorities made every effort to minimize fluctuations of the REER to maintain competitiveness in world markets.

For example, as mentioned above, in May 1964 the Government devalued the won from 190 to 256 to the dollar and made several exchange rate reforms. This new approach marked the turning point in the transition to an export-oriented industrialization policy.

Table 6.3 shows exchange rate data and subsequent changes in REER for both exports and imports for 1965–1990, taking into account two trade-related policy factors: incentives for exports and disincentives for imports. As suggested by the table, the difference between the first and the second column indicates the value of net export subsidies, tax credits, special credits, etc. (actual tariff or tariff equivalents). Adjusted export- and import-applied rates are given in columns 8 and 9, respectively.

As real exchange rates became stable and relative price changes were moderated, the Government announced the implementation of the unitary fluctuating exchange rate system in March 1965. The rate first declined to 256 won to the dollar in April, then rose to 280. After limited intervention by monetary authorities, the won was pegged at 271 to the dollar and remained at that level until 1967. The main objective was to support export-oriented industrialization policies by enhancing price competitiveness through a stable REER. In 1968, the won was allowed to depreciate gradually to a level policymakers believed reflected purchasing power parity (PPP). However, after the oil shock of the early 1970s, followed by devaluations of the dollar of approximately 10 percent in both 1972 and 1973, a significant devaluation of the won was made to correct exchange rate misalignment and compensate for huge current account deficits.

An analysis of Table 6.3 reveals the following characteristics of the Korean exchange rate system during the 1970s. First, dollar values and world prices were fairly stable, and fluctuations of PPP-adjusted official rates were less pronounced than those of nominal exchange rates. The table demonstrates that in 1973 the WPI of the country's major trading partners increased close to 30 points, while the Korean index showed an increase of only 13 points. As a result, PPP-adjusted rates rose sharply by 45.6 points and the economy enjoyed very high competitiveness gains. Second, while the official exchange rate in

Table 6.3 Effective Exchange Rates for Exports and Imports, Nominal and Adjusted for Purchasing Power Parity, 1965–1990

	Exchange Rate (won per $)			WPI and PPP Index (1965 = 100)			PPP-Adjusted Exchange Rate (won per $)			
	Nominal	Effective Rates			Major Trading			Effective Rates		Antiexport
	Official Rate	Exports[a]	Imports[b]	Korea, WPI	Partners' WPI[c]	PPP Index	Official Rate	Exports	Imports	Bias
Year	(1)	(2)	(3)	(4)	(5)	(6=100x5/4)	(7=1x6/100)	(8=2x6/100)	(9=3x6/100)	(10=8/9)
1965	265.4	275.3	293.1	100.0	100.0	100.0	265.4	275.3	293.1	0.94
1970	310.7	331.5	336.4	145.9	112.8	77.3	240.2	256.2	260.0	0.99
1971	347.7	370.5	369.5	158.5	115.4	72.3	253.1	269.7	269.0	1.00
1972	391.8	404.3	415.2	180.7	126.8	70.2	275.0	283.8	291.5	0.97
1973	398.3	407.0	417.7	193.3	155.6	80.5	320.6	327.6	336.2	0.97
1974	407.0	415.6	425.5	274.7	188.4	68.6	279.2	285.1	291.9	0.98
1975	484.0	496.9	508.9	347.4	197.0	56.7	274.4	281.7	288.5	0.98
1976	484.0	496.3	515.4	389.4	206.7	53.1	257.0	263.5	273.7	0.96
1977	484.0	493.4	519.7	424.5	226.8	53.4	258.5	263.5	277.5	0.95
1978	484.0	495.0	526.9	473.4	266.1	56.2	272.0	278.2	296.1	0.94
1979	484.0	495.0	520.0	562.5	284.1	50.5	244.4	250.0	262.6	0.95
1980	607.4	628.0	641.8	781.3	323.7	41.4	250.1	260.0	265.7	0.98
1981	681.0	696.0	715.1	940.6	341.8	36.3	247.2	252.6	259.6	0.97
1982	731.1	734.0	772.9	984.4	332.9	33.8	247.1	248.1	261.2	0.95
1983	775.8	775.8	831.7	986.7	336.9	34.1	264.5	264.5	283.6	0.93
1984	806.0	806.0	858.0	993.6	337.6	34.0	274.0	274.0	291.7	0.94
1985	870.0	870.0	920.3	1,002.5	334.6	33.4	290.6	290.6	307.4	0.95
1986	881.4	881.4	942.9	987.5	379.1	38.4	338.5	338.5	362.1	0.93
1987	822.6	822.6	888.3	992.4	410.2	41.3	339.7	339.7	366.9	0.93
1988	730.6	730.6	780.3	1,019.2	445.5	43.7	319.3	319.3	341.0	0.94
1989	671.5	671.5	705.6	1,034.5	440.6	42.6	286.1	286.1	300.6	0.95
1990	708.6	708.6	748.0	1,077.9	440.3	40.8	289.1	289.1	305.2	0.95

a Official exchange rate plus net export subsidies per dollar of export.
b Official exchange rate plus actual tariff equivalents per dollar of import.
c An average of WPIs for the US and Japan, weighted by the average shares of the US and Japan in Korea's total trade volumes with the two countries during 1963–1980. The Japanese WPI was, however, adjusted by the index of the exchange rate of the yen to the dollar.

Source : Kwang Suk Kim (1994).

the mid- to late 1970s was pegged at 484 won to the dollar, both nominal and adjusted rates for exports remained lower than those for imports. This was achieved through subsidies and import restrictions such as tariffs and tariff equivalents.

The last significant depreciation under this system occurred in January 1980, when the won fell 19.8 percent from 484 to 580 to the dollar. In February 1980, the Government adopted a multiple currency basket peg (MCBP) system , in which the won was pegged to a basket of major trading partners' currencies. After four years of balance-of-payments surpluses from 1986 to 1989, the Government abolished direct export subsidies. As a consequence, the official rate became identical to the NEER for exports (Table 6.3). However, the Government continued to intervene in the foreign exchange market to achieve policy goals through manipulating interest rates and basing decisions on outlooks of the trade balance.

The MCBP system continued until February 1990, when the market average rate system was adopted. The major purpose behind this change was to correct exchange rate misalignment by introducing increased flexibility and transparency to the exchange rate determination process. Under this system, the rate is allowed to fluctuate within a preannounced bandwidth and thus more closely reflect market forces. The permitted daily range of fluctuations was raised from 0.4 percent to 0.6 percent in September 1991 and then in gradual stages to 10 percent in November 1997. In December that year, the Ministry of Finance and Economy announced that it would abolish the 10 percent daily fluctuation limit, to stabilize the troubled financial market and discourage speculative currency demand.

As of mid-1998, the foreign currency transaction system is to be further streamlined and greatly deregulated. In addition, foreign exchange operations at nonbank financial institutions are being improved. Both domestic entrepreneurs and foreign investors, who previously faced difficulties because of the tight regulation of the Korean financial market, are expected to benefit.

Export Incentive Systems and Their Effectiveness

The export incentive systems employed after 1961 played an important role in promoting exports. In general, export incentives cover all direct and indirect measures to offset and/or compensate substantially for any antiexport bias. The major objective of providing export subsidies and other incentives was initially to improve the market competitiveness of the export industry by reducing risks from exchange rate fluctuations and by compensating for the price gap between export and domestic sales. However, alongside other liberalization attempts of the mid-1960s, the Government abandoned the direct export subsidy system in 1965, and intensified the indirect subsidy system for industries important to expanding exports through tax and financial incentives, and administrative support. These favored industries were freed from existing import duties and quotas to procure their production needs on the open market.

The following is a brief outline of selected export incentive measures.[7]

Export Incentives

Domestic tax incentives included a maximum corporate tax reduction on earnings from exports of 50 percent. This was established in 1960, but replaced in all export sectors in 1973 by the reserve fund system, which allocated to each industry government-funded credit of 1 percent of total exports. In 1977, the VAT system was introduced, under which VAT on goods and services exported for foreign currency was removed from year-end taxes. Another incentive was a tariff drawback, where refunds of a tariff on imported inputs were made on export of the finished product.

Up to 1974, domestic tax reductions and tariff exemptions were major incentives related to taxes. Between these two measures, the relative importance of the tariff exemptions increased continually. The ratio of tariff exemptions to the total amount of tax incentives rose, with a slight fluctuation, from 45 percent in 1962 to 71 percent in 1974. However, to reduce the scope of export subsidies, the prior-exemption program was abolished in 1975, with the result that tariff drawbacks became the major tariff-related incentive. The total cost

---

[7] This outline relies heavily on previous work done by Frank et al. (1975), and Chang Nam Kim et al. (1989). Unless otherwise noted, most of the indirect incentive measures introduced were effective from the 1960s to the mid-1980s.

of such tax and tariff measures for export industries increased from 565 million won in 1962 to 4,752 billion won in 1987.[8]

The main financial incentives for export activities included preferential loans for export financing, which greatly benefited the export industry under circumstances of chronic excess demand for credit in the economy. The interest-rate differential on export loans and commercial bills was very high in the early part of the export promotion period, but subsequently declined and was eliminated after 1982, when the Government abolished preferential-interest export loans.[9] Other incentives and measures included granting exporters favorable rates on, for example, railway freight and electric power, or monopoly rights to export in certain circumstances. Many of the above incentives, however, were reduced after reforms in August 1972.

The Government has created several organizations to promote exports. Since they do not entail direct monetary incentives to exports, many of them can be adopted by other developing countries. Various associations for major export industries have been organized to assist member firms by providing services in the area of marketing, advertising, inspection, and arbitration. In addition, since 1969, export industries have been protected by export insurance covering 70–90 percent of losses related to export activities. One of the main organizations is the Korea Trade Promotion Corporation. It was established in 1962 as a nonprofit government organization to carry out overseas market research and to provide export industries with information on the rapidly changing trade environment. Another export promotion activity was the Monthly Trade Promotion Meeting, held from 1965 to 1986, which oversaw the implementation of export incentives. The importance of exports can be seen in the fact that the meeting was chaired by the President of Korea. Participants were economic ministers, heads of major trading companies, and representatives from trade associations and research institutes.

Generally, until the late 1980s, the Government was instrumental in ensuring exporters access to a workforce that enhanced

[8] In nominal terms, Korean exports grew from $175.1 million to $47.3 billion during this period.

[9] Between 1964 and 1986, the average interest rate on commercial bills was 17.5 percent and that on export loans was 8.5 percent (Pyo 1990).

competitiveness. It not only assisted in wage negotiations, but also restricted trade union activities.

Finally, the Free Export Zone Establishment Act was passed in 1970 to stimulate foreign investment, promote exports, increase employment, and facilitate the transfer of technology. Two export processing zones (EPZ) were set up in Masan and Iri. Privileges granted to projects within the EPZs included tax benefits and exemptions from import and export restrictions.

Effectiveness of Export Incentives

There is much empirical evidence that the Korean economy achieved remarkable growth in exports and GDP for the period when governments applied export promoting incentives. However, the direct impact of such incentives is not easy to calculate since quantification of the effect of most measures, associated with the accuracy of estimates of REER, is difficult to derive. Furthermore, certain nonmonetary incentives could be categorized as supportive measures rather than incentives.

Whether the historically rapid export growth, in effect, is an outcome of a close relationship with export incentives is an intriguing question. Such a relationship can be examined by searching for possible correlations, using empirical analysis of the time structure of export and incentive growth. Between 1962 and 1987, there was indeed, with the exceptions of 1964 and 1980, a positive correlation in the moving pattern of exports and subsidies (Pyo 1990).[10] However, while this approach may be useful in capturing broad trends, applicability is limited because of the difficulty in identifying the exact correlation. Results of earlier empirical tests may help, though. Frank et al. (1975) suggest, on the basis of their empirical estimates of interaction between Korea's commercial policy variables and the behavior of economic aggregates for 1960–1970, that a major effect of commercial policy variables is the influence of the effective exchange rate for exports

[10] In 1964, there was a major devaluation of the Korean currency in nominal terms. The PPP-adjusted effective exchange rate for exports increased in real terms because of a net increase in export incentives. The situation in 1980 could be explained, however, as a combined effect of devaluation and the second oil shock.

on export performance and of the effective exchange rate for imports on import demand. They observe that commercial policy has been an important factor in Korea's growth. They add, however, that "in promoting exports through subsidies and low tariffs, the Government has sacrificed revenues with the result that growth has been less than optimal." In this context, and based on their estimates, they argue that deviating by more than 20 percent in either direction from historic subsidy levels results in a deterioration of the growth rate due to the resultant decrease of savings rates. The most important aspect of their approach is that they set the 1965 exchange rate as an equilibrium rate with which the same historic growth could be achieved through the elimination of all subsidies and tariffs. Therefore, their results show that the positive correlation between export subsidies and growth in exports is largely explained by the fact that the Government successfully maintained a stable REER after 1965.

Jong Man Kim (1992) also examined the effect of the country's export promotion policy by singling out the impact of export credit on export expansion. In an attempt to quantify the amount of export credit, he assumes that the Government provides a certain portion of total exports as export credit. According to his estimates, a 1 percent increase in the rate of export credit will, in turn, decrease export prices by 0.05 percent for three consecutive quarters. Under this framework, he measures the impact of export price decreases on export changes. His results, based on an estimation of a price elasticity of 1.69, reveal that a 1 percent decrease in the rate of export credit will eventually increase the amount of exports by 0.09 percent.

In sum, the econometric estimates presented here would seem to show that a positive correlation exists between export subsidies and export expansion, and that consequently, export credit may be regarded as a direct policy variable that affects exports.

DETERMINANTS OF EXPORTS

Determinants of Export Supply and Demand

The strategy of Korea's export-oriented industrialization was very successful, despite the country's small geographic size and poor natural resource base. Its main resource was a fairly well-educated and industrious labor force. Many other factors have also been identified as elements in the economy's rapid export growth, including active government export promotion, entrepreneurial talent of general trading companies, global market opportunities, and foreign capital inflows.

As stated earlier, the major policy goal of the Government when promoting exports was to maintain favorable export prices by exchange rate adjustments together with export subsidy packages. Among other factors, it was believed that the responsiveness of exports to changes in the price level (relative prices) was one of the most important determining factors of exports. Numerous studies have provided estimates of determinants of Korean export supply and demand.[11] The main debate concerns whether price elasticity of Korean export demand was high enough to ensure increased demand for exports or whether the elasticity of export demand with respect to foreign income was high enough to absorb increased proportions of Korean exports. To approach this argument, we will introduce the estimates of Korean export demand and supply functions calculated by Balassa et al. (1989), and Giorgianni and Milesi-Ferretti (1997).

In a simultaneous equation framework, Balassa et al. considered separately the effects of changes in the NEER, dollar export prices, and the prices of domestic goods. In their work, estimates were made for 1965–1979, taking into account the effect of export incentives.[12] Several features are noteworthy if we use Balassa's estimates. First, estimates of export supply indicate greater substitutability of exports

---

[11] See, among others, Frank et al. (1975), Riedel (1988), and Balassa et al. (1989).

[12] They contend that the result of price elasticities of Korean export supply shows a considerable downward bias in ordinary least square (OL_S) estimations, irrespective of whether one considers total exports or the exports of manufactured goods. For more details, see Balassa et al. (1989), p.11.

for traded rather than nontraded goods in domestic production. Second, export supply is more sensitive to changes in the NEER than to changes in the dollar price of exports. Third, an extremely high coefficient range of 5.3–5.4 is reported for the income elasticities of export demand. The majority of Korean exports comprise manufactured goods, defined as SITC sections 5 to 8, implying that Korean exports appear to be very sensitive to changes in the global economic environment. The authors summarize the characteristics of Korean export behavior in the following way.

> Estimates made for Korea indicate that exporters respond more strongly to changes in the nominal effective exchange rate than to changes in the price of export and non-export goods. These differences have been attributed to the expectation that changes in exchange rates and export incentives will not be reversed, while product prices fluctuate over time. (Balassa et al., 1989, p. 15.)

Another set of estimates pertaining to the determinants of Korean exports is presented by Giorgianni and Milesi-Ferretti (1997). The advantage of their work is its longer time coverage (1971-1995) and the inclusion of recent changes in the direction of Korean export flows. Their estimated long-run scale elasticity for export demand is 3.2, while relative price elasticity is -2. For export supply, they give a very high price elasticity of over 7, and estimate long-run cost elasticity with respect to export prices at -0.6.

The major findings of the study are as follows. First, high elasticity with respect to foreign demand reflects the growth differential between Korea and its trading partners. Second, domestic price elasticity above 2 for Korean demand also indicates that changes in Korean export volume are sensitive to price changes in foreign countries. Third, according to the forecast of the share of Korean exports, due to penetration in the economies of the Organisation for Economic Co-operation and Development (OECD) by other Asian developing economies, Korea's exports to industrial countries have been declining since the 1990s. It would also seem that Korea could maintain or increase its share of world exports by increasing its imports from other Asian economies, though admittedly, no such signs of regional integration among developing Asian economies currently exist.

Changes in Trade Structure

The disaggregation of Korean exports by commodity group clearly shows that during the 1960s, exports, such as labor-intensive manufactured goods and primary goods, made a large contribution to export growth. The Government initially focused its economic policy on light industry and on improving infrastructure, and encompassed existing industries, so as to develop such industries through utilizing the increased labor input. Due to the lack of local resources, the Government targeted the textile, plywood, and footwear industries. This required large inflows of foreign capital. Such a policy continued throughout the decade, with the result that the share of agricultural products, crude materials, and minerals declined from around 80 percent of all exports in 1960 to less than 20 percent by 1970 (Bank of Korea, *Economic Statistics Yearbook,* various years).

The share of manufactured articles in total exports was highest in 1970. However, from the 1980s the importance of textiles, and of iron and steel products fell sharply in favor of capital- and technology-intensive sectors, such as electrical appliances and electronic and transportation equipment (Lee 1993). Another significant change in the Korean trade pattern over the last four decades has been the diversification of trade partners, whose number has risen from 33 countries in 1962 to virtually the entire globe in the 1990s. Although the US and Japan are still the two largest trading partners, the Association of Southeast Asian Nations (ASEAN) and the European Union (EU) have emerged as important sources of trade, but the sharpest growth of Korean exports has been to the People's Republic of China (PRC), with its share of total Korean exports rising from 0.9 percent in 1990 to 9.9 percent in November 1997 (KOTIS database). This recent diversification bodes well for Korean success in finding new trading partners in the next century.

Comparative Advantage of Korean Exports

To investigate Korea's relative export performance and competitive abilities, Balassa's measure of revealed comparative advantage (RCA) has been adopted, as follows.

$$RCA_{ij} = (X_{ij} / C_j) / (X_i / W)$$

where

W = total OECD imports

C_j = total imports of the *j*th product

X_i = total OECD imports from the *i*th country

X_{ij}= OECD imports of the *j*th product from the *i*th country

If we examine the RCA of Korea in the OECD, the numerator in Balassa's equation denotes the share of the economy's exports of the *j*th product in total imports of *j*th product from the OECD, whereas the denominator denotes the share of the country's exports in total OECD imports. In this context, if a particular product's RCA has a value greater than one, it denotes the economy's relative strength for that product in OECD markets. Based on the shifts in comparative advantage of Korean exports measured by changes in the export share to OECD countries in the SITC level 1 product categories (Revisions 1, 2, 3), in the early 1970s, the economy's RCA was in traditional labor-intensive products. These included, primarily, products of rubber, textiles and fabrics, and of iron and steel, as well as clothing and footwear.

However, the patterns of the RCA reveal that a turnaround in Korea's competitiveness began in the early 1980s. Among the most significant shifts of comparative advantage were trends in exports of labor-intensive products and electrical machinery. Among labor-intensive products, leather manufactures and wood manufactures were the items whose comparative advantage was most seriously eroded. In addition, the comparative advantage of both textiles and clothing showed a steady decline, largely because of increasing relative labor costs.

On the other hand, in the earlier period not one of the items demonstrated a comparative advantage in machinery and transport equipment (SITC 7), a situation which was completely reversed by the 1990s. More specifically, office machines (SITC 75) and electrical machinery (SITC 77) are the two most important items whose comparative advantage has improved since the late 1980s.

THE 1996 EXPORT DECELERATION: LOSS OF COMPETITIVENESS

Trends of Exports and Imports, 1996–1998

In a dynamic scenario of constantly changing comparative advantage, Korean firms should compete more with high quality products of the industrial countries and less with lower-priced products of developing countries. This will result in upward movement on the comparative advantage ladder. Sagong and Kang (1998) argue that the country's recent export performance has been poor in one respect, that is, despite having increased the quantity of exports, the terms of trade declined substantially after 1996. This led to a considerable lower profitability of exports. The decrease in export prices can be attributed to several factors. First, the won began its long devaluation trend after July 1995, when it traded at 756 to the dollar. By the end of 1996, it had depreciated by 12 percent, and by the end of 1997, it had fallen to 1,415 against the dollar, although by mid-1998 it had appreciated to approximately 1,280 to the dollar. With a devalued local currency, Korean firms were willing to export goods at lower prices in dollar terms. Second, domestic demand for goods fell substantially, and thus firms tried to increase exports by reducing export prices. Since 1996, the Korean firms' capacity utilization rates have fallen to as low as 60 percent in manufacturing, and firms have had to look to exports as a solution for the lack of domestic demand. Third, there has been a global oversupply of the economy's major export items such as semiconductors, steel, and automobiles. (although the semiconductor market picked up in 1998, it did not return to its pre-1996 strength). Fourth, Korean industries have failed to upgrade the quality of their exports, which in turn resulted in a loss of export market share.

Until the 1980s, Korea exhibited strong export performance by producing goods with cheap, skilled labor and imported materials. Its exports accounted for 28–35 percent of GDP in the 1980s (Table 6.4). During this period, prices of Korean exports were low enough to compete with foreign products. However, in the 1990s, less developed countries began to industrialize rapidly and attract a substantial share of global trade. As a result, exports as a share of GDP declined to 24–27 percent in the first half of the 1990s.

Table 6.4 Share of Exports and Imports in GDP, 1971–1997

Year	GDP	Exports	Imports	Exports	Imports
	$ billion			Percent Share in GDP	
1971	9.5	1.1	2.4	12	25
1972	10.7	1.6	2.5	15	23
1973	13.6	3.2	4.2	24	31
1974	18.9	4.5	6.9	24	37
1975	21.3	5.1	7.3	24	34
1976	29.1	7.7	8.8	26	30
1977	37.3	10.0	10.8	27	29
1978	52.3	12.7	15.0	24	29
1979	62.7	15.1	20.0	24	32
1980	62.8	17.5	22.3	28	36
1981	70.0	21.3	26.1	30	37
1982	74.8	21.9	24.3	29	32
1983	82.7	24.4	26.2	30	32
1984	91.3	29.2	30.6	32	34
1985	94.3	30.3	31.1	32	33
1986	108.6	34.7	31.6	32	29
1987	136.3	47.3	41.0	35	30
1988	182.2	60.7	51.8	33	28
1989	222.2	62.4	61.5	28	28
1990	253.6	65.0	69.8	26	28
1991	294.1	71.9	81.5	24	28
1992	307.9	76.6	81.8	25	27
1993	332.8	82.2	83.8	25	25
1994	380.7	96.0	102.3	25	27
1995	456.5	125.1	135.1	27	30
1996	484.4	129.7	150.3	27	31
1997	442.6	136.2	144.6	31	33

Source: KOTIS database.

Korea has seen the growth rates of its exports drop sharply in recent years. The steep fall from 30 percent growth in 1995 to 3.7 percent in 1996, and then to 5 percent growth in 1997 (Table 6.1), can be attributed to a global export downturn, a sharp decrease in international semiconductor prices, the weak yen, and economic slowdown among some of the country's main trading partners. Although Korean exports grew by 3.7 percent in dollar terms in 1996, export prices declined by 12.8 percent. Prices of semiconductors, petrochemical products, and steel—all of which are major export items—dropped sharply. For instance, 16MB DRAMs sold for

$43 per chip in the beginning of 1996, but declined to $9 per chip by the end of the year.

The yen depreciated from an average yen/dollar exchange rate of 94.1 in 1995 to 108.8 in 1996. The weakened yen contributed to Korea's export deceleration in 1996. It directly affected Korean exports of automobiles, heavy industries, and steel. Korea competes with Japan in these areas. The weaker yen affected Korean exports to the US and the EU economies. The low-tech industries like textiles and apparel and footwear were already losing comparative advantage; they were unable to compete with exports from the PRC and ASEAN economies. However, more fundamental reasons might be the economy's inefficient industrial structure. The country displayed an increasing pattern of trade deficits, reaching $20.6 billion in 1996, and in 1997, though it reversed this trend significantly, it still recorded a substantial trade deficit of $8.4 billion.

In 1996, Korean exports to the US and Japan fell dramatically, while those to the PRC, ASEAN countries, Latin America, and Eastern Europe grew. However, in 1997, there was zero growth in exports to ASEAN countries and Eastern Europe, the former hit by economic and financial turbulence in July 1997 (Korea International Trade Association (KITA) and KOTIS databases).

Korea's imports posted double-digit growth during 1994–1996, reaching a record growth rate of 32 percent in 1995 (Table 6.1). In 1996, however, growth fell significantly, and in 1997 imports shrank in absolute terms by 3.8 percent, from all regions except for the PRC and ASEAN countries.

Sector Analysis of International Competitiveness

Labor-Intensive Goods

Korea has been losing ground to less developed nations in the market for labor-intensive goods. For example, footwear exports decreased rapidly from $4.3 billion (7 percent of total exports) in 1990 to $0.9 billion (less than 1 percent of total exports) in 1997 (KITA and KOTIS databases). Similarly, the economy has lost its comparative advantage to less developed countries such as Bangladesh and the PRC in other light industries, including clothing and toys, because of expensive labor. In response, Korea has emerged as a major exporter of automobiles, ships, semiconductors, steel, and chemicals. These are higher-technology products, though the country still lags far behind advanced nations such as Japan and the US at the leading edge of technology.

A more serious problem lies in the rapid growth of domestic demand for imported labor-intensive products. In the first half of the 1990s, the country's imports of such products grew at an annual rate of some 25 percent, almost double the rate for overall imports. Despite 1997's contraction in imports of 3.8 percent because of the domestic economic slowdown and the rapid depreciation of the won, imports are likely to rise again as the economy recovers. Increasing imports and decreasing exports of light industry products can be explained by price competitiveness. According to Shin (1998), the economy has been losing competitiveness by 5–10 percent annually in low value-added light industries (clothing, shoes, etc.). The steep depreciation of the won during the current Asian financial crisis may help the industry boost its exports temporarily in 1998, although exports of light industry products are expected to continue to fall in the longer term.

Machinery

Korea's domestic machinery market is estimated to have exceeded 40 trillion won in 1998. In 1997, the local machinery industry met about 70 percent of national demand. Such a high degree of self-reliance is the result of accelerated technological development in the mid-1980s and a subsequent increase in domestic production. In the 1980s, the machinery industry saw production grow rapidly at more than 20 percent a year. However, in the 1990s, as domestic companies started to embark upon structural adjustment and as the overall national economy experienced a setback, growth in the machinery industry declined to 18 percent a year. As a result of the severe economic slowdown in 1997, local demand shrunk by 6 percent compared with 1996, and domestic companies halted further investment. Consequently, machinery production grew by a mere 3.5 percent in 1996.

In terms of exports, the machinery industry showed poor performance until the 1980s as local manufacturers concentrated on meeting domestic demand. However, in the 1990s, export growth of industrial equipment grew substantially to meet growing global demand, though the industry suffered from a chronic trade deficit as the Korean economy saw a sharp increase in machinery investment due to overall expansion of production capacity. Furthermore, a strong domestic preference for imports arose in response to the low quality of domestic products.

In the machinery industry, Korea's basic production techniques such as processing and molding are comparable with those of leading industrial countries, but high value-added products are still at the imitative stage. With regard to the development of new products, production skills, and quality, Korea is still behind countries such as Japan, US, and Germany by more than 10 years. And despite considerable progress in car manufacturing-related technology, it is still at a fairly early stage in the areas of industrial robotics, production automation, and computer-integrated manufacturing.

In terms of price, Korean machinery is 10 percent cheaper than that of advanced countries. Korean engines and turbines are only slightly cheaper (by 4–6 percent) because of high production costs in the form of royalties for imported technology. However, on a non-price basis (taking an average of performance, quality, and parts availability, etc.) with foreign machinery at 100 for reference, the country's textile machinery (76) is the least competitive while high quality engines and turbines (93) are the most competitive (Inho Lee 1997). The fact that Korea's machinery is at a competitive disadvantage shows that the economy's basic technology remains relatively undeveloped.

According to a report by the Korea Development Bank (KDB), Korea's machinery production in 1998 is expected to shrink substantially as demand in the automobile industry decreases (KDB 1998). Thus, the machinery industry is expected to see production decline by 4.5 percent. However, over the longer term, it is forecast to grow by more than 6 percent a year after 2000. Such an optimistic view is based on the capital-intensive industrial promotion policy pursued by the Korean Government since 1995, and substantial private R&D investment. As local companies are likely to conduct steady investment in R&D, demand for imported machinery is likely to diminish (KDB 1996).

Semiconductors

The Korean semiconductor industry initially started production through 100 percent investment in plant and equipment by US companies in the mid-1960s. In the late 1970s, local manufacturers became increasingly involved in production. In the 1980s, the local semiconductor industry enjoyed rapid growth, largely because of concerted efforts by the Government and the private sector to develop dynamic random-access memory (DRAM) chips. As a result, Korea has emerged as a major DRAM chip producer worldwide.

In 1996, the country was the world's third largest producer of semiconductors. However, the value of its semiconductor exports dropped by 19.3 percent that year and by 2.4 percent in 1997, in dollar terms, because of a decline in world chip prices (KITA 1998). Though memory chip producers have attained the same level of technology as those in developed countries, producers of nonmemory chips still lag behind global leaders by one or two years. The country is even further behind in the fields of software programming and equipment design. Part of the problem lies in the fact that major chip makers such as Samsung, Hyundai, and LG Electronics focus too much on memory chips that generate little value-added and are subject to high international market price volatility.

Japanese producers, endowed with advanced basic technology and robotics, possess a strong competitive edge in custom-made semiconductors and nonmemory chips. Korean producers have narrowed the technological gap with them in memory chip manufacturing, but still trail far behind in basic equipment technology. This can be attributed to the fact that Japanese companies invest 11.5 percent of their sales in R&D, twice as much as those in Korea, and enjoy a mature industrial infrastructure that is not available to Korean companies.

Although the domestic semiconductor industry suffered from a drastic price decrease in the world market in the mid-1990s, prospects for semiconductors are good, according to KITA (1998). The reason is that the world semiconductor market is likely to recover in 1998, and therefore local chip makers will see increased exports to major industrial markets including the EU, Japan, and the US. Moreover, the country's major chip makers have started to change their production structure from 16 megabyte random-access memory

(MB RAM) chips to high margin 64 MB RAM chips. Also, the demand for personal computers, consuming about 70–80 percent of DRAM production, is steadily increasing. Export growth is expected to be moderate over the medium term, at about 15 percent a year. However, there are possible stumbling blocks, namely a reduction in investment in equipment due to structural adjustments in the current (1997–1998) financial crisis, and greater competition from Japan and Taipei,China, leading to falling prices. Therefore, it is not reasonable to expect this export sector to boom in the short or medium term.

Petrochemicals

In terms of exports, local petrochemical companies have been actively seeking foreign markets in an attempt to relieve the oversupply that resulted from the investment expansion of 1989–1991. Exports grew at an average annual rate of 40 percent from 1990 to 1997. Asian markets have absorbed the majority of exports, and the national petrochemical industry has grown dependent on the PRC market in particular.

To increase competitiveness, Korean petrochemical companies are currently attempting to expand into high value-added products, restructure their businesses, and take part in mergers or strategic alliances led by foreign companies. However, other Asian and Middle Eastern oil-producing countries are also actively expanding their production facilities for petrochemical products. As a result, global competition in the industry is growing more intense. Since commonly used intermediate goods such as compound vinyl and rubber vary little in quality, price is the most important factor in determining their competitiveness. In the petrochemical industry, raw materials account for 60–80 percent of production costs. Korean companies depend heavily on imported inputs, making them vulnerable to price fluctuations in the international market. In addition, because the Korean petrochemical industry uses naphtha as a production input (the US, East Asia, and the Middle East use cheaper ethylene), it operates at a disadvantage.

In terms of nonprice competitiveness, Korean firms lag behind multinational corporations in developing high quality products and in overseas marketing and service, injuring their ability to develop new markets. In addition, they need to improve their supply and distribution networks and to adopt environment-friendly technology. They also need to assess more accurately domestic and international supply and demand conditions and then make investment plans based on profitability rather than on market share. As of 1998, though the depreciated won is increasing price competitiveness, it is also leading to upward pressure on input prices. From the medium-term perspective, domestic production is forecast to increase substantially as companies continue capacity expansion through 2000. Yet as Southeast Asia, one of Korea's major markets, enters new and higher value markets through heavy investment in facilities, demand for Korean exports is expected to drop significantly, at least in the short term. Therefore, a short-term increase in petrochemical exports is unlikely.

Steel

In the steel industry, Korea has succeeded in maintaining a competitive advantage over many industrial nations based on high capacity utilization rates and relatively cheap labor. Given the low production cost of steel plates in early 1996, the domestic steel industry had a 5–25 percent price advantage over industrial nations, though any advantage over other developing countries had been eroded by lower prices there. Furthermore, producers in the EU, Japan, and the US have boosted their competitiveness through restructuring and streamlining production processes. Expansion of steel production, particularly by developing nations, is likely to produce a glut in the global market. Hence, Korea's steel industry, burdened by constantly rising labor costs and banking problems, will have to deal with greater foreign competition. In terms of nonprice factors, though the domestic steel industry is on a par with those of industrial economies in the production technology of ordinary steel products, it is at a severe disadvantage in the advanced technology required for high value-added products. In 1998, the national steel industry will have to survive low profitability from declining corporate investment in production capacity, a sharp decrease in demand from construction, and price increases of imported raw materials (Jung-ho Kim 1998). The industry is expected to experience an inventory increase, low capacity utilization rates, and a low growth rate. In addition, in spite of the weak won, exports are not expected to show much improvement as major export markets such as PRC, Japan and Southeast Asia are still suffering from an economic downturn. Korean steel companies will be able to expand export markets with improved price competitiveness, but they will see only slow export growth because of the economic turmoil in Southeast Asia and the economic slump in Japan (Korean Institute for Industrial Economics and Trade (KIET) 1997).

Automobiles

The automobile industry is approaching maturity in the Korean market, and now looks poised to expand into overseas markets and compete with those of developed nations, with which it is fairly competitive; it has a competitive edge over those in ASEAN, PRC and Mexico . Its small cars, one of the country's major exports, were 22 percent cheaper than similar-sized cars from Japan and the US in 1996 (Inho Lee 1997). However, there is some concern that the price gap is narrowing because of the depreciation of the yen and the renewed competitiveness of the US automobile industry. According to statistics on representative export items such as automobiles and household electronics goods, the share of exports out of total production has dropped sharply since 1987, implying a loss of international competitiveness.

Although Korean automobile makers possess a high level of production technology, they cannot compete with advanced economies in the area of electronic devices for automobiles.

Around 76 percent of the local automobile industry's production capacity is likely to be utilized in 1998, up from 74 percent in 1997 (Jang 1997). On the basis of 1996 production costs, the breakeven point for domestic automobile manufacturers is around 82 percent of capacity utilization. Thus, for the time being, the industry is expected to operate at a loss. In general, it will be difficult for it to achieve a full recovery until developing countries recover from the current financial crisis and world demand for automobiles increases. By mid-1998, therefore, local manufacturers had begun to launch downsizing efforts, including investment reductions, layoffs, cost reductions, and asset sales.

Cho (1997) forecasts that the domestic automobile industry will suffer from a severe shrinkage in local demand resulting from the combination of high unemployment, wage freezes and cuts, inflation, and high interest rates in 1998. Thus, domestic manufacturers will step up their efforts to seek new markets abroad. With a weaker won against the dollar, the automobile industry is expected to benefit from improved price competitiveness. However, as Southeast Asia, emerging as a major export market, is also suffering from the deepening financial crisis, demand for Korean automobiles will weaken greatly. Another factor hindering export expansion is a weakening yen, together with a possible economic slowdown in the EU and the US, and, conceivably, financial crises in Latin America and Eastern Europe.

Overall, automobile exports are estimated to grow by 11 percent in 1998, largely because of enhanced price competitiveness, diversified exports, improved quality, and more advanced business strategies (KIET 1997). In addition, imported automobiles are expected to decrease by 10 percent in value due to a sharp fall in domestic demand resulting from the Asian financial crisis, and consumers' reluctance to buy foreign "luxury" goods in the current atmosphere of financial stringency.

Shipbuilding

Korea and Japan together account for about 70 percent of the world's shipbuilding industry in gross tonnage. In 1993, the former held a 30 percent production cost advantage over the latter, though now, in terms of both price and nonprice competitiveness, the former lags behind the latter because of a low yen and the low level of shipbuilding technology in Korea. In terms of price competitiveness, the average shipbuilding costs in Japan were 5 percent lower than those of Korea at the end of 1996 (Shin 1998). Japan's relatively low costs have resulted from several favorable factors. Since June 1996, Japan's shipbuilding industry has reduced raw material costs, which comprise 60–65 percent of total costs, by 30–40 percent simply by switching from domestic to imported suppliers. Also, from 1993 to 1995, productivity improved by a substantial 36 percent, while wage increases were around 5 percent. Accordingly, Japan's shipbuilding industry has seen production costs in dollar terms drop by about 15–25 percent since 1993. In contrast, Korea's shipbuilding costs have risen by 10–15 percent on a won basis over the same period.

Japan also enjoys a comparative advantage over Korea in non-price competitiveness. Although Korea is almost on par with the

Japanese in shipbuilding technology for tankers and bulk carriers, it is falling far behind in high value-added ships such as gas carriers and passenger liners. In addition, financial support for shipbuilding is more favorable in Japan, where private merchant banks provide substantial amounts of loans at low interest rates.

Exports of Korean ships in 1998 are, however, expected to rise as long as its major markets such as the EU, Japan, the Middle East, and the US remain unaffected by the financial crisis in Asia. Furthermore, the depreciation of the won will lead to enhanced price competitiveness, which should in turn boost exports. Moreover, the long-term prospects for Korea's shipbuilding industry remain bright. For the time being, the global shipbuilding industry is forecast to maintain its current strong performance, growing steadily on into the next century. Accordingly, the domestic shipbuilding industry is expected to receive orders of some 8.4 million gross tonnes in 1997–2000 and some 7.7 million gross tonnes in 2001–2005 (KDB 1996).

Reasons for Weakening Export Competitiveness

What are the problems facing Korean exports? First of all, high costs (in both won and dollar terms) and low efficiency stand out as the biggest drags on the competitiveness of Korean industry. In dollar terms, domestic monthly wages in manufacturing increased at an annual rate of 17.6 percent from the late 1980s to 1996, the highest rate among major exporting countries. While wages in Taipei,China were 55 percent higher than in Korea in 1985, as of early 1998 they were 22 percent lower.[13] Substantial wage increases may, in fact, be regarded as the inevitable response to demands for improved working conditions and welfare. As a result, the Korean economy has been unable to maintain international competitiveness.

In addition, the foreign exchange rate, which is usually the ultimate means for balancing external trade accounts, has not helped exports. Kim et al. (1997), underlining the close relationship between the won/dollar exchange rate and the economy's exports, point out that Korean exports were adversely affected by a 7 percent

[13] According to Han (1996), in 1987-1994, wage rates in Korea grew by 6.1 percent annually, but only 4 percent in Taipei,China.

overvaluation of the won against the dollar in January 1997. The country's exports have also been closely related to the won/yen exchange rate, so that the significant appreciation of the won in 1995 worked against a trade surplus. As Korea's top 10 export items account for 43.2 percent of its total exports, five of which directly compete with Japan, a devaluation of the yen greatly hurts the competitiveness of Korean exports (Ohn and Shin 1997). When the yen appreciated from an annual average of 135.4 to the dollar in 1990 to 102.9 in 1995, Korean exports grew strongly. But as the yen depreciated from 1995, they plunged. D. H. Lee (1997), by analyzing the effects of a devalued yen on major Korean exports using an impulse response function, found that a devaluation of the yen would adversely affect all Korean industries, particularly semiconductors.

According to Inho Lee (1997), the economy's weakening competitiveness can be attributed to an unbalanced export structure characterized by high concentration on a few products. He analyzes the share of Korea's 10 largest export items in the nation's total exports based on the six-digit harmonized system classification, and concludes that Japan specializes in industries with comparative advantage and successfully pursues export diversification, while Korea concentrates on too few export items and only a handful of competitive sectors.

One of the most serious problems facing the economy is the high cost of transport. In 1995, Korean companies spent 58 trillion won on transport, equivalent to the entire national budget. These costs increased steadily from 1984 to 1995; Ahn and Hwang (1997) report that transport costs of Korean export companies represent 16.5 percent of total revenues, and that "high logistics costs are weakening the price competitiveness of export products and increasing the trade deficit." This is due to the severe lack of infrastructure such as highways, railroads, and ports.

Export profitability has been steadily eroded since 1990, except for a small surge in 1993. This decrease has been mostly because of decreasing unit export prices, higher costs of raw materials, increasing wages, and fiercer competition from less developed countries. Sagong and Kang (1998) find that nonprice competitiveness indexes of export goods, which are calculated using the degree of qualification[14] in

[14] The degree of qualification is the unit export price change divided by the average price change of all exports.

export industries, declined from 94.2 in January 1990 to 77.8 by the end of 1997. Their findings suggest that the country's export growth since 1990 has been because of increases in export volume at poorer terms of trade.

The current IMF-sponsored assistance program for structural adjustment is confined to SMEs and banks. There is no equivalent for large companies: they must attempt to enter new business areas and dispose of their assets unaided. According to Park (1997), while monopolistic state enterprises account for a substantial share of the national economy, private companies are deterred from entering their business areas because of barriers to entry such as government procurement contracts and national sales and distribution networks. Another obstacle lies in the purchase limit of other companies' equity under the Fair Trade Law, which makes it difficult for *chaebols* to expand into new business areas or acquire insolvent companies.

Regaining Export Competitiveness

A more sophisticated export policy is now necessary to adjust to the changing international environment. For instance, in addition to expanding their export volumes, SMEs need to diversify their export lines to penetrate niche markets. In general, not only can firms earn higher prices, but exports of diversified products are more profitable than those of a single item since they offer consumers selection. Even though firms know this, they have been unable to diversify their products in the past because of limited information on consumer tastes, inability to design new products, and lack of capital. One way to stimulate firms to diversify their product range is to provide them with timely information about the ever-changing market environment.

Han (1996) argues that high growth in wages has substantially weakened Korea's international competitiveness. This is an important structural factor. To cope with rising wages, firms should increase investment in automation and R&D. Furthermore, the labor market should be made more flexible, in which case the Government must create a safety net for those who are made redundant during restructuring. This entails various job assistance programs including job training, deregulation of job-creating businesses, and a national network of job information.

Given that high transport costs are also a burden, substantial investments are required in infrastructure. In addition, Ahn and Hwang (1997) suggest that "the Government should eliminate all competition-restricting regulations and explore diversified types of assistance for the logistics industry, which is falling behind in terms of technology, capital, and marketing." In addition, the Government needs to reform regulations on business.[15] Tax laws relating to company restructuring impose too large a burden on mergers and acquisitions, company splits, and asset disposal. The Government needs to introduce new laws or modify existing ones. For example, firms involved in mergers should be exempt from taxes on dividends and registration. When firms dispose of their assets for restructuring purposes, special capital gains taxes should be reduced, and acquisition and registration taxes should be removed.

Although the *chaebols* themselves recognize the need for structural changes, they are sometimes constrained by legislation. Therefore, the Government should remove the regulatory policies on large-scale investments by local companies, originally intended to prevent overinvestment and excessive competition among local firms. In addition, the Government should allow the *chaebols* to enter business areas that they choose. The *chaebols* themselves could enhance their competitiveness by changing certain business practices. In the past, they have recklessly expanded through excessive borrowing rather than structural improvement. They should abandon their long-held practices of operating in too many business areas, and instead focus on a few in which they are internationally competitive. They should pursue diversification strategies of higher value-added product differentiation.

With the establishment of WTO, the Government must now focus on enhancing national competitiveness rather than assisting specific industries. For example, it should strongly support the development of basic technology, human capital, and infrastructure, in addition to attracting foreign investment in high-technology industries. In particular, local companies need to be relieved of the risks arising from independent technology development, through increases in government support of R&D. The Government also

[15] The Federation of Korean Industries (1997) suggests that reform of regulations is the most important step to regain international competitiveness, followed by lower interest rates.

needs to devise a strategy to develop worldwide brand-name recognition. In most cases, exports under original equipment manufacturers' names, which account for more than 50 percent of total exports, are sold at lower prices than brand-name goods. Thus, without developing brand names, Korean exports will be limited in their capacity to acquire global market shares.

The Government and trade business circles should strengthen their partnership by sharing information on the economic environment of major trading partners and by discussing trade policies before their official introduction. Under the OECD and WTO frameworks, the Government has found it necessary to recast its role as trade manager to service providers in accordance with trade liberalization. It should provide one-stop marketing support for local exporters by collecting information abroad, remodeling overseas offices as information providers, and pursuing active trade diplomacy to the benefit of local exporters. SMEs in particular, which account for about 42 percent of total export volume, face greater difficulties than large businesses in terms of export information, financing, and marketing. The Government urgently needs to arrange assistance for these firms.

FUTURE PROSPECTS

Following the Asian currency crisis, the Korean economy sharply slowed due to, among other things, a tight fiscal policy and shrinking domestic demand. While the depreciated won has boosted the price competitiveness of Korean exports, the same factor at work among other Asian competitors offsets many potential gains. Many Korean companies are now suffering from an inability to generate sufficient capital from their own operations or other sources of credit, causing them to reduce substantially their capital investment plans. Meanwhile, consumption is also declining, exacerbated by increasing unemployment. Consequently, manufacturers' domestic sales are expected to decline in 1998, leading them to focus on overseas markets, in a bid to avert shrinkage and, possibly, bankruptcy.

The current financial and economic crisis facing Korea is not the simple result of a temporary weakness of economic structure and mismanagement of exchange rates; rather, more fundamental factors are at work, including worsening terms of trade, rising wages in real terms, lack of flexibility in the local labor market, high debt levels of many firms, and high interest rates. It is the mix of these fundamental factors that has led to low corporate profitability, ultimately undermining the international competitiveness of Korean products. As for the financial sector, the high insolvency rate of local companies has burdened banks with mounting levels of nonperforming loans, further contributing to the crisis.

The economy's most likely escape route from a potential economic depression is to achieve a sizable trade surplus, which can be utilized to repay emergency loans from international institutions, such as IMF and the World Bank, while boosting international investor confidence. Regaining investor confidence is a necessary pre-condition to resumption of capital inflows.

As seen before, some of the most important export products (semiconductors, steel, and petrochemicals) are unlikely to do well in the short term. Any forecast of the country's export outlook should concentrate on the close linkage of the various economies in Asia, rather than taking each country in isolation. Cheong (1998) does this, on the assumption that the crisis will remain confined to the current five economies of Korea, Indonesia, Malaysia, Philippines, and Thailand, and that no new trade barriers will be raised against their exports.

Cheong suggests that three factors—tight money supply, economic depression, and insolvency—are real and unlikely to end soon. Through forecasts of currency devaluation, unemployment rates, and physical investment reduction, he estimates that in 1998 the Korean economy will record a trade surplus of $27.7 billion. This forecast is consistent with that of the Korea Development Institute (KDI), which estimates a trade surplus for the year of $25–30 billion. However, KITA (1998) predicts a gloomy outlook for Korean exports, based on the impact of high interest rates, difficulties in accessing trade financing, unstable exchange rates, and raw materials shortages.

Among the obstacles to increased exports, difficulties that local firms are experiencing in opening letters of credit constitute potentially the most significant. Unless operating credit becomes more accessible, many companies will be unable to take advantage of increased competitiveness abroad provided by the lower won, and consequently, the trade surplus will be worse than predicted by some analysts.

In an economy as dependent on trade as Korea's, sagging exports hold the distinct possibility of fostering further economic instability.

Thus, the Government must increase access to trade financing, including encouraging the extension of trade credit by foreign financial institutions and importing countries. Furthermore, many of the inefficient regulations governing the allocation of credit need to be streamlined, while the funding of export insurance needs to be increased. At the same time, funds must be prepared for increased demand for imported raw materials.

While Korea built up a substantial trade surplus in the first five months of 1998, the structure of this balance could well undermine future economic growth. The current trade surplus is over two thirds the result of plunging imports. If gold exports[16] are excluded, first quarter 1998 exports increased by only 2.7 percent compared with the same period in 1997, while imports decreased by 35.4 percent. The first quarter growth rates fall far short of Cheong's estimates of exports growing by 21.1 percent and imports increasing by 9 percent in 1998.

The drying up of available credit, compounded by the growing structural trade imbalance, paints a fairly grim outlook for Korean exports. Furthermore, the economic difficulties of the entire region, the five countries' (as mentioned above) tight interdependence, the continuing fall of the yen, and the potential devaluation of the renminbi, all loom menacingly over any resurgence of the Korean economy through trade. Thus, taking a realistic view, export prospects for the short term are bleak. Whether they improve in the medium term depends on how Korean policymakers deal with the weakness of the export sector, and on their endeavors to contain the current financial and currency crisis.

Korea now stands at a crossroads, and the reverberations of the steps it takes are likely to be felt far outside its borders. Korean failure to overcome rapidly the current difficulties could well contribute to a long and painful period of Asian economic stagnation and demoralize countries attempting to realize strong economic growth. However, this challenge need not portend failure. Instead, this current economic hurdle may eventually be remembered as the motivating force that gave Korea true, developed country status. The

[16] Korean nongovernment organizations collected publicly held gold and exported it as a way of improving the trade balance. In the first quarter of 1998, the country exported $1.8 billion worth of gold.

Government's approach in overcoming the current crisis will likewise contain implications for international economic policy making. Successfully overcoming the crisis through continuing to liberalize its economy will provide further impetus to the growing promarket forces around the world. Success through liberalization will also likely strengthen the move toward the opening measures in Southeast Asian economies facing the same economic difficulties. Ultimately, such success would give not only hope, but also many useful examples, to the developing countries of the world.

BIBLIOGRAPHY AND REFERENCES

Ahn, Y. H, and I. S. Hwang. 1997. "Toward Developing Higher Efficiency in Korea's Logistics Industry." *KIET Economic Review* (November).

Association of Industrial Technology. 1995. *White Book for Industrial Technology.* Seoul.

Balassa, Bela, Voloudakis Evangelos, Fylaktos Panagiotis, and Suh Suk Tai. 1989. "The Determinants of Export Supply in Two Developing Countries: Greece and Korea." *International Economic Journal* 3 (1) Spring.

Bank of Korea. 1996. *Current Status of Korean Industry and its Competitiveness* (May) Seoul.

______.Various years. *Economic Statistics Yearbook.* Seoul.

______.Various issues. *Monthly Statistical Review.* Seoul.

______.Various years. *National Income Accounts.* Seoul.

Bayoumi, Tamin. 1996. "International Trade and Real Exchange Rates." Occasional Paper No. 145. Washington, DC: International Monetary Fund.

Bhagwati, Jagdish N. 1990. "Export-Promoting Trade Strategy: Issues and Evidence." In Chris Milner, ed., *Export Promotion Strategies: Theory and Evidence from Developing Countries.* New York: Harvester Wheatsheaf.

Cheong, Inkyo. 1998. "Impact of the Asian Financial Crisis on Trade Patterns." Paper presented at the Fourth APEC Roundtable: Regional Cooperation and Asian Recovery, coorganized by Brandeis University, ISEAS, and KIEP, 26-27 May.

Cho, Dong Chul. 1996. "Exchange Movements in Korea: Evaluation and Policy Implications." Working Paper No. 11. Seoul: Korea Development Institute.

Cho, Chul. 1997. "1998 Industry Outlook: Automobiles." *Industrial Economy* 116(December). Seoul.

Cho, Yoon Je, and Joo-Kyung Kim. 1995. "Credit Policy and the Industrialization of Korea." Discussion Paper No. 286. Washington, DC: World Bank.

Chun, M. K. 1998. "Analyzing the Possibility of Economic Growth by Promoting Exports." *Business Economy* (January). In Korean.

Federation of Korean Industries (FKI). 1997. "1998 Tasks of Economic Policy." *FKI Economic Issues and Forecasts.* December. In Korean.

Frank, Charles R. Kwang Suk Kim, and Larry Westphal. 1975. *Foreign Trade Regimes and Economic Development: South Korea.* New York: National Bureau of Economic Research.

Giorgianni, Lorenzo, and Gian Milesi-Ferretti. 1997. "Determinants of Korean Trade Flows and their Geographical Destination." Working Paper No. 54. Washington, DC: International Monetary Fund.

Han, J. S. 1996. "Economic Approach to High Wage Rates." *Daewoo Economic Monthly* (October).

Hong, Won Tack. 1987. "Export-Oriented Growth and Trade Patterns of Korea." In Colian I. Bradford, Jr., and William H. Branson eds., *Trade and Structural Change in Pacific Asia.* Chicago: University of Chicago Press.

Jang, Chun-rhin. 1997. "Expecting 1.69 Million Cars for Domestic Sale and 1.48 Million Cars for Export." In *1998 Industry Prospect.* Maeil Business Newspaper.

Jung, Eun-mi. 1997. "1998 Industry Outlook: Steel." *KIET Economy* (116).

Kim, Chang Nam, Sang Hee Jeong, and Akira Hirata. 1989. "Export Promotion and Trade Liberalization Policy in the Republic of Korea." Joint Research Program Series, No. 75. Tokyo: Institute of Developing Economies.

Kim, Jin Chun. 1992. *Korea's Recent Foreign Exchange Rate Systems: MCBP vs MAR System.* Seoul: Korea Institute for International Economic Policy.

Kim, Jong Man. 1992. *Impact of Exchange Rates, Interest Rates and Wages on Export Growth.* Seoul: Korea Institute for International Economic Policy. Policy Study No. 27. In Korean.

Kim, Jung-ho. 1998. "The Impact of the IMF Bailout on Korean Industry." *Samsung Economy* (68).

Kim, Kwang Suk. 1994. "Trade and Industrialization Policies in Korea: An Overview." In G. K. Helleiner, ed., *Trade Policy and Industrialization in Turbulent Times.* New York: Routledge.

______.1998. "Effects of Exchange Rates on the Trade Balance." *Industrial Economics* (February) Seoul: Korea Development Bank. In Korean.

Kim, Soo Yong. 1980. *Trade Policy and Price Fluctuation in Korea.* Seoul: Korea International Economics Institute.

Kim, Y. Y., I. C. Kim, and H. Kim. 1997. "Direction of the Supporting Policy for Korea's Corporate Restructuring." *KIET Economic Review* (August).

Kim, Yun-Hwan. 1994. "The Role of Government in Export Expansion in the Republic of Korea." *EDRC Report Series 61.* Manila: Asian Development Bank.

Korea Development Bank (KDB). 1996. *Current Status of Korean Industry and its Competitiveness.* Seoul. June.

______.1998. *KDB Monthly Bulletin.* June.

Korea Institute for Industrial Economics and Trade (KIET). 1997. *Industry Outlook under the IMF.* December. Seoul.

Korea International Trade Association (KITA). 1997. "Comparison of National Export Strategies between Korea and Japan, and the Implications." *Trade Monthly* (November). Seoul. In Korean.

______. Database.

______.1998. *Export Prospects for Korean Products by Item.* Seoul.

Korea National Statistical Office. Various years. *Major Statistics of the Korean Economy.*

Korea Trade Information Service (KOTIS)database

Krueger, Anne O. 1979. *The Developmental Role of the Foreign Sector and Aid.* Cambridge, Mass.: Harvard University Press.

Lee, D. H. 1997. "Economic Analysis of the Low Yen on Korea's Major Exports." *Daewoo Economic Monthly* (May).

Lee, Honggue. 1993. "Changing Patterns of Trade Goods and Services in the Pacific Region: Korean Case Study." Working Paper No. 13. Seoul: Korea Development Institute.

Lee, Inho. 1997. "International Competitiveness of Korea's Major Exports." *Business Economy* (October). In Korean.

Lee, Jae-duck. 1997. "1998 Industry Outlook: Textiles." *KIET Economy* (116).

Min, S. G. 1998. "How to Enhance Korea's Export Competitiveness?" *Trade Monthly* (January). In Korean.

Ministry of Industry and Resource. 1998. "Forecasts on 1998 Trade Balance" (22 April).

Ministry of Trade and Industry. 1989. *The Korean Export Processing Zones: Policy and Reflections.*

Nam, Chong-Hyun. 1990. "Export Promotion Strategy and Economic Development in Korea." In Chris Milner, ed., *Export Promotion Strategies: Theory and Evidence from Developing Countries.* New York: Harvester Wheatsheaf.

Ohn, K. H., and H. S. Shin. 1997. "The Changing Structure of Korean Exports and Imports." *KIET Economic Review* (May).

Park, H. J. 1997. "The Role of Government for Promoting Corporate Structural Adjustment." *Business Economy* (October). In Korean.

Pyo, Hak K. 1990. "Export-Led Growth, Domestic Distortions, and Trade Liberalization: The Korean Experience during the 1980s." *Journal of Asian Economics* 1(2).

Riedel, J. 1988. "The Demand for LDC Export of Manufactures: Estimates from Hong Kong." *The Economic Journal* 98(389).

Sagong, E. D., and M. H. Kang. 1998. "The Problems of Recent Exports and Imports, and Implications." *Hanhwa Economy* (February). In Korean.

Shin, H. B. 1998. "Price Competitiveness of Korean Exports." *Trade Monthly* (February).

Shin, Hyun-Soo. 1997. "Anticipated Improvement of Korea's Trade Balance." *KIET Economic Review* (December).

US Department of Labor. 1990. *Worker Rights in Export Processing Zones: Korea.* Washington, DC.

Chapter Seven

Case Study: Taipei,China

An-Chi Tung

INTRODUCTION

Taipei,China has enjoyed fast growth, stable prices, and equitable income distribution since World War II. In 1952, per capita GDP was $196; it leaped to $2,344 in 1980 and to $13,233 in 1997. Both the IMF and the World Bank have now classified Taipei,China as an advanced economy. This success has almost always been attributed to the rapid expansion of exports. Trade expanded not only with respect to GDP, but also in the world market: its share (in nominal terms) of global exports rose from 0.16 percent in 1950 to 2.23 percent in 1997 (Table 7.1). In 1996, it was the 14th largest exporter and 15th largest importer in the world, ahead of larger countries such as Brazil and richer countries such as Australia (WTO 1997).

Since exports grew faster than imports, the economy started to record a trade surplus in 1971. Its subsequent rapid expansion led to a sharp increase in foreign exchange reserves and a large-scale appreciation of the New Taiwan (NT) dollar in 1986–1987. In turn, this appreciation weakened the external competitiveness of the economy and contributed to reduced export growth which, in 1996, decreased to 3.8 percent from 20 percent in 1995, while real GDP growth fell to 5.7 percent.

In 1997, when several Asian economies were hit hard by financial crisis, Taipei,China was relatively little affected. Despite a 14.8 percent currency devaluation and a 9.3 percent decline in the stock market index in the second half of that year, real GDP growth was 6.8 percent,

Table 7.1 Exports and Imports, 1950–1997

	Trade Performance ($ million)			Share in World Market (percent)	
Year	Exports	Imports	Balance	Exports	Imports
1950	93	112	-19	0.16	0.18
1952	117	187	-71	0.17	0.24
1954	93	211	-118	0.13	0.27
1956	118	194	-75	0.12	0.19
1958	156	226	-70	0.15	0.21
1960	164	297	-133	0.13	0.23
1962	218	304	-86	0.17	0.22
1964	433	428	5	0.27	0.25
1966	536	622	-86	0.28	0.31
1968	789	903	-114	0.35	0.38
1970	1,481	1,524	-43	0.50	0.49
1972	2,988	2,514	475	0.75	0.62
1974	5,639	6,966	-1,327	0.69	0.85
1976	8,166	7,599	567	0.86	0.78
1978	12,687	11,027	1,660	1.02	0.86
1980	19,811	19,733	78	1.03	0.99
1982	22,204	18,888	3,316	1.27	1.02
1984	30,456	21,959	8,497	1.67	1.15
1986	39,862	24,182	15,680	1.96	1.14
1988	60,667	49,673	10,995	2.22	1.76
1990	67,214	54,716	12,498	1.99	1.58
1991	76,178	62,861	13,318	2.19	1.74
1992	81,470	72,007	9,464	2.18	1.87
1993	85,092	77,061	8,030	2.28	2.03
1994	93,049	85,349	7,700	2.19	1.98
1995	111,659	103,550	8,109	2.20	2.01
1996	115,947	102,370	13,577	2.20	1.90
1997	122,098	114,426	7,672	2.23	2.05

Sources: Ministry of Finance, *Monthly Statistics of Exports and Imports: Taiwan Area, The Republic of China* (various issues); and IMF, *International Financial Statistics Yearbook* (various years).

exceeding the 6.7 percent target rate. Although the economy has since performed relatively well compared with most of its neighbors, the second wave impact of the financial turmoil has, in mid-1998, just begun to be felt, especially after the plunge of the yen in June 1998. Exports contracted by 7.1 percent while real GDP growth fell to 5.5 percent in the first six months of 1998.

This study begins with an overview of Taipei,China's export expansion, and then looks into the major challenges and responses in different periods. The following two sections discuss and evaluate trade policies. The last two sections examine the recent export growth deceleration and future prospects.

EXPANSION OF EXPORTS

As summarized in Table 7.1, both exports and imports have expanded rapidly since 1950, but as exports have grown faster than imports since the 1960s, trade surpluses were recorded from 1971, except in 1974 when the economy was adversely affected by the oil crisis. In the 1990s, however, export growth became slower than import growth, and the accumulation of net foreign assets decelerated.

Commodity Composition

The merchandise composition of both exports and imports has changed continuously since the early 1950s, reflecting industrial restructuring and upgrading of industry. In 1952–1959, agricultural and processed agricultural goods dominated exports, amounting to 86.9 percent of total exports. As domestic production of textiles, apparel, and electrical and electronics products expanded in the 1960s and 1970s, the share of nonfood manufactured exports increased rapidly, to account for an average of 51.2 percent of total exports in the 1960s, 85 percent in the 1970s, 93.5 percent in the 1980s, and 96.1 percent in 1990–1997. In 1997, the three top exports were electronics (14.8 percent), textiles and apparel (13.6 percent), and information technology (IT) and telecommunications products (11.8 percent). Processed food accounted for only 1.8 percent of total exports, and agricultural products a tiny 0.3 percent.

The major imports have always been of raw materials, due to the island's lack of natural resources. In 1952-1997, an annual average of 69 percent of imports were agricultural and industrial raw materials. In 1981, every dollar's worth of exports would induce, directly and indirectly, 0.33 dollar's worth of imports (Directorate-General of Budget, Accounting and Statistics, 1985). The share of capital goods in total imports was also high (28.5 percent) in 1960–1979, but with the gradual expansion of domestic production capacity, the share fell to 16.4 percent in 1980–1997. Although the

Table 7.2 Exports and Imports of Manufactures, 1962–1997 (percent)

Industry	Processed Food	Beverages & Tobacco	Textiles	Apparel	Footwear	Leather & Products	Wood & Products	Furniture	Paper & Products	Chemical Material & Products
SITC										
Period (average)	a	11 & 12	26 & 65	84	85	21 & 61	24 & 63	82	25 & 64	5-57-57
Part A: Export Share, E_i/E										
1962-1969	33.38(1)	0.41	12.42(2)	6.40(4)	0.84	0.16	9.26(3)	0.07	1.21	3.28
1970-1979	9.70(4)	0.12	11.67(3)	15.43(1)	5.04	0.28	6.44	0.89	0.63	1.52
1980-1989	4.75	0.05	8.70(3)	10.85(2)	6.75	0.58	2.68	2.37	0.57	1.42
1990-1997	2.94	0.05	10.89(3)	4.18	2.88	0.66	0.86	1.88	0.83	2.37
Part B: Import Share, M_i/M										
1962-1969	1.72	0.78	13.78(2)	0.01	0.00	0.41	3.04	0.01	1.56	10.38(3)
1970-1979	2.56	0.66	8.76	0.04	0.00	0.83	3.79	0.01	1.21	8.90(4)
1980-1989	3.44	0.54	4.46	0.10	0.03	1.12	2.84	0.04	1.54	9.90(4)
1990-1997	2.44	0.75	2.98	0.74	0.28	0.76	2.08	0.25	1.99	10.22(3)
Part C: Net Trade Index, $(E_i-M_i)/(E_i+M_i)$										
	X	M	M→X	X	X	M	X→M	X	M	M
1962-1969	87.60	-36.75	-13.00	99.59	99.41	-57.49	47.87	51.92	-21.76	-60.14
1970-1979	58.36	-66.87	18.84	99.49	99.90	-49.74	27.45	97.76	-29.74	-69.69
1980-1989	27.84	-80.32	43.15	98.12	99.31	-18.87	8.04	97.55	-34.49	-68.51
1990-1997	13.86	-85.11	60.85	69.64	75.02	-3.31	-37.35	77.88	-36.00	-58.75
Part D: Intra-Industry Trade Index, $1-\backslash E_i-M_i\backslash/(E_i+M_i)$										
1962-1969	12.40	63.25	87.00	0.41	0.59	42.51	52.13	40.59	78.24	39.86
1970-1979	41.64	33.13	80.79	0.51	0.10	49.67	72.55	2.24	70.26	30.31
1980-1989	72.16	19.68	56.85	1.88	0.69	81.13	90.61	2.45	65.51	31.49
1990-1997	83.11	14.89	39.15	30.36	24.98	81.15	62.65	22.12	64.00	41.25

a CCC (Standard Classification of Commodities of Taipei,China) 2-SITC11 for 1962–1967, CCC 31-32 for 1971–1988, CCC 23-29 for 1968–1971, and the World Bank's top 10 industries for 1989–1997.

Notes: "→" refers to a change in the net trade position, e.g., from net imports to net exports. The leading industries are marked with (1), (2), (3), and (4) in Parts A and B.

Sources: Ministry of Finance, *Monthly Statistics of Exports and Imports: Taiwan Area, The Republic of China* (various issues).

Table 2 (continued)

Petroleum & Coal Products	Rubber & Products	Plastic & Products	Nonmetal Products	Metals	Metal Products	Machinery	Electrical & Electronics Products	Transport Equipment	Precision Instruments	Travel Goods
32 & 33	23 & 62	57 & 58	66	67 & 68	69	71 - 74	75 - 74	78 & 79	87 & 88	83
0.86	0.37	0.76	3.38	3.31	1.22	1.80	4.60	0.46	0.11	0.14
1.45	0.60	0.48	1.40	2.38	2.71	3.85	14.92[2]	2.66	1.33	1.69
1.39	0.82	1.34	2.09	2.22	4.78	8.60[4]	20.37[1]	6.58	2.06	2.60
0.71	0.80	3.00	1.25	2.73	5.48	18.81[2]	31.88	8.04[4]	2.22	0.67
6.19	1.16	1.54	0.24	9.10[4]	1.58	14.50[1]	6.44	6.99	2.02	0.00
11.74[2]	0.97	1.96	0.43	8.54	1.34	13.14[1]	11.55[3]	6.91	1.98	0.00
17.91[1]	0.81	1.86	0.74	7.68	0.94	10.45[3]	13.61[2]	6.28	2.84	0.02
7.48	0.71	2.33	1.20	9.79[4]	1.11	11.36[2]	20.98[1]	6.48	5.08	0.11
M	M→X	M→X	X	M	M→X	M→X	M→X	M→X	M	X
-79.81	-56.83	-40.46	84.31	-53.00	-22.07	-82.01	-35.92	-90.20	-91.24	88.38
-71.25	-22.96	-59.79	54.55	-55.68	33.44	-52.14	15.25	-43.01	-25.35	99.48
-81.44	13.16	-4.31	56.91	-44.98	73.24	-0.90	32.39	14.52	-2.30	98.53
-80.48	12.08	17.61	7.23	-52.27	69.57	28.01	25.95	15.15	-36.48	67.02
20.19	43.17	59.54	15.69	47.00	77.93	17.99	61.62	9.80	8.76	11.62
28.75	77.04	40.21	45.45	44.32	66.56	47.86	84.75	56.99	68.92	0.52
18.56	86.48	92.55	43.09	55.02	26.76	76.98	67.61	80.92	94.77	1.47
19.52	87.92	82.39	88.42	47.73	30.43	69.48	74.05	84.83	67.52	32.98

share of consumption goods in total imports was, on average, 16.5 percent in 1952–1954, this declined to 7.5 percent in 1955–1959 at the outset of the import-substitution period. The proportion remained low in the 1960s, 1970s, and 1980s (7.1 percent on average), but started to rise in the late 1980s because of import liberalization efforts. In 1990–1997, the share of consumption goods rose to an average of 12.6 percent a year.

Table 7.2 shows manufacturing sector exports and imports in detail. The leading export and import sectors in each period are marked in Parts A and B. It is clear that the economy specialized in food and labor-intensive industries in the early years, but exported increasingly more capital-intensive products over time. And though the share of textiles in imports was quite high (12.4 percent) in 1962–1969, since then the main import sectors have been either capital goods, or petroleum and coal products.

Part C presents the net trade position of each manufacturing sector. Four types of industries can be identified. The first group includes net importing sectors such as beverages and tobacco, leather, paper, chemicals, petroleum and coal products, metals, and precision instruments. They are either capital-intensive or based on natural resources. The second group encompasses net exporting sectors such as processed food, apparel, footwear, furniture, nonmetal products, and travel goods. They are mainly labor-intensive industries. The third type is wood and wood products, which turned from a net exporter into a net importer in the 1990s. The last group includes those sectors whose initial comparative disadvantage evolved gradually into comparative advantage over time. Textiles, electrical and electronics products, and metal products first became net exporters in the 1970s, rubber and rubber products, machinery, and transport equipment in the 1980s, and plastic and plastic products in the 1990s. These changes demonstrate the shifts in the economy's comparative advantage.

Part D shows intraindustry trade indexes. The index is at 0, the minimum, when there is no intraindustry trade at all, but at 1, the maximum, when exports equal imports. It is interesting to note that the traditional exporting sectors (apparel, footwear, travel goods, and furniture) have small intraindustry trade levels, while the indexes of capital- and technology-intensive exporting sectors (e.g., electrical and electronics products, machinery) had high levels. Five of the top 10 exports in 1997, namely machinery, electrical machinery and equipment, plastics and articles, vehicles (other than railway vehicles), and iron and steel, were also among the top 10 imports. That is to say, as the economy restructured toward capital-intensive production, it also became more integrated into the global economy through trade.

Direction of Trade

Taipei,China trades mainly with Japan and the US (Table 7.3), which together accounted for over half of the economy's total trade until the 1980s. Hong Kong, China is the third largest partner while Germany is a distant number four.

The share of imports from Japan has always been high, and remained so into the 1990s, though at slightly lower levels. This is because the economy has always relied on Japanese parts, components, and machinery for many of its imports, regardless of its own industrial upgrading. As for exports, the economy used to sell processed food and light industrial products to Japan. Although it now exports more capital- and technology-intensive products to Japan, 30 percent of its exports in 1996 were primary products, while its electronics exports had lower value-added than those imported from Japan. Given the differences in commodity composition of bilateral trade, the island's trade deficits with Japan have deteriorated over time.

The economy first registered a trade surplus with the US in 1967, when US markets began to open up. A triangular trade pattern took shape in the 1960s among Japan, the US, and Taipei,China (and other newly industrialized economies). Japan provided machinery and raw materials to Taipei,China, which then processed the materials and exported light industrial products to the US. As the economy expanded its export share in the US, it enjoyed trade surpluses there while suffering deficits with Japan.

Trade with Europe averaged only 8.5 percent of the total in 1952–1969, with Taipei,China suffering from trade deficits. The Government has made great efforts to help exporters diversify markets since the 1970s in view of potential protectionism. Both export and import shares with Europe have increased since then. Europe's share in total trade rose to 16.9 percent in 1997; Germany alone accounted for 3.8 percent. But as imports from Europe grew faster than exports, with massive procurement related to public investment or to national defense, trade deficits were recorded after 1993.

Table 7.3 Major Trading Partners, 1950–1997 (percent)

Year (average for period)	Exports: Share of Taipei,China's Exports	Exports: Share of Partner's Imports	Imports: Share of Taipei,China's Imports	Imports: Share of Partner's Exports
Japan				
1950–1959	44.87	2.27	35.54	3.71
1960–1969	25.68	1.26	36.98	2.57
1970–1979	13.72	1.59	35.67	3.66
1980–1989	11.68	2.92	29.34	4.27
1990–1997	11.26	3.78	28.76	6.30
US				
1950–1959	5.29	0.05	33.85	0.46
1960–1969	23.50	0.46	33.05	0.65
1970–1979	38.02	2.09	23.58	1.40
1980–1989	41.84	4.23	23.33	2.56
1990–1997	26.94	3.86	21.26	3.42
Hong Kong, China				
1950–1959	9.39	1.48	5.66	1.57
1960–1969	9.28	2.50	1.26	0.60
1970–1979	7.22	5.70	1.83	1.53
1980–1989	7.98	7.92	2.09	1.66
1990–1997	20.31	12.68	2.18	1.36
Hong Kong, China and PRC				
1990–1997	20.51		3.98	
Germany				
1952–1959	1.51	0.10	2.79	0.35
1960–1969	4.65	1.24	3.73	0.94
1970–1979	4.85	4.61	4.64	4.06
1980–1989	3.66	3.89	4.11	3.73
1990–1997	3.93	4.05	5.17	4.13

Sources: CEPD (1955); IMF *Direction of Trade Statistics Yearbook* (various years); Ministry of Finance, *Monthly Statistics of Exports and Imports: Taiwan Area, The Republic of China* (various issues).

Although the economy gradually lost competitiveness in labor-intensive exports to Southeast Asian economies, it started to invest there in the second half of the 1980s and exported more intermediate and capital goods to them. The share of the ASEAN economies in

Taipei,China's exports rose from 5.4 percent in 1986 to 13.3 percent in 1997, while the import share increased from 6.3 percent in 1986 to 11.6 percent in 1997.

Trade with the PRC began to boom in the late 1980s. As no direct trade is allowed by the Taipei,China authorities, and with Hong Kong, China serving as a convenient entrepôt, the export share to the latter economy rose to second position in the 1990s. Although exact statistics are unavailable, one official estimate indicates that about 70 percent of all Taipei,China's exports to Hong Kong, China were transshipped to the PRC, and the latter's share in Taipei,China's exports increased from 2.3 percent in 1987 to 16.8 percent in 1997. When transshipment is excluded, commodities headed for the PRC and Hong Kong, China were, on average, 20.5 percent of the economy's total exports in 1990–1997. The increase in imports was much slower, since the Taipei,China authorities placed more restrictions than on exports. The PRC's share in total imports was only 3.4 percent in 1997. Huge trade surpluses were recorded in favor of the island's economy every year. Thus, commercially, Taipei,China has moved close to the ASEAN economies and the PRC since the second half of the 1980s.

Cross-straits trade was also connected with the economy's foreign direct investment (FDI), which obviously affected and determined the commodity composition. The main exports from Taipei,China were intermediate goods and machinery. The main imports from the PRC were primarily low-technology electronics parts and components, labor-intensive manufactures, mineral products, and agricultural goods. Raw materials accounted for 76.8 percent of total cross-straits imports in 1996, and though much smaller than the figure of 94.8 percent in 1992, it was still higher than the figure of 69 percent for the economy's total imports.

Capital Flows

Although US aid was essential in filling both the import-export and savings-investment gaps for Taipei,China in 1951–1965 (Jacoby 1966), neither FDI nor foreign debt has been an important source of capital since the end of foreign aid in 1965. In 1997, foreign debt servicing was equivalent to a mere 0.04 percent of total exports. FDI was small, too. The amount of FDI approved by the Ministry of Economic Affairs constituted, on average, only 4.2 percent of total fixed capital formation in 1952–1997. Most FDI goes into manufacturing industries. The electrical and electronics industry is the main recipient, followed by chemicals, basic metals, metal products, and machinery. FDI into banking and insurance, trade, services, and transportation increased considerably in the 1980s and 1990s, when the Government gradually lifted investment restrictions on the tertiary sector. In 1997, 24.8 percent of total accumulated FDI was in the electrical and electronics industry, and 29.3 percent in the tertiary sector.

The surge of outward FDI was a new phenomenon in the second half of the 1980s. Earlier amounts had been a trickle. Capital fund outflows exceeded inward FDI in value terms for the first time in 1991. In 1952–1986, 60 percent of accumulated outward FDI went to the US while 32.3 percent went to Asia. With the new international division of labor in the 1990s, more outward FDI went to Southeast Asia and the PRC. In 1996, the amount of outward FDI to the PRC alone was 1.4 times as large as total inward FDI, while total outward FDI was 2.3 times that of inward FDI. The new investments to Southeast Asia headed mainly for traditional light industry. In turn, this FDI created derived demand for intermediate and capital goods. FDI to the PRC went disproportionately to labor-intensive industries (e.g., food and beverages, apparel), though the share of heavy and chemical industries (e.g., electrical and electronics products, chemicals, and metal) rose. These outward investments facilitated the economy's own industrial restructuring, upgrading it from low value-added to higher value-added products.

Factor Contents

The standard Heckscher-Ohlin predictions applied well to Taipei,China's trade in the 1960s and 1970s. A recalculation of Lin's (1973) data shows that in 1967, 50.5 percent of all manufactured exports (including sugar, but excluding other foodstuffs and simple processed products) were in the most labor-intensive group of products, while only 8.1 percent were in the highest and second highest capital-intensive groups in a five-group classification scheme (Lin 1973). To be more specific, the capital/labor ratio of exports in 1966 was estimated to be NT$52,680 per person, while that of import-competing goods was much higher, at NT$75,050. By 1971, the gap between the two had widened, with figures of NT$105,350 and NT$280,690, respectively (Liang and Liang 1975). The picture changed in the 1980s and 1990s, with the capital/labor ratio of exports increasing faster than that of imports. In 1996, the ratio of exports rose to NT$383,700 while that of imports dropped to NT$366,000. For the first time, exports were more capital intensive than imports.

A comparison of the changes in commodity composition between 1982 and 1996 by input intensity confirms the evolution of comparative advantage from labor-intensive products to capital- and technology-intensive products (Ministry of Finance, various issues). The share of exported commodities with a high capital intensity increased from 26.9 percent in 1982 to 31.8 percent in 1996, while the share of imported commodities with a high capital intensity declined from 55.4 percent to 43.4 percent over the same period. The ratio of highly labor-intensive exports fell from 47.2 percent to 33.9 percent, and that of highly labor-intensive imports rose from 31 percent to 37.9 percent over the same period. Finally, the share of exports of high technology intensity increased from 18.3 percent to 39.7 percent, while that of imports declined from 61.5 percent to 50.9 percent over this period. Although the share of R&D expenditure in GNP is still low (1.9 percent in 1996), Taipei,China had by 1995 already become the world's largest producer of 11 IT products (e.g., image scanners).

Determinants of Exports

We now review a number of studies on Taipei,China's exports in different periods and markets. In the 1950s and 1960s, the income effect dominated the price effect. An econometric exercise by Hsu (1975) shows that in 1953–1971, the foreign income elasticity for exports was 2.67–2.78. At country level, the income elasticity for its exports was 0.98 in Japan and 7.08 in the US. The price effect was statistically significant in only the US case, and was of the wrong sign for Japan. A second study by Liu (1981) on Taipei,China-Japan trade finds similar results for the period 1960–1980, though the price effect had the right sign, and was somewhat significant.

The dominance of the income effect may be due to the fact that the economy was too small a supplier to these markets, and that its exports expanded mainly with world demand (Cline 1982). It is also possible that the nominal export price was a poor proxy for the shadow export price, since it left out many explicit and implicit subsidies (discussed below). The price effect was more important later. A study by the Chung-hua Institute for Economic Research in 1996 confirms the importance of price competitiveness in determining the economy's exports in 1971–1990 in various markets, though the income effect was still more significant than the price effect in all cases. It is interesting to note that the price elasticity of developed economies toward exports was in general greater and statistically more significant than that of less developed economies. This is probably because Taipei,China exported price-elastic labor-intensive goods to Japan and the US, while exporting relatively price-inelastic capital-intensive goods to less developed countries.

Wu (1996) looks into long-term export behavior in 1965–1994. When different regions are aggregated together, and when a lag variable is included, only the income effect is statistically significant at the 10 percent level. This suggests that it is essential to examine the economy's trade behavior by period and market; otherwise, many changes may escape attention.

STAGES OF TRADE DEVELOPMENT

Import-Substitution Industrialization

Taipei,China recovered from war destruction around 1952. However, prewar export promotion for agricultural products did not continue, as sugar production never regained the prewar peak and the increase in rice production was mostly offset by the rapid inflow of migrants from the Mainland after 1949.

In 1952, the Government announced the first Four-Year Plan (1953–1956) and formally committed itself to self-sufficiency and long-term growth, with a heavy emphasis on industrialization through import substitution. Import controls were tightened, and tariff rates were raised. In addition, a multiple exchange rate system was designed to exploit agricultural exports in favor of capital and basic material imports. The NT/US dollar exchange rate that was applied to exports was, on average, only 82.8 percent of the rate applied to imports.

The priority industries included textiles, fertilizer, and electricity.[1] Textiles and fertilizer, which accounted for 29.3 percent of total imports in 1950 (CEPD 1955), benefited from a range of measures including quantitative import restrictions, high tariffs, ample supplies of electricity, government provision of raw materials, and guaranteed purchase of finished products. Although all three industries expanded rapidly, because the expansion of these industries inevitably entailed imports of parts, components, materials, and machinery, imports increased much faster than exports, and so the trade deficits worsened. As the domestic market became saturated, GDP growth declined. The Government reacted passively by periodically devaluing the overvalued NT dollar. It also introduced various subsidies to selected export industries (Lin 1973).

Labor-Intensive Export-Led Growth

As these piecemeal actions proved ineffective, the Government adopted a more comprehensive export promotion strategy in the second half of the 1950s, including exchange rate unification and depreciation, low-rate export loans, export tax rebates, export processing zones (EPZ), and enhanced entitlement to foreign exchange. In 1959, the 19-Point Financial and Economic Reform Program was announced to improve the general economic environment; in addition, some of the import-side distortions were corrected. Although most import controls remained unchanged, and industrial licensing for new firms was more forcefully implemented, the share of import items not subject to quantitative restrictions rose from 53.7 percent in 1960 to 82.1 percent in 1972. Two revisions of the tariff schedule in 1955 and 1959 brought average nominal tariff rates (with defense surtaxes included) down from 24.9 percent (in 1956–1959) to 16.6 percent (in 1960–1969).

The impact of the liberalization policies was impressive: between 1960 and 1972, real GNP grew at 10 percent annually. Labor-intensive exporting sectors expanded particularly fast, the share of textiles and apparel in total exports rising from 15.4 percent in 1961 to 28.3 percent

[1] Electricity is not an import-substitution industry, but its development is essential for the expansion of all other industries.

in 1972, and electrical products from 0.8 percent to 15.7 percent over the same period. Total exports also increased remarkably: the economy's share in world exports rose from 0.1 percent to 0.8 percent between 1960 and 1972. New constraints appeared, nevertheless. The nonexporting sectors saw little progress in productivity and efficiency because of overprotection (Ma 1994). In addition, investment in social infrastructure slowed in the 1960s and lagged behind general investment, storing up greater problems for the future.

Second-Stage Import Substitution and High-Technology Orientation

As a result of the drying up of surplus labor in the early 1970s and the subsequent loss of competitiveness in labor-intensive exporting sectors (Kuo 1983), the Government resorted to import-substitution policies once again, and under the Fifth Four-Year Plan (1969–1972) aimed to improve infrastructure and promote heavy and chemical industries. State-owned enterprises were in the forefront of the import-substitution drive. New entry was restricted, and foreign competition was restrained so as to ensure a comfortable market share for the "chartered" enterprises. In 1974–1979, basic petrochemicals saw an average annual growth rate of 32 percent, and steel of 17 percent—both chartered areas—and both exceeded the 12 percent for manufacturing as a whole.

Although specific sectors were stringently controlled and protected, liberalization continued in both exports and imports. The proportion of permissible import items increased from 59 percent in 1970 to 97.7 percent in 1974, while nominal tariff rates were reduced for many items. Export incentives were also lowered. The ratio of tax rebates to total exports decreased from 14 percent in 1971 to 4.8 percent in 1980; the interest margin between export loans and regular secured loans declined from about 5.1 percent to 3 percent.

The direction toward import substitution was modified after the second oil crisis of 1979, since capital-intensive development was neither appropriate nor sustainable for the energy-poor economy. Industrial emphasis was shifted into high technology and low energy-consuming industries instead of those merely intensive in capital use. Until then, as a small developing economy, Taipei,China had been copying, borrowing, and purchasing technology from the more advanced economies through trade, technical cooperation, and FDI. Serious attempts to develop its own technological capacity started in the early 1980s. R&D expenditure as a share of GNP increased from 0.7 percent in 1978 to 1 percent in 1985. Precision instruments, and IT/telecommunications industries were given high priority. The machinery and electrical machinery industries continued to be targeted, and the purpose was no longer to substitute for imports, but rather to upgrade the economy's technological capacity.

Globalization and Liberalization

The NT dollar appreciated against the US dollar by 28.4 percent in 1986–1987, ending 27 years of stable nominal exchange rates. Export growth slowed, as the currencies of most of its Asian competitors either appreciated very little or depreciated during this period. In the meantime, domestic production costs rose and the investment climate deteriorated. First, the lifting of martial law in 1987 opened up a process of political and social liberalization. The number of labor disputes and environmental conflicts surged (Chang 1989; Hsiao 1994). Second, economic institutions and laws did not keep pace with the changes in society and hindered economic and administrative efficiency. Third, stock and real estate prices began to soar, marking the beginning of a bubble economy. Stock prices indexes, for example, went up from an average of 746 in 1985 to 6,775 in 1990. With the worsening of domestic competitiveness, many domestic firms responded by moving abroad, and much FDI went to the ASEAN economies and the PRC, raising bilateral trade with these economies substantially. As mentioned in *Factor Contents,* above, exports as a whole became less labor-intensive, more capital-intensive, and more technology-intensive in the 1990s, while imports moved in the opposite direction.

Economic liberalization accelerated in the 1990s, partly due to increased participation in the international economy. For example, in 1991, Taipei,China joined the APEC forum. In 1992 and 1995, it obtained observer status at GATT and WTO, respectively. Accession to WTO is important to the economy, not only to reduce export barriers, but also to improve resource allocation and general production efficiency (Chou et al. 1995). The prospects of the economy's exports will be explored in more detail in the last section.

TRADE POLICIES

Foreign Exchange Management

Until the trade surpluses of the early 1970s, tight foreign exchange controls were applied. The aims were originally to preserve scarce foreign exchange and to ensure the growth of import-substitution industries. The surrendering of all foreign exchange proceeds to the Bank of Taiwan (BOT) was mandatory after the currency reforms of 1949. As there was much greater demand for, than supply of, foreign exchange in the 1950s, the Government set up various allocation rules at different times. In early 1953, the demand was so high that only 6 percent of all applications were approved, and rent-seeking was serious. In general, raw materials, fertilizer, machinery, and exportable industries' imports were favored over consumption goods (Yin 1963; Foreign Exchange and Trade Commission 1969). The ratio of consumer goods to total imports fell significantly from 19.9 percent in 1952 to 9 percent in 1955.

The controls were partially relaxed in the 1960s with the end of import-substitution industrialization. When foreign reserves began to accumulate in the early 1970s, the restrictions were further relaxed. In 1979, a foreign exchange market was set up when the exchange rate regime was changed to a managed float. In 1987, foreign portfolio investment was allowed, and all controls on the current account were removed. In 1989, foreign exchange transactions were liberalized. In 1992, the upper limit of private capital flows was, in practical terms, removed. Had these changes not occurred, the FDI outflows of the 1990s, which considerably changed the content and direction of trade, would have been dramatically reduced.

Exchange Rate Policies

Until 1957, the NT dollar was overvalued. The black market US/NT dollar exchange rate was 2.1 times the end-of-year official exchange rate in 1952, and 1.6 times in 1957. A multiple rate system prevailed, as different combinations of the Exchange Settlement Certificate and official exchange rates were assigned to different commodity groups. The system was complicated. In August 1956, for instance, the effective exchange rate that was applied to all exports by public enterprises (sugar, rice, aluminum, etc.) except for salt was NT$20.35 per US dollar; the salt rate was NT$18.55. The rate for all exports by private enterprises (except for bananas) was NT$20.43–28.99; since the Exchange Settlement Certificate rate fluctuated the banana rate was NT$18.60–23.90. The import rate for US aid or public enterprise procurement, machinery, and raw materials was NT$24.78; the rate for all other imports was NT$24.88–35.58.

In 1958–1960, the exchange rates were unified and depreciated. The degree of depreciation was especially high with respect to exportable goods. The exchange rate applicable to sugar—the share of which amounted to 44 percent of total exports in 1960—depreciated by 96.7 percent, the rate for private exporters fell by 51.2 percent, while the rate for private importers dropped by only 24 percent. The difference between the black market and official rates fell to only 5.8 percent. As nominal prices and money wages rose sharply in 1959–1961, mainly because of natural calamities, the price rises eroded some of the benefits of nominal depreciation. However, exports expanded rapidly after 1961, as did the share of trade relative to GDP.

The exchange rate was fairly stable between 1963 and 1979, with only two instances of appreciation: it rose from NT$40 per US dollar to NT$38 in 1973, then to NT$36 in 1978. The exchange rate system was converted from a fixed rate system to a managed float in February 1979. The NT dollar fluctuated along with domestic and international business cycles, but only mildly. After the 1985 Plaza Accord, the NT dollar appreciated sharply from NT$39.85 per US dollar at the end of 1985 to NT$26.16 in 1989. Since then, market mechanisms have played the dominant role, alongside the liberalization of foreign exchange transactions. The difference between black market and official rates has been below 1 percent since 1988.

Import Controls

During the import-substitution period, about half of all manufacturing importables were subject to quantitative import controls, and were regulated by foreign exchange controls and assigned different exchange rates. In the export promotion period, foreign exchange controls were significantly relaxed, and the ratio of the number of prohibited import items among all import items fell from 4.8 percent in 1956 to 3.5 percent in 1960. But import restrictions continued to be applied extensively. From 1959, any domestic industrial producer had the right to request the Government to exercise quantitative controls on the import of his product if the ex factory price did not exceed the cost, insurance and freight (CIF) import price by more than 25 percent (Lin 1973).

The price premium given to import-competing industries was reduced successively over time, to 5 percent in 1972, when 82.1 percent of all importables were freely importable. Import restrictions were greatly reduced in 1974. Although the proportion of permissible imports has remained almost unchanged since then, the proportion needing approval from the Board of Foreign Trade declined from 10.9 percent in 1989 to 3 percent in 1995; that requiring the approval of other authorities decreased from 20.1 percent to 1.5 percent; and that restricted by agency fell from 1.1 percent to 0.3 percent.

A negative list replaced the positive list in 1994. Most of those currently on the negative list are agricultural products, some of which used to be important exports in the past, such as rice. Among all agricultural imports, 193 items are classified as being "controlled" (2 percent of total import items, including rice and pork), 30 items are restricted by origin (0.3 percent), and 87 items are conditionally permissible (0.9 percent). With respect to manufacturing, 63 items are controlled (0.7 percent), 31 items are restricted by agency (0.3 percent, including petroleum and petroleum products, and raw materials for fertilizer), 18 items are restricted by origin (0.2 percent, including automobiles), and 110 items are conditionally permissible (1.2 percent). All other commodities can be imported freely.

Imports from the PRC are more tightly controlled than other imports, for political reasons. In 1992, a new set of regulations legalized trade and investment activities across the straits. By the end of 1997, 5,241 items (52.4 percent) were classified as permissible, including 4,868 items of industrial products and 350 items of agricultural products.

Import Duties

Tariffs serve the same function as quantitative import controls to protect certain sectors of the economy. In addition, import duties have been an important source of government revenue, amounting to over 20 percent of all tax revenues in 1952–1979. This proportion fell to 16.3 percent in the 1980s and to 9 percent in 1990–1997 with the gradual reduction of the average tariff burden.

After two major revisions in 1955 and 1959, the tariff schedule changed little in the 1960s. Nevertheless, due to the changes in commodity composition, the average tariff burden, not including defense surtaxes levied in fiscal years 1955–1972, was reduced from an average of 13.7 percent in the 1960s to 11.2 percent in the 1970s. Nominal tariff rates were lowered substantially in the 1980s, and the tax base was reduced from 1.2 times free on board (FOB) import prices to actual prices in 1980–1985. In 1989, the reduction of tariff rates went further, which not only lowered the average tariff burden, but also reduced the amount of refundable tariffs. In 1990–1997, the average tariff burden was only 4.5 percent.

To sum up, the tariff structure has managed to be in line with the economy's comparative advantage and consistent with the overall development strategy, despite occasional tariff redundancy and overprotection (Sun 1982; Tu and Wang 1988). A few points on the tariff structure merit further attention. First, as the economy has always been a net importer of raw materials and a net exporter of processed manufactures, the tariff rates of raw materials were set lower than those of processed manufactures, and the tariff rates of consumer goods higher than those of capital goods. Second, the exporting sectors in the 1960s (e.g., textiles) were highly protected by import tariffs, though less so in the 1970s. Third, although the economy exported mainly agricultural products in the 1950s, it is the agriculture sector that needs to be protected in the 1990s. Most of the items, since the 1995 tariff revision, that are subject to high tariff rates (20–50 percent) are agricultural or processed agricultural products.

Export Tax Rebates

Export-promoting policies were adopted much later than import-substitution policies. From 1955, exporters were allowed to apply for reimbursement of relevant tariffs and taxes on imported materials or intermediates used for export production. At first, only tariffs and defense surtaxes were refundable. Later, commodity taxes were also covered, and various other taxes, such as harbor dues, salt tax, and slaughter tax, were included over different periods. Whereas the tariff rebates offset the cost increase due to import-side distortions, the nontariff tax rebates served directly as export subsidies. In 1956–1959, the ratio of tax rebates was only 2.1 percent of the value of total exports, and 70.2 percent of all rebates were tariff rebates. In the 1960s and 1970s, the ratio of tax rebates to exports rose to an average of 9.6 percent, while the share of tariff rebates decreased to 58.2 percent. These facts signify both the elimination of import-side distortion and the strengthening of export-side incentives.

The importance of tax rebates was greatly reduced in the 1980s, because they were only applied to imports with a nominal tariff rate above 5 percent and to exports with a refundable amount above 1 percent of the FOB export value. The ratio of total rebates to exports shrank to 2.3 percent in the 1980s and to 0.2 percent in 1990–1996. The share of nontariff rebates in total rebates also fell to 25 percent in the 1980s and to 3 percent in 1990–1996.

Bonded Factories, EPZs, and Science-Based Industrial Parks

The scope of tax rebates was enlarged in the 1960s. The first bonded factory was established in 1969 to facilitate transshipment by exempting it from import taxes and reducing bureaucratic requirements. According to customs statistics, by the end of 1970, 27 bonded factories or warehouses were operational, accounting for 4.1 percent of total trade. In 1984, there were 337, accounting for 16.9 percent of total trade. Although the number of factories decreased after 1988, 265 remained in operation in 1996, accounting for 15.9 percent of total trade. In recent years, the industrial composition of the bonded factories has shifted gradually from labor-intensive industries to technically more sophisticated areas. In the

1980s, electronics, textiles, and garments were the leading industries. In 1995, 40.3 percent of bonded factories produced electronics, 10.4 percent bicycles, and 6.7 percent electrical circuit boards.

EPZs were designed not only to facilitate and promote exports, but also to create employment and attract foreign capital. The first EPZ started operations in late 1965, the second and third in 1969, and the fourth in 1997. In 1965–1973, 74 percent of all firms in the EPZs were in food, garments, or other light industries. The EPZs sought to transform themselves in the late 1980s by directing investments into high-technology industries or trade services. In 1984–1996, only 48 percent of all firms were in labor-intensive industries, while their share in the EPZs' total sales was only 12 percent. But the percentage share of the EPZ firms in total trade fell from 7.4 percent in 1973 to 5 percent in 1996. More recently, with the national development target to build Taipei,China into the Asian Pacific Region Operations Center, the role of the EPZs has been redefined. They will be transformed into warehouse transshipment zones, since all four EPZs are close to the main ports or airports. Their functions are to be enlarged to combine transshipping, high value-added manufacturing, R&D, warehousing, and services.

The Science-Based Industrial Park (HSIP)in Hsinchu is one step further from the EPZs, with a greater range of fiscal and infrastructure incentives offered. Since its establishment in 1981, 245 firms have set up in the HSIP in selected high-technology industries, including integrated circuits, computers and peripherals, telecommunications, optical-electronics, precision machinery and materials, and biotechnology. The share of the HSIP in total manufacturing sales rose from 0.7 percent in 1986 to 6 percent in 1996, and in total trade from 1.1 percent to 8.3 percent over the same period. The industries in the HSIP are export-oriented, including semiconductors, personal computers, image scanners, and solid-state diodes, and often have significant shares of world markets. For example, over 60 percent of the economy's personal computer network cards are produced in the HSIP, a product in which the economy has had a world market share of about 20 percent in recent years. In view of the success of the HSIP, a second and larger science-based industrial park in Tainan in the south started production in 1998. The new park focuses on microelectronic and precision instruments, semiconductors, and agro-biological technology products.

Export Loans and Other Export Incentives

The provision of cheap export loans is another policy that aims directly at promoting exports. From 1957, exporters could obtain short-term loans at low interest rates from the BOT, and later, other banks. This was a great help to private exporters. The interest rate was 6 percent if repaid in foreign exchange and 11.9 percent if repaid in NT dollars, but 19.8 percent for regular secured loans (July 1957). Although the interest margin became smaller over time, it was at least 3.5 percent before 1981. As the interest margin shrank to almost zero after 1985, the demand for such cheap loans fell. Following the methodology of Hsiao (1994), the ratio of export loans was estimated to be 3.1 percent of the value of total exports in 1996, compared with 21.2 percent in 1972.

There are other positive export incentives. In the 1950s and 1960s, the Government helped several industries organize export cartels to regulate production and explore export markets. Such cartels were formed in the paper, textiles, canned mushroom, canned asparagus, steel products, rubber products, cement, and monosodium glutamate industries, among others (Lin 1973; Foreign Exchange and Trade Commission 1969). The Government still provides help in quality inspection, export insurance, and marketing for exports, and in the provision of information and training of human capital through the parastatal China External Trade Development Council and the Central Trust of China, a public enterprise.

FDI Policies

Although FDI has not been significant to the economy quantitatively, it has been important in the introduction of new technology (electronics in particular—see Hsiao 1994), and in the expansion of exports (Schive 1994).

The impending phaseout of US aid in the late 1950s made pressing the need for foreign capital and led to the revision of existing laws and regulations concerning investment capital inflows. More important, the Statute for Encouragement of Investment of 1960 offered a variety of incentives to foreign nationals, overseas Chinese, and local residents. In 1965, this statute was amended to provide tax benefits to selected enterprises or industries. The fiscal incentives included tax holidays, reductions, and exemptions. With the EPZs helping attract foreign capital, the proportion of FDI in total investment rose from 1.2 percent in 1952–1959 to 5.4 percent in 1960–1969, and then dropped slightly to 5 percent in 1970–1979.

With the deterioration of the investment environment since the mid-1980s, the growth of FDI has slowed. In 1990, the Statute for Upgrading Industries was enacted upon the expiration of the Statute for Encouragement for Investment. The new statute offered similar fiscal incentives as the earlier one, but these were only applied to industries that would upgrade the economy's industrial base. The absolute amount of foreign investment started to decline after 1989, though this was not a worry as the economy had been a net exporter of capital since 1988. The share of FDI in gross investment rose again after 1994, with the removal of several investment restrictions as part of wider liberalization efforts. In 1997, the amount of FDI was 6.8 percent of gross investment.

Outward FDI accelerated in view of the new economic realities from the second half of the 1980s. Financial market liberalization after 1987 further facilitated capital outflows. In 1987–1989, more than 300 cases of outward FDI were approved by the Investment Commission, Ministry of Economic Affairs, compared with only 284 cases in the previous 28 years. Although some investment plans were not realized, many cases were not officially registered. The underreporting was particularly serious with respect to FDI to the PRC because such investment was banned by Taipei,China. In 1991, this ban was lifted. Although all investments had to go through a third country and to only a limited number of industries, excluding services, the PRC has become the largest recipient of the island's outward FDI since 1992. When the restrictions were further loosened in 1993, new applications and ex post registrations pushed the annual total for 1993 to the PRC to double the amount to the rest of the world. With the revision of the Statute Governing the Relations between Peoples of the Taiwan Area and the Mainland Area in 1997, which further relaxed investment constraints, an additional $2 billion was registered.

EVALUATING TRADE POLICIES

To evaluate the impact of the various trade policies on trade performance, we shall construct a number of indexes. The first index is the ratio between the exchange rates actually applicable to exports and to imports, with subsidies, taxes, and tax rebates[2] considered (the final column of Table 7.4). The index shows how well trade incentives as a whole maintain the neutrality between exports and import substitution. The second and third indexes are the nominal effective exchange rate (NEER) and real effective exchange rate (REER) indexes, which illustrate the economy's competitiveness in world markets (Table 7.5). To highlight the competition in the US and Japanese markets, the NEER and REER are calculated against major competitors (CNEER and CREER), rather than against partners. This provides interesting results (Tables 7.6 and 7.7).

Neutrality between Exports and Import Substitution

Table 7.4 provides summary statistics on the impact of major trade incentives in terms of exchange rates applicable to exports and imports. The export exchange rate (E-rate) and the import exchange rate (M-rate) are the weighted averages of exchange rates applied to different commodities in different time periods when the multiple rate system prevailed. During the single rate period, they are the export and import converter between the NT and US dollar values. The de facto export exchange rate (E-rate') includes the subsidies from cheap loans and tax rebates, but excludes tariff exemptions. The de facto import exchange rate (M-rate') includes the actual tariffs collected (including defense taxes). Both the E-rate' and M-rate' are underestimated because of lack of data. Specifically, random subsidies on export loss and tax reductions on investment are excluded; and nontariff import restrictions are not quantified, though they were extensively used during the 1950s, 1960s, and 1970s (Foreign Exchange and Trade Commission 1969).

---

[2] See notes to Table 4.

Table 7.4 Export and Import Exchange Rates, 1952–1997

					Export/Import Exchange Rate Ratio (percent)	
Year	E-rate (a)	E-rate′ (b)	M-rate (c)	M-rate′ (d)	Without subsidies etc. (a)/(c)	With subsidies etc. (b)/(d)
1952	11.39	11.39	11.40	13.74	99.94	82.93
1954	15.54	15.54	18.76	23.99	82.86	64.79
1956	21.37	21.41	25.08	31.19	85.23	68.65
1958	27.20	27.98	26.82	34.83	101.44	80.35
1960	38.93	40.71	39.16	44.96	99.39	90.53
1962	39.87	42.00	40.01	46.86	99.66	89.62
1964	40.00	41.96	40.10	47.00	99.75	89.29
1966	40.00	42.27	40.10	46.74	99.75	90.43
1968	40.00	42.44	40.10	47.61	99.75	89.13
1970	40.00	42.81	40.10	45.82	99.75	93.43
1972	40.00	42.06	40.10	45.00	99.75	93.46
1974	37.90	39.35	38.10	41.93	99.48	93.86
1976	37.95	39.39	38.05	42.07	99.74	93.61
1978	36.93	38.14	37.03	41.23	99.71	92.52
1980	35.95	36.54	36.05	38.98	99.72	93.74
1982	38.92	39.34	38.97	41.80	99.88	94.11
1984	39.55	39.93	39.66	42.82	99.74	93.24
1986	37.81	38.02	37.92	40.88	99.69	93.00
1988	28.55	28.57	28.65	30.30	99.64	94.30
1990	26.82	26.82	26.90	28.35	99.71	94.61
1992	25.14	25.14	25.23	26.53	99.62	94.77
1994	26.39	26.40	26.50	27.76	99.61	95.10
1996	27.40	27.40	27.50	28.48	99.63	96.19
1997	28.52	...	28.63	29.51	99.61	...

Notes: 1. For 1952–1964, E-rate and M-rate are average nominal exchange rates of various commodities weighted by their export or import shares; for 1965–1997, E-rate and M-rate are export and import converters. 2. E-rate′ includes interest subsidy (1957–1985) and tax rebates (1956–1996) but excludes tariff rebates. 3. M-rate′ includes actual tariffs and defense tax collected, but excludes the effects of quantitative restrictions.

Sources: Ministry of Finance, *Yearbook of Tax Statistics, Republic of China* (various years); Ministry of Finance, *Monthly Statistics of Exports and Imports: Taiwan Area, The Republic of China* (various issues).

The last two columns of Table 7.4 present rough estimates of the neutrality between exports and import substitution. The last but one column shows the preadjustment ratios. As import substitution was favored over exports in the 1950s, the ratio of the E-rate to the M-rate was small and the bias was large. From the export promotion period, the distortion was small. The changes are much more pronounced in the last column. The average ratio of E-rate' to M-rate' was only 73.8 percent in 1952–1959, indicating a strong bias toward import substitution. It rose to 90.2 percent in the 1960s with the major reduction in import bias and the strengthening of export incentives. The ratio rose continuously in the following decades, when both the import-side and export-side distortions were reduced with faster import liberalization. When the export incentives were almost completely removed in the 1990s, import biases were also substantially reduced, and the ratio rose to an average of 95.2 percent in 1990–1996. As can be seen, over time, the trade incentives with regard to exports and import substitution have become more neutral.

Nominal Effective Exchange Rates

To look at Taipei,China's exchange rate compared with its trading partners, we now construct an NEER index by taking the inverse of the price of the domestic currency in units of foreign currencies, calibrated at 1969–1971 value, and weighted by trade shares. The NEER index is defined as

$$NEER_t = \Sigma_i \left(\frac{er_t}{er_0}\right)_i \times s_i \times 100$$

where

er_t = foreign currency per NT dollar in time t

er_0 = foreign currency per NT dollar in time 0

s_i = trade share of country i

As the NT dollar appreciates (or depreciates), the NEER rises (or falls). When NEER = 100, the exchange rate is equal to the level of the base period, which was chosen because it manifests a certain degree of equilibrium. As the economy recorded a trade surplus in 1971, we take 1969–1971 as the base period (Table 7.5). Official yearly average nominal exchange rates are used in the calculation. The bilateral exchange rate indexes are then weighted by the trade shares of trading partners in the base period.

The NT exchange rates were seriously overvalued in the import-substitution industrialization period, the NEER being 292.15 in 1953

Table 7.5 NEER and REER, 1953–1997 (1969–1971 base period)

Year	NEER	REER
1953	292.15	189.71
1955	193.92	136.53
1957	167.29	144.70
1959	106.76	98.20
1961	98.53	110.13
1963	99.09	107.34
1965	99.62	100.98
1967	99.68	99.08
1969	100.22	102.70
1971	99.35	96.82
1973	92.71	88.90
1975	96.12	112.14
1977	93.97	104.92
1979	92.90	103.62
1981	93.96	118.20
1983	93.33	109.67
1985	100.48	107.32
1987	111.18	111.84
1989	130.95	128.15
1991	130.29	122.84
1993	131.13	123.45
1995	125.98	120.88
1997	124.62	119.64

Sources: IMF, *Direction of Trade Statistics* (various years); IMF, *International Financial Statistics Yearbook* (various years); Ministry of Finance, *Monthly Statistics of Exports and Imports: Taiwan Area, Republic of China* (various issues); Central Bank of China (various issues).

and over 100 throughout the 1950s. The NEERs remained somewhat stable in 1960–1985 when the nominal exchange rates were pegged to the US dollar. It began to rise above 100 after 1985 when the NT dollar appreciated relative to its trading partners' currencies. It then declined after 1993, implying a certain degree of undervaluation (Table 7.5).

Real Effective Exchange Rates

We now calibrate the NEERs by relative prices. The REER thus calculated is a measure of competitiveness.

$$\text{REER}_t = \Sigma_i \left(\frac{er_t}{er_0}\right)_i \times \left(\frac{CPI^T}{CPI_i}\right) \times s_i \times 100$$

where

er_t = foreign currency per NT dollar in time t

er_0 = foreign currency per NT dollar in time 0

s_i = trade share of country i

CPI^T, CPI_i = consumer price index of Taipei,China or country i

When the NEER rises or when the inflation rate in Taipei,China is higher than in its trading partners, the REER increases. That is to say, when the REER is greater than 100, the NT dollar is overvalued in real terms and is less competitive than in the base year. The CPI is used here, as it is the only consistent set for all relevant economies. Although it has a number of problems, it is close to the measure of the consumer expenditure deflator, and is close to the GDP deflator adjusted for the impact of changes in the terms of trade, and is thus an appropriate choice (Wright 1993).

The REER was well above 100 in 1953–1958 (see Table 7.5), implying that the economy was not very competitive in world markets during the import-substitution period. But the degree of real overvaluation was much less than the NEER, since Taipei,China's prices were relatively low in the 1950s against the 1969–1971 base period when compared with those of its trading partners, the US in particular. In 1953, the REER was only 189.71, 64.9 percent of the NEER figure. The REER improved substantially after 1953 and remained fairly constant in the 1960s, 1970s, and early 1980s. The REER declined from the second half of the 1980s with nominal appreciation, but improved in the 1990s because of low inflation.

Since the trading partners in the first three decades after 1953 were quite different from those of the last decade or so, the REER and NEER for 1985–1997 have been recalculated, with 1989–1991 as the base period. The figures indicate that the economy became more competitive after 1992, as its inflation rates have been low in comparison with those of its trading partners. The REER was below

94 in 1995–1997, suggesting (at least before the Asian financial crisis) that there was room for a 6 percent nominal appreciation for the economy to remain competitive, provided that the inflation rate was not higher than those of its trading partners.

Real Effective Exchange Rates against Competitors

Taipei,China competes with countries that may be small partners but large competitors in the major markets. In particular, Korea exports products which replace Taipei,China's products rather than complement them. To give proper weights to these competitors, we now calculate a new set of NEER and REER indexes, based on the export shares of each competitor in Japan and the US, the two main export markets. We focus on Taipei,China's Asian competitors in the 1989–1991 period, and exclude weak competitors whose market shares were smaller than one fifth of its own share in each of the two markets (Table 7.6). Those commodities (at SITC 4-digit level) that the economy does not export are also excluded. We thus have a CNEER and a CREER for both Japan and the US (Table 7.7).

In Table 7.6, we group trading partners with a market share no smaller than 1 percent by four categories. In addition to (A) the four major partners identified in the section *Direction of Trade* (of this chapter), we also consider (B) the Asian economies, many of which are competitors of Taipei,China; (C) industrial countries, whose trade shares with Taipei,China are increasing; and (D) oil-exporters, as the economy remains highly dependent on imported energy.

Although the CNEER and CREER series (as defined above) are very sensitive to the choice of market and of base period, the results are interesting. The CNEERs in both the Japanese and US markets are smaller than the NEERs before 1990, but larger afterwards, reflecting that the NT dollar has appreciated much more than competitors' currencies (Table 7.7). Yet because the inflation rate is lower than in competing economies, the CREER is closer to equilibrium than the CNEER, meaning that the economy has been fairly competitive in the world market in recent years. However, as the CREER has been higher than the REER in the 1990s, Taipei,China is more competitive against its trading partners than against its competitors, indicating the existence of competitive pressure from its neighbors.

Table 7.6 Major Trading Partners and Competitors (percent)

Trading Partner	Share in Taipei,China's Total Trade 1969–1971	Share in Taipei,China's Total Trade 1989–1991	Competitor	Share in Total Imports of: Japan Base Period 1989–1991	Share in Total Imports of: US Base Period 1989–1991
(A) Largest Four					
Japan	29.02	20.46			
US	31.27	28.24			
Hong Kong, China	5.16[a]	8.78	Hong Kong, China	0.95	1.97
Germany	4.42	4.74			
(B) Asia					
PRC		2.59	PRC	5.47	3.25
Indonesia	1.33[a]	1.64	Indonesia	5.34	0.73
Korea	1.27	2.09	Korea	5.46	3.80
Malaysia	1.29	1.71	Malaysia	2.48	1.10
Philippines	1.37		Philippines	0.96	
Singapore	1.39	2.71	Singapore	1.45	1.94
Thailand	2.05	1.42	Thailand	1.90	1.10
Viet Nam	2.02[a]				
(C) Industrial Countries			Memo item: Taipei,China	3.91	4.49
United Kingdom	1.39	2.47			
France		1.74			
Italy		1.40			
Netherlands	1.39	2.05			
Switzerland		1.07			
Canada	2.66	2.07			
Australia	2.35	2.50			
(D) Oil Exporters					
Kuwait	1.40[b]				
Saudi Arabia		1.64			
Number of Trading Partners in NEER Calculation	12	18	Number of Competitors in CNEER Calculation	8	7

[a] Excluded from calculation owing to incomplete CPI data.
[b] Excluded from calculation owing to incomplete CPI and exchange rate data.

Source: Ministry of Finance, *Monthly Statistics of Exports and Imports: Taiwan Area, Republic of China* (various issues).

Table 7.7 NEER and CNEER,1985–1997 (1989–1991 base period)

Year	NEER	CNEER[a] in the Markets of Japan	CNEER[a] in the Markets of US
1985	84.05	58.98	67.41
1986	76.90	65.81	73.14
1987	85.92	81.08	85.56
1988	91.61	87.85	90.97
1989	101.73	94.71	96.13
1990	99.47	99.88	100.10
1991	98.83	105.33	103.71
1992	103.62	114.33	112.05
1993	98.40	112.01	109.05
1994	98.04	126.52	123.58
1995	94.86	124.12	119.37
1996	94.17	121.83	116.35
1997	95.14	130.70	120.02

Year	NEER	CNEER[a] in the Markets of Japan	CNEER[a] in the Markets of US
1985	89.73	71.54	80.47
1986	82.04	78.15	85.72
1987	89.87	92.75	97.33
1988	93.21	93.56	96.53
1989	102.96	97.37	98.52
1990	99.60	100.48	100.53
1991	97.71	102.41	101.33
1992	103.30	109.36	108.05
1993	97.32	101.87	100.72
1994	97.05	106.86	105.81
1995	93.90	99.46	97.52
1996	93.89	94.72	92.97
1997	93.40	98.95	93.95

[a] Calculated as the relative exchange rates of Taipei,China against its competitors according to the competitors' market shares in either Japan or the US.

Sources: As Table 7.5.

RECENT DEVELOPMENTS

The trade performance of Taipei,China can be summarized in five points. First, the accumulation of foreign reserves accelerated after the 1960s as exports grew faster than imports, but the increase in the trade surplus moderated in the 1990s with the implementation of further import liberalization. Second, the comparative advantage of the economy has shifted from natural resource goods and labor-intensive commodities toward capital- and technology-intensive ones. Third, in the 1960s and 1970s, it traded mainly with Japan and the US under a triangular trade-production relation. With the entrance of Southeast Asia, and later the PRC, into the world system of the division of labor in the late 1980s, Taipei,China developed a new relation with these economies through trade and FDI. Fourth, while trade policies have become less restrictive over time, policy packages have been altering in accord with the development of the economy. Finally, despite its initial overvaluation, the NT dollar's exchange rate has been more or less in line with the economy's real purchasing power since the end of the import-substitution industrialization period. If 1989–1991 is taken as the base period, the low REERs of recent years imply that, at least before the Asian financial crisis, there was still room for the NT dollar to appreciate.

Export Deceleration in 1996

Real GDP grew by only 5.7 percent in 1996, the lowest rate since 1991, and considerably below the 6.8 percent target rate. Although real private consumption and government consumption expanded by 6.2 percent and by 5.2 percent, respectively, at 1991 constant prices, real gross fixed capital formation increased by only 2.6 percent. Factors that led to the general economic slowdown included a GDP growth deceleration in Asia as a whole (WEFA April 1998), a worldwide decline, or a cyclical demand downturn, in the electronics and IT/ telecommunications products, severe damages inflicted by Typhoon Herb, and the heightened tension across the straits before and after Taipei,China's first direct presidential election in March. The poor export performance of 1996 (3.8 percent) became conspicuous because of the high growth (20 percent) of 1995. In 1997, there was a marginal improvement to 5.3 percent. Another noteworthy feature was that the deceleration of export growth in 1996 took place in all major markets and all major exports.

In 1996, the largest exports were electronics products (Table 7.8). As worldwide prices of semiconductors declined in 1996, electronics export growth fell from 31.8 percent in 1995 to 2.4 percent in 1996. Export growth of textiles and apparel lost momentum as well. They rose by only 0.3 percent in 1996, down from 11.6 percent in 1995. Stagnation in two of the largest markets, namely, the PRC and Hong Kong, China on the one hand and the US on the other was largely due to continuous import substitution in the former and the keen

Table 7.8 Major Exports and Imports, 1995–1997

Exports	Total	Electronics	Textiles and Apparel	IT/Telecommunications
Value ($ million)				
1995	111,659	16,253	15,621	9,910
1996	115,947	16,636	15,674	12,536
1997	122,081	18,004	16,659	14,453
Percent Share				
1995	...	14.56	13.99	8.87
1996	...	14.34	13.51	10.81
1997	...	14.75	13.64	11.84
Percent Growth				
1995	20.00	31.78	11.57	45.95
1996	3.84	2.36	0.34	26.50
1997	5.29	8.22	6.28	15.29
Imports	**Total**	**Electronics**	**Machinery**	**Minerals**
Value ($ million)				
1995	103,550	16,823	10,346	8,247
1996	102,370	16,212	11,155	9,277
1997	114,425	18,642	11,469	10,294
Percent Share				
1995	...	16.25	9.99	7.96
1996	...	15.84	10.90	9.06
1997	...	16.29	10.02	9.00
Percent Growth				
1995	21.33	37.17	28.08	18.32
1996	-1.14	-3.63	7.82	12.49
1997	11.78	14.99	2.81	10.96

Source: Customs data.

competition with other exporters in the latter. Although IT/ telecommunications exports grew at a high (26.5 percent) in 1996, it was much lower than the 46 percent attained in 1995.

As noted, value of exports to major markets either stagnated or contracted in 1996. For instance, the PRC-Hong Kong, China market, which accounted for 23.6 percent of total exports, expanded only by 3.5 percent. The low growth in this market was due to cross-straits political tensions and because of reduction in import growth in the PRC from 14.2 percent in 1995 to 5.1 percent in 1996. Second, the deceleration in the Japanese market (3.9 percent) and contraction in the German market (-5.1 percent) were both caused by relative appreciation of the NT dollar against the yen and the deutsche mark. Third, because of slow growth in the demand for electronics and contraction in the demand for textiles and apparel, exports growth to the US decelerated sharply (1.8 percent) in 1996. Fourth, the growth rate of exports to the ASEAN market decelerated from 30.5 percent in 1995 to 3.1 percent in 1996, reflecting weak import demand. Finally, exports to other European countries (France, Italy, Netherlands, and UK) did expand by 6.8 percent, largely because of a better performance by the IT sector; but these economies were minor markets and accounted for only 7.8 percent of total exports.

Thus, the 1996 deceleration was the consequence of internal (domestic recession), external (slow growth in the ASEAN economies, cyclical downturn in the demand for electronics products, and currency appreciation), and noneconomic (political tensions) factors. The weight of each one of these three factors varies according to commodity and destination. It bears repeating that the CNEER and CREER indexes in both the important markets (Japan and the US) declined during 1996, indicating nominal and real depreciation against competitor economies, resulting in an improvement of competitiveness. This explains why the economies suffered less than its other Asian competitors. For instance, the export growth of South Korea decelerated from 30.3 percent to 3.7 percent during the 1995–1996 period (WEFA 1998).

Financial Turmoil in 1997

As the economy started to recover from the trough of the business cycle in the last quarter of 1996, demand from the private sector expanded rapidly. In 1997, real GDP growth reached 6.8 percent, the wholesale price index decreased by 0.5 percent, and the unemployment rate fell to 2.8 percent. However, recovery in export was less satisfactory. While total imports increased by 11.8 percent, exports rose by a meager 5.3 percent, less than the world average of 10.4 percent. Exports destined for Japan contracted by 14.4 percent because the yen was weak and a foot-and-mouth epidemic slashed domestic pork production. Exports of animal and animal products to Japan fell by 55.6 percent, and their share in total exports to Japan declined from 17.8 percent (1996) to 9.3 percent (1997). In the Korean and Thai markets, exports declined by 11.1 percent and 8.2 percent respectively, due mainly to the depression of these two economies following the financial crisis. Exports to the ASEAN economies (not including Brunei, Lao People's Democratic Republic, and Myanmar) as a whole fell in absolute terms. The percentage share of PRC-Hong Kong, China together in total exports rose slightly from 23.6 percent in 1996 to 24 percent in 1997, because of the increase in demand for industrial intermediates from the PRC's own export expansion.

Among the major exports, electronics products were 8.2 percent higher in 1997 than the previous year. Exports to PRC-Hong Kong, China rose by 36.5 percent, so that together their share in total electronics exports reached 22.6 percent, very close to the figure for the largest market, the US (23.5 percent). Exports of textiles and apparel rose moderately, since exports to the largest market of PRC-Hong Kong, China decreased a little in absolute terms, and the second largest market of the US grew only modestly. Finally, exports of IT/ telecommunications products grew by 15.3 percent, but again lower than in 1996 (26.5 percent), because exports to Japan declined by 18.4 percent. Thus, weak demand continued to plague exports in 1997.

The financial turmoil began on 2 July 1997, when Thailand devalued its currency against the US dollar and triggered a currency crisis that soon spread to many other Asian economies. Besides Thailand, Indonesia and Korea were hard hit, and all three requested IMF assistance and adopted IMF restructuring packages. The baht, rupiah, and won depreciated by 46.1 percent, 52.3 percent, and 47.6 percent, respectively, in the second half of 1997, and the stock markets in these economies collapsed. During the same period, the currencies of Malaysia; Philippines; Singapore; Taipei,China; and Japan also depreciated sharply, and stock prices plunged. Both Hong Kong, China and the PRC had linked their currencies to the US dollar: the former saw its stock prices fall by 29.4 percent, though the latter's remained stable, perhaps because of the fact that its capital markets were closed and therefore sheltered from external disturbances.

Although the NT dollar depreciated by 14.8 percent against the US dollar in the second half of 1997, and the stock index decreased by 9.3 percent, Taipei,China suffered the least damage among the economies in the region, except for the PRC. The sum of currency depreciation and stock price falls was 24.1 percent, lower than for Singapore (40.2 percent) and Japan (39.5 percent); in Hong Kong, China, stock prices alone fell by 29.4 percent.

The reason why Taipei,China has suffered relatively lightly is because the characteristics of the economy are considerably different from those of the troubled economies. To begin with, the economy's financial performance is quite strong. It has run a current account surplus since 1971, and, unlike most other economies in the region, it has ample foreign exchange reserves, with public foreign debt of about 0.15 percent of total foreign reserves in 1997. Second, its financial institutions are relatively sound. The bad debt ratio was only 4 percent in 1997, compared with 19 percent in Thailand. Third, although the Central Bank attempted to stabilize the NT dollar in July–September 1997, it desisted in October 1997 and let the market determine the exchange rate. Although the NT dollar fell sharply from NT$28.597 per US dollar by the end of the third quarter to NT$32.638 by the end of the fourth quarter, the Central Bank did not lose too much of its foreign reserves in defense of the currency, as happened in Thailand, where the baht was already overvalued after the rapid appreciation of the US dollar in 1995 through a loose peg arrangement. Domestic financial activities were therefore not much affected. Last and more fundamentally, the implementation of economic liberalization and industrial upgrading policies over the past decade has proceeded in a gradual and orderly way, and has largely removed government protection. The ability of the real economy to compete in international markets has therefore improved over time.

Thus, because of sound financial institutions, the flexibility of the NT exchange rate to reflect its true purchasing power, and continued industrial upgrading, the economy has weathered the financial turmoil relatively well. The damage to the real economy was minimized, and real GDP grew by 6.8 percent in 1997, the highest rate since 1992.

FUTURE PROSPECTS

The financial turmoil that started in 1997 brought along further changes. Although the economy survived the crisis fairly well in 1997, and the financial markets of the afflicted economies settled somewhat in mid-1998, the volatility of the region remains high. To address the important issue of how the crisis is going to affect the growth and composition of Taipei,China's exports, we examine the income and price effects on its trade given the competitive and complementary relations between the ASEAN economies, Japan, Korea, and itself.

More broadly, we ask "Where do we go from here?" after considering the ongoing efforts at liberalization and industrial upgrading. The success of the Uruguay Round and formation of WTO spearheaded the global trend toward more economic freedom. In the meantime, competition from both the high and low ends of product markets has required the redefinition of Taipei,China's comparative advantage in the global system of production and trading. In response, the economy has sought to upgrade its technological capacity while adopting an import liberalization policy.

After the Asian Crisis

Since the second half of 1997, the forecast of Wharton Econometric Forecasting Associates (WEFA) for real GDP growth in nine Asian economies[3] in 1998 has been revised downward on successive occasions. In April 1998, the average was projected to be -0.2 percent, compared with 0.4 percent in January 1998 and 4.7 percent in November 1997. Although Taipei,China was not severely battered, the Government lowered the target rate of real GDP growth from 6.7 percent to 6 percent by early 1998; by mid-1998, however, its forecast of GDP growth was revised downward to 5.3 percent. Both Taipei,China's exports and imports have fallen in the first eight months of 1998 compared with the same period of 1997: exports fell

[3] Hong Kong, China; Indonesia; Korea; Malaysia; Philippines; Singapore; Taipei,China; Thailand; and Viet Nam.

by 7.4 percent and imports by 6.9 percent, and both had already fallen in the last quarter of 1997. External demand was weak, therefore, in the first eight months of 1998; exports destined for all the crisis economies decreased enormously. Exports to Indonesia fell by 52.5 percent, to Korea by 41.7 percent, to Singapore by 30.8 percent, and to Japan by 23.9 percent. In contrast, exports to the US rose by 1.8 percent and to Europe by 9.1 percent. Although exports to Hong Kong, China (PRC not included) decreased by 8.2 percent, PRC-Hong Kong, China (together), US, and Japan remained the top three markets.

It is obvious that the decrease in exports to the ASEAN economies, Japan, and Korea can be ascribed to reduced real income and the lower currency value of these economies. As exports to them were 24.8 percent of total exports in 1997, the economic recession in these economies had an adverse impact on export performance through both income and price effects.

As mentioned in *Commodity Composition* above, the import content of the economy's exports is high; therefore, total imports decreased by 6.9 percent in the first eight months of 1998. Imports from the US, the largest source, declined by 13.1 percent; but the decrease in imports from countries battered by the Asian crisis was less than the average. Imports from Korea, for example, increased by 12.8 percent. The distribution of trade among countries clearly reflects the various degrees of the NT dollar's real appreciation against trading partners' currencies.

The relative depreciation of the currencies of Korea and the ASEAN economies also affected Taipei,China's exports as these economies compete in various markets. Korea's exports of consumer electronics, machinery, electrical machinery, and petrochemicals are close substitutes for those from Taipei,China, which also competes with the ASEAN economies in electronics, textiles, and many other industries. When competitors' currencies depreciate, total exports are adversely affected. Although the estimated competition effect is insignificant, it is the low-technology or labor-intensive sectors that are more seriously affected than the capital-intensive or high-technology sectors (Wang 1998).

The currency depreciation and subsequent export expansion of these economies affect the island's exports in another way. Under the current international division of labor, these economies import more from Taipei,China when their own exports increase. The percentage increase is highest with intermediate exports, such as textiles, chemical materials, and metal products. As the derived demand largely offsets the direct competition effect, the net impact of a relative 10 percent export expansion of these economies on Taipei,China's exports is only an absolute 0.1 percent decrease. The net increase is the largest in chemical materials and chemical products, while the labor-intensive sectors suffer from an export decline (Wang 1998).

This finding is similar to what has always happened between Taipei,China and Japan: as the former depends heavily on the latter's supply of key parts and components, export expansion in the former may lead it to increase its imports and register worse trade balances with the latter. By the same token, the relative appreciation of the NT dollar against the currencies of its Southeast Asian neighbors may not affect its total exports very much when derived demand is considered. In view of the depth of the present financial crisis, however, the income effect may dominate the competition effect, as is the case found in the section *Determinants of Exports* (of this chapter). The prospects for the immediate future would not seem very bright.

Liberalization and Industrial Upgrading

Internationalization and liberalization have been the major guiding principles of the economy's development policies since 1984. Preparation for accession to WTO in the 1990s has further accelerated the pace of liberalization, but Taipei,China still needs to lower its tariff and nontariff barriers, and to open its markets to a range of goods that have long been protected by nontariff barriers. Agriculture and automobiles may be severely affected, and infant industries such as biotechnology will not receive the protection they used to.

While import industries are under pressure to liberalize, export industries are facing continuous competitive pressures from both developed and developing economies, and they need to upgrade their technological capacity to remain competitive. The share of high technology-intensive exports in all exports rose from 18.3 percent in 1982 to 39.7 percent in 1997. Specifically, textiles and electronics, which have been the leading exports for several decades, have gradually restructured toward higher technology content and higher value-added.

The major benefit of WTO membership is, of course, the reduction of barriers to exports, as free trade is at the core of WTO.

Although the opening up of previously protected markets to imports will cause adjustment problems for a number of industries, more efficient resource allocation and improved productivity will, in the long run, make up for the short-run costs. If Taipei,China becomes a member of WTO, real GDP growth will rise from the basic forecast of 5.6 percent to 6.2 percent during 1995–2002 (Chou et al. 1995).

The nominal tariff rate for industrial products is currently 6.5 percent, and 83 percent of all items are subject to a tariff rate of 10 percent or lower. Although tariff rates have been falling since the 1970s, the average tariff rate has to be reduced further to 4.7 percent in the first year of membership of WTO, and to 3.8 percent in the sixth year. Specifically, the first year tariff rate for agricultural products is 13.1 percent, and the sixth year rate is 12.3 percent, whereas the nominal tariff rate is currently around 20 percent. Clearly, there is still a long way to go.

The products subject to high tariffs are also protected by nontariff restrictions. Automobiles are subject to import origin constraints, and local content constraints of parts and components. Agricultural products are sheltered both by restrictions on imports, and price support or other indirect subsidies on production. These measures need to be removed. In addition, the authorities have to abolish the state monopoly on wine and tobacco, open up the markets for service industries, and follow (among others) the Trade Related Intellectual Property Right Statement, the Agreement on Government Procurement, and the General Agreement on Trade in Services.

The impact of trade liberalization on each industry can be discussed within the framework of the work of Chou et al. (1995). The rates of increase in automobile imports (200.5 percent) and agricultural imports (51.6 percent) would be extremely high in the long run, because these sectors have been heavily protected. The rate of import expansion in textiles and garments would be the third highest (48.9 percent) due to both the relaxation of protection and the increase in intraindustry trade. Exports of textiles, machinery, and electrical and electronics products would increase considerably. Yet exports of industries with low export ratios (such as agriculture, mining, paper, nonmetal products) would fall because of resource reallocation into the more export-oriented sectors. As for value-added, the low-traded service industries (construction, electricity, gas, and water) would expand fastest among all sectors, because they grow with the overall growth of the economy, and most of the increased demand would be satisfied by domestic rather than foreign production. The increase in textiles and garments would be high, while machinery, household electrical appliances, and electronics products would also expand. Automobiles would record negative growth as expected. Steel production would decrease, since the import ratio is higher than the export ratio and the increase in imports would displace domestic production.

A tricky issue is the possibility of increased dependence on agricultural imports from the PRC, which is politically undesirable. The Government has placed more constraints on imports from the Mainland than on imports from the rest of the world; among all imports from the PRC, agricultural products are subject to the most restrictions. When both Taipei,China and the PRC become members of WTO, the displacement of domestic agricultural products by cheap imports from the other side of the straits may be inevitable.

Electronics and IT/Telecommunications

By way of concluding the paper, we look into the most dynamic exports in the 1990s, which are electronics, and IT/telecommunications products. Their shares in total exports were 14.8 percent and 11.8 percent, respectively, in 1997 (Table 7.8), compared with 13 percent and 0.7 percent in 1981. They have been the top and third largest exports of recent years, with textiles the second largest. The two industries were among the 10 priority industries identified by the Government in the early 1990s; the expansion rates of semiconductors and IT/telecommunications products in 1992–1995 were the highest, with average annual growth rates of 58.4 percent and 20.5 percent, respectively, while the average actual growth rate for the 10 industries was 17.7 percent.

The rapid development of the electronics industry is based mainly on original equipment manufacturing OEM or own design manufacturing ODM. Although worldwide prices of electronics products declined in 1996, electronics exports registered some growth (2.3 percent) due to a stronger vertical division of labor across national borders and the improvement of marketing techniques. In 1997, electronics exports grew by 8.3 percent. The major markets were US (23 percent); PRC-Hong Kong, China (23 percent); and Singapore (12 percent). The major suppliers were Japan (28 percent),

US (21 percent), Malaysia (11 percent), Korea (8 percent), and Singapore (6 percent). In both the US and Japanese markets, the economy is gradually losing competitiveness to PRC, Korea, Malaysia, and Singapore, especially with respect to integrated circuits.

Taipei,China is relatively more competitive in IT/telecommunications exports. The major markets in 1997 were US (43 percent), Netherlands (11 percent), and Japan (10 percent), while the major suppliers were Japan, US, and Singapore. Again, PRC, Korea, Malaysia, Singapore, and Thailand were the chief competitors in the US and Japanese markets. In 1997, export growth of IT/telecommunications products fell to 15.3 percent from 26.6 percent in 1996 for several reasons. First, as the international division of labor expanded further, more production processes were moved abroad. Second, the prices of central processing units, dynamic random-access memory (DRAM) chips, and some peripherals fluctuated and decreased. Third, two of the chief OEM/ODM customers, Packard Bell NEC and Apple, lost significant shares in the world market for personal computers. Fourth, demand from Japan and many European countries declined because of the strong US dollar.

In spite of the fact that some of the factors mentioned above were short term in nature, the economy will face tougher competition in the future. Although the OEM/ODM pattern has helped absorb market uncertainties, Taipei,China needs to upgrade domestic technology capacity to ensure long-term competitiveness. Yet its R&D expenditure is clearly insufficient. For example, the setup cost of an eight-inch wafer plant producing 64 MB DRAM chips requires about NT$40 billion (Chung-hua Institute for Economic Research 1997), while the entire R&D expenditure in 1995 was only NT$125 billion. In Singapore, the Government and multinational corporations share R&D expenditure in electronics and IT/telecommunications industries; in Korea, the *chaebols* and the Government share R&D costs. As foreign participation in R&D is low (0.1 percent in 1995) in Taipei,China, and as most firms are small, the Government needs to play a more active role in R&D investment or to help induce more foreign technology transfer.

BIBLIOGRAPHY AND REFERENCES

Central Bank of China. Various issues. *Financial Statistics, Taiwan District, The Republic of China.* Taipei: Economic Research Department.

Chang, Ching-hsi. 1989. "A Study on the Labor Market in Taiwan." Paper presented at 1989 Joint Conference on the Industrial Policies of Taipei,China and the Republic of Korea: 11-32. Taipei: Chung-hua Institute for Economic Research. In Chinese.

Chou, Ji, Shiu-tung Wang, and Shu-ling Perng. 1995. "The Impacts of Access to the WTO on Taiwan's Economy." *Economic Papers* (167): 1, 14-5. Taipei: Chung-hua Institute for Economic Research. In Chinese.

Chung-hua Institute for Economic Research. 1996. "The Construction and Application of a Trade-Oriented Quarterly Macroeconomic Model: Taiwan's Trade Forecast for 1996/1997." Taipei. In Chinese.

______. 1997. "Changes in the Taiwan's Competitiveness of Electronics, Information and Communication Products and Trade Prospects." *Quarterly Forecast on Trend of External Trade* 3:151-60. In Chinese.

Cline, W. R. 1982. "Can the East Asian Model of Development Be Generalized?" *World Development* 10:81-90.

Council for Economic Planning and Development (CEPD). 1955. *Industry of Free China* 4(4):53, 75-9, 80-1. Taipei.

Directorate-General of Budget, Accounting and Statistics. 1985. *Report on the Compilation of Input-Output Table 1981*:53, 66-7, 82-4. Taipei. In Chinese.

Foreign Exchange and Trade Commission. 1969. *Fourteen Years of the Foreign Exchange and Trade Commission*: 20-3, 357. Taipei. In Chinese.

Hsiao, Feng-hsiung. 1994. *Taiwan's Industrial Policy and Industrial Development*: 205, 279-85. Taipei: Far Eastern Economic Research Consulting Institute. In Chinese.

Hsing, Mo-huan. 1971. *Industrialization and Trade Policies in Taiwan.* Monograph Series No. 2. Taipei: Institute of Economics, Academia Sinica.

Hsu, Jo-ho. 1975. "Income and Price Elasticity of Taiwan's Imports and Exports." In Chen Sun, ed., *Collected Papers on Taiwan's External Trade*: 247-62. Taipei: Linking Publication Company. In Chinese.

Hu, Yong-an. 1997. "The Impact of the Lifting of Local Content Constraints on the Automobile Industry." *Economic Situations and Review* 3(2):19-28. In Chinese.

International Monetary Fund (IMF). Various years. *International Financial Statistics Yearbook.* Washington, DC.

______. Various years. *Direction of Trade Statistics Yearbook.* Washington, DC.

Jacoby, Neil. 1966. *US Aid to Taiwan: A Study of Foreign Aid, Self-help and Development.* New York: Praeger Publishers.

Kuo, Shirley, W. Y. 1983. *The Taiwan Economy in Transition:* 53. Boulder: Westview Press.

Liang, Kuo-Hsu, and Ching-Ing Hou Liang. 1975. "Exports and Employment in Taiwan," *Conference on Population and Economic Development in Taiwan.* Taipei: Academia Sinica.

Liang, Kuo-Hsu, and Ching-Ing Hou Liang. 1981. "Trade and Incentive Policies in Taiwan." *Conference and Lessons of Economic Development in Taiwan.* Taipei: Academia Sinica.

Lin, Ching-Yuan. 1973. *Industrialization in Taiwan, 1946-1972: Trade and Import-Substitution Policies for Developing Countries*: 95, 108. New York: Praeger Publishers.

Liu, Tai-ying. 1981. "Sino-Japanese Input-Output Correlation and The Way to Balance Trade." *Conference on Taiwan's External Trade:* 585-634. Taipei: Academia Sinica. In Chinese.

Ma, Kay. 1994. "The Evolution of Taiwan's Industrial Policy." In K. Ma, ed., *Collected Papers on Taiwan's Industrial Development.* Taipei: Linking Publication Company. In Chinese.

Mathews, John A. 1997. "A Silicon Valley of the East: Creating Taiwan's Semiconductor Industry." *California Management Review* 39(4): 26-54.

Ministry of Economic Affairs, Investment Commission. 1997. "Report on the Overseas Chinese and Foreign Investment, Technical Cooperation, Outward Investment, Outward Technical Cooperation 1996." Taipei. In Chinese.

Ministry of Finance. Various issues. *Monthly Statistics of Exports and Imports: Taiwan Area, The Republic of China.* Taipei: Department of Statistics.

______. Various years. *Yearbook of Tax Statistics, Republic of China.* Taipei: Department of Statistics.

Nam, Chong-Hyun. 1995. "The Role of Trade and Exchange Rate Policy in Korea's Growth." In Takatoshi Ito and Anne Krueger, eds., *Growth Theories in Light of the East Asian Experiences.* Chicago: University of Chicago Press.

Schive, Chi. 1994. "FDI and Technology Transfer." In Kuo-Hsu Liang, ed., *Collected Articles on Taiwan's Economic Development in Memory of Professor Yen Hua.* Taipei: Times Publication Company. In Chinese.

Sun, Ke-nan. 1982. "Tariff Protection, Industrial Restructuring and Trade Expansion." *Conference Proceedings on Current Fiscal Problems.* Taipei: Chinese Economic Association. In Chinese.

Tu, C. H. and W. T. Wang 1988. "Trade Liberalization in the Republic of China, and the Economic Effects of Tariff Reductions." Paper presented at 1988 Joint Conference on the Industrial Policies of the Republic of China and the Republic of Korea: 42-100. Seoul: Korea Development Institute.

Wade, Robert. 1990. *Governing the Markets.* Princeton: Princeton University Press.

Wang, Shu-ching. 1998. "Development in East Asian Trade and Evaluation of the Impacts of Financial Turmoil." *Economic Conditions and Review Quarterly* 3(4):84-106. In Chinese.

Wharton Econometric Forecasting Associates (WEFA). Various issues. *World Economic Outlook.* Eddystone, Pennsylvania.

World Trade Organization (WTO). 1997. *Annual Report 1997.* Geneva.

Wright, Stephen. 1993. "Measures of Real Effective Exchange Rates." Working Paper No. 16. Department of Applied Economics, University of Cambridge.

Wu, Chung-shu. 1996. "An Annual Macroeconometric Model of Taiwan." In Chung-shu Wu, ed., *Proceedings of Macroeconometric Models of Taiwan.* Taipei: Academia Sinica. In Chinese.

Yin, K. Y. 1963. *My Views Toward Taiwan's Economy.* Taipei: Council for US Aid. In Chinese.

Chapter Eight

Case Study: Malaysia

Mahani Zainal-Abidin

MALAYSIAN TRADE REGIME AND EXPORT PERFORMANCE

Exports have always been important to the Malaysian economy, and over the years this importance has increased. In the initial years after independence in 1957, the ratio of exports to GDP was 0.46 (1960) but by 1996 this ratio had become 0.81. Exports became particularly important for economic growth during the 1980s and early 1990s. In 1980–1989, they grew at an average annual rate of 10.9 percent, more than double GDP growth of 5.2 percent (World Bank 1997). Exports grew much faster during 1990–1995 at 14.4 percent a year, compared with GDP growth of 8.7 percent a year.

Export Promotion Strategy and Trade Regime

Malaysia has always been an open trading nation and as such it has adopted a relatively liberal trade policy. A moderate degree of protection was implemented during the import-substitution period, but this weakened during export-oriented industrialization, then strengthened again during the period of heavy industrialization. After 1987, the trade policy stance was liberalized once more.

Import Substitution

After independence and until the late 1960s, import-substitution industrialization was the policy used to create an industrial base to provide higher growth and alleviate unemployment. Consequently, the contribution of the manufacturing sector to GDP rose from 6 percent in 1957 to 11 percent in 1965, with the main industries producing final consumer goods and some consumer durables. Tariffs were applied but they were not excessive: in 1963 the nominal rate of protection (NRP) was 10 percent while the effective rate of protection (ERP) was 24 percent, much lower rates than other developing countries.

Export-Oriented Industrialization

Export-oriented industrialization was introduced both to overcome some of the constraints of import substitution and in response to the flow of capital from industrial countries. Although economic growth rates under import substitution were reasonably high, there were signs that such growth might not be sustainable since the domestic market was too small and existing industries showed no sign of venturing into export markets. The shift to exports was appealing mainly because Malaysia had abundant low-cost labor.

Heavy Industrialization

A second round of import substitution in the form of heavy industrialization was applied in the early 1980s. The main objectives were to encourage capital deepening and expansion of the domestic industrial base, as the previous two policies had failed to do this. In addition, heavy industrialization was also instrumental in creating opportunities for Malaysian industrial entrepreneurs through the development of intermediate industries to support selected heavy industries, such as steel, automobiles, cement, aerospace, petrochemicals, and pulp and paper.

Liberalization

The severe recession of 1985–1986 was a catalyst for a rethink of the Malaysian industrialization and trade strategies. The recession was caused by fiscal budget and trade deficits. Since 1980, there had been a massive increase in public expenditure, in part to finance heavy industrialization. Public development expenditure as a share of GNP almost doubled from 14.3 percent in 1976–1980 to over 27 percent in 1981–1982. In addition, the external sector had incurred a deficit due to the collapse of primary commodity prices. In 1985, GDP contracted by 1 percent and unemployment rose to 7 percent. To revive the economy, the Government adopted two strategies—reducing the role and size of the public sector, and promoting exports. These strategies depended on liberalization of the domestic investment environment and of the trade regime. The targeted source of growth also shifted from the public to the private sector.

An increasingly liberal trade regime was created for exporters to enhance their competitiveness and to reduce discrimination against exports. The aim was to guarantee that exporters paid no more than world prices for tradable inputs, which meant an exemption from tariffs and from indirect taxes on imported inputs. Liberalization and the large inflow of FDI (see below) were major elements in boosting exports after 1986 (Table 8.1). The recession in 1985–1986 had been accompanied by a significant depreciation of the Malaysian ringgit and this has been cited as one of the factors that contributed to the rapid recovery of the economy and the quick expansion of exports. Since then, the ringgit has been kept competitive to ensure continued export growth.

Export Performance

Malaysia's share of global trade has increased significantly since 1976 as shown in Table 8.1. In 1957, its share of world exports was 0.87 percent but declined to a low of 0.43 percent in 1972 as a result of declining exports of rubber and tin. Its share began to increase after the effects of export-oriented industrialization were felt; between 1970 and 1995, it rose from 0.57 percent to 1.48 percent. The two main features of Malaysia's exports have been their rapid growth, and

Table 8.1 Growth of Exports, 1957–1997

Year	Malaysia ($ billion)	World ($ billion)	Percent of World Exports
1957	0.914	105.3	0.87
1960	1.187	118.1	1.01
1965	1.236	170.4	0.73
1970	1.687	298.3	0.57
1971	1.644	333.9	0.49
1972	1.722	397.7	0.43
1973	3.049	553.3	0.55
1974	4.236	820.1	0.52
1975	3.843	843.5	0.46
1976	5.295	950.9	0.56
1977	6.079	1,076.5	0.56
1978	7.404	1,245.8	0.59
1979	11.079	1,604.2	0.69
1980	12.945	1,920.8	0.67
1981	11.765	1,899.7	0.62
1982	12.031	1,752.9	0.69
1983	14.130	1,712.0	0.83
1984	16.590	1,817.9	0.91
1985	15.442	1,848.7	0.84
1986	13.753	2,034.5	0.68
1987	17.939	2,391.7	0.75
1988	21.110	2,729.4	0.77
1989	25.053	2,965.5	0.84
1990	29.416	3,379.1	0.87
1991	34.349	3,477.6	0.99
1992	40.713	3,723.0	1.09
1993	47.122	3,712.4	1.27
1994	58.756	4,222.2	1.39
1995	74.045	5,013.9	1.48
1996	77.304	5,265.8	1.46
1997	77.871	5,734.4	1.35

Source: IMF (various years).

concentration on a few main products—electrical and electronics products, textile products, palm oil, and timber. In 1995, exports grew by 26.4 percent. In 1996, their growth rate decelerated to 4.4 percent and in 1997, the growth rate fell further to 0.7 percent.

Structure

The structure of exports has changed markedly over the last four decades: primary commodity exports constituted some 80 percent of total exports in 1960, but only 15 percent in 1997. Manufactured exports have risen substantially and their share is now about 79 percent. There have also been changes in the composition of primary commodity exports: in 1960 rubber and tin were the largest export items, accounting for about 69 percent and 17 percent of total exports, respectively. Their shares have since declined to 9 percent and 2 percent, respectively. Among the newer primary commodity exports, sawlogs registered a significant gain in export share between 1960 and 1970, but this has fallen in the 1990s. Another timber-based export, sawn timber, has been prominent since the late 1980s.

The changing structure of primary commodity exports was the result of national endowment as well as policy initiatives. Crude petroleum became an export when a vast reserve was discovered in the waters off Malaysia. The government policy to promote palm oil was implemented through the launch of a special land plantation scheme. Another export product that is growing in importance is liquefied natural gas (LNG). The growth of this export item started in the early 1980s, and in terms of value, exports now nearly match those of crude petroleum.

Prior to 1975, the major manufactured exports were textiles, apparel, and footwear, wood products, and petroleum products (Table 8.2). After that date, electrical and electronics products and machinery emerged as the single most important item in manufactured exports, reaching 69 percent in 1996. They also registered the highest average annual growth among all manufacturing industries, growing by 25 percent a year in 1975–1996. The growth of electrical and electronics exports is attributed directly to FDI, which has made Malaysia a key global player in the semiconductor industry. Textiles, apparel, and footwear; wood products; and chemicals grew reasonably (with average annual growth rates of 17.2 percent, 16.9 percent, and 22.1 percent, respectively) but slower than electrical and electronics exports; as a result, their share of total manufactured exports declined.

Table 8.2 Structure of Manufactured Exports, 1968–1996

Year	Food, Beverages, and Tobacco $ M	%	Textiles, Apparel, and Footwear $ M	%	Wood Products $ M	%	Rubber Products $ M	%	Chemicals and Chemical Products $ M	%	Petroleum Products $ M	%	Nonmetallic Mineral Products $ M	%	Iron and Steel and Metal Manufactures $ M	%	Electrical & Electronics Products, Machinery $ M	%	Transport Equipment $ M	%	Other Manufactures $ M	%	Total $ M	% of Total Exports %
1968	29.7	21	8.8	6	14.0	10	3.6	3	10.8	8	56.1	40	3.3	2	2.9	2	...	...	6.9	5	4.2	3	140.3	10
1969	28.3	19	9.7	7	21.4	15	4.5	3	11.0	7	52.3	35	4.5	3	5.5	4	...	...	5.8	4	4.5	3	147.8	9
1970	33.8	20	10.1	6	29.2	17	5.2	3	9.7	6	51.6	30	5.8	3	5.8	3	...	...	6.5	4	11.7	7	169.5	10
1971	33.4	19	15.5	9	40.3	23	6.2	4	11.0	6	37.9	22	4.8	3	5.2	3	...	...	9.7	6	10.7	6	174.8	10
1972	40.2	19	27.4	13	59.8	28	7.1	3	13.2	6	32.7	15	4.6	2	8.2	4	...	...	8.2	4	14.9	7	216.4	13
1973	57.6	14	46.1	12	111.8	28	8.6	2	22.0	6	41.6	10	6.1	2	10.6	3	..	..	28.6	7	67.3	17	400.4	13
1974	70.6	10	68.0	9	108.2	15	13.9	2	26.0	4	64.9	9	8.2	1	14.3	2	...	...	86.1	12	268.8	37	729.0	17
1975	115.6	18	84.1	13	79.3	12	16.7	3	33.7	5	40.7	6	9.0	1	23.9	4	195.7	30	25.6	4	17.3	3	641.7	18
1976	115.4	14	123.6	15	128.0	15	18.7	2	32.7	4	55.2	7	11.7	1	29.4	4	258.6	31	32.6	4	27.5	3	833.5	16
1977	130.8	13	146.1	14	130.8	13	21.9	2	37.4	4	43.4	4	12.6	1	34.9	3	389.4	38	34.9	3	33.9	3	1,016.1	16
1978	143.8	9	210.5	13	168.0	11	29.8	2	47.5	3	43.3	3	19.1	1	51.6	3	763.5	49	58.2	4	31.1	2	1,566.4	20
1979	175.8	8	259.5	12	215.7	10	34.2	2	63.5	3	60.5	3	22.6	1	78.3	4	1,100.7	52	57.1	3	51.9	2	2,119.9	19
1980	234.5	9	363.2	13	211.5	8	37.7	1	84.5	3	85.2	3	27.4	1	112.4	4	1,358.4	50	100.4	4	126.5	5	2,741.8	22
1981	302.7	11	350.1	13	212.2	8	36.9	1	89.0	3	100.6	4	22.7	1	94.5	3	1,447.4	52	37.1	1	75.4	3	2,768.5	23
1982	264.9	8	352.7	11	183.8	6	38.2	1	22.2	4	123.5	4	31.1	1	89.0	3	1,782.3	57	86.2	3	61.8	2	3,135.7	25
1983	297.4	7	402.9	10	210.2	5	41.7	1	193.6	5	255.6	6	44.2	1	102.7	3	2,269.1	56	146.5	4	76.0	2	4,039.9	29
1984	346.9	7	472.8	9	176.1	4	44.0	1	272.8	5	381.5	8	56.7	1	123.3	2	2,782.0	56	244.0	5	92.9	2	4,992.9	32
1985	322.7	7	532.5	11	150.9	3	46.7	1	252.1	5	430.3	9	62.1	1	147.4	3	2,683.0	54	234.0	5	98.5	2	4,960.3	32
1986	369.5	7	599.7	11	206.3	4	92.0	2	292.6	5	277.0	5	73.4	1	201.2	4	3,266.3	58	199.1	4	103.2	2	5,680.2	42
1987	492.9	6	815.5	10	342.0	4	194.7	2	372.4	5	335.7	4	121.0	2	308.9	4	4,417.7	57	281.5	4	132.3	2	7,814.9	44
1988	512.1	5	873.4	9	336.3	4	337.4	4	507.7	5	282.3	3	166.1	2	428.0	5	5,594.7	59	186.5	2	181.5	2	9,406.1	47
1989	664.6	5	1,146.6	9	398.2	3	423.3	3	521.1	4	372.0	3	243.6	2	529.7	4	7,703.5	61	438.5	3	263.4	2	12,704.6	51
1990	763.5	5	1,447.1	9	499.0	3	501.4	3	543.7	3	476.0	3	285.6	2	584.0	4	9,815.7	61	714.1	4	393.0	2	16,023.0	56
1991	832.2	4	1,728.9	8	633.1	3	645.8	3	662.0	3	422.5	2	326.5	2	665.3	3	13,083.3	63	1,205.6	6	597.0	3	20,802.4	61
1992	934.8	4	1,961.1	8	891.0	4	826.3	4	877.1	3	566.2	2	341.8	1	877.0	3	15,930.5	63	1,568.4	6	680.6	3	25,354.9	66
1993	944.9	3	1,993.7	6	1,494.9	5	913.2	3	1,047.3	3	617.9	2	391.5	1	1,132.1	4	20,418.1	66	1,358.6	4	739.9	2	31,052.2	71
1994	1,222.3	3	2,365.5	5	1,864.8	4	1,074.5	2	1,776.5	4	835.4	2	559.1	1	1,419.6	3	29,831.0	67	2,278.4	5	989.7	2	44,217.0	76
1995	1,423.3	3	2,566.3	5	1,950.3	4	1,286.5	2	2,463.2	4	1,230.9	2	660.1	1	1,832.9	3	38,089.7	68	2,067.6	4	2,101.6	4	55,672.5	79
1996	1,548.8	3	2,785.2	5	2,435.6	4	1,434.5	2	2,694.8	4	1,312.4	2	656.3	1	2,001.2	3	41,711.6	69	1,817.6	3	2,461.2	4	60,859.3	79

Sources: Government of Malaysia (various issues).

Export Markets

The most important markets for Malaysian exports are the US, Japan, and Europe. (Exports are often sent to final markets via Singapore, giving Singapore the largest market share, but almost all is entrepôt trade, with the goods reexported without further processing.) The trend now is for other Asian nations, in particular Malaysia's neighbors in ASEAN, to have a greater share of the total. For example in 1980, the total share of exports of the US, Japan, and Europe was 56 percent, falling to 45 percent in 1996, while the Asian market (excluding Japan) rose from 16 percent to 26 percent in the same period (Bank Negara Malaysia, various issues). Hong Kong, China; Korea; and Taipei,China are among the most prominent new markets for Malaysian goods. The expansion of trade with these markets can be attributed to these economies' high capital investment in Malaysia.

POLICIES AFFECTING EXPORT DEVELOPMENT

Trade Regime

Tariff Regime

After independence, tariffs were regarded as a tool to protect infant and import-substitution industries. However, as stated earlier, tariff protection was not excessive. In the 1950s, tariff rates were low and in the 1960s increased only slightly. Nevertheless, there were incidences of very high protection for selected industries, such as automobiles. Although the export promotion period began in the early 1970s, further increases to import tariffs were made, until the NRP reached a peak of 22 percent in 1979. There were wide variations in the NRP and the ERP among industries. Heavy industrialization transformed the protective structure from production (and protection) of consumer goods to the manufacture of heavy industrial products and consumer durables. The latter were the least protected in 1963, but were the most protected in the 1970s and early 1980s; their ERP increased from −11 percent in 1963 to 165 percent in 1982. However, after the mid-1980s, the ERP of consumer durables declined sharply.

The recession of the mid-1980s spurred the Government into accelerating exports, particularly manufacturing, because of the shortcomings of the heavy industrialization policy and fluctuating primary commodity prices. Tariff liberalization began in the middle of the 1980s and was important in creating a more export-conducive environment. The average unweighted tariff rate decreased from 13.6 percent in 1984–1987 to 12.8 percent in 1991–1993; the reduction of the import-weighted average tariff rate was steeper: from 14.7 percent to 11.2 percent over the same period (APEC 1995). More recently, Malaysia has intensified tariff liberalization as part of its commitments within multilateral and regional trading arrangements, namely the WTO and the ASEAN Free Trade Area (AFTA). In its WTO commitments, the Government has offered to reduce and bind tariffs for about 6,000 products. The Post-Uruguay Round trade-weighted average nominal tariff rate for Malaysia is now only 9 percent, compared with 11.2 percent previously. In addition, there are only a few quantitative restrictions, thus limiting the scope for discretionary trade measures, and making the trade regime relatively transparent. The AFTA schedule calls for tariffs on intra-ASEAN trade to be no more than 5 percent by 1 January 2003. The AFTA tariff cuts use the Common Effective Preferential Tariff (CEPT) formula, which is based on sectors and hence has a comprehensive product coverage. In recent years, the Government has unilaterally cut tariffs on the most favored nation basis. Since 1993, it has reduced or abolished import duties on some 4,000 items.

Exchange Rate Regime

In June 1973, given the prevailing uncertainty in international markets and following moves by other governments, the Government decided to float its currency. The influence of the exchange rate on the balance of payments was not fully evidenced until then. As mentioned earlier, the role of the exchange rate in determining export competitiveness was singularly noticeable after the middle of the 1980s when it superseded tariffs as the main trade policy instrument. Even though there was a massive capital inflow into Malaysia from the late 1980s, the real effective exchange rate (REER) declined, helping keep exports competitive (Gan 1992).

The currency float of 1973 was not "clean." The Central Bank continued to defend the ringgit (RM) at its upper intervention limit of RM2.5947 to the dollar, to moderate excessive fluctuations. Subsequently, in September 1975, the ringgit was pegged to a basket of major trading partners' currencies, in an attempt to keep exchange rate fluctuations moderate while allowing it to reflect underlying exchange rate trends. After the Plaza Accord in 1985, the exchange rate regime moved toward a coordinated floating arrangement (Gan and Kwek 1994).[1]

The state of the exchange rate regime is best analyzed by examining the REER pattern. The REER index continued to rise from 1983 to reach a peak in the third quarter of 1984 (Table 8.3). This was linked to the petroleum price rises in the second oil shock of 1979 and later to the increase in public expenditure in the first half of the 1980s.

The adverse consequence of an overvalued ringgit in the first half of the 1980s prompted the Government to adopt an exchange rate policy to push the REER lower. This led to the recovery of exports and made the export sector the veritable engine of growth. During 1987–1988, the upward pressure on the exchange rate came from the improvement in the terms of trade, which rose by an average of 8 percent a year. The accumulated reserves were then used to repay some external debt. However, foreign capital continued to flow in because of the widening of interest differentials between domestic and foreign rates, causing a sharp appreciation of the REER from the first quarter of 1992 until the first quarter of 1993.

Foreign investment inflows in 1989 rose by 140 percent compared with the previous year, and by 1991, inflows were almost double those of 1989. Such huge inflows could have been allowed to cause a substantial appreciation of the exchange rate. Instead, the NEER and REER continued to decline; the lowest REER was in the second quarter of 1995. Foreign reserves doubled between 1990 and 1996. Through its strong sterilized intervention, the Government showed a firm commitment to contain currency appreciation and maintain a competitive, export-oriented exchange rate.

[1] This section draws heavily on Gan and Kwek (1994).

Table 8.3 Quarterly Indexes of the Ringgit REER and NEER, 1983–1996

Year	Quarter	REER	NEER	Year	Quarter	REER	NEER
1983	1	156.3	151.8	1990	1	103.5	102.4
	2	155.2	151.1		2	104.0	103.4
	3	156.1	151.4		3	99.2	99.6
	4	154.5	150.0		4	94.2	94.6
1984	1	158.4	151.2	1991	1	95.4	95.0
	2	156.4	152.2		2	97.5	96.5
	3	161.6	155.3		3	95.9	95.1
	4	157.2	152.9		4	93.6	92.8
1985	1	153.7	150.4	1992	1	98.5	96.5
	2	153.2	150.6		2	103.0	100.3
	3	153.3	146.6		3	102.1	98.7
	4	140.0	138.1		4	102.3	98.7
1986	1	132.6	132.2	1993	1	102.7	96.4
	2	122.1	118.9		2	98.1	94.3
	3	117.2	113.8		3	97.7	93.8
	4	119.9	115.8		4	98.7	94.1
1987	1	118.8	115.1	1994	1	94.0	89.2
	2	117.0	114.1		2	94.5	89.6
	3	115.9	113.3		3	94.1	89.3
	4	111.3	109.5		4	94.4	89.0
1988	1	107.0	104.6	1995	1	94.4	87.5
	2	105.1	103.1		2	93.3	85.7
	3	106.9	104.1		3	95.4	88.7
	4	101.6	99.0		4	96.6	89.0
1989	1	100.7	97.8	1996	1	98.7	89.6
	2	103.5	102.0		2	101.2	91.9
	3	105.7	104.1		3	101.5	92.4
	4	104.6	103.2		4	101.8	92.3

Source: Based on data provided by the Malaysian Institute of Economic Research, Kuala Lumpur.

Quantitative Restrictions

In the first round of import-substitution industrialization, import restrictions or quotas were based either on the industry's expected production capacity or the previous year's imports. By any standard, import restrictions and quotas were never pervasive; in 1973, items under quantitative restrictions (including quotas, total prohibition, and import licensing) constituted only about 6.9 percent of the total number of imported products. This proportion increased to

10.7 percent in 1990. Shortly after the introduction of a less restrictive trade policy, there was a move away from quotas to import licensing: 119 items were under quota in 1973, but after 1984 no products were subject to quota. In contrast, the number of items requiring import licenses increased from 86 in 1973 to 1,121 in 1990 (Aslam 1993). At present, quantitative restrictions and import licenses are in force only in some heavy industries (automobiles), selected agricultural products (poultry), and textiles (batik). Automotive industries have the highest nontariff protection.

Incentives

Investment Incentives

The major investment incentive policy of the 1985–1995 First Industrial Master Plan was the Promotion of Investment Act (PIA), introduced in 1986. It offered a wider range of incentives and to more industries than earlier acts, with incentives for investment, reinvestment, exports, capital expenditure, and industrial location. Another feature of the PIA was its focus on capital: larger benefits could be secured with greater total capital invested. In addition to an investment tax allowance, capital-related incentives included a reinvestment allowance of 25 percent of capital expenditure for expansion purposes, an accelerated depreciation allowance, and a 60 percent capital allowance for plant and machinery used in agriculture. High-technology industries, training, strategic projects such as aerospace, and R&D projects received tax allowances. In addition, the export incentives included the following: export credit refinancing, with a preferential credit facility for exporters; exemption from import duty on direct raw materials and components; a drawback on excise duty on parts, ingredients, and packaging materials; a drawback on sales tax on materials used in manufacturing; and an exemption from import duty and sales tax on machinery and equipment.

Free Trade Zones

The Free Trade Zone Act was passed in 1971 and there are now 12 such zones, used exclusively for exports. Companies locating in these areas enjoy exemption from import duties for inputs, export taxes, excise tax, and simplified customs procedures and formalities in their import of raw materials, parts, machinery, and equipment, as well as in the export of their finished goods. When it is neither practical nor desirable to establish a free trade zone, a similar facility called a "licensed manufacturing warehouse" is accorded to a particular company. This facility was introduced in 1975. Like free trade zones, this facility is granted to companies that export at least 80 percent of their products.

Foreign Direct Investment

FDI in Malaysia has acted as a vehicle for capital movement, technology transfer, and skills development. However, although it has developed industrial competence in some sectors, it has left many sectors largely untouched. It has helped build a completely new economic sector for Malaysia, namely electronics and semiconductors. It also greatly expanded the existing textiles and apparel industry. FDI flows into Malaysia grew more than tenfold between 1980 and 1996, from $329 million to $3,750 million, but at a variable rate because of occasional, exceptionally large investments in some years, mainly in petrochemicals (Government of Malaysia, various issues). Two major growth periods may be distinguished: 1980–1982, in response to the intensive promotion of the Government to attract FDI; and 1986 onwards, when the Government liberalized the economy and the flow reached its peak year of 1992 ($6,809 million). An important characteristic of this latter inflow was the relocation by Japanese manufacturers to lower-cost production centers due to the appreciation of the yen. Since then flows have declined, partly because of increased competition from other locations, especially the People's Republic of China (PRC).

The profile of FDI has undergone major changes over the years in terms of sources and types of investment and industries. FDI in Malaysia is dominated by the Asia-Pacific countries, the share of which rose from 64.5 percent in 1982 to 81.3 percent in 1990 (Government of Malaysia, various issues). By contrast, the share of the European Union declined sharply from 21.8 percent to 6.3 percent over the same period. Japan accounted for about 24 percent of the approved FDI in 1990, while the share of the newly industrialized economies (NIEs) increased dramatically from 1.3 percent to 41.8 percent between 1982 and 1990. Taipei,China accounted for as much as 36 percent of approved investments in 1990, overtaking Japan. Korea, a newcomer, more than tripled its stake in Malaysia in terms of approved investments in 1989–1990, but still accounted for a small proportion of the total (3.7 percent in 1990). Singapore has always been a major source of FDI for Malaysia, owing mainly to its geographic proximity and historical ties. It is the biggest foreign investor in terms of stock, although it is overshadowed by others in flow terms. A striking feature of more recent FDI is that it has flowed largely into small and medium enterprises (SMEs).

Indirect Policies

Macroeconomic Policies

The Government can be credited with pursuing prudent macroeconomic management policies that provided a stable base for economic growth and export expansion. However, there have been two periods where the macroeconomic alignment could have created a disincentive to export activities. In the first—the early 1980s—public sector expansion was at a very high level with the Government engaging directly in business activities. The second period was 1994–1996, when massive capital inflows caused a "bubble" economy.

Institutions

Institutions that were established to promote industrial development and facilitate exports played a critical role in the exceptional performance of the export sector. The Malaysian Industrial Development Authority (MIDA), which is under the Ministry of International Trade and Industry, acted as a one-stop agency to encourage investment, process and approve investment applications, approve incentives, and provide support for various industries. In addition, trade financing institutions were formed, such as the Malaysian Export Credit Insurance Berhad, incorporated in 1977, to provide export credit insurance and guarantee schemes to trading firms and manufacturing exporters.

Labor Policy

The growth of the export sector was based on relatively abundant, low-cost labor. Malaysia became the world's largest exporter of electronics components, which were produced by utilizing labor-intensive technology. This approach met the national needs of generating employment. Manufacturing employment grew at an average rate of 23.6 percent in 1968–1973 and 12.4 percent in 1973–1981 (Soon 1987). In addition, export-oriented industries, in particular the electrical and electronics industry, managed to suppress wage increases through certain wage policies such as restriction of trade union activity and the absence of minimum wage legislation. However, during the high growth period (from 1988) the supply of unskilled labor was almost exhausted, resulting in increased upward pressure on wages.

DETERMINANTS OF EXPORTS

Comparative Advantage

Evolution of Comparative Advantage

The evolution of comparative advantage in Malaysia can be separated into three stages: the natural resources endowment phase that ran from preindependence to the late 1960s; export-oriented industrialization from the 1970s to the mid-1980s; and liberalization and rapid growth, from 1986 to the present. Though the main factors affecting Malaysia's comparative advantage have remained unchanged, additional factors have emerged as a result of domestic developments and external changes. In all three phases external influences were as important as, if not more than, domestic influences in shaping Malaysia's comparative advantage. In a sense, the openness of the economy worked as a critical factor. It provided the discipline to be responsive to global competitive elements. Changes in comparative advantage were also made possible by the willingness of the Government to introduce policies that would nurture newly emerging comparative advantage.

Determinants of Comparative Advantage

The two comparative advantage indicators, namely revealed comparative advantage (RCA) and domestic resource cost (DRC),[2] both show that Malaysia's export strength lies with industries that utilize abundant factors, namely labor and natural resources. Some of these industries, in particular the electrical and electronics industry, achieved very high RCA gains in a few years. However, competitiveness is not only determined by underlying factor endowment but also by imported factors of production, namely capital and skills. Studies have shown that, generally, fundamental competitiveness has remained with industries using natural factor endowment; industries exporting capital-intensive goods have gained comparative advantage as shown by their improved RCA and DRC (Gan 1987; Rokiah 1996).

Gan (1987) compared the RCA ranking of 34 two-digit SITC commodity exports (SITC 5–8 excluding 68) for the years 1973, 1978, and 1984. Three variations of RCA were used: RCAI refers to the ratio of net exports of SITC commodity i from Malaysia to world exports of that commodity; RCAII refers to the ratio of exports of SITC commodity i from Malaysia to net imports of that commodity into Malaysia; and RCAIII refers to the ratio of exports of commodity i to world exports of that commodity, relative to the ratio of total Malaysian exports of manufactures to world exports of manufactures. The reason for using the various measures of RCA is that RCAII may not reflect the true situation because imports can be influenced by changes in protection measures and therefore the export/import ratio may not reflect the underlying comparative advantage. Thus, export share is a more accurate indicator provided it is viewed with respect to its share in total exports.

---

[2] The RCA measures the export share of commodity i from country j in the world market relative to its production share. An RCA value of more than unity indicates that the country has captured more export share than that of production and thus it has a comparative advantage. The DRC, on the other hand, measures the domestic factor costs relative to the value-added at free trade prices. Thus, a DRC of less than one implies that the domestic industry can produce at lower cost than its competitors in the international market.

In 1973, the export of cork and wood manufactures was ranked the highest by RCAIII. Among the top 10 export products with RCAIII values greater than unity, two were resource-based (wood and rubber products), three were unskilled and labor-intensive (textiles, apparel, and footwear), and the rest belonged to capital-intensive categories (medicinal and pharmaceutical products, fertilizers, scientific equipment, and office machinery). Products with the lowest rankings were capital-intensive ones such as photographic equipment, iron and steel, and metalworking. By 1984, the comparative advantage of Malaysian exports had changed considerably, with electrical machinery, apparatus, and appliances having the highest ranking. Telecommunications apparatus joined the top 10 products in comparative advantage. Resource-based exports and unskilled, labor-intensive exports (which had long been in the top 10) remained in that group, albeit with lower rankings. At the lower end of the ranking scale, iron and steel, metalworking, and road vehicles remained very uncompetitive (Gan 1992).

More detailed estimates of the RCA were made by Fong (1986), though they cover a shorter period, namely the 1970s. These estimates track the RCA in five selected industries: electronics, textiles, plastics, iron and steel, and plywood. The electronics industry did not have a comparative advantage when it was launched in 1970, but by 1978 it had established a strong position. Its RCA increased from 0.19 in 1970 to 11.09 in 1978. Textiles also underwent a significant improvement, while plastic products and plywood had a more stable pattern of comparative advantage, with an RCA of around 1 for most of the period. The iron and steel industry was clearly an import-substitution activity, with a very low RCA.

A study of the competitiveness of infant industries, based on 1987 estimates of DRC, by Rokiah (1996) confirmed the earlier findings that resource-based industries (defined to include labor-intensive activities) were more competitive than nonresource-based ones. For example, of the 15 industries that registered a DRC of less than unity, nine were resource based. Quite a large number of the products of those industries were import-substitution products, such as food manufactures, and soap and cleaning preparations. The export industries included in the competitive groups were textiles, rubber, and wood products. The electronics industry was not included in the study because it is FDI driven, and thus was not nurtured by domestic resources. The competitive industries were also analyzed according to their level of capital intensity. Rokiah concluded that, as in the resource-based comparison, there was no clear link between comparative advantage and capital intensity.

Comparing the DRC estimates of 1979 and 1987, Rokiah (1996) also showed that infant industries had improved their competitiveness. In 1979, only 15 industries had a DRC of less than unity but this number increased to 25 by 1987. This improvement was largely attributed to gains in total factor productivity.

Factors Limiting Exports

The rapid economic growth of 1987–1996 has caused some rigidities and constraints in exports. These limiting factors are found in both the manufacturing sector and in its relationship with the wider economy. The trade regime itself was further liberalized in this period and is not, therefore, an impediment to the future growth of exports. The rigidities primarily concern technological capability and capacity, the relationship between labor cost and productivity, skills levels, and the structure of the manufacturing sector. The constraints relate to resource allocation between the manufacturing and nonmanufacturing sectors—namely returns of the tradable and nontradable sectors and the allocation of capital. Some of these limiting factors, such as technology and skills levels, may severely affect exports in the medium term, whereas others, such as labor costs, allocation of credit, and relative sector returns, may have a more immediate impact.

Structure of Manufacturing Sector

Some major industries have minimal linkages with one another and with the rest of the economy; most of their inputs are imported and almost all of their products are exported. Estimates of forward and backward linkages for 1988 by Aziz (1991) show that industries with the highest linkages are those catering to the domestic market, except for textiles and apparel. (However, this study did not have a comprehensive coverage of all the industries in the manufacturing sector and thus its results are indicative only.) Industries with high forward linkages are machines and related industries (1.51), food processing (1.17), textiles and apparel (1.12), and palm oil (1.11), whereas the lowest are petroleum products (0.98), mineral-based industries (0.74), and wood and paper products (0.74). Estimates of backward linkages show stronger links than those of forward ones. Industries with high backward linkages are textiles and apparel (1.8), food processing (1.35), wood and paper products (1.29), machines and related industries (1.22), and palm oil (1.13). Those with lower backward linkages are beverages and tobacco (1.0) and petroleum products (0.88). Another good example is the electrical and electronics industry. The import content is so high that, according to some estimates, for every one ringgit of output about 0.8 ringgit is needed for imports, hence generating very little value-added.

Technology Base

Malaysia has become heavily dependent on foreign technology, as it does not have its own adequate domestic technological capability. The electrical and electronics industry, the main exporter, is dominated by multinational corporations (MNCs) that conduct their research overseas. Malaysian R&D expenditure at 0.37 percent of GDP is much lower than that of Japan at 2.8 percent; Korea at 2.3 percent; and Taipei,China at 1.8 percent (Mahani 1996). Moreover, foreign technology has not been transferred successfully and there is very little upgrading and development work on it. What R&D that exists is carried out mainly by the Government, while private sector R&D investment represents a small part of the total.

FDI activities have also tended to concentrate on specific stages within the overall manufacturing process, with intermediate products imported or exported as needed. This has helped develop a pool of technically skilled managers and engineers, but few have enough exposure to the whole manufacturing process to be able to build indigenous counterparts to FDI-funded operations. Although the specific transfer of technology in selected manufacturing industries has recently been both complete and in-depth, it covers only a small fraction of the industrial base and is therefore of limited use for strengthening domestic development. For domestic companies, the acquisition of technology is done normally through technical arrangements with the design franchise holders, and covers very specific and limited areas.

Human Resources

The high economic growth of 1987–1996 created a tight labor market and changed its structure. It also led to rapid wage rises. In 1985–1990, employment grew at an annual average rate of 3.4 percent while the labor force expanded by 3.4 percent (World Bank 1995). However, in 1990–1994, the respective figures were 3.3 percent for employment and 2.8 percent for the labor force. The increase in employment was higher in manufacturing (9.1 percent) than nonmanufacturing (3.7 percent).[3] As a result, the average real wage per worker in the manufacturing sector rose by 10.9 percent in 1995–1997 compared with 4.4 percent in 1989–1994 (Department of Statistics, various issues).

Shortages of labor in the manufacturing industry have several negative impacts. First, the paucity of unskilled labor, temporarily relieved by the inflow of unskilled foreign labor, has encouraged labor-intensive industries to remain in production despite loss of comparative advantage. Manufacturers have therefore been able to postpone upgrading into more capital-intensive and higher knowledge-based activities. Second, the shortage of skilled labor is hampering companies' efforts to move upmarket since there are too few qualified workers in technical areas, particularly engineering and information technology (IT). As just mentioned, a significant problem is the rapid rise in wage levels: in 1991–1993, real monthly wages rose by 3.7 percent a year. They were not accompanied by corresponding increases in productivity. Lee (1996) has shown that during 1985–1993 the real value-added per worker increased by only 2.5 percent a year.

EXPORT DECELERATION OF 1996–1997

Introduction

After registering an average annual export growth rate of 17 percent since 1988, the Malaysian economy received a jolt in 1996, when its export growth rate plummeted to 4.4 percent. Manufactured exports

---

[3] The average employment growth rate was 3.3 percent because agricultural employment contracted by 3 percent.

rose by only 8.1 percent and this rate was far below the average performance of 22 percent a year of 1993–1995. The slowdown in the agriculture sector was even more alarming, with exports falling by 8.5 percent. For an economy that is heavily dependent on exports, high export growth was crucial to achieving the targeted GDP annual growth of 7.5 percent.

Export performance in 1997 was equally unimpressive. The first half of 1997 showed some signs of recovery but the Asian financial crisis that began in mid-1997 has slowed export recovery. However, the currency depreciation caused by the crisis benefited Malaysian exports. This is best illustrated by the different growth rates when exports are recorded in US dollar or ringgit terms: export value grew by only 0.7 percent in US dollars but by 12 percent in ringgit.

This development brought into question the competitiveness of Malaysian, as well as other Asian, exports. Were they losing their comparative advantage or were other global factors altering the world export pattern? Was the 1996 export performance a blip in a more stable upward trend or was it the precursor of a new trend? This section analyzes both domestic causes such as increasing labor costs, low productivity, and overvaluation of the exchange rate, and external factors such as global overcapacity.

Onset of Export Deceleration

The overall export growth rate began to fall after reaching a peak in 1994; exports increased in 1995 by 26.4 percent, but in 1996 the growth rate decelerated to 4.4 percent. A more disaggregated analysis shows a slightly different picture. Manufacturing export growth declined from 33.9 percent in 1994 to 22.9 percent in 1995 and to 8.1 percent in 1996 (Government of Malaysia, various issues). On the other hand, the growth performance for primary commodities was mixed—the increase in 1994 was quite small at 4.5 percent but 1995 proved to be a better year with 12 percent. Yet exports contracted in 1996 by 1.6 percent. From this observation of the disaggregated pattern between manufacturing and nonmanufacturing exports, the underlying competitiveness of manufactured exports appears to be changing: there was a steady decline in the manufacturing export growth rate in 1994–1996. The fluctuating performance of nonmanufacturing exports suggests the influence of short-term factors.

Manufacturing exports can be further segregated into two groups —resource-based and nonresource-based goods. Electrical and electronics goods, the most important manufacturing export product and one which belongs to the nonresource-based category, suffered a sharp reversal, moving from a 38.5 percent increase in 1994 to only 7.6 percent growth in 1996 (Government of Malaysia, various issues). Transport equipment exports fared even worse. During the same period, growth of 60.2 percent reversed itself into a fall of 13.4 percent. Conversely, resource-based manufacturing exports such as wood, rubber, and petroleum products fared much better, registering healthy but somewhat fluctuating growth. This, however, is a relatively low value-added group of products.

In general, the performance of most primary commodity exports was much worse than manufacturing exports, including rubber, palm oil, and sawlogs and sawn timber. However, crude oil and LNG compensated, with the latter registering the best increase of this group with growth of 40.6 percent in 1996. The dramatic increase in exports is most likely because of the decision by the National Petroleum Company to fully utilize its gas reserves, as well as to higher demand from Japan and Korea.

The electronics exports to the US declined steadily. In 1993, 33 percent of total electronics exports were destined for the US. By 1966, this proportion fell to 25 percent. An identical trend was observed for textiles and apparel; the US share declined from 31 percent to 23 percent over the same period. Singapore and Japan reduced their shares in the exports of chemicals from Malaysia. Korea's share in rubber exports fell by 4 percent over the same period while Japan's share fell by 2 percent. Similarly, the proportion of exports of sawlogs declined for Korea and the PRC by 4 and 3 percent, respectively, over the 1993–1996 period.

The dismal export performance was not confined to selected groups of products but was an across-the-board decline. Because of the large share of electrical and electronics exports in total manufacturing exports (53 percent), the low growth rate has raised fears about the external sector's ability to fuel economic growth. This concern is further compounded by the fact that the source of the decline was electronics components, the mainstay of the industry and a key input for many final electrical and electronics products, including computers. This could imply that consumer demand for these products has gone down.

To ascertain the underlying pattern of the general export decline, it is important to analyze it in the context of the share of specific exports in the world market. Due to the unavailability of 1996 data on exports by commodity sector classification, an examination of the share for 1992–1995 is made instead. Almost all of the export products that saw a fall in 1996 had enjoyed increasing global market share prior to 1996; in particular, electrical machinery had augmented its share in the world market from 3.7 percent in 1992 to 4.8 percent in 1995 (UN 1995). Other products with similar performance were chemicals and chemical products, and manufactures of metals, palm oil, and LNG. Products that showed a decreasing trend were textiles and apparel, rubber products, wood (sawlogs and sawn timber), and tin. Based on these trends, it would seem that the 1996 export reduction was not entirely because of a loss of international competitiveness for products that were enjoying increasing global share, but more likely because of external factors such as a reduction in global demand or world oversupply. On the other hand, products that experienced decreasing share in 1992-1995, including labor-intensive exports such as textiles and apparel, and primary commodities such as wood and rubber, clearly indicated their declining competitiveness.

The gloomy export performance in 1996 and the prospect that this may be a permanent trend have two serious implications for the country. First, single-digit growth of electrical and electronics exports exposed the structural weakness of Malaysian external trade. It is chronically dependent on a single industry and a large reduction in the growth rate of this industry will have a potent impact on the economy, particularly on employment and export earnings. In addition, the electrical and electronics industry has small per unit net export earnings because of its high import content and as such it requires a large growth rate to make a substantial contribution to total net export revenue. In addition, since Malaysia is losing comparative advantage in labor-intensive activities (as seen above) and if productivity does not grow fast enough, some of the MNCs that are a major force in the industry may relocate to other countries in the region. There has already been some relocation of production of lower-value electrical and electronics products to the PRC and Viet Nam.

The second implication about the 1996 reversal is that it has forced a fundamental review of the competitiveness of exports. The slowdown of labor-intensive exports (electronics and textiles) has highlighted the urgency of shifting to technology-and knowledge-intensive activities. Similarly, sharply fluctuating primary commodity exports emphasize the need not to rely on such exports but to promote more downstream activities. A reasonably strong and steady performance of resource-based manufacturing exports has raised the significance of such industries.

Factors Responsible for Export Deceleration

The preceding analysis has given some broad indications of the causes of the export deceleration. The changing domestic supply conditions and the relative returns to the tradable and nontradable sectors are among the key causes as to why some of the export industries lost their comparative advantage. The most prominent among them is labor, in terms of increased costs and the lack of skilled workers that has restricted the ability of these industries to move to higher value-added activities. However, the internal factors alone are insufficient to explain the sharp reduction of exports in 1996, since some of these export products have increased their share in the global market. For them, external factors, such as global oversupply, have played a bigger role in the deceleration.

Macroeconomic Policies

The Government has largely ceded its role as an active economic promoter to the private sector through its privatization policy. This policy has encouraged investment in the nontradable sector, in particular infrastructure, as manifested by the allocation of credit given by the financial institutions. The concentration of domestic investment in the nontradable sector has left most of the investment in export industries to be made by FDI. In view of the keen competition from other countries for FDI in the international market, the decreasing FDI inflow was not compensated for by high domestic investment. Gan et al. (1997) show that overcapacity and poor cash flow among Malaysian companies in telecommunications, property, transportation, infrastructure, and selected industries in the manufacturing sector are indications of the failure to allocate resources to their most productive uses. As a result, these industries are experiencing a declining rate of return on assets. Returns to the tradable sector have been further eroded because producers of tradables are price-takers and so cannot adjust prices, unlike those in the nontradable sector.

Since the middle of 1980s, the Malaysian trade regime has been substantially liberalized. The post-Uruguay Round average tariff rate is only 9 percent and most of the quantitative restrictions were abolished. Yet, there were some selected domestic industries that were protected and received government support, such as automobile. Because of protection, these industries have enjoyed high rates of return. As opposed to this, exporters had to operate in a more competitive environment, with little government support. Therefore, the new market entrants had difficulty in breaking into export markets. Established export industries such as electronics have strong export marketing links through the network of multinational companies. Another problem was that of capital scarcity for technological upgrading: although an Industrial Technical Assistance Fund does exist, it is targeted for selected industries and requires complicated procedures. Failure to attract new investments into the manufacturing sector has hampered efforts to move to higher value-added industries in the recent past. This stalled the process of movement to products in which Malaysia has comparative advantage. In short, the macroeconomic policies adopted by the Government since the middle of the 1980s have made the tradable sector unattractive, thus threatening export capabilities.

Domestic Supply Conditions

High economic growth since the mid-1980s created constraint in the labor market–logistics services technological capability–which adversely affected the domestic supply conditions. These bottlenecks eroded Malaysia's cost competitiveness, particularly in labor-intensive exports. They also effectively slowed the transformation to higher value-added products. A tight labor market affects the export industry in two ways. First, rising wage levels increase the costs of production and cause labor-intensive export industries to lose their comparative advantage against countries that still have relatively low-cost labor in abundance. This condition is especially prevalent in textiles and apparel, and rubber products. Second, the tight labor market also means a shortage of labor, leading frequently to high turnover; this has limited companies' ability to expand production. The World Bank (1995) found that the degree of difficulty in recruiting local technical personnel in Malaysia was the same as that in the Philippines and Thailand, whereas it was much less in PRC, Indonesia, and Viet Nam.

A tight labor market is, in theory, supposed to foster the restructuring of the industry sector and encourage it to move to higher value-added activities. In Malaysia, this process has been impeded because foreign workers have not been allowed to meet the demand. However, employment of foreign workers in itself has hidden costs in terms of administrative uncertainty. For example, the policy on the importation of foreign unskilled workers is at the best of times unclear and it changes quite frequently. Many of these changes are done without prior consultation with the industry groups affected and are often introduced at short notice. Such labor policy uncertainties seriously hinder the smooth functioning of large labor-intensive export production units, most of which are part of MNCs' international production networks. For smaller local exporting firms, these uncertainties affect their export production schedules and they may lose export orders as a consequence.

Two other factors that could have contributed indirectly to the loss of competitiveness are the high logistics costs and technological limitations. The domestic logistics industry is still fragmented, where separate operators handle each portion of the transport system. For example, container operators only transport goods from the factories to the warehouse yards, while freight forwarders only carry out freight services. Similarly, insurance for exports and insurance for imports are handled separately. In other words, the total logistics system in moving goods from factories to their export destinations is not integrated and is inefficient. It could provide comprehensive services at a much lower rate if it were reformed. For example, many Malaysian exporters use Singapore to export their products because the real cost is lower because of greater efficiency and timeliness.

Technological limitations have prevented the expansion of vertical product differentiation in the export structure. Malaysian industrialization started with the assembly of low value-added final goods and components. This specialization has been mastered very well and Malaysia, until the advent of high labor costs, gained a comparative advantage in this activity. The export market for this type of products is now saturated with emerging countries that have lower labor costs. To meet this challenge, the economy must move to higher level processes and upgrade its products. Because of its limited technological capability, it has yet to develop competency in higher level products, and thus some export products may face declining demand from developed countries. For example, Malaysia's current advantage in furniture exports is fast eroding because the market for low-end mass-produced furniture is limited and there is now competition from other low-cost producers such as Indonesia, and this may be the reason for Malaysia's declining share in wood products in 1995. Thus, limitations in domestic supply conditions have contributed significantly to the weakening of Malaysia's export performance.

Exchange Rate

After the second half of 1992, Malaysia allowed the ringgit to appreciate against the currencies of its major trading partners, namely the US dollar and the Singapore dollar. The ringgit's REER continued to rise against those of certain trading partners and competitors, reaching a first peak at the end of 1993 through early 1994. It then depreciated slightly but continued to increase and reached a second peak in the middle of 1997, that is, at the beginning of the Asian financial crisis. The rise in the ringgit's REER is most noticeable when compared with the movements of the REERs of Korea and Taipei,China. Both these economies took an opposite exchange rate stance from that of Malaysia in that their currencies, in terms of REER, were kept competitive. Higher interest rates, large increases in foreign capital inflows, especially short-term, and a perception that the ringgit was undervalued supported the currency's appreciation. The high growth experienced by the Malaysian economy since the late 1980s has attracted a large volume of short-term capital inflows, particularly into the equity market. As a result of signs of overheating, the Government adopted higher interest rates to control inflation, leading to further inflows of capital and the ringgit's appreciation.

Such appreciation and its effect on exports are often viewed in the context of the yuan's devaluation in 1994. This made the PRC's exports very competitive and many commentators have attributed the cause of ASEAN export deceleration in 1996 to this. But the link is rather weak because the time lag is long, i.e., about two years, though changes in export orders can take some time to filter their way through the system. However, the Malaysian exports that suffered a reduction in 1996 are different from those exported by the PRC, which is a large producer of electrical appliances (not of electronics components). The 1996 export deceleration did not involve electrical appliances, which grew by 17 percent. The ringgit's appreciation has affected textiles and other labor-intensive exports, particularly those aimed at the US market. The North American Free Trade Agreement (NAFTA) has given the US better access to Mexico, another exporter of labor-intensive products.

Global Factors

The global factors at work on the export deceleration of 1996 are the worldwide oversupply of certain products and the emergence of new competitors. The sharp drop in electrical and electronics exports in 1996 affected other Asian exporters as well. Korean electronics exports plunged by 22.5 percent, Singapore's by 6.5 percent, and Taipei,China's by 13 percent (*Far Eastern Economic Review,* 26 October 1996). Export deceleration encountered by the major producers of electronics components points to the fact that the cause is external.

Oversupply is also seen in the decline in the export prices of goods such as dynamic random-access memory (DRAM) chips, which fell by as much as 90 percent in 1996 (*Far Eastern Economic Review,* 26 October 1996). Since 1990, there had been a massive investment in production capacity of semiconductors by domestic companies in Korea, and to a lesser extent in Singapore and Taipei,China. When those investments began production, competition became very keen and price was used to gain market share.

Competition for agricultural exports came from neighboring countries, particularly Indonesia. Because of the rising cost of labor and better returns on the alternative use of land, some Malaysian companies, starting in the early 1990s, opened up vast plantations overseas for palm oil and rubber. This move to source new locations coincided with Indonesia's effort to intensify large-scale commercialization of its agriculture sector to generate employment.

Large areas of land in Sumatra and Kalimantan were earmarked for estate-type plantation development.

The effect of competition can also be seen from the movement of export prices. The overall export price index increased—except for a slight drop of 1.5 percent in 1992, by 49 percent from 1987 to 1995—with an average annual rate of increase of 5.8 percent. The average export price of manufactured exports rose by 5.7 percent a year, lower than that of agriculture. However, export prices fell substantially in 1996 and 1997, with manufacturing registering the largest drop of 3.4 percent, followed by agriculture with 2.7 percent. The sharp export price drop compared with the earlier increases for both manufactured and agricultural exports indicates excess supply in the world market. As a result of the higher rate of increase in export prices than import prices in 1987–1995, the terms of trade were in Malaysia's favor. Thus, the export expansion in the first half of the 1990s was not only due to an increase in volume but also to higher export prices.[4]

Export Performance in 1997–1998

As noted earlier, performance for both primary commodities and manufactured exports in 1997 was dismal. In 1997, even though in ringgit terms the growth rate was reasonable at 12 percent, in US dollar terms it was only 1 percent. The growth rate in dollar terms reflected a more accurate picture because in the second half of 1997, Malaysian exports by value benefited from currency depreciation. At a more disaggregated level, total exports of major primary commodities decreased by 0.14 percent in dollar terms while manufactured exports contracted by 25 percent (Bank Negara Malaysia, various issues). But in ringgit terms, the export performance was much better because of the exchange rate depreciation: primary commodity exports increased by 30 percent and manufactured exports by 12.9 percent. In dollar terms, textiles and apparel exports continued to decline steeply in 1997, with wood and chemical products performing a little better. Electrical and electronics exports

[4] The estimated export volume index showed that export volume increased by 206.7 percent from 1987 to 1997. See Government of Malaysia, *Treasury Economic Report*, 1997/98.

were further reduced by 25 percent in 1997; monthly exports registered negative performance except for January, March, and August.

Although export data for the first quarter of 1998 are preliminary, they show an interesting pattern. In January almost all export products experienced a contraction, a continuation of the pattern since October 1997. In February and March, most manufactured exports rebounded; for example, the electrical and electronics machinery increase for February was 24.6 percent and for March 13.7 percent. An improvement was also noted for iron, steel, and metal manufactures, and chemicals and chemical products. In comparison, the performance of primary commodity exports was mixed, with most products enjoying an export increase for one month but registering a decline in the other month.

Although the sharp depreciation of the ringgit from July 1997 was expected to boost demand for exports, the actual performance of exports has been contrary to expectations. Time lag could be a factor here because the REER only started to depreciate significantly in October 1997. A clearer pattern of the benefits of the depreciation emerged only after February 1998, a time lag of five months after the depreciation, when exports showed an improvement. This effect should, however, be seen in the context of the even sharper depreciation by neighboring competitors such as Indonesia and Thailand, and lower demand as a result of the slowdown in the economies of major importing countries, namely Korea and Japan.

PROSPECTS AND POLICY RECOMMENDATIONS

Export Prospects

The success of the export-led growth policy has made the Malaysian economy open and dependent on exports as its engine for growth. There is, therefore, little possibility that this policy will be reversed or that the role of exports will be reduced, especially in light of the dismal export performance of 1996 and 1997. Both the Government and the business community understand the need to examine export fundamentals and competitiveness.

Thus the future of Malaysian exports will very much depend on the success of nurturing the new areas of comparative advantage and the removal of existing impediments. One of the issues to be addressed is the structure of exports, which depend heavily on the electrical and electronics industry. Other existing export industries need to be developed to play a bigger role in export growth. The industries that have the potential to expand (the sunrise industries) include rubber, palm oil, and petroleum products. Malaysia has advanced expertise and technology in the first two industries, where the Government has invested in research work to develop upstream and downstream activities. Malaysia also has the capability to carry out research work and product development to create new rubber products, particularly those for industrial use. In addition, the country has a large supply of raw materials needed for petroleum-based products such as plastic resin. Advanced petroleum products could have good demand prospects because they are inputs for products with higher returns; for example, there is a potential for greater use of specialized plastic products in vehicles. For the electrical and electronics industry, it is likely that the loss of labor's comparative advantage will induce the industry to move to higher value-added products, such as multimedia and IT products.

The restructuring of exports should also include the phasing out of industries that may no longer be competitive. Two such industries are textiles and apparel, and wood products. As a labor-intensive industry, textiles and apparel has been adversely affected by higher labor costs. The industry will have to move to higher quality products but the environment and expertise for such development is still limited as compared with, for example, Hong Kong, China. With regard to wood products, furniture constitutes the bulk of Malaysia's exports, with some manufacturers producing as subcontractors for established global producers. As the supply of raw materials becomes scarce, the costs of production will increase. For this industry, the main competitor is Indonesia, which possesses abundant raw materials but has lower expertise, and can offer better prices.

During the boom period of exchange rates (1987–1995) the highest rate of export growth was about 20 percent a year. This rate can be achieved again in the medium term both when the global market recovers and when Malaysia regains its comparative advantage, but this time in higher value-added products. A market recovery alone would suggest a growth rate of 12 percent. Growth of 10 percent is possible with improved comparative advantage, but in a weak market. In the worst case, i.e., in a weak market and with no improvement in comparative advantage, exports may expand by only 4 percent a year. In the most favorable situation, Malaysia can achieve its previous excellent export growth rate of 20 percent a year, but recovery from the current economic and currency crisis is expected to take some time. Using an optimistic forecast of a recovery period of two years, exports are likely to grow at about 4 percent during this period.

The possibility of Malaysian exports achieving their former high performance requires more concerted efforts to encourage manufacturers to find new areas of comparative advantage and to move to higher value-added export products. For this purpose, the following policies are suggested.

Policy Recommendations

After the depletion of their low-cost labor pools, economies such as Korea and Taipei,China moved into a new phase of industrialization, which focused mainly on technology and knowledge-based activities. Malaysia has now reached that stage with the tightening of the labor market and the relocation of some lower-end labor-intensive activities to countries with lower labor costs. Malaysia's quest for new comparative advantage has to be directed to six areas—labor, technology, exchange rate, investment environment, incentives, and expansion of downstream activities.

Labor

There are two policy thrusts regarding labor issues: reducing the number of unskilled foreign workers and increasing the skills level of domestic workers. The de facto or unannounced policy of maintaining wage levels and enlarging the labor supply through immigration of foreign labor should be eliminated. Programs to reduce the number of these foreign workers should be implemented.

There is evidence that the skills intensity in the manufacturing sector declined between 1985 and 1991 (World Bank 1995). The ratio of skilled labor is measured by the proportion of managerial and professional classes to skilled workers; this ratio fell from 0.43 in 1985 to 0.35 in 1991. This finding holds across most manufacturing industries. The reversal of this trend is fundamental if labor productivity is to rise, and it can only be done when the supply of skilled workers has been augmented. Thus, the proportion of the population enroling in secondary and higher education must be increased. This requires the expansion of mid-level technical training schemes, particularly vocational training, and encouragement of in-house training by increasing the benefits of the existing incentive packages.

The proportion of tertiary level enrollment in science and engineering subjects is very much lower when compared with Japan and the NIEs such as Korea (Lall 1996). This category of worker is critical for the development of technological capacity. Greater promotional efforts and direct incentives may be needed.

Technology

Expansion of technological capacity and capability is a necessary complement of the requirement of higher labor productivity. Policy recommendations in this area may be divided into two: those for MNCs and those for domestic firms.

The MNCs' technological capability is based outside Malaysia, making the scope for technology transfer limited. The establishment of MNCs' R&D centers in Malaysia will strengthen the domestic technological capacity through the transfer of technology. These centers are likely to train local researchers and help develop capacity for product development. Consequently, the relocation of MNCs' R&D centers to Malaysia should be promoted for selected products. Tax incentives have been introduced for this purpose, but additional measures can be introduced such as easier recruitment of foreign technical experts and more stringent application of intellectual property rights.

Domestic technological R&D is still in its infancy and most of it lies in the domain of the public sector. In addition, there is a lack of coordination between the producers of the R&D (the public sector) and the users (the private sector). Efforts should be concentrated to match these two groups so that the results of R&D can be used commercially in the most effective way. The Government has already provided tax incentives for private companies to sponsor research work in public and private institutions or to carry out their own research activities. In addition, the formation of industry-specific research institutions should be encouraged, where companies participating in these industries could be the shareholders of the institutions. Public research institutions could take a lead role in these industry-based research institutions, as well as becoming shareholders in them.

Another essential area is the development of the machine tool industry. Malaysia lacks a strong product design and development capability, and this hinges on the availability of a well-developed machine tool industry. This will allow producers to quickly develop new products to respond to market changes. In many countries this industry is made up of SMEs. However, in view of the limited capability of the SMEs to initiate such activities, the public sector should take a lead in strengthening the industry.

Exchange Rate

The export performance of 1995 to the first half of 1997 has shown the importance of maintaining a real exchange rate level that can induce the domestic economy to respond to internal as well as external changes. An overvalued exchange rate diverts resources to the nontradable sector and erodes export competitiveness. Hence, Malaysia's exchange rate regime should be flexible to reflect the changes in the domestic economy, such as relative prices and wage movements, along with the changes in competitors' exchange rates.

Investment Environment

The right investment conditions with transparent and consistent regulations, reasonable real interest rates, and efficient infrastructure, are not only necessary to attract FDI but also to increase domestic investment. FDI still plays an important role in Malaysian manufacturing output and exports—as a provider of capital, technology, management skills, marketing networks, and export earnings. At present, competition for FDI is keen and FDI providers may place greater demands on host countries before making their investments. On the domestic front, the investment environment should encourage capital flows into productive and tradable sectors. Any new measures must also be WTO consistent.

Incentives

To improve the investment environment, products and activities that form the basis of incentives should be reviewed regularly to support the objective of strengthening workers' skills, technological capability, and R&D. A variation of an incentive measure is a matching grant for the above areas to secure the interest of firms. For example, in the training of workers, the Government can give a grant matching the amount spent by firms to train their workers. A number of countries, such as Singapore, have implemented this scheme and the response has been positive.

An area that has seen very slow development and yet is critical to export expansion is trade facilitation, which includes customs procedures, standards, and data management. Streamlining of customs procedures and harmonization of standards will expedite the movement of goods at points of entry. Similarly, efficient data processing relating to customs clearance will also facilitate exporting and importing but, more important, it will reduce delays that raise the cost of doing business. In addition, export credit refinancing facilities such as those given to finance insurance facilities have proven to be beneficial to exporters, and therefore they should be continued and expanded.

Increasing the efficiency of the service industries that support exports is another significant part of an overall target of reducing the cost of export activities. The relevant service industries include banking, insurance, and business services. Efficiency improvements could involve increased automation and/or liberalization. Although service activities are relatively labor-intensive, productivity gains can be derived from a more efficient use of capital. A similar policy of not allowing unskilled low-cost foreign workers to enter these labor-intensive industries should be pursued and increasing labor costs must be met with productivity gains through automation and skills improvement. Incentives to allow larger tax exemptions for automation could be introduced.

Another aspect of improved efficiency is the introduction of competition: entry barriers, in particular license requirements, should be minimized to reduce the initial costs of doing business. For example, entry of operators of integrated transport and logistics systems should be liberalized, to reduce costs to exporters by enabling them to maintain lower stock levels.

Expansion of Downstream Activities

Malaysia can develop a strong comparative advantage in downstream resource-based activities because of its advanced research capability, particularly in rubber and palm oil, and the availability of raw materials. Malaysia is the world's leading research center for these two industries and has the capability to develop advanced related products. Since the production of rubber and palm oil is likely to meet keen competition from emerging competitor countries and Malaysia may not be able to meet this challenge effectively due to increasing costs, it should intensify its efforts in the export of downstream products. What is still lacking is the large investment required in these products and the link with the global market. It is suggested that FDI should also be channeled into these industries to help develop the critical export links.

BIBLIOGRAPHY AND REFERENCES

Ariff, M. 1991. "The Changing Role of Foreign Direct Investment." In H. Yokoyama and T. Mokhtar, eds., *Malaysian Economy in Transition.* Tokyo: Institute of Developing Economies.

Asia-Pacific Economic Cooperation (APEC) Forum. 1995. "Survey of Impediments to Trade and Investment in the APEC Region." Report by the Pacific Economic Cooperation Council for APEC.

Aslam, Mohamed G. H. 1993. "Tariff Reduction and Trade Performance: The Case of Malaysia." M. Ec Dissertation, Faculty of Economics and Administration, University of Malaya, Kuala Lumpur. Mimeo.

Aziz, A. R. 1991. "Magnitude and Structure of Agriculture Price Protection in Malaysia." Occasional Paper No. 19. Centre for Agriculture Policy Studies, Universiti Pertanian Malaysia, Kuala Lumpur. September.

Bank Negara Malaysia. Various issues. *Quarterly Economic Bulletin.* Kuala Lumpur.

Bautista, R. 1981. "Exchange Rate Changes and LDC Export Performance under Generalised Currency Floating." *Welwirtschaftliehes Archiv* 17(3):443-468.

Chen, Y. L. 1991. "Protection Cost: A Case Study of the Manufacturing Industries in Malaysia, 1987." Thesis submitted for M. Soc. (Ec), School of Social Science, Universiti Sains, Malaysia.

Department of Statistics. Various issues. *Monthly Manufacturing Statistics.*

Edwards, C. 1990. "Malaysian Industrial Policy in the 1990s: Look East?" Mimeo.

Far Eastern Economic Review. 1996. 26 October.

Fong, C. O. 1986. *Technological Leap: Malaysian Industry in Transition.* Singapore: Oxford University Press.

Gan, W. B. 1987. "Macroeconomic Policy, Real Exchange Rate and International Competitiveness: The Malaysian Experience during the 1980s." Faculty of Economics and Administration, University of Malaya, Kuala Lumpur. Mimeo.

______. 1989. "The Ringgit Exchange Rate and the Malaysian Economy." In Z. A. Mahani and K. C. Lim, eds., *Strategy For Growth: Towards a More Competitive Economy*. Kuala Lumpur: Malaysian Economic Association.

______. 1992. "Macroeconomic Adjustment and the Real Exchange Rate: Implications for Growth of the Manufacturing Sector in Malaysia." Paper Presented at the ISIS-HIID Conference on the Malaysian Economy, Kuala Lumpur.

Gan W. B., and K. T. Kwek. 1994. "Exchange Rate Intervention and Sterilisation in Malaysia." Malaysian Institute of Economic Research Conference paper.

Gan, W. B., L. Y. Soon, and C. C. Soh. 1997. "Asia's Financial Crisis and Lessons for Malaysia." Paper presented at a Seminar on the East Asian Financial Crisis, Malaysian Economic Association, Kuala Lumpur.

Government of Malaysia. Various issues. *Treasury Economic Report*. Kuala Lumpur.

Government of Malaysia/UNDP/World Bank. 1984. "Malaysian Industrial Policy Studies Project Report No. 1: Tariff and Tariff Related Incentives in Malaysia." Mimeo.

Ministry of International Trade and Industry. 1996. *The Second Industrial Master Plan: 1996-2005*.

International Monetary Fund (IMF). Various years. *International Financial Statistics Yearbook*. Washington, DC.

Jomo, K. S. 1990. *Growth and Structural Change in the Malaysian Economy*. London: Macmillan.

______. ed. 1993. *Industrialising Malaysia: Policy, Performance, Prospects*. London: Routledge.

______. ed. 1997. *Southeast Asia's Misunderstood Miracle*. Boulder: Westview Press.

Krueger, Anne O. 1978. *Foreign Trade Regime and Economic Development: Liberalisation Attempts and Consequences*. Cambridge, Mass.: Ballinger Press.

Lall, S. 1996. "Technology Policy and Challenges." Paper presented at the Conference on Globalisation and Development: Lessons for the Malaysian Economy, Faculty of Economics and Administration, University of Malaya, Kuala Lumpur.

Lee, K. F. 1990. "Export Expansion and Industrial Growth: The Malaysia Experience, 1968-86." M. Ec. Dissertation. University of Malaya, Kuala Lumpur. Mimeo.

Lee, K. H. 1986. "The Structure and Causes of Malaysian Manufacturing Sector Protection." In C. Findlay and R. Garnaut, eds., *The Political Economy of ASEAN and Australia.* Sydney: Allen and Unwin.

______. 1996. "Labour Market Issues: Skills Training and Labour Productivity." Paper presented at the National Convention on the Seventh Malaysia Plan, Malaysian Economic Association, Kuala Lumpur.

Mahani, Z. A. 1994. "Economic Liberalisation and Structural Reform: The Malaysian Experience." In D. T. Nguyen and K. Roy, eds., *Economic Reforms, Liberalisation and Trade in the Asia Pacific Region.* New Delhi: Wiley Eastern.

______. 1996. "The Malaysian New Industrial Policy: The Next Phase of Development." Paper presented at the Fifth Convention of the East Asian Economic Association, Bangkok.

______. 1997. "Malaysia Industrial and Trade Policies Under the New International Trading System." Study submitted for the UN Commission for Latin America and the Caribbean.

Mahani, Z. A., and K. C. Lim, eds. 1989. *Strategy for Growth: Towards a More Competitive Economy.* Malaysian Economic Association, Kuala Lumpur.

McGee, T. G. et al. 1986. "Industrialisation and Labour Force Processes: A Case Study of Peninsular Malaysia." Research School of Pacific Studies, Australian National University, Canberra.

Nagaraj, S., and K. H. Lee, eds. 1991. *The Malaysian Economy Beyond 1990: International and Domestic Perspectives.* Malaysian Economic Association, Kuala Lumpur.

Panchamukhi, V. R. 1972. "Effective Protection and Intra-Regional Trade: A Case Study of Malaysia." Bangkok: ESCAP Secretariat. Mimeo.

Power, J. H. 1971. "The Structure of Protection in West Malaysia." In B. Balassa and Associates, eds., *The Structure of Protection in Developing Countries.* Baltimore: Johns Hopkins University Press.

Rana, P. B. 1981. *ASEAN Exchange Rates: Policies and Trade Effects.* Singapore: Institute of Southeast Asian Studies.

Rao, B. V. V. 1980. *Malaysia: Development Pattern and Policy.* Singapore: Singapore University Press.

Rasiah, R. 1993. "Free Trade Zones And Industrial Development in Malaysia." In K. S. Jomo, ed., *Industrialising Malaysia: Policy, Performance, Prospects.* London: Routledge.

Rating Agency of Malaysia. 1997. *Research Bulletin.*

Rokiah, A. 1996. *Industrialisation in Malaysia: Import Substitution Strategy and Infant Industry Performance.* London: Routledge.

Soon, L. Y. 1987. "Wages and Labour Welfare in Malaysia: An Analysis of the Impact of Export-led Industrialisation." Faculty of Economics and Administration, University of Malaya, Kuala Lumpur.

Tan, E. C. 1990. "Malaysia External Trade: Does A Currency Depreciation Help?" *Asian Economies* (74).

Teh, K. P. 1977. "Protection, Fiscal Incentives and Industrialisation in West Malaysia since 1957." Monograph Series. University of Malaya, Kuala Lumpur.

United Nations (UN). 1995. *Yearbook of International Trade Statistics.*

Von Rabenau, K. 1975. "Trade Policies and Industrialisation in a Developing Country: The Case of West Malaysia." Economic Discussion Paper No. 55. Regenburgh: University of Regenburgh.

Warr, P. G. 1987. "Malaysia's Industrial Enclaves: Benefits and Costs." *Developing Economies* 25(1):30-55.

World Bank. 1989. *Malaysia: Matching Risks and Rewards in A Mixed Economy Program.* Washington, DC.

______. 1995. *Malaysia, Meeting Labor Needs: More Workers and Better Skills.* Washington, DC.

______. 1997. *World Development Report 1997: The State in a Changing World.* New York: Oxford University Press for the World Bank.

Yokoyama, H., ed. 1990. *Malaysian Economy: Policy and Structural Change.* Tokyo: Institute of Developing Economies.

Yokoyama, H., and T. Mokhtar, eds. 1991. *Malaysian Economy in Transition.* Tokyo: Institute of Developing Economies.

Zellner A. 1963. "Estimators of Seemingly Unrelated Regressions: Some Exact Finite Sample Results." *Journal of the American Statistical Association* 58:977-992.

CHAPTER NINE

Case Study: Thailand

Peter G. Warr

INTRODUCTION

Over the two and a half decades ending in 1995, Thailand was one of the fastest growing of the world's developing countries, and for the last eight years of this period it was *the* fastest growing economy in the world. This growth performance was led by high levels of investment, both domestic and foreign, and by a dramatic export growth. Over the decade ending in 1995, export growth exceeded 20 percent a year, in real terms. From being predominantly an agricultural exporter, Thailand moved toward much greater specialization in labor- and capital-intensive manufactured exports. By 1995, exports of garments and textiles alone outweighed all its agricultural exports combined. In 1996, a severe and unanticipated slowdown in export growth followed the appreciation of the US dollar, to which the Thai currency was loosely tied. The combination of these events produced a financial crisis leading, in July 1997, to the floating of the currency and subsequently to intervention by the International Monetary Fund (IMF) in Thailand's financial management. Export growth, or the lack of it, played a central role in all these matters. The determinants of Thailand's export performance are therefore crucial to an understanding of the country's overall economic growth in the past and are a key to its future prospects.

THAILAND'S EXPORT PERFORMANCE, 1970–1997

Thailand's economic experience over the past three decades has been a classic example of export-led growth. As a share of GDP, exports of goods and factor services grew from 15 percent in 1970 to 42 percent in 1995. Periods in which GDP growth was greatest were, in general, periods in which exports as a proportion of GDP expanded most significantly. This is clearest during the economic boom years of 1987 to 1995. GDP growth increased from an average rate of 6.3 percent over the previous decade to an average rate of 9.9 percent over this nine-year period. During the same nine-year period, the ratio of

Table 9.1 Export and Import Growth, 1975–1997

	Exports		Imports		
Year	Value ($ million)	Percent change	Value ($ million)	Percent change	Percent of World Exports
1975	2,230	...	3,183	...	0.26
1976	2,984	33.8	3,634	14.2	0.31
1977	3,440	15.3	4,605	26.7	0.31
1978	4,100	19.2	5,348	16.1	0.32
1979	5,310	29.5	7,191	34.5	0.33
1980	6,532	23.0	9,230	28.4	0.33
1981	7,066	8.2	9,976	8.1	0.36
1982	6,982	-1.2	8,523	-14.6	0.38
1983	6,389	-8.5	10,278	20.6	0.36
1984	7,466	16.9	10,384	1.0	0.40
1985	7,185	-3.8	9,236	-11.1	0.37
1986	8,913	24.1	9,149	-0.9	0.43
1987	11,605	30.2	13,076	42.9	0.47
1988	16,030	38.1	20,329	55.5	0.57
1989	20,319	26.8	25,286	24.4	0.67
1990	23,256	14.5	33,151	31.1	0.68
1991	28,982	24.6	37,617	13.5	0.82
1992	33,061	14.1	40,657	8.1	0.87
1993	37,669	13.9	46,200	13.6	1.00
1994	45,961	22.0	55,135	19.3	1.07
1995	56,912	23.8	74,050	34.3	1.11
1996	56,380	-0.9	73,660	-0.5	1.06
1997	57,211	1.5	64,361	-12.6	1.09

Source: Author's calculations based on IMF, *Direction of Trade Statistics* database.

exports to GDP rose from 29 percent to 42 percent, reflecting faster export growth than that of GDP. Again over the nine-year period 1987 to 1995, exports grew at an average annual rate of 22 percent, expressed in dollars, having grown at just over half that rate in the preceding decade. Merchandise exports grew faster than exports in general and therefore faster than exports of factor services.

Destination and Composition of Exports

The destination of Thailand's exports has moved away from Europe and increasingly toward other Asian nations, as shown in panels 1 and 2 of Table 9.2. Until 1996 PRC; Hong Kong, China; and Taipei,China together accounted for a rising share of Thailand's exports, as did the countries of ASEAN, while the share of the 12 countries of the European Community (EC-12) declined. In 1996, of the regional groupings shown, the economies of the North American Free Trade Agreement (NAFTA) were the largest market for Thailand's exports, followed by ASEAN, Japan, and the EC-12.

The third panel shows the growth rate of each country or regional component of total exports. The fourth and fifth panels are designed to facilitate decomposition of the changes in exports by destination. "Net effects" draws upon the mathematical fact that the growth rate of the sum of exports to all destinations is equal to the share-weighted sum of the growth rates of exports to each individual destination. Each of the entries in this fourth panel is the share-weighted growth rate of exports to that destination. This is the share of that destination in total exports shown in the first panel multiplied by the growth rate of exports to that destination shown in the second panel. For example, in 1995, Thailand's total exports grew by 23.8 percent. The sum of each of the regional entries shown in the fourth ("net effects") panel is also 23.8 percent, making it possible to see the total contribution that the growth of exports to each destination makes to the growth of total exports. The fifth panel ("normalized net effects") differs from this only in that it divides each of the regional entries by 23.8 and multiplies it by 100. The regional entries in this panel thus sum to 100 and each expresses the individual destination's percentage contribution to the growth of total exports.

Table 9.2 Exports by Destination-Decomposition, 1984–1997

	1984	1985	1986	1987	1988
Export Value ($ million)					
PRC; Hong Kong, China; Taipei,China	604	706	793	1,048	1,533
EC-12	1,535	1,358	1,898	2,585	3,314
Japan	965	951	1,260	1,732	2,545
Korea	123	133	244	153	255
ASEAN	1,054	1,031	1,270	1,584	1,862
Australia, New Zealand	134	133	173	238	326
NAFTA	1,385	1,496	1,729	2,338	3,496
Rest of world	1,666	1,376	1,546	1,927	2,698
World	7,466	7,185	8,913	11,605	16,030
Composition (percent)					
PRC; Hong Kong, China; Taipei,China	8.1	9.8	8.9	9.0	9.6
EC-12	20.6	18.9	21.3	22.3	20.7
Japan	12.9	13.2	14.1	14.9	15.9
Korea	1.6	1.9	2.7	1.3	1.6
ASEAN	14.1	14.3	14.2	13.6	11.6
Australia, New Zealand	1.8	1.9	1.9	2.1	2.0
NAFTA	18.6	20.8	19.4	20.1	21.8
Rest of world	22.3	19.2	17.3	16.6	16.8
World	100	100	100	100	100
Growth (percent)					
PRC; Hong Kong, China; Taipei,China		17.1	12.2	32.2	46.3
EC-12		-11.5	39.8	36.2	28.2
Japan		-1.5	32.5	37.5	46.9
Korea		8.1	83.5	-37.3	66.7
ASEAN		-2.2	23.2	24.7	17.6
Australia, New Zealand		-0.7	30.1	37.6	37.0
NAFTA		8.0	15.6	35.2	49.5
Rest of world		-17.4	12.4	24.6	40.0
World		-3.8	24.1	30.2	38.1
Net Effects					
PRC; Hong Kong, China; Taipei,China		1.4	1.2	2.9	4.2
EC-12		-2.4	7.5	7.7	6.3
Japan		-0.2	4.3	5.3	7.0
Korea		0.1	1.5	-1.0	0.9
ASEAN		-0.3	3.3	3.5	2.4
Australia, New Zealand		0.0	0.6	0.7	0.8
NAFTA		1.5	3.2	6.8	10.0
Rest of world		-3.9	2.4	4.3	6.6
World		-3.8	24.1	30.2	38.1
Normalized Net Effects					
PRC; Hong Kong, China; Taipei,China		-37	5	9	11
EC-12		63	31	26	16
Japan		5	18	18	18
Korea		-4	6	-3	2
ASEAN		8	14	12	6
Australia, New Zealand		0	2	2	2
NAFTA		-40	13	23	26
Rest of world		103	10	14	17
World		100	100	100	100

Source: Author's calculations based on IMF, *Direction of Trade Statistics* database.

1989	1990	1991	1992	1993	1994	1995	1996	1997
1,802	1,755	2,274	2,724	3,355	4,431	6,059	6,795	5,163
3,840	4,978	6,160	6,377	6,304	6,744	8,199	8,550	8,944
3,422	3,969	5,135	5,686	6,300	7,728	9,477	9,373	8,742
300	394	459	533	461	571	801	1,013	1,097
2,304	2,623	3,367	4,127	5,936	8,547	10,760	10,314	11,428
417	413	483	553	575	715	870	939	1,056
4,687	5,628	6,558	7,853	8,611	10,207	10,744	10,694	12,304
3,547	3,495	4,546	5,207	6,127	7,017	10,002	8,702	8,477
20,319	23,256	28,982	33,061	37,669	45,961	56,912	56,380	57,211
8.9	7.5	7.8	8.2	8.9	9.6	10.6	12.1	9.0
18.9	21.4	21.3	19.3	16.7	14.7	14.4	15.2	15.6
16.8	17.1	17.7	17.2	16.7	16.8	16.7	16.6	15.3
1.5	1.7	1.6	1.6	1.2	1.2	1.4	1.8	1.9
11.3	11.3	11.6	12.5	15.8	18.6	18.9	18.3	20.0
2.1	1.8	1.7	1.7	1.5	1.6	1.5	1.7	1.8
23.1	24.2	22.6	23.8	22.9	22.2	18.9	19.0	21.5
17.5	15.0	15.7	15.7	16.3	15.3	17.6	15.4	14.8
100	100	100	100	100	100	100	100	100
17.5	-2.6	29.6	19.8	23.2	32.1	36.7	12.1	-24.0
15.9	29.6	23.7	3.5	-1.1	7.0	21.6	4.3	4.6
34.5	16.0	29.4	10.7	10.8	22.7	22.6	-1.1	-6.7
17.6	31.3	16.5	16.1	-13.5	23.9	40.3	26.5	8.3
23.7	13.8	28.4	22.6	43.8	44.0	25.9	-4.1	10.8
27.9	-1.0	16.9	14.5	4.0	24.3	21.7	7.9	12.5
34.1	20.1	16.5	19.7	9.7	18.5	5.3	-0.5	15.1
31.5	-1.5	30.1	14.5	17.7	14.5	42.5	-13.0	-2.6
26.8	14.5	24.6	14.1	13.9	22.0	23.8	-0.9	1.5
1.7	-0.2	2.2	1.6	1.9	2.9	3.5	1.3	-2.9
3.3	5.6	5.1	0.7	-0.2	1.2	3.2	0.6	0.7
5.5	2.7	5.0	1.9	1.9	3.8	3.8	-0.2	-1.1
0.3	0.5	0.3	0.3	-0.2	0.3	0.5	0.4	0.1
2.8	1.6	3.2	2.6	5.5	6.9	4.8	-0.8	2.0
0.6	0.0	0.3	0.2	0.1	0.4	0.3	0.1	0.2
7.4	4.6	4.0	4.5	2.3	4.2	1.2	-0.1	2.9
5.3	-0.3	4.5	2.3	2.8	2.4	6.5	-2.3	-0.4
26.8	14.5	24.6	14.1	13.9	22.0	23.8	-0.9	1.5
6	-2	9	11	14	13	15	-138	-196
12	39	21	5	-2	5	13	-66	47
20	19	20	14	13	17	16	20	-76
1	3	1	2	-2	1	2	-40	10
10	11	13	19	39	31	20	84	134
2	0	1	2	0	2	1	-13	14
28	32	16	32	16	19	5	9	194
20	-2	18	16	20	11	27	244	-27
100	100	100	100	100	100	100	100	100

The composition of Thailand's exports has changed more dramatically than the distribution of exports by destination. Until the 1970s, most of Thailand's export industries were agro-based, such as milled rice, frozen seafood, and canned fruit, which use agricultural products as raw materials. From 1980, these exports became more diversified. Table 9.3 summarizes changes in Thailand's exports, classified by SITC 1-digit category, with data from 1985 to 1996. The large change in the composition of Thailand's exports is the decline in the relative importance of agro-based exports (SITC 0) and the increased importance of manufactured goods (SITC 7 and 8). This can be seen from the "net effects" panel where it is apparent that the largest contributors to the growth of exports over the period 1985 to 1995 were SITC 7 and 8. Thailand's experience was typical of rapidly growing economies: agricultural exports declined as a share of total exports, reflecting the decline of agriculture as a share of total output. Further details on these developments are provided in Table 9.4, which shows data for the 30 SITC 3-digit categories that contributed most to total exports in 1996.

In 1970, rice was the largest single export category, followed by rubber and vegetables. Garments became increasingly important, overtaking rice in 1986, and by 1990 garments had become by far the largest category, followed by rice, office machines, and rubber. By 1996, rice was the ninth most important export category, garments third, rubber fourth, and vegetables 20th. The two most important export categories in 1996 were office machines (SITC 714) and electrical machinery (SITC 729). Together, they accounted for 25 percent of the total value of Thailand's exports in 1996. The most important components of these two categories are statistical machines (SITC 7143) and transistors and valves (SITC 7293). These are primarily electronic calculators and computer parts. With manufactured categories such as these, it is very important to emphasize the distinction between gross and net exports. A high proportion of the inputs into the production of these commodities is imported. The most important contributors to gross exports are not necessarily the most important in terms of net exports or of value-added. Regrettably, data on value-added generated by these SITC categories are not available.

Table 9.3 Export Performance by SITC 1-Digit Category, 1985–1996

SITC Section	1985	1986	1987	1988	1989	1990	1991	1992	1993	1994	1995	1996
Composition												
0 Food and Live Animals	44.8	43.5	36.3	34.1	33.7	28.2	26.5	25.5	21.4	20.6	19.0	18.6
1 Beverages and Tobacco	0.9	0.7	0.5	0.4	0.3	0.4	0.5	0.5	0.4	0.4	0.3	0.3
2 Crude Matls. excl. Fuels	10.5	8.9	8.9	9.1	7.1	5.7	5.0	4.9	4.4	5.0	5.8	6.0
3 Mineral Fuels, etc.	1.3	0.8	0.7	0.8	0.7	0.8	1.0	1.0	1.1	0.8	0.7	0.9
4 Animal, Vegetable Oil, Fat	0.3	0.1	0.1	0.0	0.0	0.0	0.0	0.0	0.0	0.1	0.0	0.0
5 Chemicals	1.3	1.6	1.6	1.6	1.7	2.0	2.5	2.5	2.8	2.8	3.8	3.0
6 Basic Manufactures	17.5	16.3	16.5	14.4	13.3	13.7	12.7	12.0	12.2	12.1	11.9	10.8
7 Machines, Transport Equip.	8.8	10.7	11.9	15.4	16.1	19.8	21.8	24.3	27.7	30.8	31.5	39.7
8 Misc. Manufactured Goods	13.8	16.6	22.5	23.5	26.0	28.2	28.8	28.2	28.5	26.9	26.1	19.2
9 Goods not Classd. by Kind	0.8	0.7	0.9	0.7	1.0	1.2	1.2	1.1	1.5	0.7	0.9	1.3
Growth												
0 Food and Live Animals	-13.5	21.1	10.5	28.3	24.1	-3.5	15.7	10.2	-4.1	17.2	14.9	-6.7
1 Beverages and Tobacco	-15.6	-2.3	-6.4	25.2	-0.7	29.9	47.6	27.8	-11.4	9.9	-12.8	28.9
2 Crude Matls. excl. Fuels	-7.7	6.0	32.6	39.7	-2.1	-7.9	8.6	11.1	2.4	38.5	45.8	-1.5
3 Mineral Fuels, etc.	20.0	-23.1	17.7	49.2	19.7	31.6	47.5	13.1	23.2	-11.0	14.9	24.1
4 Animal, Vegetable Oil, Fat	13.9	-59.1	49.6	-42.5	-16.5	1.8	6.8	6.7	18.5	20.0	-5.8	-3.3
5 Chemicals	32.9	50.4	35.7	35.0	29.6	34.8	57.9	15.4	26.7	21.1	69.6	-25.0
6 Basic Manufactures	4.9	16.1	33.5	19.4	16.6	18.0	14.0	8.7	15.9	20.8	22.4	-13.0
7 Machines, Transport Equip.	24.3	51.2	46.7	77.2	31.5	41.4	35.5	27.9	30.6	35.0	27.8	19.9
8 Misc. Manufactured Goods	6.9	49.8	79.3	42.3	39.1	25.2	25.8	12.1	15.4	14.6	21.5	-30.2
9 Goods not Classd. by Kind	0.0	8.7	73.8	4.2	83.6	36.0	24.2	0.5	62.7	-43.3	55.1	47.1
Total	*-3.1*	*24.5*	*32.4*	*36.7*	*25.6*	*15.2*	*23.1*	*14.6*	*14.3*	*21.7*	*24.7*	*-4.8*
Net Effects												
0 Food and Live Animals		9.4	4.6	10.3	8.2	-1.2	4.4	2.7	-1.1	3.7	3.1	-1.3
1 Beverages and Tobacco		0.0	0.0	0.1	0.0	0.1	0.2	0.1	-0.1	0.0	0.0	0.1
2 Crude Matls. excl. Fuels		0.6	2.9	3.6	-0.2	-0.6	0.5	0.6	0.1	1.7	2.3	-0.1
3 Mineral Fuels, etc.		-0.3	0.1	0.3	0.2	0.2	0.4	0.1	0.2	-0.1	0.1	0.2
4 Animal, Vegetable Oil, Fat		-0.2	0.1	0.0	0.0	0.0	0.0	0.0	0.0	0.0	0.0	0.0
5 Chemicals		0.7	0.6	0.6	0.5	0.6	1.1	0.4	0.7	0.6	1.9	-0.9
6 Basic Manufactures		2.8	5.5	3.2	2.4	2.4	1.9	1.1	1.9	2.5	2.7	-1.5
7 Machines, Transport Equip.		4.5	5.0	9.2	4.8	6.7	7.0	6.1	7.4	9.7	8.5	6.3
8 Misc. Manufactured Goods		6.9	13.2	9.5	9.2	6.5	7.3	3.5	4.4	4.2	5.8	-7.9
9 Goods not Classd. by Kind		0.1	0.5	0.0	0.6	0.4	0.3	0.0	0.7	-0.7	0.4	0.4
Total		*24.5*	*32.4*	*36.7*	*25.6*	*15.1*	*23.1*	*14.6*	*14.3*	*21.6*	*24.7*	*-4.8*
Normalized Effects												
0 Food and Live Animals		38.5	14.1	28.0	32.1	-7.8	19.1	18.6	-7.4	17.0	12.4	26.5
1 Beverages and Tobacco		-0.1	-0.1	0.3	0.0	0.7	0.8	0.9	-0.4	0.2	-0.2	-1.5
2 Crude Matls. excl. Fuels		2.5	9.0	9.7	-0.8	-3.7	2.1	3.8	0.8	7.8	9.2	1.8
3 Mineral Fuels, etc.		-1.2	0.4	0.9	0.6	1.5	1.7	0.9	1.6	-0.5	0.5	-3.6
4 Animal, Vegetable Oil, Fat		-0.8	0.2	-0.1	0.0	0.0	0.0	0.0	0.0	0.0	0.0	0.0
5 Chemicals		2.7	1.8	1.6	1.9	3.8	4.9	2.6	4.7	2.7	7.8	19.7
6 Basic Manufactures		11.5	16.9	8.7	9.3	15.9	8.3	7.5	13.4	11.7	10.9	32.1
7 Machines, Transport Equip.		18.4	15.4	24.9	18.9	44.0	30.3	41.6	52.0	44.9	34.5	-130.7
8 Misc. Manufactured Goods		28.1	40.8	25.9	35.8	43.1	31.5	24.0	30.6	19.2	23.3	164.3
9 Goods not Classd. by Kind		0.3	1.6	0.1	2.3	2.4	1.3	0.0	4.7	-3.0	1.6	-8.6
Total		*100*	*100*	*100*	*100*	*100*	*100*	*100*	*100*	*100*	*100*	*100*

Source: Author's calculations based on IMF, *Direction of Trade Statistics* database.

Table 9.4 Top 30 Exports by SITC 3-Digit Category, Ranking Based on 1996 Values

($'000)

Rank	SITC Heading	1970	1975	1980	1985	1986	1990	1995	1996
1	Office Machines	-	376	3,093	52,876	60,152	1,560,287	5,484,114	9,449,768
2	Electrical Machinery, n.e.s.	189	17,722	11,365	84,959	151,522	1,032,635	3,705,535	4,265,678
3	Clothing, not of Fur	878	53,500	266,587	572,647	824,474	2,825,598	4,842,561	2,957,660
4	Rubber, Crude, Synthetic	108,165	170,561	604,158	500,255	573,087	922,925	2,462,008	2,422,204
5	Fish, Fresh, Simply Preserved	15,956	86,069	214,215	329,828	486,160	1,264,873	2,856,100	2,375,378
6	Telecommunications Equipment	113	1,918	8,847	4,550	7,443	563,551	2,003,748	2,140,686
7	Elec. Power Mach., Switchgear	88	2,637	305,884	332,374	526,970	201,421	1,960,965	1,810,169
8	Machines, n.e.s., Nonelectric	266	2,153	18,623	88,105	96,962	442,843	1,780,626	1,749,484
9	Rice	120,998	287,177	952,770	829,567	769,097	1,086,122	1,951,536	1,562,223
10	Fish, etc., Tinned, Prepared	4	9,962	87,313	284,966	444,965	993,130	1,590,429	1,434,303
11	Pearls, Precious, Semi-p. Stones	6,607	38,737	158,608	236,504	319,258	879,072	1,197,886	1,211,213
12	Sugar and Honey	6,707	303,263	163,320	259,353	315,117	739,639	1,228,394	1,179,123
13	Sound Recorders, Producers	4	122	799	1,736	2,270	538,827	1,233,073	1,167,292
14	Gold, Silverware, Jewelry	849	4,297	29,592	85,052	202,399	565,068	927,891	1,006,312
15	Instruments, Apparatus	-	1,522	7,472	22,687	18,346	111,435	733,740	936,595
16	Footwear	11	740	17,381	84,188	114,490	743,305	2,087,799	855,758
17	Toys, Sporting Goods, etc.	199	749	3,140	19,835	29,990	462,313	743,897	790,808
18	Furniture	20	3,116	29,399	48,780	72,050	309,255	752,574	779,804
19	Special Transactions	22,226	47,888	183,300	52,696	57,472	271,997	479,244	707,659
20	Veg., etc., Fresh, Simply Prsvd.	62,448	231,939	745,494	588,980	709,710	898,719	544,981	681,426
21	Fruit, Preserved, Prepared	2,680	18,189	88,654	160,733	167,758	402,950	566,490	672,050
22	Plastic Materials, etc.	8	3,070	11,636	28,132	46,723	132,753	722,672	555,231
23	Domestic Electrical Equipment	1	398	1,550	1,539	4,348	268,374	627,918	547,452
24	Electr. Distributing Machinery	8	607	3,397	7,767	30,232	190,870	518,883	505,990
25	Textile, Yarn, and Thread	1,555	9,620	75,637	103,782	133,880	211,956	511,696	504,659
26	Watches and Clocks	815	3,079	14,412	23,352	33,170	185,221	445,029	464,285
27	Articles of Plastic, n.e.s.	443	4,567	29,810	46,481	53,544	224,123	1,772,809	451,310
28	Chemicals, n.e.s.	734	732	5,002	18,979	23,384	134,345	369,372	442,653
29	Travel Goods, Handbags	39	646	13,920	16,352	27,796	234,085	452,480	394,666
30	Woven Textiles, Noncotton	2,101	27,219	116,816	167,901	215,229	358,479	686,642	368,938
	Sum of Top 30	354,112	1,332,575	4,172,194	5,054,956	6,517,998	18,756,171	45,241,092	44,390,777
	Sum of Others	331,044	829,595	2,196,936	2,001,131	2,268,470	4,246,269	11,041,242	9,188,856
	Total Value of Above	685,156	2,162,170	6,369,130	7,056,087	8,786,468	23,002,440	56,282,334	53,579,633

Note: n.e.s. = not elsewhere specified.

Source: Author's calculations based on IMF, *Direction of Trade Statistics* database.

Factor Intensity of Exports

A more helpful picture of the changing composition of Thailand's exports is obtained by classifying exports by factor intensity. Table 9.5 represents an effort to do this. SITC commodity categories are classified into four groups: land intensive, mineral intensive, capital intensive, and labor intensive. The striking feature of the table is the growth in the importance of capital-intensive and labor-intensive exports and the relative decline of land-intensive exports. The comparative advantage of the economy was moving in favor of capital- and labor-intensive commodities, and away from land- and mineral-intensive exports.

Table 9.5 Composition of Gross Exports by Factor Intensity Selected Years

Year	Land Intensive	Mineral Intensive	Labor Intensive	Capital Intensive	Total
1970	77.4	16.6	1.5	1.2	100
1975	76.3	11.0	7.1	3.4	100
1980	59.5	16.5	11.4	9.7	100
1985	57.1	9.4	18.2	14.6	100
1986	54.5	6.9	20.0	17.9	100
1987	47.6	6.6	24.9	20.0	100
1988	44.5	6.2	24.8	23.7	100
1989	42.2	5.8	25.3	25.7	100
1990	35.5	6.0	26.6	30.6	100
1991	33.1	5.3	27.5	32.9	100
1992	32.1	4.5	26.3	36.1	100
1993	27.4	4.6	26.9	39.6	100
1994	27.2	4.2	24.6	43.3	100
1995	26.1	4.0	24.1	45.0	100
1996	25.9	4.3	16.0	52.4	100

Source: Author's calculations based on IMF, *Direction of Trade Statistics* database.

Commodity Classification by Factor Intensity and SITC Number

Land-Intensive

SITC	Commodity
0	Food and Live Animals
1	Beverages and Tobacco
21	Hides, Skins, Furs, Undressed
22	Oil Seeds, Nuts, Kernels
23	Rubber Crude, Synthetic
24	Wood Lumber and Cork
25	Pulp and Waste Paper
26	Textile Fibers
29	Crude Animal, Veg. Mat, n.e.s.
4	Animal, Vegetable Oil, Fat
61	Leather, Dressed Fur, etc.
63	Wood, Cork Manufactures., n.e.s.

Mineral Intensive

SITC	Commodity
27	Crude Fertil., Minerals, n.e.s.
28	Metalliferous Ores, Scrap
3	Mineral Fuels, etc.
661	Cement, etc. Building Prod.
662	Clay, Refractory Bldg. Prod.
663	Other Nonmetal Mineral Manufactures
667	Pearls, Prec., Semi-p. Stone
671	Pig Iron, etc.
68	Nonferrous Metals

Capital-Intensive

SITC	Commodity
5	Chemicals
62	Rubber Manufactures, n.e.s.
64	Paper, Paperboard and Manufactures
672	Iron, Steel Primary Forms
673	Iron and Steel Shapes
674	Iron, Steel Univ, Plate, Sheet
675	Iron, Steel Hoop, Strip
676	Railway Rails, etc. Iron, Steel
677	Iron, Steel Wire excl. w Rod
678	Iron, Steel Tubes, Pipes, etc.
679	Iron, Steel Castings, Unwkd.
69	Metal Manufactures, n.e.s.
71	Machinery, Nonelectric
714	Office Machines
722	Elec. Pwr. Mach., Switchgear
723	Elec. Distributing Mach.
724	Telecommunications Equip.
725	Domestic Elec. Equip.
726	Elec. Medical, X-ray Equip.
729	Electrical Machinery, n.e.s.
731	Railway Vehicles
732	Road Motor Vehicles
733	Road Vehicles, Nonmotor
734	Aircraft
86	Instruments, Watches, Clocks
891	Sound Recorders, Producers
892	Printed Matter
896	Works of Art, etc.
897	Gold, Silverware, Jewelry

Labor-Intensive

SITC	Commodity
65	Textile, Yarn, Fabric, etc.
664	Glass
665	Glassware
666	Pottery
735	Ships and Boats
81	Plumbg, Heatng, Lghtng Equip.
82	Furniture
83	Travel Goods, Handbags
84	Clothing
85	Footwear
893	Articles of Plastic, n.e.s.
894	Toys, Sporting Goods, etc.
895	Office Supplies, n.e.s.
899	Other Manufactured Goods
951	War Firearms, Ammunition

Note: n.e.s. = not elsewhere specified.

Table 9.6 takes this analysis a step further, focusing on the period since 1984. From the panel "net effects" it is clear that until 1988 the largest contribution to the growth of gross exports came from land-intensive commodities. The most important contributors since then have been capital-intensive and labor-intensive commodities, especially the former. The vital qualification that must be made is that the classification of final commodities (gross exports) by factor intensity is not the same as the classification of the production processes occurring in Thailand by factor intensity. For example, some capital-intensive intermediate goods may be imported into Thailand and then reexported with small amounts of value having been contributed. The most important point is not the factor intensity of the final export—meaning the overall factor intensity of all the processes required to produce the final product—but the factor intensity of the value-adding processes occurring in Thailand. Even though the final gross export may be capital-intensive, the value-adding processes in Thailand could be labor-intensive. This is true of several of the assembly-type exports classified as capital-intensive.

Table 9.6 Gross Export Performance Decomposed by Factor Intensity, 1984–1996

	1984	1985	1986	1987	1988	1989	1990	1991	1992	1993	1994	1995	1996
Export Value													
Land Intensive	4,554	4,029	4,786	5,540	7,083	8,430	8,176	9,373	10,409	10,143	12,252	14,671	13,883
Capital Intensive	800.7	1,030	1,576	2,322	3,766	5,131	7,047	9,319	11,717	14,692	19,550	25,339	28,090
Labor Intensive	1,237	1,282	1,756	2,891	3,948	5,057	6,117	7,793	8,528	9,965	11,116	13,538	8,567
Mineral Intensive	630.8	659.9	608.6	772.1	993.6	1,155	1,388	1,498	1,457	1,723	1,885	2,250	2,319
Not Classified	56.5	55.1	59.4	103.9	111.4	202	274	341	341	557	315	484	720
Total	7,279	7,056	8,786	11,629	15,902	19,975	23,002	28,324	32,452	37,080	45,118	56,282	53,579
Composition													
Land Intensive	62.6	57.1	54.5	47.6	44.5	42.2	35.5	33.1	32.1	27.4	27.2	26.1	25.9
Capital Intensive	11.0	14.6	17.9	20.0	23.7	25.7	30.6	32.9	36.1	39.6	43.3	45.0	52.4
Labor Intensive	17.0	18.2	20.0	24.9	24.8	25.3	26.6	27.5	26.3	26.9	24.6	24.1	16.0
Mineral Intensive	8.7	9.4	6.9	6.6	6.2	5.8	6.0	5.3	4.5	4.6	4.2	4.0	4.3
Not Classified	0.8	0.8	0.7	0.9	0.7	1.0	1.2	1.2	1.1	1.5	0.7	0.9	1.3
Total	100	100	100	100	100	100	100	100	100	100	100	100	100
Export Growth													
Land Intensive		-11.5	18.8	15.8	27.9	19.0	-3.0	14.6	11.1	-2.6	20.8	19.7	-5.4
Capital Intensive		28.6	53.0	47.3	62.2	36.2	37.3	32.2	25.7	25.4	33.1	29.6	10.9
Labor Intensive		3.6	37.	64.6	36.6	28.1	21.0	27.4	9.4	16.9	11.6	21.8	-36.7
Mineral Intensive		4.6	-7.8	26.9	28.7	16.2	20.2	7.9	-2.7	18.3	9.4	19.4	3.1
Not Classified		-2.5	7.8	74.9	7.2	81.3	35.6	24.5	0.0	63.3	-43.4	53.7	48.8
Total		-3.1	24.5	32.4	36.7	25.6	15.2	23.1	14.6	14.3	21.7	24.7	-4.8
Net Effects													
Land Intensive		-7.2	10.7	8.6	13.3	8.5	-1.3	5.2	3.7	-0.8	5.7	5.4	-1.4
Capital Intensive		3.2	7.7	8.5	12.4	8.6	9.6	9.9	8.5	9.2	13.1	12.8	4.9
Labor Intensive		0.6	6.7	12.9	9.1	7.0	5.3	7.3	2.6	4.4	3.1	5.4	-8.8
Mineral Intensive		0.4	-0.7	1.9	1.9	1.0	1.2	0.5	-0.1	0.8	0.4	0.8	0.1
Not Classified		0.0	0.1	0.5	0.1	0.6	0.4	0.3	0.0	0.7	-0.7	0.4	0.4
Total		-3.1	24.5	32.4	36.7	25.6	15.2	23.1	14.6	14.3	21.7	24.7	-4.8
Normalized Net Effects													
Land Intensive		235.4	43.8	26.5	36.1	33.1	-8.4	22.5	25.1	-5.7	26.2	21.7	29.2
Capital Intensive		-102.8	31.6	26.2	33.8	33.5	63.3	42.7	58.1	64.3	60.4	51.9	-101.8
Labor Intensive		-20.2	27.4	39.9	24.7	27.2	35.0	31.5	17.8	31.1	14.3	21.7	183.9
Mineral Intensive		-13.0	-3.0	5.8	5.2	4.0	7.7	2.1	-1.0	5.7	2.0	3.3	-2.6
Not Classified		0.6	0.2	1.6	0.2	2.2	2.4	1.3	0.0	4.7	-3.0	1.5	-8.7
Total		100	100	100	100	100	100	100	100	100	100	100	100

Source: Author's calculations based on *UN International Trade database*.

Revealed Comparative Advantage or Competitiveness

Which are the "sunrise" and "sunset" industries in Thailand or, (almost) equivalently, in which industries is Thailand exhibiting improved comparative advantage and in which industries is the reverse occurring? Before turning to data on this issue, we first present a measure of the export performance of an industry designed to reveal the degree to which that industry is competing successfully in international markets. This index of trade performance is based on the earlier work of Balassa and others on "revealed" comparative advantage, but is intended to improve upon these earlier measures. We shall call it the net export performance ratio (NEPR):

$$N_j^T = \frac{(X_j^T - M_j^T)/X_j^W}{X_*^T / X_*^W},$$

where

N_j^T = Thailand's NEPR for industry j
X_j^T = Thailand's gross exports of commodity j
M_j^T = Thailand's gross imports of commodity j
X_j^W = world exports of commodity j
X_*^T = Thailand's total exports of all goods
X_*^W = total world exports of all goods

Thus the index measures the degree to which Thailand's net exports of commodity j, as a share of world exports of that commodity, exceed (NEPR > 1) or fall short of (NEPR < 1) Thailand's share of world exports in general. NEPR < 0 indicates that the commodity is a net import.

Tables 9.7 and 9.8 present data on the NEPR at two levels of aggregation. From our discussion above (see Table 9.3), SITC category 7 (machines and transport equipment) is a large contributor to gross exports, but from Table 9.7 it is clear that imports of this category are even larger. The NEPR of this aggregate category is therefore negative in all periods shown. The SITC categories 0 (agriculture) and 8 (miscellaneous manufactured articles) are the ones showing the greatest "revealed" comparative advantage. More useful information is obtained by looking at a more disaggregated level. Table 9.8 does this, focusing again on the 30 largest gross exports, as shown in Table 9.4, above. Rapid increases in the NEPR of office machines (714), domestic electrical equipment (725), footwear (851), toys and sporting goods (894), and jewelry (897) are especially notable.

Table 9.7 NEPR by SITC 1-Digit Category, 1979–1996

SITC Section	1979-1981	1982-1984	1985-1987	1988-1990	1991-1993	1994-1996
0 Food and Live Animals	4.82	5.27	4.20	3.24	2.40	2.10
1 Beverages and Tobacco	0.02	0.18	-0.15	-0.36	-0.19	-0.21
2 Crude Matls. excl. Fuels	0.86	0.48	0.33	-0.36	-0.62	0.12
3 Mineral Fuels, etc.	-1.78	-1.79	-1.37	-1.19	-1.06	-0.81
4 Animal, Vegetable Oil, Fat	-1.11	-0.49	0.08	-0.25	-0.29	-0.17
5 Chemicals	-2.34	-2.19	-1.69	-1.46	-1.12	-0.91
6 Basic Manufactures	-0.14	-0.40	-0.24	-0.83	-0.88	-0.64
7 Machines, Transport Equip.	-1.23	-1.18	-0.72	-0.99	-0.76	-0.63
8 Misc. Manuf. Goods	0.43	0.62	1.24	1.60	1.62	1.26
9 Goods not Classd. by Kind	-2.65	-2.49	-2.43	-1.53	-0.79	-0.32
Total	*-0.45*	*-0.44*	*-0.14*	*-0.34*	*-0.27*	*-0.18*

Source: Author's calculations based on *UN International Trade* database.

PROTECTION AND EXPORT PROMOTION POLICIES

Protection Policies

As with most low- and middle-income developing countries, Thailand's product market policies imply taxation of agriculture and subsidization of industry. Export taxes have historically been applied to several agricultural export commodities, but have been slowly phased out. Rubber is now the only commodity subject to an export tax. Tariffs and quantitative import restrictions are used to protect part of the manufacturing sector. The production of these commodities is highly competitive, with a couple of exceptions mentioned below.

Table 9.8 NEPR of the Top 30 Exports, 1979–1996

SITC Heading	1979-1981	1982-1984	1985-1987	1988-1990	1991-1993	1994-1996
031 Fish, Fresh, Simply Presvd.	5.82	5.51	3.36	2.26	3.74	4.72
032 Fish, etc., Tinned, Prepared	9.39	19.47	23.98	24.53	18.61	15.32
042 Rice	62.65	68.14	60.05	52.33	30.73	24.13
053 Fruit, Preserved, Prepared	6.66	6.83	7.43	6.48	6.24	4.37
054 Veg., etc., Fresh, Simply Presvd.	25.78	24.80	16.39	8.81	5.02	2.19
061 Sugar and Honey	6.34	14.06	11.60	10.87	7.11	7.06
231 Rubber, Crude, Synthetic	19.50	17.29	17.79	14.96	13.13	14.80
581 Plastic Materials, etc.	-2.08	-1.83	-1.41	-1.32	-0.97	-0.67
599 Chemicals, n.e.s.	-3.04	-2.83	-1.83	-1.15	-0.86	-0.66
651 Textile, Yarn, and Thread	0.85	0.38	0.51	-0.19	0.37	0.81
653 Woven Textiles, Noncotton	0.87	0.85	0.65	0.07	-0.17	-0.21
667 Pearls, Precious, Semi-p. Stones	2.14	3.15	2.58	-0.08	-0.65	0.41
714 Office Machines	-0.47	-0.69	-0.71	0.06	0.65	1.41
719 Machines, n.e.s., Nonelectric	-1.52	-1.59	-1.15	-1.42	-1.39	-1.44
722 Elec. Power Mach., Switchgear	-0.80	-0.88	-1.89	-1.94	-1.75	-0.83
723 Elec. Distrib. Machinery	-1.26	-1.47	-0.83	-0.06	0.28	0.25
724 Telecoms. Equip.	-0.84	-1.58	-1.29	-0.61	0.24	-0.04
725 Domestic Electrical Equip.	-0.81	-0.59	-0.36	0.94	1.43	1.27
729 Electrical Machinery, n.e.s.	-1.07	-0.84	0.48	-0.76	-0.93	-0.84
821 Furniture	0.68	0.86	1.14	1.51	1.51	1.39
831 Travel Goods, Handbags	1.37	1.67	2.03	4.51	4.44	3.46
841 Clothing not of Fur	2.23	2.84	3.61	4.01	3.34	2.38
851 Footwear	0.58	1.45	1.77	3.31	3.59	3.93
861 Instruments, Apparatus	-0.78	-1.10	-0.49	-0.61	-0.29	-0.26
864 Watches and Clocks	-0.22	-0.17	-0.50	-0.33	0.28	0.72
891 Sound Recorders, Producers	-0.35	-0.60	-0.34	0.32	0.55	0.14
893 Articles of Plastic, n.e.s.	0.02	0.31	0.02	-0.14	0.55	0.64
894 Toys, Sporting Goods, etc.	-0.38	-0.29	0.38	2.22	2.66	1.80
897 Gold, Silverware, Jewelry	1.56	1.81	5.88	5.95	4.43	3.99
931 Special Transactions	-3.26	-3.16	-2.95	-1.53	-0.83	-0.31
Total	*-0.45*	*-0.44*	*-0.14*	*-0.34*	*-0.27*	*-0.18*

Note: n.e.s. = not elsewhere specified.

Source: Author's calculations based on *UN International Trade* database.

Agricultural Taxation

Agriculture receives little direct government support and is taxed lightly. Agricultural goods are exempted from the value-added tax system introduced in 1992, along with industries supplying inputs for agricultural use. Until 1986, rice exports were taxed by a combination of instruments: the rice premium (a specific export tax), an export duty (an ad valorem export tax), and a reserve requirement (equivalent to an ad valorem export tax). The effect was to keep both consumer prices and prices received by farmers well below international prices.

Manufacturing Protection

Parts of the manufacturing sector are highly protected and inefficient, but the manufacturing sector is generally competitive and less highly regulated than those elsewhere in Southeast Asia. Thailand does not practice free trade, but its protection levels are moderate and relatively stable.

A measure of the way in which government interventions affect the structure of incentives for producers in different sectors is the effective rate of protection (ERP). This focuses in particular on the effects of protection policy—the most important single method of intervention in Thailand—in altering the profitability of producing in different sectors. It measures the value-added per unit of output in each sector (the value of output minus the value of intermediate inputs divided by the volume of output) with and without protection, and relates the difference between them to unit value-added without protection. Thus the ERP is an estimate of the proportion by which protection has *increased* unit value-added in an industry relative to what it would have been in the absence of protection. Detailed input-output tables are required for this work, in addition to estimates of nominal rates of protection by industry.

There have been several studies of protection policies in Thailand, most estimating ERPs—the proportion by which the overall structure of protection raises the value-added received by an industry per unit of output relative to what it would be under free trade. Unfortunately, the various empirical studies of ERP have used different types of data, different product definitions, and different methodologies. For example, some studies use the official tariff rates, while others use tariff rates estimated from customs duty collections or from price comparisons. It is thus difficult to compare the results of these studies over time. Nevertheless, the ERP studies show a similar pattern over the past three decades.

The protection system has been biased against the agro-based industries and toward the manufacturing sector, both import-competing and nonimport-competing. This is the typical pattern of protection found in developing countries. Estimates for 1995 imply value-added weighted ERPs for export industries of -12 percent and similar average rates for import-competing sectors of 180 percent (Budsayavith 1996). Studies of this kind are difficult and the estimates obtained are always open to dispute. The implication is clear, however, that Thailand is far from being a free-trading country and that the system of protection works strongly against the export sectors.

Quantitative Restrictions in International Trade

Apart from tariffs and export taxes, the trade regime in Thailand has several restrictive measures, such as quantitative import and export controls. At present, there are import bans on 18 commodities, and special permission is required to import another 30. The Ministry of Commerce imposes and supervises import controls. Commodities under control include those produced in the socialist countries, weapons and strategic firearms, rice, and sugar. The controls on rice and sugar are to prevent reimporting after the products have been exported. Export controls are in place on 38 commodities, 16 of which are outright bans. The export controls are meant to ensure domestic supplies for local consumption at low prices. Exports of items such as paper, pesticide, flat iron sheets, polyfiber, and cement are regulated to ensure local supplies.

Besides direct controls on imports and exports, the Ministry of Commerce also administers price controls on "essential products." This has been possible with the passage of the Price Setting and Anti-Monopoly Act of 1979. As of early 1998, there were 21 commodities under price control. This does not mean that their prices are actively regulated, but that the Director of the Department of Internal Trade has been authorized by the Cabinet to impose price controls on any of these commodities if the Director deems it necessary. The scope left for discretionary behavior on the part of public officials is obvious. Only two commodity prices were actively controlled as of early 1998: sugar and cooking oil.

Exchange Rate Controls

Exchange rate management is in the policy domain of the Bank of Thailand, but input from the Ministry of Finance is important. From 1955, when the multiple exchange rate system was abolished, until the devaluations of 1981 (see below), the baht was maintained at a relatively fixed parity with the dollar, at a rate of between 20 and 21. The main argument for this peg was the stability and the confidence it was believed to provide. Between 1955 and 1977, the dollar depreciated against other currencies and the baht/dollar rate was slightly adjusted five times, to maintain parity with the depreciated dollar.

The volatility of the dollar and the enlarged trade deficits in the late 1970s following the second oil shock prompted the Government to reconsider its exchange rate policy. Although much of Thailand's trade is denominated in dollars, less than 20 percent of exports and imports are with the US. Pegging to the overvalued dollar in the late 1970s had worked to increase the country's balance of payments deficits. In March 1978, the Bank of Thailand announced that the baht would no longer be tied to the dollar but that its value would be linked to a basket of currencies in which the dollar would be a major component. The new system was, however, short-lived. In November 1978, a system of daily fixing was introduced, in effect putting the baht back in parity to the dollar at a rate of 19.8.

In 1979 and 1980, Thailand experienced severe trade deficits that reached a record 4.6 percent of GDP. The deficits resulted from an artificially strong dollar—to which the baht was still pegged, militating against Thai exports—and strong growth in domestic spending. In an effort to address the problem of external balance, the Government devalued the baht twice in 1981, bringing the parity rate down to 23 to the dollar. It also abandoned the daily fixing system. Such a drastic move, particularly the second devaluation, which at 8.7 percent was then the largest in recent history, proved to be politically unpopular and led to the resignation of a deputy finance minister. To build up confidence in the baht after these two devaluations, in 1981 the

Government introduced a "currency swap" to guarantee that those bringing in foreign funds would not have to pay back more than the amount they had borrowed from abroad when their loans fell due.

The abandonment of the daily fixing system was tantamount to returning to the old single-rate fixed exchange system. In 1984 the baht was devalued again by 14.5 percent to curb the growing trade deficit. The fixed exchange system was also abandoned and was replaced by a "flexible exchange rate system" under which the baht was tied to a basket of currencies. This was intended to provide greater flexibility in the management of the country's foreign exchange. The composition of the basket was never revealed by the Bank of Thailand, but it was obvious from the narrow range within which the baht/dollar rate remained that the basket was heavily dominated by the dollar. From 1984 until the float of July 1997, approximate parity to the dollar was maintained in spite of the dollar's realignment relative to other currencies.

Export Promotion Policies

A central feature of government intervention in Thailand's industry has been the attempt to promote exports. A major instrument of intervention has been the promotion of private investment, administered through the Board of Investment (BOI), established in 1959. BOI uses a combination of various investment promotion schemes, tariff policies, tax regimes, and trade and price controls to direct the pattern of private investment. During the 1960s and early 1970s, industrial policies strongly favored import substitution. Import tariffs were raised significantly to protect local industries, with incentives strongest for production of final goods based on imported intermediate and capital goods. With the passage of the Investment Promotion Act of 1972 the officially stated emphasis of industrial promotion policy shifted toward promotion of exports.

The incentives offered by BOI include tax and tariff exemptions, guarantee of government protection from nationalization and from direct competition by state enterprises, and guarantees of rights of profit and capital repatriation. The range of incentives differs significantly between industries, reflecting priority rankings in the promotion policy. A list of industries eligible for promotion privileges is drawn up by BOI using, as a broad framework, the five-year development plans developed by the Government's economic planning agency, the National Economic and Social Development Board (NESDB). In addition to BOI, the Ministries of Industry, Commerce, and Finance, as well as the Bank of Thailand, formulate and administer policies that directly affect industrial development. For example, the Ministry of Finance operates a comprehensive tax refund system for all taxes incurred in the production process; the Bank of Thailand provides a rediscount facility at subsidized interest rates to export-oriented firms; and the Ministry of Commerce provides technical assistance through its Export Service Center.

Discussions of Thailand's industrial and trade policies have frequently characterized the period since the mid-1970s as one of export promotion, contrasted with the preceding two decades of import substitution. In this often-heard account of Thailand's industrial policy, the overall direction of policy supposedly shifted away from discriminating against export industries toward favoring them. The growth of nontraditional exports is attributed to this supposed policy shift.[1] The belief that the apparent shift in policy stance caused the greatly increased growth of exports arises because the change in the ideology and rhetoric of the development planners coincided, very roughly, with significantly improved exports of manufactured goods from Thailand. There is good evidence that, from around the mid-1970s, there was a shift in the views of economic planners and their academic advisers away from the desirability of import-substitution industrialization policies. "Export promotion" became the intellectual fashion among economists in Thailand, as it did elsewhere. This is clear from the text accompanying the five-year development plans. Beginning with the Third Economic Development Plan (1972–1976), export promotion was stressed over import substitution in plan documents.

However, while the views of the development planners may be important, they are not in themselves policy. Was there really a shift in policy and was it significant enough to produce the dramatic surge in exports that subsequently occurred? Or was this change of language

---

[1] See, for example, Suphachalasai (1992) and Tambunlertchai (1993). This assumption continues to be reflected in government policy documents. For example, the Eighth Five-Year Development Plan, 1997-2001, states : "To come to grips with the current account deficit problem, which is currently worsening, the government must step up the promotion of exports and reduce imports by promoting local production of intermediate products and capital goods." (NESDB 1996).

more a matter of intellectual fashion than policy commitment? Protection of inefficient import-competing manufacturing sectors actually increased during the mid- to late 1970s, at the same time as national planning documents emphasized the importance of export promotion (Warr 1993). Along with increased protection of some industries, "export promotion" policies were indeed introduced in the 1970s, supposedly to promote manufactured exports. But were the industries favored by this system subsequently successful? We shall explore this issue by examining the statistical relationship between the trade performance of industries and the Government's interventions to promote them. We draw upon the measure NEPR, as discussed above. We shall focus on five instruments of intervention, chosen both for their importance and because they are capable of being quantified from available data: ERPs by industry, the allocation of subsidized loans through the Industrial Finance Corporation of Thailand (IFCT), the number of BOI-approved projects, Customs Department tax drawbacks, and the allocation of tax rebates by the Fiscal Policy Office of the Ministry of Finance.

Table 9.9 shows the correlation coefficients between export performance and each of the above five instruments of intervention. Table 9.10 shows the correlation between the changes *over time* in each industry's trade performance[2] and the changes *over time* in each of the five instruments of intervention. The results show that export performance is negatively related to all five measures. Moreover, the absolute magnitude of these negative correlation coefficients increases over time, suggesting that the degree to which industrial policy has favored industries that perform poorly in terms of exports actually increased from the 1970s to the mid-1990s. Finally, the change over time in net export performance is negatively related to the change in all five instruments. Increasing levels of support were granted to those industries whose export performance *worsened* over time, not those whose performance improved.

In the case of import protection these results are hardly surprising. Protection is explicitly an incentive to import-competing production and (implicitly) a disincentive to exporting. But the

[2] They are agriculture, tobacco, textiles, wood products, furniture, paper, printing, rubber, chemicals, petroleum, nonmetal products, metal products, machinery, electrical machinery, transport, and other manufacturing.

Table 9.9 Correlation Coefficients Across Industries of Trade Performance and Industry Policy

	ERP				IFCT Loan Allocation				
NEPR	1974	1984	1987	1995	1960-1979	1980-1985	1986-1990	1990-1992	1993-1995
1970-1974	-0.12	-0.12	-0.15	-0.22	-0.10	0.09	-0.17	-0.04	-0.05
1975-1979	0.14	-0.23	-0.20	-0.25	-0.15	-0.03	-0.26	-0.11	-0.20
1980-1984	0.23	-0.31	-0.21	-0.24	-0.18	-0.11	-0.30	-0.14	-0.29
1985-1989	0.10	-0.30	-0.22	-0.27	-0.27	-0.27	-0.40	-0.31	-0.43
1990-1992	0.19	-0.38	-0.26	-0.24	-0.33	-0.44	-0.52	-0.43	-0.63
1993-1995	0.11	-0.40	-0.31	-0.30	-0.28	-0.37	-0.50	-0.36	-0.63

	BOI ProjectsTax				Drawback			Tax Rebates		
NEPR	1983-1985	1987-1989	1990-1992	1993-1995	1986-1989	1990-1992	1993-1995	1986-1989	1990-1992	1993-1995
1970-1974	-0.01	-0.21	-0.46	-0.47	-0.08	-0.12	-0.10	-0.27	-0.30	-0.23
1975-1979	-0.07	-0.29	-0.47	-0.51	-0.05	-0.09	-0.07	-0.26	-0.33	-0.22
1980-1984	-0.10	-0.35	-0.43	-0.49	0.01	-0.03	-0.02	-0.24	-0.33	-0.15
1985-1989	-0.27	-0.33	-0.41	-0.48	0.11	0.11	0.13	-0.16	-0.15	-0.02
1990-1992	-0.40	-0.35	-0.33	-0.43	0.13	0.17	0.18	-0.12	-0.07	0.07
1993-1995	-0.35	-0.30	-0.33	-0.43	0.12	0.15	0.17	-0.09	-0.03	0.06

Source: Author's calculations.

negative correlation with export performance is even higher in the case of the BOI instruments, as well as IFCT loans. Far from being instruments of export promotion the IFCT loans, tax drawbacks, tax rebates, and most especially the BOI investment promotion schemes, turn out to be surprisingly similar to industry protection in their allocation across industries. At the industry level, poor performers are promoted by these measures, not successful exporters. In view of these results it is surely impossible to attribute Thailand's pre-1996 export performance to "export promoting" industrial policy.

The political economy behind these results is presumably that industries, which are well organized for lobbying purposes, put proportionately more resources into the behavior that secures bureaucratic support than industries that are less well organized. But the former are not necessarily performing well in economic terms—our results suggest the reverse. Thus policy measures intended to promote exports are captured by the system of rent-seeking and in fact support roughly the same poorly performing industries that are favored by the system of protection.

Table 9.10 Correlation Coefficients Across Industries of Changes in Trade Performance and Industry Policy

Change in NEPR	Change in ERP 1974-1987	1974-1984	1984-1987	1987-1995	Change in IFCT Loan Allocation (1960-1979) to (1986-1990)	(1960-1979) to (1980-1985)	(1980-1985) to (1986-1990)	(1986-1990) to (1990-1992)	(1990-1992) to (1993-1995)
(1975-1979) to (1970-1974)	-0.82	-0.82	-0.05	-0.08	-0.08	-0.22	0.14	-0.07	-0.25
(1980-1984) to (1975-1979)	-0.46	-0.47	0.14	0.01	-0.06	-0.23	0.18	-0.02	-0.38
(1985-1989) to (1980-1984)	0.37	0.37	0.03	0.06	0.06	-0.19	0.28	-0.23	0.13
(1990-1992) to (1985-1989)	-0.24	-0.24	-0.02	0.15	-0.11	-0.34	0.23	-0.15	-0.23
(1993-1995) to (1990-1992)	0.46	0.47	-0.15	-0.16	-0.11	0.16	-0.32	0.38	-0.13

Source: Author's calculations.

Change in NEPR	Change in BOI-Promoted Projects (1983-1985) to (1987-1989)	(1987-1989) to (1990-1992)	(1990-1992) to (1993-1995)	Change in Drawbacks (1986-1989) to (1990-1992)	(1990-1992) to (1993-1995)	Change in Rebates (1986-1989) to (1990-1992)	(1990-1992) to (1993-1995)
(1975-1979) to (1970-1974)	-0.07	-0.04	-0.11	-0.04	-0.08	-0.12	0.04
(1980-1984) to (1975-1979)	-0.12	0.17	-0.35	-0.22	-0.27	-0.04	0.36
(1985-1989) to (1980-1984)	0.45	0.24	-0.16	0.15	-0.20	0.07	0.22
(1990-1992) to (1985-1989)	0.34	0.32	-0.40	0.20	-0.16	0.03	0.19
(1993-1995) to (1990-1992)	-0.11	0.13	-0.02	-0.10	0.04	-0.06	-0.12

Source: Author's calculations.

RELATIVE PRICES: TERMS OF TRADE AND REAL EXCHANGE RATE

Terms of Trade

Thailand's external terms of trade—the ratio of export prices to import prices—surged with the international commodity price boom of 1973. The petroleum price shocks of the early and late 1970s reduced the terms of trade significantly and this trend continued with the world recession of the early 1980s. Since then the terms of trade have remained remarkably stable, with very little movement since 1982. But since that year, the country's volume of exports has surged dramatically. This experience provides no apparent support for the assumption that a country which increases its exports will suffer a decline in its terms of trade. No effect of this kind is apparent from the data for Thailand.

To go beyond these very broad observations, a more formal statistical approach is required. Our principal interest is in the elasticity of demand for Thailand's exports, both short-run and long-run. Given the simultaneous determination of export supply and demand, both supply and demand must be modeled together. Two models of Thailand's export supply and demand are presented below. They differ in the treatment of the export supply equation, but because of the simultaneous estimation of the supply and demand equations in the two models, the difference on the supply side has potential implications for the behavior of the demand side. We shall discuss the demand equation first.

The traditional framework for analyzing the demand for commodity exports is set out by Goldstein and Khan (1978). Although the specification of this model differs between studies, for example, with respect to dynamics and supply structure, the core of the underlying (long-run) framework is usually a demand equation for a particular country's exports of a given commodity, or group of commodities, with the quantity of exports on the left-hand side of the estimating equation. This methodology, in particular the treatment of quantity demanded as the dependent variable (normalization in quantities), has been criticized on the grounds that ordinary least square (OLS) estimates of the demand elasticities will be biased downward. Riedel (1988) and Athukorala and Riedel (1991), referring to previous studies of developing country exports of manufactures, argue that it is preferable to estimate the demand equation normalized in prices when using OLS since, in this manner, the "small country" hypothesis that demand is infinitely elastic with respect to price can be tested. Athukorala and Riedel state:

> If the country were truly a price-taker, [the foreign and domestic prices for exports] would be perfectly, or at least very highly, collinear. In this case, the relative price variable would exhibit very little, if any, variability. Therefore, for a true small country, the coefficient on the relative price variable cannot be precisely estimated, and may turn out relatively low (and statistically insignificant) even though its true value is extremely high (Athukorala and Riedel 1991).

As they note, the high income elasticities of demand, combined with low price elasticities obtained in some previous studies, could point to the "false" notion that less developed country exports of manufactures are sensitive to the level of income of developed countries. Indeed, using two-stage least squares and specifying a partial adjustment mechanism for the demand and supply equations, they find that, for the case of Korean exports of machinery and transport equipment, an inverse export demand equation supports the small country hypothesis, while the usual demand equation specification typically points to a low price and a high income elasticity of demand for these commodities.

In each of the two models presented below, export demand is estimated with the price of Thailand's exports relative to competing countries' exports (PX_t / PW_t) specified as the dependent variable. The independent variables are the quantity of Thailand's exports relative to the exports of competing countries (X_t / W_t), the lagged value of this variable (X_{t-1} / W_{t-1}), and the lagged value of the dependent variable (PX_{t-1} / PW_{t-1}). In addition, a shifter variable is included, which is the share of the foreign capital stock within Thailand in the total capital stock (KF_{t-1} / KA_{t-1}). This variable is intended to capture the possibility that foreign capital shifts the demand function for exports by changing their composition.

The treatment of export supply differs in the two models. In Model 1, the production of goods for export is distinguished from the supply of goods for the home market. The overall level of real output is treated as predetermined and the supply equation relates to its division between the two forms of output, export, and domestic supply (X_t / D_t). Export supply is then related to the relative prices of export and domestic output (PX_t / PD_t), the lagged value of this relative price (PX_{t-1} / PD_{t-1}), and to its own lagged value (X_{t-1} / D_{t-1}). There is also a shifter variable for the foreign capital stock relative to the total capital stock (KF_{t-1} / KA_{t-1}) to allow for the possibility that foreign capital shifts the supply function for exports through the introduction of new technology.

Because of the presence of cointegration among the variables of the system, error correction methods are used to estimate both systems. Estimation was through three-stage least squares, using the values of the predetermined and exogenous variables as instruments. The results are summarized below.

Model 1: Export Demand

$$
\begin{aligned}
D(\ln(PX_t/PW_t) = {} & \underset{(0.01)}{0.005}\, D(\ln(X_t / W_t) - \underset{(3.47)}{0.96} \ln(PX_{t-1} / PW_{t-1}) \\
& \underset{(0.09)}{-0.07} \ln(X_{t-1} / W_{t-1}) + \underset{(2.63)}{0.54} \ln(KF_{t-1} / KA_{t-1}) \\
& \underset{(0.68)}{-0.017}\, T - \underset{(2.26)}{1.05}
\end{aligned}
$$

$\bar{R}^2 = 0.52$
$DW = 1.75$
Run = -1.11

Short-run elasticity = 210.98 (0.01)
Long-run elasticity = 13.72 (0.33)

Model 1: Export Supply

$$D(\ln(X_t/D_t)) = \underset{(2.47)}{0.95}\, D(\ln(PX_t/PD_t) - \underset{(4.24)}{0.53} \ln(X_{t-1}/W_{t-1})$$

$$+ \underset{(2.32)}{0.7} \ln(PX_{t-1}/PD_{t-1}) + \underset{(2.47)}{0.40} \ln(KF_{t-1}/KA_{t-1})$$

$$+ \underset{(5.16)}{0.046}\, T - \underset{(0.06)}{0.024}$$

$\bar{R}^2 = 0.57$
$DW = 2.38$
Run $= 0.24$

Short-run elasticity = 1.05 (2.47)
Long-run elasticity = 0.75 (2.16)

In Model 2, export supply is related to potential total output, denoted YH_t. The dependent variable is the ratio between these two variables (X_t / YH_t). The independent variables are the price of exports relative to the GDP deflator (PX_t / PY_t), its lagged value, the lagged value of the dependent variable, and a shift variable for the foreign capital stock, (KF_{t-1} / KA_{t-1}), whose purpose is as described for Model 1 above.

Model 2: Export Demand

$$D((\ln(PX_t/PW_t) = \underset{(1.84)}{0.94}\, D(\ln(PX_t/PY_t) - \underset{(3.28)}{0.49} \ln(X_{t-1}/YH_{t-1})$$

$$+ \underset{(1.68)}{0.69} \ln(PX_{t-1}/PY_{t-1}) + \underset{(0.67)}{0.097} \ln(KF_{t-1}/KA_{t-1})$$

$$+ \underset{(3.56)}{0.03}\, T - \underset{(2.01)}{0.83}$$

$\bar{R}^2 = 0.48$
$DW = 1.64$
Run $= 1.11$

Short-run elasticity = -4.32 (0.63)
Long-run elasticity = 214.32 (0.02)

Model 2: Export Supply

$$\mathrm{Dln}(X_t/YH_t)) = \underset{(1.84)}{0.94}\ \mathrm{D}(\ln(PX_t/PY_t) - \underset{(3.28)}{0.49}\ \ln(X_{t-1}/YH_{t-1})$$

$$+ \underset{(1.68)}{0.69}\ \ln(PX_{t-1}/PY_{t-1}) + \underset{(0.67)}{0.097}\ \ln(KF_{t-1}/KA_{t-1})$$

$$+ \underset{(3.56)}{0.03}\ T - \underset{(2.01)}{0.83}$$

$\bar{R}^2 = 0.36$
$DW = 1.65$
Run $= 1.50$

Short-run elasticity = 1.06 (1.84)
Long-run elasticity = 0.70 (1.66)

The results from Models 1 and 2 are identical as regards the elasticity of foreign demand. It is not possible to reject the hypothesis that the coefficient on the quantity variable in the demand equation is zero. This applies to the current value of the quantity variable as well as its lagged value. This implies that the hypothesis that the elasticity of export demand is infinite is similarly not rejected, either as regards the long-run or short-run value of this demand parameter. The supposition that expansion of Thai exports implies a worsening of Thailand's external terms of trade must therefore be rejected.

Real Exchange Rate

Data on the relative prices of traded and nontraded goods are summarized in Figure 9.1. The data are presented monthly for the years 1988 to 1998. This figure updates similar calculations presented in Warr and Nidhiprabha (1996), which used monthly domestic price data to calculate an index of traded goods' prices (using 33 individual wholesale prices for goods that approximately match the analytical concept of traded goods) relative to nontraded goods (using 42 individual consumer prices for goods and services that approximately match the analytical concept of nontraded goods).[3] In the earlier study, data were presented for the period 1968–1988. Over this period the index took values between a maximum of 1.7 and a minimum of 0.68 (indexed to August 1973 = 1). At the end of the data series (January 1988) the value of this index was 0.7.

Figure 9.1 Real Exchange and Competitiveness, Monthly, 1988–1998

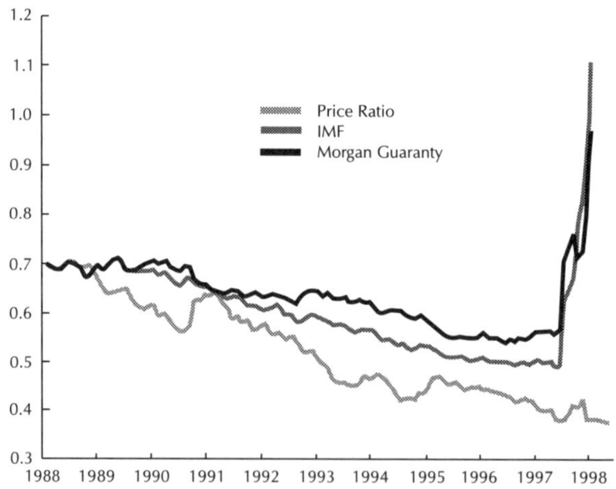

Sources: Author's calculations using data from Department of Business Economics, Ministry of Commerce, Bangkok; Bank of Thailand; and IMF (various issues).

---

[3] For a full discussion of this index and its composition, see Warr and Nidhiprabha (1996), pp. 221-26.

For comparison with the earlier series, Figure 9.1 is indexed to begin at 0.7 in January 1988, and the composition of the index shown is identical to the one used in the earlier study. Short-term fluctuations aside, the index declined steadily from 1990. By April 1997 its value was just 0.43; a very large real appreciation had occurred. The real exchange rate, as measured, had fallen to 37 percent less than its lowest value over the two decades prior to the boom. Do external exchange rate changes explain this outcome? The question arises because it is now well understood that the depreciation after 1995 of the Japanese yen and other currencies relative to the dollar meant that any currency pegged to the dollar would suffer a real appreciation. The answer, though, is no.

The real appreciation demonstrated in Figure 9.1 was not at all confined to the period after 1995, when the dollar was appreciating. A large real appreciation can also be seen in the first five years of the 1990s, when the dollar was depreciating relative to the yen and other currencies. Most of the real appreciation from 1990 to mid-1997 was already evident by mid-1994, well before the appreciation of the dollar began. External exchange rate changes were clearly relevant, but they were not the main causal factor. The principal cause of the real appreciation resided in forces operating within the Thai economy—not external exchange rate adjustments. The principal factors were the demand effects of large foreign capital inflows, only partially sterilized. The real appreciation undermined the competitiveness of Thailand's traded goods industries, meaning their capacity to attract resources within the domestic economy in competition with nontraded goods sectors.

Figure 9.1 also shows two other measures of real exchange rates, also described as measures of the "competitiveness" of domestic traded goods producers. These measures are both obtained by looking at nominal exchange rates and adjusting them by price levels in the home country and abroad. The two shown are the Morgan Guaranty index (the export share-weighted sum of trading partner wholesale price indexes, each multiplied by the bilateral exchange rate divided by the domestic wholesale price index) and the IMF index (which has the same numerator but the denominator is the domestic consumer price index). These measures are frequently interpreted as proxies for the relative prices of traded and nontraded goods within the domestic economy. Interpreted in this way, both these measures significantly understate the magnitude of a real appreciation. Both also greatly exaggerate the gain in export competitiveness resulting from a depreciation, and distort the pattern of its changes over time.

1996 EXPORT SLOWDOWN: TRIGGER TO THE 1997 CURRENCY CRISIS

From Tables 9.1 to 9.4 it is obvious that there was a serious slowdown of exports in 1996. This did not *cause* the crisis of 1997. It *triggered* a crisis to which Thailand had become vulnerable for macroeconomic reasons. If it had not been for this vulnerability, the export slowdown of 1996 would have caused little more than a temporary balance of payments problem, requiring the country to borrow abroad to smooth out import capacity until exports recovered. The mechanism by which the export slowdown triggered the crisis was by damaging investor confidence in the Bank of Thailand's capacity to maintain its fixed exchange rate, provoking a capital outflow that was very much larger than anyone expected. The vulnerability lay in the potential size of this outflow, but that is beyond the scope of this study. Here we ask what caused the export slowdown of 1996.

Over the five years prior to 1996, total exports of goods and services had grown at an annual average rate of around 16 percent and merchandise exports at 22 percent. In 1996, the volume of exports actually contracted slightly. Alternative data sources differ as to the amount of the contraction, but a 2 percent decline, measured in dollars, seems to be approximately correct. The point is that export growth stopped completely and this seriously unnerved market participants.

The aggregate export slowdown was due to large absolute declines in exports of a few major commodities: garments, shoes and parts, frozen shrimps, and textiles (*Bangkok Post,* December 1996). It should be noted that, with the possible exception of frozen shrimps, these are all labor-intensive industries. The apparent export slowdown has attracted many attempts at explanation. We review them here, arranged in what would seem to be increasing order of importance—that is, with the least important first, followed by the most important.

Theories for the 1996 Export Slowdown

Politics

The Government of Prime Minister Banharn Silpa-archa had taken office after the elections of July 1995, but was disrupted by repeated scandals and by allegations of corruption and other misdemeanors. The public perception was also one of weakness in economic management and other areas. In November 1996 the Government was forced by the threat of a parliamentary censure motion to call a general election. Economic management was a major issue in the campaign and the Banharn Government was blamed for a range of economic problems including the export slowdown, the deterioration in the current account, and slumps in both the property market and the stock exchange.

Corruption and incompetence of the levels attributed to the Banharn administration were nothing new for Thailand. In the past, corruption at the top of government had not led to serious economic failure because policy continued to be controlled primarily by technocrats, rather than by politicians. For this reason it seems unlikely that the Banharn Government was truly responsible for more than a little of the export slowdown. The Government's apparent incompetence seems to have been more a source of public embarrassment than of extensive policy failure. There were worrying instances in which the Banharn Government had attempted to interfere with the bureaucracy's economic management, including an apparent challenge to the independence of the Bank of Thailand, but it would seem that, to some extent, the Banharn Government was merely unlucky to have been in office when more powerful economic forces induced the economic problems of 1996. However, the Government's political failings would seem inadequate to explain the 1996 export slowdown.

Monetary Policy

The Bank of Thailand responded to normal inflation in 1995 by tightening monetary policy. Inflation eased, but the apparent effect on real output was greater than expected. By early 1996 an export slowdown was already evident and slower growth for the whole of 1996 was being forecast. The Bank of Thailand eased its monetary policy and interest rates declined. Monetary tightness in late 1995 and early 1996 may have contributed to the export slowdown, but to only a limited degree. There is no obvious reason why exporters should be more negatively affected by a tight monetary policy than producers for the domestic market, and no reason why labor-intensive exporters should be affected the most.

Liberalization of the movement of capital into and out of Thailand has reduced the Bank of Thailand's capacity to control the domestic money supply, but exchange rate expectations have powerful effects on financial markets. Expectations of exchange rate adjustments have major effects on capital movements, and rumors of impending devaluation of the baht had circulated in Bangkok financial circles since as early as May 1996. By inducing capital outflow such expectations have a contractionary effect on the domestic money supply. These financial movements could not reasonably be cited as a cause of the export slowdown, but they do provide a credible explanation for the property and stock market slumps of 1996.

It was apparent from the impending failure of some large financial institutions that there was a failure of supervision from the Bank of Thailand. This, at least, was the implicit assessment of the chief of IMF, Michael Camdessus, while also expressing confidence in the current set of policies. Speaking in Hong Kong, China, in early 1997, he said that Thailand's financial institutions

> ... have not been maintained in sufficiently tight supervision and discipline. ... In Asia and elsewhere, prudential regulation and supervision have not kept pace with the new complexities of the banking business. ... Thailand is in a difficult phase after a very remarkable period of development. It is now in a period of adjustment and the measures are sound (*Australian Financial Review*, 10 March 1997).

Trade Liberalization

As noted earlier, during the late 1980s and early 1990s, Thailand liberalized its import protection regime significantly. The expected effect of this liberalization was a gain in overall economic efficiency, reflected partly in a surge of exports. Such efficiency gains raise overall productivity and the *level* of exports permanently, but they will not necessarily raise growth *rates* permanently. That is, the gains are expected to be primarily static rather than dynamic. The surge in export growth rates experienced in the late 1980s and early 1990s thus reflected, in part, the efficiency gains from earlier liberalization, and by the mid-1990s these had been fully realized. The level of exports had been permanently raised, but the export growth *rate* had been raised only temporarily, and would have been expected to slow around the mid-1990s. Trade liberalization may therefore explain some of the export slowdown of 1996, but not all of it.

Congested Infrastructure

The unprecedented rate of Thailand's industrial expansion from the late 1980s, concentrated on export-oriented production, placed an enormous strain on the country's already congested infrastructure facilities. Despite very high levels of public investment in infrastructure during the Seventh Five-Year Plan (1992–1996), it had not been possible to keep up with the demand. Average levels of infrastructure investment over this period exceeded 250 billion baht per year ($10 billion at the exchange rate of the time). Of this, transportation accounted for 40 percent, energy 35 percent, telecommunications 18 percent, and other utilities 7 percent. Roads, ports, and telecommunications were increasingly overused. The congestion of infrastructure clearly contributed to the export slowdown, but could not in itself explain its apparent severity and suddenness.

Falsified Export Data

A new value-added tax (VAT) system was introduced in the early 1990s. Under this scheme, exporters may receive rebates of VAT at the rate of 7 percent of the value of goods exported. The rebates are paid on documentary evidence that the exports are actually made. By 1995, a market had developed in falsified export documents, so that VAT rebates were being claimed for nonexistent exports. Empty containers were reportedly being shipped abroad as part of this form of tax fraud. It has been estimated that of the 1,406 billion baht of exports officially declared for 1995, at least 100 billion baht were fictitious (*Bangkok Post,* December 1996).

If this estimate was correct and the official export data for both 1994 and 1996 were both correct, the true growth rate for 1995 would have been lower than the reported rate. Similarly, the true export growth rate for 1996 would then have been higher than the reported rate because the true 1995 base on which it was calculated would have been below the reported level. If the 100 billion baht estimate for export overstatement in 1995 was correct, export growth for the years ending 1995 and 1996 would have been 14.8 percent and 7.2 percent, respectively, rather than the 23.6 percent and 1.6 percent reported. If the true overstatement of 1995 exports was 150 billion baht, the true growth rates for 1995 and 1996 would have been 10.4 percent and 11.4 percent, respectively.

Calculations of this kind have led some observers to conclude that the sudden export slowdown of 1996 may have been at least partly a statistical artifact. The overstatement of exports for the purpose of claiming VAT rebates presumably began a year or two earlier than 1995, when it was officially uncovered. This means that the true growth rates for 1994 and 1995 were also presumably lower than the reported rates and the 1996 export slowdown was correspondingly smaller than what the official data indicate. In short, the overstatement of exports could have disguised a moderate slowdown in exports that actually began a year or two earlier.

A test of the importance of this explanation for the apparently large slowdown in 1996 is possible using trade data. Thai exporters may well have recognized a tax advantage in overreporting export values to the authorities. But if so, this incentive would not have existed with respect to the reports made by importers abroad to their authorities. By comparing the two it is possible to ascertain whether this explanation is valid. Using two trade data sets, from IMF and UN, to compare reported exports to the world with importing countries' reported purchases from Thailand, no significant change in the relationship between reported exports and importing countries' reported imports from Thailand can be seen between 1985 and 1996. This theory for the 1996 slowdown—that it was an artifact of the reporting system—can therefore be dismissed.

Real Appreciation

During 1995 and 1996, the nominal baht/dollar exchange rate depreciated somewhat, from an average of 24.9 to 25.5 baht to the dollar—a depreciation of 2.4 percent. Much more significant, however, was that the yen depreciated against the dollar, from an average of 93.5 to 107.5 yen to the dollar—a depreciation of 15 percent in just one year. This means that the baht appreciated against the yen by more than 12 percent.

When these calculations are conducted in real terms, to take account of differences in rates of inflation, the story is even more dramatic. The 2.4 percent nominal depreciation of the baht against the dollar was offset by the difference in rates of inflation between the two countries, as measured by consumer price index movements — 5.8 percent for Thailand and 2.8 percent for the US. Thailand's real exchange rate against the dollar barely changed; there was in fact a small real appreciation of 0.6 percent. But Japan's rate of inflation was only 0.2 percent, so the yen depreciated in real terms against the dollar by a striking 17.6 percent. The baht appreciated in real terms against the yen by more than 18 percent. In 1996, Thailand's overall real exchange rate with respect to all trading partners appreciated by about 5 percent compared with 1995.[4]

Along with the goods of other countries that peg their exchange rates more or less to the dollar, Thai goods became less competitive in Japanese markets as a result of this large real appreciation. For the same reason, Thai goods also became slightly less competitive in US export markets relative to US goods and markedly less competitive in US markets relative to Japanese goods. Nevertheless, Figure 9.1 reveals that the real appreciation of the baht preceded these external events. It began at around 1990 and, although there was some acceleration in the rate of real appreciation after 1995, the largest part of the absolute real appreciation that occurred since 1990 had actually happened *before* 1995. The real appreciation was therefore primarily a result of forces internal to the Thai economy, rather than external exchange rate movements. There is one obvious explanation

[4] Since we are interested in the implications for Thailand's export industries, this calculation uses Thailand's export shares to weight the bilateral real exchange rates with respect to individual trading partners.

—the "Dutch disease" effects of prolonged and massive capital inflows that fueled the boom of 1988–1995.

The large real appreciation explains part of Thailand's export slowdown in 1996, but it does not explain why labor-intensive industries suffered the most.

Demand Slowdown in Importing Countries

In 1996, export growth declined relative to the previous year in almost all Asian countries, with Thailand's reported slowdown one of the largest. The principal reason was a slowdown of demand from major importing countries, especially Japan. To the extent that international demand-side factors were responsible, the 1996 slowdown does not indicate a decline in the Asian countries' export competitiveness. There is little that these countries can do about a decline in international demand. To some extent, they must wait for demand to recover and maintain their efficiency in the meantime. Desperate schemes intended to "promote" exports have the potential to introduce inefficiencies that will only impede their capacity to respond efficiently to increased international demand when recovery occurs.

The slow growth in international demand for electronics products is well known and was also significant for Thailand, but they were not the slowest growing of Thailand's exports. Exports of labor-intensive products such as garments, textiles, and footwear actually fell the most. Once again, slow growth of international demand does not account for that difference. Internal factors, operating within the Thai economy, must be responsible.

Real Wages

Recently available data on real wages provide the single most significant explanation for Thailand's export slowdown and its concentration in labor-intensive industries. Work at the Thailand Development Research Institute has recently produced a reliable series of real wage data for Thailand. These data are reproduced in Figure 9.2 for the years 1982 to 1994. The data describe an index of nominal wages for the manufacturing sector deflated by the consumer price index and are indexed in such a way that the level for 1982 is 100. Over the 13 years

Figure 9.2 Real Wage Data, 1982–1994

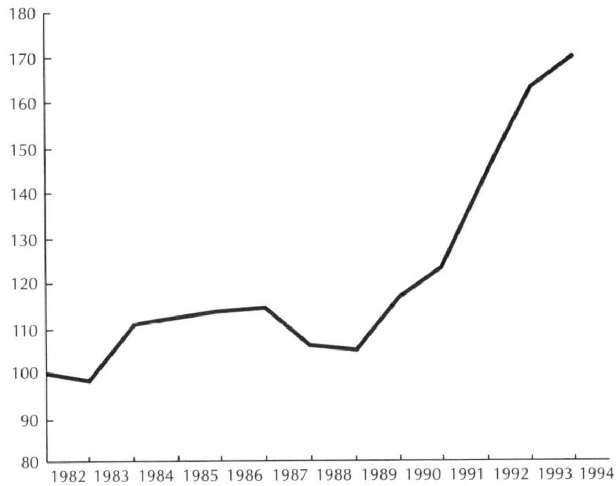

Source: Author's calculations.

from 1982 to 1994, real wages increased by 70 percent, but this increase was heavily concentrated in the years after 1990. Over the years from 1982 to 1990, the increase was from an index of 100 to 117, an average compound rate of increase of 2 percent. But over the following four years to 1994, the real wage increased to an index of 170, an average annual rate of increase in real wages of almost 10 percent.

Why the sudden increase in real wages? During the early stages of Thai economic growth, the rising demand from the industry and services sectors for labor could be met from a very large pool of rural labor with relatively low productivity. The potential supply of unskilled rural labor was so large that as workers moved from agriculture to more productive jobs in the manufacturing and services sectors, it was possible for these sectors to expand their levels of employment without significantly bidding up real wages. But as this process continued the pool of cheap rural labor was largely used up, so that by the early 1990s labor shortages were becoming evident. Agriculture was itself experiencing serious problems of seasonal labor shortages. Further increases in the demand for labor outside agriculture then led to rising wages.

Thailand's export industries are especially vulnerable to increases in real wages for two basic reasons. First, many of Thailand's most successful export industries are highly labor-intensive, implying that a given increase in real wages has large effects on their costs. Second, these export industries face highly competitive international markets for their products, where they must act as price-takers. This means that cost increases cannot be passed on in the form of increases in product prices. Producers for the domestic market may have greater scope for doing so.

The implication of rising real wages is a loss of competitiveness in the labor-intensive export-oriented industries that have been the basis of much of the country's growth over the past decade. This information helps explain the export slowdown of the mid-1990s. With the end of the era of cheap labor, Thailand's labor-intensive exports faced the prospect of declining competitiveness. The importance of this point is confirmed by the fact that the export slowdown was concentrated in labor-intensive industries such as garments, footwear, and textiles.[5]

For the labor-intensive export-oriented industries, large real wage increases raise serious problems. They mean that the export competitiveness of these industries has declined permanently, given their present technology. They must adjust or face a steadily declining market share. To adjust, these industries must find less labor-intensive and more capital- and skills-intensive ways of producing their goods. Thailand as a whole must move out of these industries as wages continue to rise and move into more skills-intensive industries. Here, the education sector must supply the skilled labor force required.

However, past indications raise serious concerns about the capacity of the education sector to do this. Primary school enrollment is virtually universal, but the rates of secondary school enrollment are among the lowest of any country in Thailand's income category. There are several reasons for this. First, secondary school is not cheap. This is especially true for rural people, who constitute over 60 percent of the population. Secondary schools are heavily concentrated in urban areas, especially Bangkok.[6] But for rural people to send their children to upper secondary school, they must often send them to live away from home, at considerable expense. In addition, the

---

5 The frozen shrimp industry is a special case, where US import restrictions were important, effectively banning nonfarm shrimp imports from Thailand. These bans were lifted in 1997.

6 Thailand has the highest "urban primacy ratio" of any country in the world with a population of over 10 million. This measures the proportion of the total urban population of the country that resides in the largest single city.

curriculum of secondary schools, especially at the upper levels, is rigid and is designed to prepare students for university entrance. The education received is not necessarily useful for a student aiming at a technical or blue-collar career.[7] The structure of the education system is therefore not serving Thailand well. Greater privatization with government support in the form of education subsidies to the students themselves is likely to be beneficial.

FUTURE PROSPECTS

Thailand's future economic prospects are heavily dependent on the performance of its export industries. In this section we present an assessment of their prospects, drawing upon the above analysis.

Export Competitiveness

The competitiveness of Thailand's labor-intensive exporters was reduced by the increase in real wages that occurred over the five years prior to the crisis. The massive nominal depreciation that occurred since the floating of the baht on 2 July 1997 will reverse that decline, at least temporarily. Preliminary data on nominal wages since mid-1997 suggest that they are at best stagnant and in some cases, such as the construction sector, even declining. At the same time, the depreciation of the currency can be expected to induce a higher than normal rate of inflation, especially in traded goods. The result is therefore expected to be a decline in real wages that will, in itself, restore the profitability of some labor-intensive industries such as garments and footwear, so badly affected by the events of 1996 and 1997.

The depreciation implies a major reorientation of domestic prices, with tradable goods prices (exportables and import substitutes) rising relative to nontradables, especially services and construction. Data on relative prices since the crisis are worrying in this respect. Figure 9.1 shows that little increase in the prices of tradable goods relative to nontradables is yet evident from the data on relative prices observable within Thailand. The massive increase in competitiveness indicated

7 For further details, see Sirilaksana (1993).

by the IMF and Morgan Guaranty indexes of real effective exchange rates is not evident from the data. To some extent, the increases in competitiveness suggested by these indexes are statistical artifacts. (This point is argued in detail in the section *Relative Prices: Terms of Trade and Real Exchange Rate* of this chapter.) Even so, the apparent lack of increase in the tradables to nontradables price ratio is puzzling and, in a different form, is already an issue of concern among policymakers.

In Thai policy circles, it has been claimed that domestic prices of exportables, measured at the farm or factory gate, have not adjusted fully to the baht's depreciation. If this is true, it is a matter of great concern because if the prices received by producers for exportable commodities do not respond to the depreciation, aggregate production of these commodities will presumably not occur. The only avenue for expanding exports would then be to divert an increasing amount of total production from domestic sales to export sales. This is a response that may be expected in any case, but the scope for increasing the total volume of exports in this way is clearly limited by the total output of the industries concerned. Sustained expansion of exports requires production to expand, and for this to occur production must become more profitable.

According to data on the price of rice, which is monitored with care and in great detail by the Thai Ministry of Agriculture and Cooperatives, and though only nine months of data are presently available since the depreciation of July 1997, rice prices at the farm gate have been slow to adjust to the exchange rate adjustment. It must be emphasized that further data are required before firm conclusions can be drawn, but the record to date suggests that close monitoring of this situation is important. If the apparent failure of farm gate prices to respond to the depreciation persists, and is confirmed for other major exports, this will be a matter of great policy concern.

It would not seem reasonable to attribute this apparent outcome to monopolistic behavior on the part of marketing agents. Thai rice markets have been studied in depth and have been found to be highly competitive. A more reasonable explanation may relate to exchange rate risk. Following the depreciation, the baht/dollar exchange rate was unstable and this led to great uncertainty on the part of traders. The increases in the margins between FOB prices and farm gate prices that followed the depreciation may correspond to a premium for the greatly increased exchange rate risk that exporters were accepting in purchasing rice for subsequent export at a highly uncertain exchange rate. If so, that situation was temporary because one year after the depreciation, exchange rate stability had largely been restored, albeit with a floating rate and not one pegged by the Bank of Thailand. Full adjustment of farm and factory gate prices would then be expected, but with a delay.

As domestic prices respond, the profitability of traded goods industries will increase. The net consequences for the path of unemployment will depend in part on the flexibility of resource allocation. The more rapidly resource allocation can adjust in response to the change in incentives, the smaller will be unemployment. Resources will be released by the services and construction sectors and reabsorbed by exporters. The question is: To what extent can resources be moved efficiently from services sectors that are now laying off workers to the export industries that are now becoming so much more profitable? The less flexible is resource reallocation, the greater will be frictional unemployment. The flexibility of the economy is now being tested.

Expansion of Aggregate Exports

To recover from the present crisis Thailand must expand its exports. There is no doubt that 1998 has been a very difficult year. Financial reform and facilitation of the response of exports to the increased profitability created by the baht's depreciation are the priority areas for policy. Poverty incidence will increase at a rate determined by the rate at which labor can relocate from the services and construction industries, which are contracting, to the more profitable export industries. Financial reform will be an important determinant of the success of this adjustment.

Many observers have said that the economic fundamentals for Thailand are good and that rapid growth will soon be restored. They may be right, but it is worrying that the commentators seldom specify what these fundamentals actually are. The baht's depreciation may be expected to increase the profitability of exports in the short to medium term. During that period, rapid growth will be possible as resources made idle by the crisis are reabsorbed into productive use. But closer examination raises doubts about the possibilities of restoration of very rapid growth once that recovery has taken place.

First, the domestic resource that fueled the boom—cheap unskilled labor—will no longer be abundant once the unemployed workers released by the current recession are reabsorbed. When these workers reenter the workforce, the era of cheap labor will be over. The evidence for this view is the dramatic increase of real wages in the early 1990s (described above). The failure of the education system to supply the skilled labor required to facilitate movement to more skills-intensive modes of production, especially for export, will then be critical. The problem is the low rates of secondary school participation, rather than failure at either the primary or tertiary levels.

Second, foreign investment also fueled the boom because it brought with it advanced technology and skills. This area is difficult to predict because the future of foreign investment is so dependent on events outside Thailand, including Japan, the US, and the newly industrialized economies, especially Hong Kong, China; Singapore; and Taipei,China. In the short term, foreign investment could be substantial as foreigners move to take advantage of assets made cheap by the depreciation and domestic recession. Nevertheless, it seems doubtful that, after this period of bargain-hunting, foreign investment will return to levels similar to those experienced during the boom. Following the crisis, investors will now surely be more cautious. In early 1998, there were promising signs of a recovery of foreign direct investment, but it was still too early to distinguish adequately between temporary bargain-hunting in asset markets and a long-term commitment to introduce new capital. The future of Thailand's export performance greatly depends on this matter.

Third, public infrastructure, especially transport, was badly congested by 1996. The severe cutbacks in public investment now in place mean that little can be done in the immediate future to address this problem. The largest public infrastructure projects are idle. The campaign of privatization has reduced the dependence of some projects on the Government's fiscal policy, but high domestic interest rates have also affected these projects significantly. The construction sector is in severe recession. After the recovery has restored output and thereby also restored pressure on public infrastructure, the constraint of inadequate physical infrastructure will again be strongly felt.

Finally, and most unpredictably, the recovery of exports remains dependent on Thailand's customers, notably Japan and the US. Japanese import demand will only recover when the economy has emerged from its present recession, and this in turn requires the deep problems with the financial system to be addressed. The uncertainty as regards the US is not merely whether the present high levels of the current account deficit will be tolerated, but whether an increase in them will be. To recover from their crises, Thailand and several other Asian countries must turn their present current account deficits into surpluses. This will need the rest of the world to accept larger deficits (or smaller surpluses) than at present. Whether the US will accept this remains in question, especially if there is a dramatic decline in the stock markets there.

Thailand's future as an exporter of labor-intensive products is surely limited. Once the workers laid off during the crisis are reabsorbed, it will no longer be competitive as a cheap labor country. Even during the recovery phase, it remains to be seen whether unemployment will produce declines in real wages large enough to restore the competitiveness of labor-intensive industries in a regional economy where several countries are in Thailand's position. The major point is that after recovery has occurred, the economy will no longer be competitive as an exporter of "cheap labor" commodities. It must move its productive capacity to more skills- and capital-intensive modes of production. The performance of the education sector therefore remains the single most important determinant of Thailand's future export performance and of its economic prospects in general. In short, a thorough overhaul of secondary education is required.

There is every reason to expect that Thailand can return to moderate rates of output growth, potentially around 6 percent or even 7 percent, and possibly even as early as the second half of 1999, though recovery in 2000 now seems more probable. Substantial growth of exports will be a prerequisite. Nevertheless, the extraordinary growth of exports and output that Thailand experienced during the boom years of 1988 to 1995 will almost certainly not be repeated.

Future Composition of Exports

Table 9.3 showed that, as a share of total exports, agricultural exports fell steeply between 1985 and 1996. This trend will probably be reversed temporarily as agricultural exports, during the recovery, become more important than in recent years. These exports are less affected by the problems of the financial system than exports of manufactured goods. In addition, vast numbers of urban workers laid off by the recession, perhaps as many as two million, have returned to rural areas. To the extent that they find employment in rural areas, they will boost agricultural exports. Nevertheless, once recovery has occurred, it may be expected that the process of decline of agriculture as a share of total output and total exports will resume. In the longer term, agricultural exports will continue to move away from staple foods and toward nontraditional commodities such as aquaculture products, flowers, fruits, and processed foods.

Manufactured exports will continue to dominate exports. The baht's depreciation will restore the profitability of labor-intensive goods such as garments, footwear, and textiles, whose competitiveness was reduced by the real wage increases of the early to mid-1990s. The long-term future of manufacturing depends on whether the deficiencies in the supply of skilled labor can be rectified. Table 9.5 showed that the factor intensity of exports shifted dramatically between 1970 and 1996, away from land-intensive goods toward capital-intensive goods. This shift reflected the greatly increased levels of capital accumulation in Thailand during this period, but it must be recalled that these data reflect the factor intensity of all the production processes involved in producing a good and not necessarily the factor intensity of the production processes occurring within Thailand. The export slowdown of 1996 and 1997 was heavily concentrated in labor-intensive goods exports, and these exports may expand during the recovery from the crisis, but the long-term lesson is that the economy's future export prospects do not lie in this area. Continuation of the long-term process of increasing capital intensity must be expected.

The destination of exports has moved increasingly toward other Asian countries and away from the traditional markets of Europe and North America. The expansion of exports to other ASEAN countries (see Table 9.2) mirrors the increasing share of these countries in global trade. The crisis in Southeast Asia will surely reverse this trend for several years at least. The prospects for exports to Japan must also be in some doubt, unless that country sees a recovery within the near future. Improved access to European and North American markets will therefore be important for Thailand. In this, Thailand is competing with other Asian countries affected by the crisis.

Policy Environment

A large depreciation of the baht has now occurred. Although traded goods prices have been slow to respond to the depreciation, this adjustment must be expected sooner or later. The Government is attempting to restore investor confidence by intervening in foreign exchange markets to stabilize the baht/dollar exchange rate; it remains to be seen whether a level of around 40 baht to the dollar is sustainable. Overall, however, it seems that the exchange rate adjustment necessary for the restoration of export competitiveness has now been made.

In the past, the Government emphasized the use of policy instruments designed to promote the development of industries that would expand exports. These instruments of "export promotion" are widely thought to have encouraged the expansion of exports that occurred in Thailand since the mid-1970s. In the section *Protection and Export Promotion Policies* of this chapter, strong evidence was presented which suggests that these instruments were ineffective in promoting exports. The correlation between receipt of these "export promotion" instruments and actual export success was negative. The industries promoted were, on average, the poor performers in terms of exports. This means that to the extent that these schemes shifted resources away from nonpromoted industries and toward promoted ones, they were in fact shifting resources away from the more successful exporters and toward less successful ones. Total exports were presumably *reduced* by these schemes.

Since the crisis of 1997, the Government has renewed its commitment to export promotion and proposes to expand the use of existing instruments of promoting exports. The record of the past suggests that this is a mistake. Government officials are not good at picking winners in terms of export performance or of any other criterion of commercial success. Probably more important is that the instruments of export promotion have been captured by the rent-seeking processes that have led to the inefficient structure of industrial protection in Thailand. There is little reason to expect that this pattern will change. Rather than attempting to pick winners in export terms and promote the industries chosen, the Government would be better advised to reduce substantially the overall levels of protection. The structure of industrial protection is a clear disincentive to expansion of exports; by reducing the levels of protection the Government could be assured that it was pursuing a policy that would promote efficient expansion of its export industries.

One year after the crisis of 1997, Thailand's banking system has been frozen by the presence of high levels of nonperforming loans. The problems of the banking system resemble Japan's in this respect and are closely related to them. The banks must be required to face up to nonperforming loans and take the capital losses that are implied. A period of recapitalization will then be necessary and this will inevitably require greater foreign participation. Until this is done, the ultraconservative policies at present pursued by the banks—a consequence of their high levels of nonperforming loans—will continue to mean poor performance of the banking system and ongoing liquidity problems for exporters and others.

Longer-term policy measures that are required include development of secondary education, especially in rural areas, and continued improvement of the infrastructure base. Because of the fiscal constraints facing the Government and the strictness of the IMF reform package, it is clear that privatization must play an expanded role in these developments. Ways must be found to achieve greater private sector involvement in secondary and vocational education. Relaxation of restrictions on foreign ownership, including foreign ownership of banks, must also be prioritized.

BIBLIOGRAPHY AND REFERENCES

Athukorala, P., and J. Riedel. 1991. "The Small Country Assumption: A Reassessment with Evidence from Korea." *Weltwirtschaftliches Archiv* 127:138-151.

Australian Financial Review. 10 March 1997:8.

Balassa, Bela. 1979. "The Changing Pattern of Comparative Advantage in Manufactured Goods." *Review of Economics and Statistics* 61(May): 259-266.

Bangkok Post. 1996. "Year-End Economic Review." (December): 26.

Bank of Thailand database.

Budsayavith, S. 1996. "Estimates of Effective Rates of Protection for Thailand." Ramkhamhaeng University, Bangkok. Mimeo.

Department of Business Economics, Ministry of Commerce Database Bangkok.

Goldstein, M., and M. S. Khan. 1978. "The Supply and Demand for Exports: A Simultaneous Approach." *Review of Economics and Statistics* 60:275-286.

Goldstein, M., and M. S. Khan. 1985. "Income and Price Effects in Foreign Trade." In W. Jones and P. B. Kenen, ed., *Handbook of International Economics.* Vol II. Amsterdam: Elsevier.

International Monetary Fund (IMF). *Direction of Trade Statistics* database.

______. Various Issues. *International Financial Statistics.* Washington D.C.

Krugman, P. 1989. "Differences in Income Elasticities and Trends in Real Exchange Rates." *European Economic Review* 33:1031-1054.

National Economic and Social Development Board (NESDB). 1996. *Eighth Five-Year Development Plan* (October).

Pinthong, C. 1984. "Distribution of Benefit of Government Rice Procurement Policy in Thailand." *Thammasat University Journal* 13:166-187. In Thai.

Riedel, J. 1988. "The Demand for LDC Exports of Manufactures: Estimates from Hong Kong." *Economic Journal* 98:138-148.

Robinson, David, Yangho Byeon, and Ranjit Teja. 1991. "*Thailand:*

Adjusting to Success, Current Policy Issues." Occasional Paper No. 85. Washington, DC: International Monetary Fund.

Roumasset, J., and S. Setboonsarng. 1988. "Second-Best Agricultural Policy: Getting the Price of Thai Rice Right." *Journal of Development Economics* 28:323-340.

Siamwalla, Ammar, and Suthad Setboonsarng. 1989. "Trade, Exchange Rate and Agricultural Pricing Policies in Thailand: Comparative Studies on the Agricultural Pricing Policy." Washington, DC: World Bank.

Siamwalla, Ammar, and Suthad Setboonsarng. 1991. "Thailand." In A. O. Krueger, M. Schiff, and A. Valdes,eds., *The Political Economy of Agricultural Pricing Policy.* Vol. II. Asia. Baltimore: Johns Hopkins University Press.

Siamwalla, A., S. Setboonsarng, and D. Patamasiriwat. 1993. "Agriculture." in Peter G. Warr, ed., *The Thai Economy in Transition*: 81-117. Cambridge: Cambridge University Press.

Sirilaksana, Khoman. 1993. "Education Policy." in Peter G. Warr,ed., *The Thai Economy in Transition:* 325-354. Cambridge: Cambridge University Press.

Suphachalasai, Suphat. 1992. "Export-led Industrialization in Thailand." Paper presented at the conference on The Making of a Fifth Tiger? Thailand's Industrialization and its Consequences, Australian National University, 7-9 December 1992.

Tambunlertchai, Somsak. 1993. "Manufacturing." In Peter G. Warr, ed., *The Thai Economy in Transition.* Cambridge: Cambridge University Press.

Taylor, J. B. 1980. "Aggregate Dynamics and Staggered Contracts." *Journal of Political Economy* 80:1-23.

UN International Trade database.

Warr, Peter G. ed. 1993. *The Thai Economy in Transition.* Cambridge: Cambridge University Press.

Warr, Peter G., and Bhanupong Nidhiprabha. 1996. *Thailand's Macroeconomic Miracle: Stable Adjustment and Sustained Growth.* Washington, DC: World Bank, and Kuala Lumpur: Oxford University Press.

World Bank. 1992. *World Development Report 1992.* New York: Oxford University Press for the World Bank.

______. 1993. *East Asia's Economic Miracle.* New York: Oxford University Press for the World Bank.

Chapter Ten

Rejuvenating Asian Exports

Dilip K. Das

THE TRANSITION

Export expansion has been a vitally important policy platform of Asian economic growth. In 1996, when the platform seemed no longer steady, policymakers and scholars became concerned. The question of whether this transition to a low export growth rate was permanent or a passing phase began to be asked in various national, regional, and international forums. In an attempt to answer this, this volume reviews the export regimes and recent performance, including the slump, in five Asian economies.

The principal objectives of this chapter are to present a summary of the findings of the policy-related chapters, and to summarize the causes behind deceleration in export growth and short- and medium-term project scenarios, based on the five case studies. This is followed by policy prescriptions for restoring the vigor and competitiveness of Asian exports. Some generalizations emerge and can be applied to groups of countries, although none is so sweeping that it can be applied to all.

Outer-Oriented Strategy

Anne Krueger (Chapter 2) begins with a much-discussed stylized prescription of export-led growth. Consistent with her earlier works,

Krueger identifies openness of the economy, uniformity of incentives for most economic activities, and relatively low levels of protection against imports as powerful incentives for the flow of new resources into export industries. Outer-oriented strategies promote growth by encouraging investment in industries in which the economy has a comparative advantage, and then exporting the output to the world market, thereby removing the domestic market constraint. In a developing economy, the boundary of this constraint is reached quickly. The small domestic market leads to low-scale economies that in turn cause the capital/output ratio to rise. Therefore, even large savings and investment rates are offset by the increase in the incremental capital/output ratio.

An outer-oriented trade strategy can succeed only when the framework of incentives for potential exporters and other producers provides reasonable economic efficiency. Misallocation of resources—which can result from unrealistic exchange rates, severe quantitative restrictions, and bureaucratic selection of industries—is greatly reduced under an outer-oriented trade policy regime. Such a policy regime resulted in rapid export expansion and growth in the newly industrialized economies (NIEs)[1] and the ASEAN-4 economies.[2] However, Asian economies present a range of experiences with different trade regimes. India has only a few years of experience with liberalizing trade restrictions, as do Bangladesh, Nepal, and Pakistan, where the vestiges of an inner-oriented trade strategy are still evident.

Krueger believes that the export debacle of 1996 was largely caused by the downswing of the business cycle. A demand slump in electronics, particularly semiconductors, contributed to this, although it was not the only cause. Soon after, the financial and currency crisis of 1997 began. This was caused by factors such as unrealistic real exchange rates, unsustainable current account deficits, and large borrowings from the international capital markets. Some weak fundamentals (such as the banking and financial system) hastened the onset of the crisis. But in the electronics industry, periods of excess and feeble demand alternate, thus when the business cycle picks up again the Asian economies will pull

[1] Hong Kong, China; Republic of Korea; Singapore; and Taipei,China.

[2] Indonesia, Malaysia, Philippines, and Thailand.

themselves out of the export slump. Satisfactory demand growth in the industrial world, particularly Japan, will be beneficial. However, resolving the difficulties of the banking and financial sector in the affected economies is a precondition for recovery.

Twin-Shock Explanation

Takatoshi Ito (Chapter 3) draws attention to the pattern of industrialization in developing Asia that evolved during the 1980s. This involved imports of machinery and parts from Japan and other industrial economies, and assembling of manufactured products for export to the US and Japan. He establishes, through a regression exercise, that this pattern increased the sensitivity of the Asian economies' real exchange rates to movements against the dollar and the yen. He identifies the two 1996 shocks as the steep yen depreciation and the recession in the global electronics industry. The first made Asian exports uncompetitive in Japan, the US, and other large markets, while the second effectively contracted the export sector of several Asian economies. Because the Asian economies have large intraregional trade, these shocks were amplified.

Although Ito calls the 1996 deceleration "cyclical," he has ascribed it to the two above-identified shocks. He implies that if the deceleration was caused by two adverse external factors, then once these causal factors are remedied, Asian exports will no longer suffer from deceleration. As of late 1998, his prognosis has not been realized. He has tried to explain this by stating that although there were signs of minor recovery in the second and third quarters of 1997 in some export sectors, the onset of the Asian crisis changed the economic structure and competitiveness of the regional economy entirely.

Multilateral Trading Environment

The external environment is of material significance for expansion or stagnation of trade. Improvements in the multilateral trading environment brought about by various rounds of the General Agreement on Tariffs and Trade were partly responsible for the stellar export performance of several Asian economies. David Greenaway (Chapter 4) focuses on the recent improvements in the multilateral trading environment and regional integration, extensively documenting developments in both. The 1990s have been marked by the completion of the Uruguay Round, one of the most ambitious rounds of multilateral trade negotiations (MTNs), and a concurrent rise in regional integration in Asia. The two can possibly work at cross purposes, that is, regional trading arrangements (RTAs) can limit the effectiveness of MTNs. However, this does not seem to be the case in Asia in the 1990s. In fact, the deceleration in Asian exports occurred despite an improvement in the global trading environment.

CAUSES OF EXPORT DECELERATION

Global or Regional Factors

According to the World Trade Organization[3] statistics, growth in the value of world merchandise trade decelerated from 20 percent in 1994 to 4 percent in 1995. This weakness in global demand adversely affected Asian exporters. Continued weak performance of the Japanese economy and slow growth in Germany in 1996 affected the export performance of several Asian economies. Japan, the largest regional economy, is an important regional export market, while Germany is an important European market. Second, massive investment in Asia's electronics industry contributed to conditions of oversupply. Hindsight reveals that several Asian economies, in particular Malaysia, Korea; and Taipei,China, overinvested in electronics. Therefore inventory buildups were large in the region. The consequent precipitous fall in prices and downturn in global demand for electronics were the other major reasons affecting the export of electronics, information technology, and computer-related products from Hong Kong, China; Korea; Malaysia; Singapore; Taipei,China; and Thailand. For several regional economies this product category was one of their principal revenue earners.

---

[3] World Trade Organization. *Annual Report 1997*, Geneva, Table II.4.

Changing Exchange Rate Configuration

Two developments on the exchange rate front worsened the competitiveness of Asian exports during this period. First, in 1994 the yuan was devalued by almost 45 percent, leading to a loss of competitiveness of several export sectors in the other Asian economies, in particular ones with low technology. Exports from the People's Republic of China (PRC) displaced their exports of low value-added products. Second, as the dollar appreciated the real effective exchange rate (REER) began to rise in several Asian economies because their currencies were actually linked to the dollar (Frankel and Wei 1994; and Ito 1999). The currencies of Korea, Pakistan, and Thailand had appreciated since 1995. The Malaysian ringgit had gradually started appreciating in 1992 and the Korean won was considered considerably overvalued in 1995. The climbing REER made the export sector less competitive in all these countries.

Korean exports, and to a limited extent those from Taipei,China, had an additional problem. Export performance in Korea was closely related to the won/yen exchange rate because Korea and Japan compete in a large number of product markets. The yen began depreciating in mid-1995 and this greatly deteriorated the competitiveness of the exports from Korea and Taipei,China, particularly those that were high-tech and high value added. Although the reasons behind the rising REER were economy-specific, there was a common factor, that is, prolonged and massive capital inflows, which fueled boom conditions in several Asian economies. At the same time they encouraged the regional currencies to appreciate and create a "Dutch disease"-like situation.

Value and Volume Growth

If exports for the NIEs and the ASEAN-4 economies are decomposed in value and volume terms, one observes that between March 1995 and March 1996, value and volume changed in parallel for exports from Hong Kong, China; and Singapore, and export prices declined only slightly more than volume. Although decline of export volumes was common for the ASEAN economies, the value trends were different. The Philippines recorded mild value gains, while the other

ASEAN economies experienced stable prices. One of the principal reasons for a decline in export volume seems to have been loss of competitiveness.

Infrastructure Bottlenecks

Infrastructure development had not kept pace with economic and industrial development in most of the high-performing Asian economies. In almost all the successful exporting economies energy supply was insufficient, roads and ports were congested, and telecommunications circuits overloaded. Korea had the highest cost of transport in the region (16.5 percent of revenue): this affected the price competitiveness of its exports. Some, like Malaysia; Taipei,China; and Thailand had made large investments in infrastructure, yet weaknesses in this sector persisted. Exports from India and Pakistan have suffered from infrastructure-related weaknesses for a long time, in particular from power shortages. Pakistan suffered from an additional weakness, that of its banking sector.

Skill Shortage and Soaring Real Wages

The high rate of GDP growth pushed wages up in several Asian economies during the 1990s. As these economies grew, so did their needs for skilled labor. Human resource development in several Asian economies did not keep pace with changes in the comparative advantage of their export sectors. Because of poor human resource planning, the increased skilled labor need could not be met locally. Skill shortages were more pronounced in the ASEAN-4 economies than in the NIEs. This led to further upward pressure on wages in general, and on wages of skilled labor in particular. Real wages rose faster in Korea, Malaysia, and Thailand than in other Asian economies. Rising real wages caused production costs to rise, which in turn led to loss of competitiveness in export markets. For instance, initially Korea had a 5–15 percent price advantage in steel in the international marketplace; this was gradually eroded by its rising labor costs. Wages in the manufacturing sector increased at an annual rate of 17.6 percent between 1990 and 1996; this was much higher than in other competing economies. Several Asian economies lost comparative advantage in labor-intensive products because of rising wages. In Thailand real wages rose by 75 percent during 1991–1995, leading to a loss of competitiveness in textiles and garments, shoes, and frozen shrimps. Skill shortages made it difficult to move to higher value-added products. For instance, by the mid-1990s Korea, Malaysia, and Thailand all lagged behind in the production of nonmemory chips. They had so far focused on memory chips, which were low in terms of value added and subject to high price volatility.

Maintaining and Enhancing Quality Standards

A related problem was failure to upgrade the quality of export products. Not adopting state-of-the-art technology had high costs in terms of inability to upgrade product quality. In many successful exporting economies, where products were price competitive, nonprice competitiveness was low. For instance, Korea had price competitiveness in machines, engines, and turbines, but lacked the quality edge needed in the international marketplace, this eroded competitiveness and affected exports. Similarly, manufactured exports from India and Pakistan have long suffered because their prices are not competitive in the international marketplace.

High Degree of Concentration

A common structural weakness of the export sector in many Asian economies was the high concentration in a handful of industries, making them vulnerable to changes in global market conditions. A remarkable aspect of Asia's export performance was the rapid shift from resource- and labor-intensive industries to more skill- and capital-intensive exports. Between 1990 and 1996, there was a dramatic change in the export structure in Asia. Malaysia and Singapore doubled their share of exports in high-technology products. Thailand, which had started from a low base in 1990, almost tripled its share, while Indonesia reduced its share of resource-based exports but was still low on the technology ladder for most exports. Thus, a noteworthy characteristic of the 1990s is the speed of the transformation of the composition of exports. Both-push and-pull factors contributed to this rapid transformation. Push factors include rising real wages, labor-intensive methods, and low-tech goods products all of which were being slowly phased out. Pull factors include foreign direct investment (FDI) from industrialized countries —the driving force—and the relocation of production bases by Korea, Japan, and Taipei,China to neighboring Asian countries. These led to a heavy concentration of exports in a small number of products, which in turn affected the export performance of Korea; Malaysia; Taipei,China; and Thailand. Pakistan—and to some extent India— already had heavy concentration of exports in a small number of products during the early 1990s, which had persisted.

Monetary Policy

In 1995, India, Pakistan, and Thailand, in an attempt to rein in inflation, adopted stringent monetary policies. In addition, banks in India and Pakistan suffered from a high ratio of default to total loans in their portfolios and therefore restricted lending. Consequently, a severe credit crunch was created, contributing to export slowdown.

Country-Specific Factors

There were also some country-specific factors that led to export deceleration. Economic activity decelerated sharply during the 1990s. In Pakistan this was particularly severe from 1995 to 1997. The agriculture sector performed poorly and the industry sector stagnated. In addition, the country suffered from a high degree of macroeconomic instability. All these factors told on Pakistan's export performance. Taipei,China was hit by the devastating typhoon, Herb. Cross-strait tensions with the PRC affected economic and trade performance. Although liberalization and trade policy reforms did take place in India and Pakistan during the 1990s, they were too little and too late. In addition, the export incentive packages were and continue to be complex and cumbersome to implement.

The 1996 deceleration of PRC exports was caused by three government policy changes. First, the value-added tax rebate that exporters were entitled to was lowered in July 1995 and January 1996. Second, before 1996 enterprises with foreign investments were exempt from tariffs on imports of machinery and equipment. The new policy eliminated this privilege. Both of these policy changes had a severe negative effect on export performance because enterprises with foreign investments accounted for almost one third of the country's total exports in 1995. The third policy change was the introduction of the duty security account for processing trade. Processed exports, based on imported raw materials, accounted for almost half of the PRC's exports in 1995. Initially the imported raw materials for these exports were free from tariff duties. However, it was observed that some industries and exporters were abusing this privilege. They avoided paying duties on the pretext that the final product from their imported raw material would be exported. Sometimes they succeeded in proving this with false documents. To eliminate this malpractice, the Government introduced the duty security account in designated banks: all importers of raw materials had to pay duty into these accounts. However, once the output of the imported raw materials was exported, the duty was reimbursed to the exporter's bank. The exporters found this policy cumbersome as reimbursements were made only after repeated reminders, an inordinate bureaucratic foot-dragging, and long delays. It increased their transaction costs, thus adversely affecting exports.

THE TRIGGER FOR 1996 DECELERATION

An important question has so far remained unanswered. Since many of these factors existed all through the 1990s, why was there this sudden and steep deceleration in 1996? Principal factors that caused the 1996 deceleration are (i) a dramatic fall in the world export growth rate, (ii) depreciation of the yen, (iii) appreciation of the REER in some Asian countries, and (iv) a significant decline in the price of major export products. All these four factors are cyclical in nature. The fall in the world export growth rate from its cyclical peak in 1995 was the largest in the last 15 years—from 20 percent in 1995 to 4 percent in 1996 in dollar terms. The sharp depreciation of the yen in 1995 compounded the negative impact of the slowdown in world exports on many Asian countries. Japan is both a major market for other Asian products as well as a competitor in the international marketplace. Although the 1992–1994 yen appreciation sent import growth soaring, the sharp depreciation had a reverse impact. Japan's imports—

including those from Asia—fell sharply. In addition, because of the fall in the value of the currency, Japan's exports began to compete with those from Korea; Hong Kong, China; and Taipei,China in the markets of other developing economies. This was particularly true with Korea, whose real export growth has tended to mirror changes in the yen-dollar exchange rate, that is, rising with an appreciation of the yen and falling with depreciation. In mid-1995, several Asian economies began experiencing appreciation in REER. The appreciating trend continued in Indonesia, Philippines, and Thailand until the second quarter of 1997, and hurt export competitiveness in those countries.

In addition, several Asian economies suffered from a significant price decline in their major export products resulting in massive terms of trade losses. The US experienced the sharpest fall in prices for imports from Asian countries, which dropped by 25 percent. Only the Philippines had rising unit export prices at the time of the onset of the crisis. The largest price declines occurred in the electronics industry, especially in computers, semiconductors, and information technology-related products. Several Asian economies (Korea, Malaysia, and Taipei,China) had large parts of their exports concentrated in this industry sector. Korea was particularly hard hit when the 16MB DRAM chips, which accounted for a large share of electronics exports, fell from a peak of $150 per unit to $10 between 1995 and 1997. Prices of labor-intensive manufactured goods, such as textiles and apparel, were also unsteady during 1996. These factors coalesced to trigger the 1996 export deceleration in Asia. It bears repeating that some of the structural weaknesses affecting export performance had already existed.

EXPECTATION OF ACCELERATION IN 1997

Although the Asian financial and currency crisis began in Thailand in July 1997, the contagion soon took over and the crisis spread to the other economies. The currency crisis in the NIEs and the ASEAN-4 caused instability in currency values; in many cases the depreciations were steep. For instance, between June 1997 and August 1998 the Indonesian rupiah depreciated by 82.9 percent vis-a-vis the US dollar, the Malaysian ringgit 40.9 percent, the Philippine peso 39.3 percent, the Thai baht 39.7 percent, the Korean won 33.3 percent, the New Taiwan dollar 19.6 percent, and the Singapore dollar 18.4 percent. Being on a fixed exchange rate, the Hong Kong dollar and the yuan did not depreciate.

Theoretical models generally predict that variability in exchange rate, including currency depreciation, has a strong negative effect on exports. The Akhtar-Hilton (1984) model posits that increased instability in currency value will lead to a lower level of trade under the assumption that traders are risk averse. Exchange rate variability and the resulting price uncertainty may, if other factors remain unchanged, lead to a gradual reduction in the volume of trade through backward shifts in demand and supply schedules. The size of the shift will depend on exporters' and importers' perceptions of the risk involved, on the extent of exchange rate variation, and on the elasticities of supply and demand. Also, firm behavior is not independent of exchange rate variability because price uncertainty adversely affects procurement and output, and discourages exports as well as imports. Using pooled time-series data for 10 developing countries, Grobar (1993) provides empirical evidence of the negative relationship between changes in the real exchange rate and manufactured exports. Based on this theoretical evidence, one can easily infer that the possible short-term impact of currency depreciation in Asia was the slowing of trade in general and exports in particular.

General expectations were that once the initial phase of uncertainty was over, such steep currency depreciations would have a significant price effect and improve the export competitiveness of Asian economies. Therefore, possibilities of dramatic export revival were seen in the steep depreciations. The export revival in turn was seen as a vehicle of economic recovery. The regional rescue programs of the IMF were also partly based on the assumption that currency depreciations will provide an impetus to exports. Theoretically these expectations and assumptions were not irrational. However, much to the chagrin of these economies, in 1997 the dramatic export revival proved to be a mirage. Total export growth from Asia was 6.7 percent in 1997, a minuscule improvement over the growth rate in 1996. Intra-Asian trade contracted by 2.7 percent in 1997. While there were several reasons behind the failure to recover in 1997, the principal ones are short- and long-term elasticities, supply-side bottlenecks, and demand-side constraints.

Short- and Long-Term Elasticities

Short-run price elasticities in international trade are likely to be much smaller than long-term elasticities. This is illustrated by the short-term and long-term effects of a currency depreciation on a country's trade balance. Immediately after a currency depreciation, the trade balance generally worsens before improving later on. This is essentially because of the tendency of the domestic currency prices of imports to rise faster than export prices soon after the depreciation, with quantities (of both imports and exports) initially not changing very much.

Because the domestic currency prices of imports rise immediately and the import content of many export lines in Asia is inordinately high,[5] the immediate impact of a currency depreciation is loss of competitiveness of exports. In Indonesia, Malaysia, Philippines, and Thailand, exporters, on an average, imported 30 percent of the raw materials used in the production process. Two of the most import-intensive export sectors in the region are electronics and auto assembly. In these two sectors import content ranges from 60 to 90 percent. The increased input costs offset any advantage that low wages provided. Thus, the immediate impact of currency depreciation was loss of export competitiveness in many important export lines and, therefore, exports failed to recover in 1997.

Supply-Side Bottlenecks

After the onset of the financial and currency crisis in Asia, credit became one of the biggest supply-side constraints. The banking and financial sector in the crisis-stricken Asian economies was in a state of disarray. In fact, this was partly responsible for the emergence of the crisis situation. A large number of banks were weighed down by massive bad debts. In addition, they could not lend because they were short of meeting the 8 percent capital adequacy ratio stipulated by IMF.[6] Consequently, an environment of severe credit shortage emerged

---

5 For instance, the import content of Nike shoes exported from various Asian locales is as high as 70 percent.

6 The 8 percent capital adequacy norm was originally determined by the Bank for International Settlements, Basle, Switzerland. It is part of the so-called Basle accord.

in the crisis-stricken economies. Trade finance virtually dried up and so did the working capital loans. This severe credit crunch hampered the ability of Asian firms to take advantage of the currency depreciations. Export orders were received, but there was little liquidity available to purchase the necessary inputs, both domestic and imported. The fact that the banking sector in many Asian economies was in a state of disarray was well known internationally; therefore, letters of credit from banks in these countries were not acceptable to foreign banks. In the initial period of economic adjustment, financial costs also soared because interest rates in many economies soared to extremely high levels. It was considered necessary by central banks as well as IMF to keep the exchange rates from depreciating abysmally. It was also believed that high interest rates will eventually help stabilize the respective currencies.

Demand-Side Constraints

Recent intraregional trade has made an increasing contribution to export growth in Asia. In 1996, the share of intraregional trade accounted for about 40 percent of total exports, up from 32 percent in 1990. If Japan is included, the share rises to 50 percent. Intraregional trade is the single most important trade flow in Asia. It is more important than Asia's trade with the US or other G-7 economies.[7] In fact, it is more important than Asia's trade with the rest of the world. According to *the Annual Report 1997* of the World Trade Organization, intra-Asian trade, including Japan, accounted for 52 percent of total exports.[8] This concentration of trade within Asia reflects an ongoing process of regional integration and of specialization in countries of the region. The country with the lowest dependence on trade with other Asian economies is the Philippines, which sends only 25 percent of its total exports to other Asian economies. At the other end of the spectrum are Malaysia; Hong Kong, China; and Singapore having the greatest dependence, 40-45 percent, on trade with other Asian economies.

---

[7] G-7 is the group of largest seven industrial countries. It includes the United States, Japan, Germany, France, Italy, Canada, and the United Kingdom.

[8] World Trade Organization. *Annual Report 1997*. Vol. II. Geneva. Table III.3. p. 23.

The magnitude and interdependency of these trade links was one of the features of the so-called Asian miracle that fueled rapid regional growth. But after the 1997 crisis, these links became a liability because they provided a perfect channel for the contagion to spread swiftly to other Asian economies. The acute recession that started in several Asian economies led to weak import demand in the region. Intraregional trade growth decelerated from 23.4 percent in 1995 to 4.8 percent in 1996 and further to 6.4 percent in 1997.

Until the first quarter of 1998, the Asian economies were still in the throes of the crisis. The growth rate of intratrade was low at 6.4 percent in 1997; it registered a further (2.8 percent) decline in the first quarter of 1998. Data for the five crisis-stricken countries (Indonesia, Korea, Malaysia, Philippines, and Thailand) indicate a drop in exports to Japan in the first quarter of 1998 of about 14 percent relative to the same period in 1997 (IMF 1998). Over this period, Japanese domestic demand fell by 5 percent. In addition, the yen depreciated against the dollar by 10 percent, reducing the competitiveness of Asian exports in the Japanese market. In 1997, intraregional exports from all four NIEs contracted, and so did those from India, Malaysia, Pakistan, and Thailand. The economies that began to show marked improvement during the first quarter of 1998 were PRC, Hong Kong, China; and Philippines. It is essential that intra-Asian trade links once again become an asset and a means to spread economic recovery.

Associated with this is the micro factor of export price pass-through.[9] That is, how much price decline due to currency depreciation is passed on by exporting firms in the exporting country to importing firms in the importing country. Large importers, who were aware of the depreciating currencies, began demanding either complete pass-through in their import prices, or at least price cuts ranging from 35 to 60 percent. However, the costs incurred by Asian exporters did not fall much because of a steep rise in the cost of imported inputs. They could barely afford 10 percent price cuts. Therefore, expectations of large price pass-through in importing countries were not met, which in turn affected the fresh batches of export orders in the short term.

[9] The concept of export price pass-through was posited by Paul Krugman in 1987.

In addition, price elasticity of demand can only help raise export volumes in the short term when there is a meaningful fall in prices. A small price decline will not be able to raise export volumes in the short term unless the price elasticity is extremely high. For some large export items, like electronics, machinery, textiles, and apparel, the price elasticity is low.

EXPORT VOLUME GROWTH IN 1998

Both the 1996 deceleration and the 1997–1998 financial and currency crisis have inspired appropriate responses, including strategic adjustments in exporting firms and industries. These adjustments and currency depreciations, after a time lag, have spawned some encouraging results. Export volumes gradually surged in Korea; in fact since the third quarter of 1997, the volume surge has been substantial. It continued in 1998; during the months of July and August the index numbers of value were 97.1 and 94.2 (1995 = 100). In comparison, the index numbers for volume were 166.2 and 165.

Likewise, in Hong Kong, China; Indonesia; and Singapore, export volumes started rising in mid-1997 and continued during 1998. Since the Hong Kong dollar was not devalued by the Hong Kong Monetary Authority, the difference between value and volume indexes was small. In August 1998, the two indexes stood at 106.3 and 111.9. But in the case of Indonesia and Singapore, the volume index was substantially higher than in mid-1998. In comparison, export volumes have not risen in the Philippines or Taipei,China. In these two economies export value indexes have risen over the same period because of a rise in the unit prices of their exports. The rise in the unit prices of exports was in turn influenced by recovering electronics goods prices, which form a significant part of the total exports from these two countries.

Of the countries for which export volume data are available, the maximum volume increase has been observed for Indonesia and Korea. The rising volume trend was not noticed in Thailand until December 1997. This shows that the effect of currency depreciation was felt after a relatively longer time lag in Thailand. For the five crisis-stricken Asian economies, during 1998 the index of export volume remained considerably higher than that of export value. On average, their export volume growth has been estimated at 25 percent year-on-year (World Bank 1998).

Thus viewed, export volumes have indeed responded to policy adjustments by exporting firms and exchange rate depreciation. This response was lagged, and the surge in export volumes was more than offset by a sharp drop in unit value of exports as well as currency depreciations. The US import data show that the pace of decline in prices from Asian economies has accelerated—from 6 percent annually in the third quarter of 1997 to 12 percent in the second quarter of 1998. The fall in prices could also result from competition in relative prices. Asian countries tend to compete more intensely with one another than with other non-Asian exporters (Muscatelli and Montagna 1994). This is partly because of greater similarity in export structures. This implies that if several Asian countries lowered their export prices simultaneously, no one will be able to increase the market share. The final outcome will be lower export prices and slippage in terms of trade. This may be a significant factor in the crisis countries, especially for electronics. At the macroeconomic level, however, rising export volumes will help in propping up output and employment. This in turn could lay the foundation of an export as well as an economic recovery.

POLICY MEASURES NEEDED TO RESTORE COMPETITIVENESS AND REJUVENATE EXPORTS

New strategies, or modifications of the old ones, are sorely needed to restore the competitiveness of exports. The principal policy measures that need to be applied in an earnest and timely manner fall in 10 areas.

Macroeconomic Stability and Reforms

Macroeconomic stability is one of the essential elements for the success of the outer-oriented policy regime. While the NIEs paid a great deal of attention to it when launching into their outer-oriented regimes, the opposite examples are also available. For instance, Chile and later on Pakistan lost their export vigor because of macroeconomic instability. Lower inflation rates, current account and budget deficits, as well as a stable and realistic exchange rate regime are some of the prerequisites for the successul operation of outer-oriented policy regimes.

When Asian economies adopted their outward-oriented strategies, they began their process of market-oriented reforms and opened their economies. Markets replaced the governments; consequently resources were directed at more productive sectors and utilized optimally. Such a movement of productive resources favorably influenced their productivity level. Subsequently these economies embarked on developing their incentive structures, knowing well that neutrality of incentives is needed to promote exports. However, export strategies and incentives that induced rapid export growth at early stages of development may be inadequate to sustain export performance when economies are more advanced (refer to Chapter 2). The reform process is a continuous one. As the economy moves to a higher level of export growth, new rigidities appear in the system. The reform process should anticipate these and eliminate them before they become effective barriers for exports. Alternatively, policymakers should address them as soon as the rigidities are identified. Cumbersome policy changes should be avoided because they have the potential to stifle exports, as occurred in the PRC in 1996.

Banking and Financial Sector Reforms

Although banking and financial sector weaknesses were not among the causal factors behind the export deceleration, they did deter several Asian economies from recovering from the export slump. In these economies, the financial sector was in such a disarray after the crisis began that it could not provide working capital loans to exporters. In addition, exporters having firm export orders could not open letters of credit and execute their export orders.

A smoothly functioning banking sector is an important determinant of export performance. This sector performed particularly poorly in several Asian economies (particularly in Indonesia, Korea, Malaysia, and Thailand) where massive lending took place without proper credit analysis. The situation was aggravated by inadequate regulatory and prudential standards and a weak supervision framework. The result was large nonperforming assets. When banks are saddled with nonperforming assets, they avoid fresh lendings.

All these Asian economies need to restructure and consolidate their banking and financial sectors, write off capital losses, and recapitalize their financial institutions. In addition, regulatory and prudential norms need to be strengthened so that excesses and omissions that occurred during the 1990s are not repeated in the future. Commercial banks should periodically assess the quality of their assets. An independent financial supervisory agency should be established to carry out the supervisory responsibilities.[10] Consolidation and restructuring would decisively entail closures and mergers. To that end, bankruptcy laws need to be made more flexible than they currently are. In some economies consolidation cannot be achieved without foreign participation. Export performance is sure to respond favorably to sectoral strengthening.

Real Effective Exchange Rate

An important lesson learned from the experiences of the mid-1990s is the significance of maintaining a competitive REER. An abrupt rise in the REER can be detrimental to trade: if it is not carefully managed, investible resources will be diverted to nontrade sectors and competitiveness of exports eroded. Changes in the REER should be such that they respond to domestic and external factors in a flexible manner and keep the trading sectors competitive. Domestic price movements, real wages, and changes in competitors' exchange rates should be fully and swiftly reflected in the REER. Delays in adjustment of the REER can potentially lead to high costs in terms of lost export markets.

Changes in Comparative Advantage

Comparative advantage is a dynamic concept. It changes as the economy moves up its growth path. Therefore, a successful export strategy requires that sectors be monitored carefully. Sectors that are losing their comparative advantage and, therefore, are needed to be

[10] Such an agency has been established in Japan, with operations beginning in June 1998.

phased out and those that are to be promoted because the comparative advantage is moving on to them, must be clearly identified. A study of revealed comparative advantage is of enormous benefit in this regard. Computing domestic resource costs is the other analytical tool. Both should be periodically calculated by the responsible government agency. Generally Asian economies did a fairly good job of keeping up with the changes in their comparative advantage. However, there were cases of failure—or incomplete adjustment. In Thailand, for example, the economy was locked into labor-intensive exports for an inordinate length of time. Hindsight reveals that its movement out of labor-intensive sectors and into capital- and skill-intensive sectors should have been faster. Asian economies should be more conscious of this, as such policy errors have high costs.

Technological and Industrial Upgrading

Associated with the concept of keeping up with changing comparative advantage are the measures needed to technologically upgrade the industry sector, particularly for exports. In some traditionally successful export areas like textiles and apparel, machinery and equipment are more than two decades old. Obsolescence of plants and machinery is an issue in some other export areas also. These plants and machinery need to be replaced by modern ones, embodying contemporary technology. Asian economies also need to develop productive capacity in skill- and capital-intensive sectors that cannot be achieved without moving up the technological curve. The ratio of high-tech exports to total exports needs to continue to increase in these economies.

Higher technology content has a high and positive correlation with value added, which in turn means a more profitable export sector. Second, as the technology level of the manufacturing sector rises, exports become more competitive in the international marketplace. Third, movement to a higher technological level also allows industries to adopt higher level processes, which in turn help them differentiate their products and perform better in export markets. Thus, technological upgrading is an effective and essential tool needed by Asian economies to move out of their present morass and enhance their future competitiveness.

Asian economies also need to learn from their past in this regard. Historically, FDI has made a large contribution and helped Asian economies to transform their technological scenarios. Malaysia is an excellent example of FDI bringing in state-of-the-art technology and in the process improving domestic technological standards. FDI-related technology transfer succeeded in giving an impetus to exports in many Asian economies. The same tried and tested strategy, with further refinements, can be used in the future.

Demand-Based Human Capital Development

Accompanying the need for technological upgrade is a critical demand for the development of technological education in Asian economies. In many, education systems have not only failed to meet the demand for trained personnel having high and intermediate technological skill levels, but also trained personnel with financial and managerial skills. These bottlenecks affected export performance in many Asian economies, particularly the ASEAN-4 economies. These economies must formulate plans for demand-based skill development. Such plans cannot be developed in the short term; it takes time for skill development. Therefore, in the short term they may have to depend on imported skilled personnel.

Easing Infrastructure Bottlenecks

Poor infrastructure was an endemic frailty of the export sector in Asia, leading to high costs and consequent loss of competitiveness. Measures must be taken to ease the road and port congestion and bring about a balance in the demand and supply of power. This has been talked about for some time, and some Asian economies—particularly the NIEs and ASEAN-4—have already made large investments in infrastructure development throughout the 1990s. Others, like India and Pakistan, have not made adequate progress in this regard, and inadequate infrastructure continues to be a binding constraint on exports. Such economies need to plan and make adequate investments without delay. In addition, for rapid development of this sector, governments should avoid all competition-restricting regulations, like entry barriers, so that the private sector may also take up infrastructure development.

A related factor is the provision of export infrastructure and support services, like insurance, business services, and market research assistance. They enhance the efficiency of capital invested in exports and lead to productivity gains.

Diversification

Asian economies have commonly concentrated on a small number of products that account for a large proportion of export revenue. Diversification must be two-pronged. First, more sectors or product lines should be developed to avoid concentration of export products. Second, greater product diversity should be developed by exporting firms. This would enable them to retain their export markets for longer periods, allow them to penetrate niche markets, and improve their profit performance. To this end, firms need to collect more information on consumer demand, and to improve their design capabilities. Even some of the most successful exporting economies of Asia need to pay attention to this aspect of exports.

Corporate Governance and Restructuring

Reckless expansion[11] and unrelated diversification through excessive borrowing caused a great deal of problems for many large firms, particularly in Korea. Firms need to concentrate on a small number of competitive sectors rather than a large number of noncompetitive ones. To be sure, firms should pursue well-conceived diversification strategies but they should only target various levels of goods within the same or related lines. They need to ensure that a synergy develops between various sectors. In the aftermath of the Asian crisis, corporate restructuring has started in several affected Asian economies. By early 1999, it had made sufficient progress in Korea.

In addition, in adjusting to the new ground realities Asian firms need to reinvigorate themselves through mergers, acquisitions, sellouts, and asset swaps. To be sure, there has been some action but the aggregate numbers of mergers and acquisitions are not as large

[11] Paul Krugman (1998) considers diversification strategies of the Korean *chaebol* as "ego-driven."

as expected. According to the data put out by the accounting and consulting firm KPMG, the number of merger deals in Asia (excluding Japan) was 67 in 1998, which was less than that in Latin America (82 deals).[12] In Korea, which was one of the earliest to start in this direction, the *chaebols* have made some progress in reshuffling assets among each other. Singapore has also seen mergers in the banking, manufacturing, and property sectors. Several large conglomerates in the region have sold their assets and returned to their "core businesses." In Thailand, some foreign financial institutions have bought into Thai banks and brokerage houses. However, corporate restructuring has been slow because of two principal reasons. First, Asian firms are reluctant to cede majority control, partly because majority of them are family-owned. Second, there is a problem of valuation. Present owners believe that the acquirers demand outrageously low prices, while the acquirers think Asian asset owners are unrealistic. If Asian firms have to rejuvenate themselves fast and be competitive in the international markets, not only governments but also societies will need to adjust to the completely new corporate landscapes.

Electronics, Information Technology, and Telecommunications

This was the most dynamic export sector in PRC; Hong Kong, China; Korea; Malaysia; and Taipei,China during the 1990s. However, it suffered from both overinvestment and a demand slump in mid-1996; adjustment process—including disinvestment—was vigorously pursued from 1997 to 1999. These industries are largely based on original equipment manufacturing and own design manufacturing. Their main customers are large transnational corporations like Apple, Bell, NEC, and Packard. In some Asian countries this area needs technological upgrading, which is largely done through FDI. Other than technological upgrading, vertical division of labor across national boundaries needs to be strengthened. Asian economies also need to strengthen their marketing skills in this area.

---

[12] Khanna (1999).

PROSPECTS

In 1998 prospects for world trade were clouded to some degree by the Asian financial and currency crisis. According to estimates made by the World Trade Organization, world trade volume was expected to grow at 4.6 percent in 1998, or half the 9.8 percent recorded for 1997 (WTO 1998). This in turn adversely affected the Asian export recovery endeavors during 1998. The export growth rate forecast for 1999 is a tepid 5.3 percent (OECD 1998).

Short-Term Prospects

Given the background of the financial and currency crisis, there is a pressing need to expand exports. There were marginal improvements in the growth rates of Asian exports in value terms during the first three quarters of 1997, when quarterly growth rates were 4.8 percent, 7.6 percent, and 9 percent. But these improvements were small and could not be called a recovery. The financial and currency crisis added to uncertainties and anxieties. In the fourth quarter of 1997 and the first two quarters of 1998, under the influence of the crisis, the growth rate of exports declined again. In fact, after declining to close to zero in the first quarter of 1998, the export growth rate contracted by 4.2 percent in the second. It continued to be a difficult year for the Asian economies. Neither the external nor domestic economic environment was conducive to export expansion in the short term.

The crisis scenario made it impossible for Asian economies to expand their manufacturing activities and promote exports. If anything, GDP growth rates in several Asian economies either stagnated or contracted in 1998. The average GDP growth rate for Asia fell from 6.1 percent in 1997 to 1.8 percent in 1998. This had a negative income effect on exports, and because of weak domestic demand intraregional exports suffered substantially during the two years. They decelerated to 4.6 percent and 6.8 percent during 1996 and 1997. Intratrade further decelerated (2.8 percent) in the first quarter of 1998. In addition, the Japanese economy was in recession in 1998; therefore, it could not be expected to be an engine of Asian export growth. The yen depreciated considerably during 1997 and the first half of 1998. To add to the uncertainties, there were similar apprehensions regarding the yuan and Hong Kong dollar during 1998. Such an unstable external environment was not conducive to rejuvenating exports in the region during 1997 and 1998. The financial and banking sectors of several Asian economies were in dire straits. Although interest rates had declined substantially in mid-1998, they were still high in some Asian economies. For instance in Indonesia they were 26 percent, Philippines 18 percent, Korea 17 percent, Thailand 16 percent, and India close to 15 percent. These high rates made investment difficult and exacerbated the problems of export industries. By early 1999, they declined further.

Several Asian currencies have recorded steep depreciations. Between June 1997[13] and August 1998, the Indonesian rupiah depreciated by 83 percent, the Malaysian ringgit 41 percent, the Thai baht 40 percent, the Philippine peso 39 percent, the Korean won 33 percent, the New Taiwan dollar 20 percent, the Singapore dollar 18 percent, the Indian rupee 16 percent, and the Pakistan rupee 9 percent. However, the export industries were not able to benefit from the steep currency depreciations. The US dollar value of their exports did not rise in 1998, largely because of the ongoing financial and banking sector crisis. In addition, as stated earlier, in many Asian economies exports were highly import intensive. Steep currency depreciations made imported raw materials very expensive. To make things more difficult, high interest rates in the domestic financial markets made any borrowing from local banks a difficult proposition, and were an additional deterrent to export expansion. Because of the problems of the banking sector (discussed earlier), it was neither able to provide working capital loans to exporters nor take care of their export financing needs. Enterprises having export orders were not able to open letters of credits, and therefore could not execute their export orders. Finance became a binding constraint on export performance in all the crisis-stricken economies. Besides, for whatever they could export, Asian countries competed against each other. Intense competition led to falling unit export prices and declining terms of trade.

The two Asian economies that more or less bucked the trend were the PRC and the Philippines, where exports picked up after a short-

[13] The advent of the Asian financial and currency crisis can be dated back to 2 July 1997, when Thailand depreciated its currency.

lived decline in 1996. A noteworthy short-term effect of currency depreciation was the reversal of comparative advantage to (i) labor-intensive, (ii) primary sector, and (iii) low-technology exports in several Asian economies. This could be called economic and technological retrogression. In countries like Korea and Thailand, depreciation has restored comparative advantage to garments and footwear. Korea had lost comparative advantage in these products during the 1980s and Thailand during the early 1990s. These dramatic changes in comparative advantage are changing the direction of trade radically. For instance, during the late 1980s and early 1990s, exports from the PRC and Korea were largely complementary, i.e., they rarely competed in the international marketplace. While the PRC exploited the low price end of the market, Korea offered higher price and up-market products. The currency depreciation has changed this comfortable relationship. With the new value of the won, higher quality Korean products began to cost less in dollar terms in 1998. Investors from Korea and Taipei,China are either closing down export-oriented plants in other Asian economies or reducing production in these plants. These countries are also competing directly with exports from the PRC and other Asian countries. The PRC exports of textiles, shipbuilding, and steel have been affected because of direct competition from Korea and Taipei,China (Kynge 1998).

Although exports from the NIEs and the ASEAN-4 economies did not start expanding in dollar terms, according to the preliminary export volume data, they did rise in volume terms during the first half of 1998 (Burton 1998; *The Economist* 1998). This rise in volume ranged between 20 and 30 percent, but was not reflected in the dollar value of exports because of a sharp drop in their dollar value and falling prices. However, at a macroeconomic level, rising export volumes will help to raise output and employment levels in Asian economies, which in turn will support their GDP growth rate in the immediate future. As domestic demand has slumped in these economies, imports have recorded sharp declines. This development has brought about large improvements in their current account balances during 1998. Thanks to these factors, the wild currency swings of 1997 subsided by the third quarter of 1998. The currencies stabilized enough for some central banks to cut interest rates further, which in turn should help their real economies.

Are there realistic prospects for a short-term recovery of Asian exports? Let us pull all the logical strands together and decide. Given the sluggish growth in world trade in volume terms, reversal of private capital flows from Asia, continued strength of the dollar, recession in Japan, and virtual collapse of intraregional trade, realistic prospects for a short-term recovery of Asian exports in value terms are not bright. In the aftermath of the Asian economic and financial crisis, the short-term outlook is laden with downside risk.

To counter this pessimistic indication, there are two favorable indicators. First, export volumes have started rising in several Asian economies and, second, export value recorded a marginal rise in the first quarter of 1998, providing a glimmer of hope for the beginning of an export recovery. However, in the edging up of these two indicators, one can only see weak prospects for a pickup because so far (first quarter of 1999) we do not have the export data for the remaining two quarters of 1998. The remaining quarters may well show more residual effects of the Asian crisis on regional export performance. For instance, the preliminary export data for the PRC show zero growth for the latter half of 1998 and those for Taipei,China a fall of over 10 percent (NRI 1999). The Asian crisis is the principal causal factor behind these developments.

Asian economies are expected to do better in 1999. The Asian Development Bank estimates their GDP growth rate will rise to 3.5 percent, although Indonesia and Malaysia are likely to record negative GDP growth rates in 1999. A slowdown has been forecast for the US and the OECD economies for 1999. This leads us to conclude that the demand stimulus that the Asian economies badly need will not be available from the regional or industrial economies. These factors indicate that Asian exports, at best, are likely to stabilize during 1999.

Medium-Term Prospects

While realistic prospects for export expansion are not encouraging for the short term, they are much better for the medium term. Indonesia, Korea, and Thailand (the so-called IMF-three) and Malaysia were restructuring their banking sector during 1997 and 1998 in earnest. Once the banking and financial sector restructuring has progressed sufficiently, the steep currency depreciations will have a price effect on exports and improve regional export performance.

The new postdepreciation currency configuration is not all that is likely to influence export performance. Large investments were made in physical infrastructure by several Asian economies during the 1990s, and this investment activity was continuing in the late 1990s. Some of these infrastructure projects will soon start coming onstream and the bottleneck on exports will be eased. Export deceleration and the financial crisis have focused the attention of policymakers on demand-based human resource development, particularly the development of skilled labor. It has become apparent that middle-level skills in general, and managerial and financial skills in particular, are in short supply in the ASEAN-4 economies. During the mid-1990s, Malaysia and Thailand started taking measures to redress this imbalance in their economic structures. However, addressing these skill shortages in the short term span is a difficult proposition; they can only be managed in the medium term. With progress in (i) financial sector restructuring, (ii) structural adjustments, and (iii) demand-based skill development, exports are bound to improve their performance.

The composition of Asian exports and division of labor in the region will also change in the medium term. The distortions caused in comparative advantage by steep currency depreciations will work themselves out and currency values will return to values close to their purchasing power parities. Low-technology industries will again move back to countries like the PRC, India, and Viet Nam. The sectors that suffered from overinvestment will have time to adjust to changed price and demand conditions. To be sure, some disinvestment or readjustment will take place in the electronics, information technology, and telecommunications sectors. Also, the technological and industrial upgrading required in the NIEs and ASEAN-4 will have progressed, resulting in an improvement of their export performance. These changes are likely to be hastened by the crisis. It bears repeating that none of these measures are short term. Implementing them will take time and their impact on export performance can only be realistically expected over the medium term.

By the first quarter of 1999, the Asian currencies had substantially stabilized, the stock market had picked up, and the yen had appreciated. Also, around this time financial sector constraints began to ease somewhat, and interest rates were far below their peak levels. This should stimulate the real economy. It is likely that with the passage of time, more credit will become available and the trade credit situation will ameliorate further, improving medium-term prospects for export expansion. In November 1998, the G-7 leaders proposed a set of measures to strengthen the global economy, and Japan announced a $500 billion financial revitalization package to stimulate domestic demand. Also in that month, during the APEC summit, Japan, the US, the World Bank, and the Asian Development Bank announced stabilization packages to assist the crisis-ridden Asian economies. These domestic and international initiatives have begun to create an appropriate environment for economic stability in Asia. In January 1999, credit rating agencies like Standard and Poors (S&P) lifted the credit rating of Korea and Thailand to investment grade.[14] In addition, the PRC confirmed that its exchange rate policy is not likely to change in the near future and that the yuan is not likely to be devalued. These developments have managed to underpin a rebound in market sentiment. As the regional economy stabilizes in 1999 and world export growth picks up in 2000 (as forecast by OECD), Asian export growth is likely to pick up as well.

Over the last quarter century, the NIEs and the ASEAN-4 established themselves as outward-looking economies. Their basic structure and economic orientation is not likely to be changed by the current export slump and crises. After making adjustments to the new situation, these economies will naturally move on to business as usual. However, they will only be able to do so by 2000-2001.

We began this chapter with a rhetorical question: Is the deceleration in Asian exports permanent or a passing phase? It is now possible to answer this. The present deceleration is not permanent. It was caused by structural, cyclical, and country-specific problems, as well as the confluence of some cyclical factors in 1996. It was subsequently exacerbated by the financial and currency crisis that started in July 1997. With the passage of time, as (i) financial sector restructuring, (ii) structural adjustments, and (iii) skill development proceed, along with the other necessary measures, Asian export growth is likely to resume. As for the growth rates, those achieved during the initial stages of export expansion in Asian economies are not likely to be repeated. However, there is little cause for doubting a return to robust export growth over the medium term in Asia. An amber signal is warranted here. The return to robust export growth

---

[14] Although at this point Moody's graded both of these economies as speculative, the international capital market expected it to soon fall in line with S&P.

rates would only be feasible if the policy measures needed to restore competitiveness are earnestly implemented.

SUMMING-UP

Since export is an overarching sector in several successful Asian economies and is considered an important variable in their past economic success, deceleration in its growth rate in 1996, continued poor performance in 1997, and failure to recover in 1998 caused a great deal of concern among Asian policymakers. The deceleration was aggravated by the financial and currency crisis that followed. This crisis effectively managed to deter Asian economies from launching into a full export recovery.

Asian economies suffered from several structural infirmities during the 1990s: severe infrastructure bottlenecks, crucial skill shortages, rising real wages, and a high degree of concentration of exports in a small number of sectors. The 1996 deceleration was essentially caused by several cyclical factors working in confluence with each other and with the structural infirmities that already existed. The principal cyclical factors were (i) a weak export demand in the industrial economies during 1996, causing a steep fall in the global export growth rate, (ii) a global electronic demand slump and overinvestment, (iii) a steep depreciation in the yen, (iv) a changing exchange rate configuration that worked against Asian exporters, (v) stringent monetary policies, (vi) price declines that affected the terms of trade adversely, and (vii) country-specific factors.

Realistic prospects of a short-term recovery for Asian exports are bleak, but they are much better for the medium term. After analyzing various contributing and retarding factors, we conclude that a steady improvement in export expansion in Asia can be realistically expected from 2000 to 2001. However, exports will not be rejuvenated without earnestly implementing new strategies or modifiying the old ones. The following measures are needed to restore the competitiveness of the export sector: maintain macroeconomic stability and continue reforms, especially financial and banking sector reforms; keep up with changes in comparative advantage, technological upgrading, and demand-based human capital development; dispell infrastructure bottlenecks; address high real wages; diversify exports; improve corporate governance; and make structural adjustments in the electronics subsector. The present deceleration in Asian export growth is not permanent. It has been caused by a confluence of structural, cyclical, and country-specific problems. The financial and currency crises that followed exacerbated the situation and made it impossible for the export sector to recover.

BIBLIOGRAPHY AND REFERENCES

Akhtar, M.A. and R.S. Hilton. 1984. "Exchange Rate Uncertainty and International Trade: Some Conceptual Issues and New Estimates for Germany and the United States." Research paper No. 8403. New York: Federal Reserve Bank of New York. May.

Burton, J. 1998. "Juggernaut in Trouble." *The Financial Times,* 27 August.

The Economist. 1998. "Better News in Asia." 29 August, page 70.

Frankel, J. A., and S.J. Wei. 1994. "Yen Bloc or Dollar Bloc? Exchange Rate Policies of East Asian Economies." In T. Ito and A.O. Krueger, eds., *Macroeconomic Linkages: Savings, Exchange Rates, and Capital Flows.* Chicago: University of Chicago Press.

Grobar, L.M. 1993. "The Effect of Real Exchange Rate Uncertainty on LDC Manufactured Exports." *Journal of Development Economics* 41:67-376.

International Monetary Fund. 1998. *World Economic Outlook.* Washington, DC. October.

Ito, T. 1999. (Chapter 3 of this volume).

Khanna, V. 1999 "Why Asia's Corporate Clean-up is Lagging." *Business Times.* Singapore. 1 February.

Krugman, P. 1998. "Pricing to Market when the Exchange Rate Changes." In S.W. Arndt and J.D. Richardson, eds., *Real Financial Linkages Among Open Economies.* Cambridge, MA: The MIT Press.

Kynge, J. 1998. "Manufactures Cry Foul." *The Financial Times.* 27 August.

Muscatelli V.A., and C. Montagna. 1994. "Untra-NIE Competition in Exports of Manufacturers." *Journal of International Economics* 37:29-47.

Nomura Research Institute (NRI). 1999. *Emerging Asia.* Tokyo. 8 January.

Organisation for Economic Co-operation and Development. 1998. *OECD Economic Outlook.* Paris.

World Bank. 1998. *Global Economic Prospects.* Washington, DC.

World Trade Organization. 1997. *Annual Report 1998.* Vol. 1. Geneva.

AUTHOR INDEX

SUBJECT INDEX

A

B

C

D

E

R

S

T

U

V